C-3661   CAREER EXAMINATION SERIES

This is your
PASSBOOK for...

Canal Section Superintendent

Test Preparation Study Guide
Questions & Answers

NATIONAL LEARNING CORPORATION®

COPYRIGHT NOTICE

This book is SOLELY intended for, is sold ONLY to, and its use is RESTRICTED to individual, bona fide applicants or candidates who qualify by virtue of having seriously filed applications for appropriate license, certificate, professional and/or promotional advancement, higher school matriculation, scholarship, or other legitimate requirements of education and/or governmental authorities.

This book is NOT intended for use, class instruction, tutoring, training, duplication, copying, reprinting, excerption, or adaptation, etc., by:

1) Other publishers
2) Proprietors and/or Instructors of "Coaching" and/or Preparatory Courses
3) Personnel and/or Training Divisions of commercial, industrial, and governmental organizations
4) Schools, colleges, or universities and/or their departments and staffs, including teachers and other personnel
5) Testing Agencies or Bureaus
6) Study groups which seek by the purchase of a single volume to copy and/or duplicate and/or adapt this material for use by the group as a whole without having purchased individual volumes for each of the members of the group
7) Et al.

Such persons would be in violation of appropriate Federal and State statutes.

PROVISION OF LICENSING AGREEMENTS – Recognized educational, commercial, industrial, and governmental institutions and organizations, and others legitimately engaged in educational pursuits, including training, testing, and measurement activities, may address request for a licensing agreement to the copyright owners, who will determine whether, and under what conditions, including fees and charges, the materials in this book may be used them. In other words, a licensing facility exists for the legitimate use of the material in this book on other than an individual basis. However, it is asseverated and affirmed here that the material in this book CANNOT be used without the receipt of the express permission of such a licensing agreement from the Publishers. Inquiries re licensing should be addressed to the company, attention rights and permissions department.

All rights reserved, including the right of reproduction in whole or in part, in any form or by any means, electronic or mechanical, including photocopying, recording, or by any information storage and retrieval system, without permission in writing from the Publisher.

Copyright © 2025 by
National Learning Corporation

212 Michael Drive, Syosset, NY 11791
(516) 921-8888 • www.passbooks.com
E-mail: info@passbooks.com

PASSBOOK® SERIES

THE *PASSBOOK® SERIES* has been created to prepare applicants and candidates for the ultimate academic battlefield – the examination room.

At some time in our lives, each and every one of us may be required to take an examination – for validation, matriculation, admission, qualification, registration, certification, or licensure.

Based on the assumption that every applicant or candidate has met the basic formal educational standards, has taken the required number of courses, and read the necessary texts, the *PASSBOOK® SERIES* furnishes the one special preparation which may assure passing with confidence, instead of failing with insecurity. Examination questions – together with answers – are furnished as the basic vehicle for study so that the mysteries of the examination and its compounding difficulties may be eliminated or diminished by a sure method.

This book is meant to help you pass your examination provided that you qualify and are serious in your objective.

The entire field is reviewed through the huge store of content information which is succinctly presented through a provocative and challenging approach – the question-and-answer method.

A climate of success is established by furnishing the correct answers at the end of each test.

You soon learn to recognize types of questions, forms of questions, and patterns of questioning. You may even begin to anticipate expected outcomes.

You perceive that many questions are repeated or adapted so that you can gain acute insights, which may enable you to score many sure points.

You learn how to confront new questions, or types of questions, and to attack them confidently and work out the correct answers.

You note objectives and emphases, and recognize pitfalls and dangers, so that you may make positive educational adjustments.

Moreover, you are kept fully informed in relation to new concepts, methods, practices, and directions in the field.

You discover that you are actually taking the examination all the time: you are preparing for the examination by "taking" an examination, not by reading extraneous and/or supererogatory textbooks.

In short, this PASSBOOK®, used directedly, should be an important factor in helping you to pass your test.

CANAL SECTION SUPERINTENDENT

DUTIES
As a Canal Section Superintendent, you would direct the work of canal employees in the operation and maintenance of a canal section and instruct them in the methods of performing varied maintenance work. You would perform supervisory activities that include monitoring staff performance, completing performance evaluations, counseling employees and conducting investigations, as necessary and determining staff assignments. You would investigate accidents, complaints, requests for permits, and violations of canal regulations; participate in the development and supervise the implementation of construction and maintenance programs; approve payrolls, purchase orders, and vouchers; and have overall responsibility for preparing/monitoring the Section budget.

SCOPE OF THE EXAMINATION:
The written test is designed to test for knowledge, skills, and/or abilities in such areas as:
1. **Work Planning and Scheduling** - These questions test for knowledge of the principles used in developing and implementing work plans and for the ability to arrange work assignments in a manner that will achieve work goals while staying within scheduling criteria. This may include setting up vacation or work schedules, taking into consideration such factors as seniority, work skills, duty hours, and shift coverage.
2. **General construction, inspection, repair & maintenance of floating plants, banks, movable bridges, locks, dams, piles & other canal structures** - These questions test for knowledge of the proper construction, inspection, maintenance and repair procedures to use on the canal infrastructure, including pile driving, concrete mixing and placement, lock-wall, valve and gate maintenance, embankment and dam repair, and floating plant operation.
3. **Preparing written material** - These questions test for the ability to present information clearly and accurately, and to organize paragraphs logically and comprehensibly. For some questions, you will be given information in two or three sentences followed by four restatements of the information. You must then choose the best version. For other questions, you will be given paragraphs with their sentences out of order. You must then choose, from four suggestions, the best order for the sentences.
4. **Channel excavation and bank protection including usage of equipment** - These questions test for knowledge of the proper procedures and typical equipment used in constructing and maintaining embankments and similar canal channel and bank protective structures.
5. **Construction, operation, maintenance, testing and repair of canal mechanical, hydraulic and electrical equipment** - These questions test for knowledge of the characteristics and operating procedures of the canal locks, lift bridges and other structures on the State Canal System and the mechanical, electrical, and hydraulic principles involved in the testing, maintenance, and repair of the equipment used on these structures.
6. **Administrative supervision** - These questions test for knowledge of the principles and practices involved in directing the activities of a large subordinate staff, including subordinate supervisors. Questions relate to the personal interactions between an upper level supervisor and his/her subordinate supervisors in the accomplishment of objectives. These questions cover such areas as assigning work to and coordinating the activities of several units, establishing and guiding staff development programs, evaluating the performance of subordinate supervisors, and maintaining relationships with other organizational sections.

HOW TO TAKE A TEST

I. YOU MUST PASS AN EXAMINATION

A. WHAT EVERY CANDIDATE SHOULD KNOW
Examination applicants often ask us for help in preparing for the written test. What can I study in advance? What kinds of questions will be asked? How will the test be given? How will the papers be graded?

As an applicant for a civil service examination, you may be wondering about some of these things. Our purpose here is to suggest effective methods of advance study and to describe civil service examinations.

Your chances for success on this examination can be increased if you know how to prepare. Those "pre-examination jitters" can be reduced if you know what to expect. You can even experience an adventure in good citizenship if you know why civil service exams are given.

B. WHY ARE CIVIL SERVICE EXAMINATIONS GIVEN?
Civil service examinations are important to you in two ways. As a citizen, you want public jobs filled by employees who know how to do their work. As a job seeker, you want a fair chance to compete for that job on an equal footing with other candidates. The best-known means of accomplishing this two-fold goal is the competitive examination.

Exams are widely publicized throughout the nation. They may be administered for jobs in federal, state, city, municipal, town or village governments or agencies.

Any citizen may apply, with some limitations, such as the age or residence of applicants. Your experience and education may be reviewed to see whether you meet the requirements for the particular examination. When these requirements exist, they are reasonable and applied consistently to all applicants. Thus, a competitive examination may cause you some uneasiness now, but it is your privilege and safeguard.

C. HOW ARE CIVIL SERVICE EXAMS DEVELOPED?
Examinations are carefully written by trained technicians who are specialists in the field known as "psychological measurement," in consultation with recognized authorities in the field of work that the test will cover. These experts recommend the subject matter areas or skills to be tested; only those knowledges or skills important to your success on the job are included. The most reliable books and source materials available are used as references. Together, the experts and technicians judge the difficulty level of the questions.

Test technicians know how to phrase questions so that the problem is clearly stated. Their ethics do not permit "trick" or "catch" questions. Questions may have been tried out on sample groups, or subjected to statistical analysis, to determine their usefulness.

Written tests are often used in combination with performance tests, ratings of training and experience, and oral interviews. All of these measures combine to form the best-known means of finding the right person for the right job.

II. HOW TO PASS THE WRITTEN TEST

A. NATURE OF THE EXAMINATION

To prepare intelligently for civil service examinations, you should know how they differ from school examinations you have taken. In school you were assigned certain definite pages to read or subjects to cover. The examination questions were quite detailed and usually emphasized memory. Civil service exams, on the other hand, try to discover your present ability to perform the duties of a position, plus your potentiality to learn these duties. In other words, a civil service exam attempts to predict how successful you will be. Questions cover such a broad area that they cannot be as minute and detailed as school exam questions.

In the public service similar kinds of work, or positions, are grouped together in one "class." This process is known as *position-classification*. All the positions in a class are paid according to the salary range for that class. One class title covers all of these positions, and they are all tested by the same examination.

B. FOUR BASIC STEPS

1) Study the announcement

How, then, can you know what subjects to study? Our best answer is: "Learn as much as possible about the class of positions for which you've applied." The exam will test the knowledge, skills and abilities needed to do the work.

Your most valuable source of information about the position you want is the official exam announcement. This announcement lists the training and experience qualifications. Check these standards and apply only if you come reasonably close to meeting them.

The brief description of the position in the examination announcement offers some clues to the subjects which will be tested. Think about the job itself. Review the duties in your mind. Can you perform them, or are there some in which you are rusty? Fill in the blank spots in your preparation.

Many jurisdictions preview the written test in the exam announcement by including a section called "Knowledge and Abilities Required," "Scope of the Examination," or some similar heading. Here you will find out specifically what fields will be tested.

2) Review your own background

Once you learn in general what the position is all about, and what you need to know to do the work, ask yourself which subjects you already know fairly well and which need improvement. You may wonder whether to concentrate on improving your strong areas or on building some background in your fields of weakness. When the announcement has specified "some knowledge" or "considerable knowledge," or has used adjectives like "beginning principles of…" or "advanced … methods," you can get a clue as to the number and difficulty of questions to be asked in any given field. More questions, and hence broader coverage, would be included for those subjects which are more important in the work. Now weigh your strengths and weaknesses against the job requirements and prepare accordingly.

3) Determine the level of the position

Another way to tell how intensively you should prepare is to understand the level of the job for which you are applying. Is it the entering level? In other words, is this the position in which beginners in a field of work are hired? Or is it an intermediate or advanced level? Sometimes this is indicated by such words as "Junior" or "Senior" in the class title. Other jurisdictions use Roman numerals to designate the level – Clerk I, Clerk II, for example. The word "Supervisor" sometimes appears in the title. If the level is not indicated by the title, check the description of duties. Will you be working under very close supervision, or will you have responsibility for independent decisions in this work?

4) Choose appropriate study materials

Now that you know the subjects to be examined and the relative amount of each subject to be covered, you can choose suitable study materials. For beginning level jobs, or even advanced ones, if you have a pronounced weakness in some aspect of your training, read a modern, standard textbook in that field. Be sure it is up to date and has general coverage. Such books are normally available at your library, and the librarian will be glad to help you locate one. For entry-level positions, questions of appropriate difficulty are chosen – neither highly advanced questions, nor those too simple. Such questions require careful thought but not advanced training.

If the position for which you are applying is technical or advanced, you will read more advanced, specialized material. If you are already familiar with the basic principles of your field, elementary textbooks would waste your time. Concentrate on advanced textbooks and technical periodicals. Think through the concepts and review difficult problems in your field.

These are all general sources. You can get more ideas on your own initiative, following these leads. For example, training manuals and publications of the government agency which employs workers in your field can be useful, particularly for technical and professional positions. A letter or visit to the government department involved may result in more specific study suggestions, and certainly will provide you with a more definite idea of the exact nature of the position you are seeking.

III. KINDS OF TESTS

Tests are used for purposes other than measuring knowledge and ability to perform specified duties. For some positions, it is equally important to test ability to make adjustments to new situations or to profit from training. In others, basic mental abilities not dependent on information are essential. Questions which test these things may not appear as pertinent to the duties of the position as those which test for knowledge and information. Yet they are often highly important parts of a fair examination. For very general questions, it is almost impossible to help you direct your study efforts. What we can do is to point out some of the more common of these general abilities needed in public service positions and describe some typical questions.

1) General information

Broad, general information has been found useful for predicting job success in some kinds of work. This is tested in a variety of ways, from vocabulary lists to questions about current events. Basic background in some field of work, such as sociology or economics, may be sampled in a group of questions. Often these are principles which have become familiar to most persons through exposure rather than through formal training. It is difficult to advise you how to study for these questions; being alert to the world around you is our best suggestion.

2) Verbal ability

An example of an ability needed in many positions is verbal or language ability. Verbal ability is, in brief, the ability to use and understand words. Vocabulary and grammar tests are typical measures of this ability. Reading comprehension or paragraph interpretation questions are common in many kinds of civil service tests. You are given a paragraph of written material and asked to find its central meaning.

3) Numerical ability

Number skills can be tested by the familiar arithmetic problem, by checking paired lists of numbers to see which are alike and which are different, or by interpreting charts and graphs. In the latter test, a graph may be printed in the test booklet which you are asked to use as the basis for answering questions.

4) Observation

A popular test for law-enforcement positions is the observation test. A picture is shown to you for several minutes, then taken away. Questions about the picture test your ability to observe both details and larger elements.

5) Following directions

In many positions in the public service, the employee must be able to carry out written instructions dependably and accurately. You may be given a chart with several columns, each column listing a variety of information. The questions require you to carry out directions involving the information given in the chart.

6) Skills and aptitudes

Performance tests effectively measure some manual skills and aptitudes. When the skill is one in which you are trained, such as typing or shorthand, you can practice. These tests are often very much like those given in business school or high school courses. For many of the other skills and aptitudes, however, no short-time preparation can be made. Skills and abilities natural to you or that you have developed throughout your lifetime are being tested.

Many of the general questions just described provide all the data needed to answer the questions and ask you to use your reasoning ability to find the answers. Your best preparation for these tests, as well as for tests of facts and ideas, is to be at your physical and mental best. You, no doubt, have your own methods of getting into an exam-taking mood and keeping "in shape." The next section lists some ideas on this subject.

IV. KINDS OF QUESTIONS

Only rarely is the "essay" question, which you answer in narrative form, used in civil service tests. Civil service tests are usually of the short-answer type. Full instructions for answering these questions will be given to you at the examination. But in case this is your first experience with short-answer questions and separate answer sheets, here is what you need to know:

1) **Multiple-choice Questions**

Most popular of the short-answer questions is the "multiple choice" or "best answer" question. It can be used, for example, to test for factual knowledge, ability to solve problems or judgment in meeting situations found at work.

A multiple-choice question is normally one of three types—
- It can begin with an incomplete statement followed by several possible endings. You are to find the one ending which *best* completes the statement, although some of the others may not be entirely wrong.
- It can also be a complete statement in the form of a question which is answered by choosing one of the statements listed.

- It can be in the form of a problem – again you select the best answer.

Here is an example of a multiple-choice question with a discussion which should give you some clues as to the method for choosing the right answer:

When an employee has a complaint about his assignment, the action which will *best* help him overcome his difficulty is to
- A. discuss his difficulty with his coworkers
- B. take the problem to the head of the organization
- C. take the problem to the person who gave him the assignment
- D. say nothing to anyone about his complaint

In answering this question, you should study each of the choices to find which is best. Consider choice "A" – Certainly an employee may discuss his complaint with fellow employees, but no change or improvement can result, and the complaint remains unresolved. Choice "B" is a poor choice since the head of the organization probably does not know what assignment you have been given, and taking your problem to him is known as "going over the head" of the supervisor. The supervisor, or person who made the assignment, is the person who can clarify it or correct any injustice. Choice "C" is, therefore, correct. To say nothing, as in choice "D," is unwise. Supervisors have and interest in knowing the problems employees are facing, and the employee is seeking a solution to his problem.

2) True/False Questions

The "true/false" or "right/wrong" form of question is sometimes used. Here a complete statement is given. Your job is to decide whether the statement is right or wrong.

SAMPLE: A roaming cell-phone call to a nearby city costs less than a non-roaming call to a distant city.

This statement is wrong, or false, since roaming calls are more expensive.

This is not a complete list of all possible question forms, although most of the others are variations of these common types. You will always get complete directions for answering questions. Be sure you understand *how* to mark your answers – ask questions until you do.

V. RECORDING YOUR ANSWERS

Computer terminals are used more and more today for many different kinds of exams.

For an examination with very few applicants, you may be told to record your answers in the test booklet itself. Separate answer sheets are much more common. If this separate answer sheet is to be scored by machine – and this is often the case – it is highly important that you mark your answers correctly in order to get credit.

An electronic scoring machine is often used in civil service offices because of the speed with which papers can be scored. Machine-scored answer sheets must be marked with a pencil, which will be given to you. This pencil has a high graphite content which responds to the electronic scoring machine. As a matter of fact, stray dots may register as answers, so do not let your pencil rest on the answer sheet while you are pondering the correct answer. Also, if your pencil lead breaks or is otherwise defective, ask for another.

Since the answer sheet will be dropped in a slot in the scoring machine, be careful not to bend the corners or get the paper crumpled.

The answer sheet normally has five vertical columns of numbers, with 30 numbers to a column. These numbers correspond to the question numbers in your test booklet. After each number, going across the page are four or five pairs of dotted lines. These short dotted lines have small letters or numbers above them. The first two pairs may also have a "T" or "F" above the letters. This indicates that the first two pairs only are to be used if the questions are of the true-false type. If the questions are multiple choice, disregard the "T" and "F" and pay attention only to the small letters or numbers.

Answer your questions in the manner of the sample that follows:

32. The largest city in the United States is
    A. Washington, D.C.
    B. New York City
    C. Chicago
    D. Detroit
    E. San Francisco

1) Choose the answer you think is best. (New York City is the largest, so "B" is correct.)
2) Find the row of dotted lines numbered the same as the question you are answering. (Find row number 32)
3) Find the pair of dotted lines corresponding to the answer. (Find the pair of lines under the mark "B.")
4) Make a solid black mark between the dotted lines.

VI. BEFORE THE TEST

Common sense will help you find procedures to follow to get ready for an examination. Too many of us, however, overlook these sensible measures. Indeed, nervousness and fatigue have been found to be the most serious reasons why applicants fail to do their best on civil service tests. Here is a list of reminders:

- Begin your preparation early – Don't wait until the last minute to go scurrying around for books and materials or to find out what the position is all about.
- Prepare continuously – An hour a night for a week is better than an all-night cram session. This has been definitely established. What is more, a night a week for a month will return better dividends than crowding your study into a shorter period of time.
- Locate the place of the exam – You have been sent a notice telling you when and where to report for the examination. If the location is in a different town or otherwise unfamiliar to you, it would be well to inquire the best route and learn something about the building.
- Relax the night before the test – Allow your mind to rest. Do not study at all that night. Plan some mild recreation or diversion; then go to bed early and get a good night's sleep.
- Get up early enough to make a leisurely trip to the place for the test – This way unforeseen events, traffic snarls, unfamiliar buildings, etc. will not upset you.
- Dress comfortably – A written test is not a fashion show. You will be known by number and not by name, so wear something comfortable.

- Leave excess paraphernalia at home – Shopping bags and odd bundles will get in your way. You need bring only the items mentioned in the official notice you received; usually everything you need is provided. Do not bring reference books to the exam. They will only confuse those last minutes and be taken away from you when in the test room.
- Arrive somewhat ahead of time – If because of transportation schedules you must get there very early, bring a newspaper or magazine to take your mind off yourself while waiting.
- Locate the examination room – When you have found the proper room, you will be directed to the seat or part of the room where you will sit. Sometimes you are given a sheet of instructions to read while you are waiting. Do not fill out any forms until you are told to do so; just read them and be prepared.
- Relax and prepare to listen to the instructions
- If you have any physical problem that may keep you from doing your best, be sure to tell the test administrator. If you are sick or in poor health, you really cannot do your best on the exam. You can come back and take the test some other time.

VII. AT THE TEST

The day of the test is here and you have the test booklet in your hand. The temptation to get going is very strong. Caution! There is more to success than knowing the right answers. You must know how to identify your papers and understand variations in the type of short-answer question used in this particular examination. Follow these suggestions for maximum results from your efforts:

1) Cooperate with the monitor
The test administrator has a duty to create a situation in which you can be as much at ease as possible. He will give instructions, tell you when to begin, check to see that you are marking your answer sheet correctly, and so on. He is not there to guard you, although he will see that your competitors do not take unfair advantage. He wants to help you do your best.

2) Listen to all instructions
Don't jump the gun! Wait until you understand all directions. In most civil service tests you get more time than you need to answer the questions. So don't be in a hurry. Read each word of instructions until you clearly understand the meaning. Study the examples, listen to all announcements and follow directions. Ask questions if you do not understand what to do.

3) Identify your papers
Civil service exams are usually identified by number only. You will be assigned a number; you must not put your name on your test papers. Be sure to copy your number correctly. Since more than one exam may be given, copy your exact examination title.

4) Plan your time
Unless you are told that a test is a "speed" or "rate of work" test, speed itself is usually not important. Time enough to answer all the questions will be provided, but this does not mean that you have all day. An overall time limit has been set. Divide the total time (in minutes) by the number of questions to determine the approximate time you have for each question.

5) Do not linger over difficult questions

If you come across a difficult question, mark it with a paper clip (useful to have along) and come back to it when you have been through the booklet. One caution if you do this – be sure to skip a number on your answer sheet as well. Check often to be sure that you have not lost your place and that you are marking in the row numbered the same as the question you are answering.

6) Read the questions

Be sure you know what the question asks! Many capable people are unsuccessful because they failed to *read* the questions correctly.

7) Answer all questions

Unless you have been instructed that a penalty will be deducted for incorrect answers, it is better to guess than to omit a question.

8) Speed tests

It is often better NOT to guess on speed tests. It has been found that on timed tests people are tempted to spend the last few seconds before time is called in marking answers at random – without even reading them – in the hope of picking up a few extra points. To discourage this practice, the instructions may warn you that your score will be "corrected" for guessing. That is, a penalty will be applied. The incorrect answers will be deducted from the correct ones, or some other penalty formula will be used.

9) Review your answers

If you finish before time is called, go back to the questions you guessed or omitted to give them further thought. Review other answers if you have time.

10) Return your test materials

If you are ready to leave before others have finished or time is called, take ALL your materials to the monitor and leave quietly. Never take any test material with you. The monitor can discover whose papers are not complete, and taking a test booklet may be grounds for disqualification.

VIII. EXAMINATION TECHNIQUES

1) Read the general instructions carefully. These are usually printed on the first page of the exam booklet. As a rule, these instructions refer to the timing of the examination; the fact that you should not start work until the signal and must stop work at a signal, etc. If there are any *special* instructions, such as a choice of questions to be answered, make sure that you note this instruction carefully.

2) When you are ready to start work on the examination, that is as soon as the signal has been given, read the instructions to each question booklet, underline any key words or phrases, such as *least, best, outline, describe* and the like. In this way you will tend to answer as requested rather than discover on reviewing your paper that you *listed without describing*, that you selected the *worst* choice rather than the *best* choice, etc.

3) If the examination is of the objective or multiple-choice type – that is, each question will also give a series of possible answers: A, B, C or D, and you are called upon to select the best answer and write the letter next to that answer on your answer paper – it is advisable to start answering each question in turn. There may be anywhere from 50 to 100 such questions in the three or four hours allotted and you can see how much time would be taken if you read through all the questions before beginning to answer any. Furthermore, if you come across a question or group of questions which you know would be difficult to answer, it would undoubtedly affect your handling of all the other questions.

4) If the examination is of the essay type and contains but a few questions, it is a moot point as to whether you should read all the questions before starting to answer any one. Of course, if you are given a choice – say five out of seven and the like – then it is essential to read all the questions so you can eliminate the two that are most difficult. If, however, you are asked to answer all the questions, there may be danger in trying to answer the easiest one first because you may find that you will spend too much time on it. The best technique is to answer the first question, then proceed to the second, etc.

5) Time your answers. Before the exam begins, write down the time it started, then add the time allowed for the examination and write down the time it must be completed, then divide the time available somewhat as follows:
    - If 3-1/2 hours are allowed, that would be 210 minutes. If you have 80 objective-type questions, that would be an average of 2-1/2 minutes per question. Allow yourself no more than 2 minutes per question, or a total of 160 minutes, which will permit about 50 minutes to review.
    - If for the time allotment of 210 minutes there are 7 essay questions to answer, that would average about 30 minutes a question. Give yourself only 25 minutes per question so that you have about 35 minutes to review.

6) The most important instruction is to *read each question* and make sure you know what is wanted. The second most important instruction is to *time yourself properly* so that you answer every question. The third most important instruction is to *answer every question*. Guess if you have to but include something for each question. Remember that you will receive no credit for a blank and will probably receive some credit if you write something in answer to an essay question. If you guess a letter – say "B" for a multiple-choice question – you may have guessed right. If you leave a blank as an answer to a multiple-choice question, the examiners may respect your feelings but it will not add a point to your score. Some exams may penalize you for wrong answers, so in such cases *only*, you may not want to guess unless you have some basis for your answer.

7) Suggestions
    a. Objective-type questions
        1. Examine the question booklet for proper sequence of pages and questions
        2. Read all instructions carefully
        3. Skip any question which seems too difficult; return to it after all other questions have been answered
        4. Apportion your time properly; do not spend too much time on any single question or group of questions

5. Note and underline key words – *all, most, fewest, least, best, worst, same, opposite,* etc.
6. Pay particular attention to negatives
7. Note unusual option, e.g., unduly long, short, complex, different or similar in content to the body of the question
8. Observe the use of "hedging" words – *probably, may, most likely,* etc.
9. Make sure that your answer is put next to the same number as the question
10. Do not second-guess unless you have good reason to believe the second answer is definitely more correct
11. Cross out original answer if you decide another answer is more accurate; do not erase until you are ready to hand your paper in
12. Answer all questions; guess unless instructed otherwise
13. Leave time for review

   b. Essay questions
   1. Read each question carefully
   2. Determine exactly what is wanted. Underline key words or phrases.
   3. Decide on outline or paragraph answer
   4. Include many different points and elements unless asked to develop any one or two points or elements
   5. Show impartiality by giving pros and cons unless directed to select one side only
   6. Make and write down any assumptions you find necessary to answer the questions
   7. Watch your English, grammar, punctuation and choice of words
   8. Time your answers; don't crowd material

8) Answering the essay question

Most essay questions can be answered by framing the specific response around several key words or ideas. Here are a few such key words or ideas:

M's: manpower, materials, methods, money, management
P's: purpose, program, policy, plan, procedure, practice, problems, pitfalls, personnel, public relations

   a. Six basic steps in handling problems:
   1. Preliminary plan and background development
   2. Collect information, data and facts
   3. Analyze and interpret information, data and facts
   4. Analyze and develop solutions as well as make recommendations
   5. Prepare report and sell recommendations
   6. Install recommendations and follow up effectiveness

   b. Pitfalls to avoid
   1. *Taking things for granted* – A statement of the situation does not necessarily imply that each of the elements is necessarily true; for example, a complaint may be invalid and biased so that all that can be taken for granted is that a complaint has been registered

2. *Considering only one side of a situation* – Wherever possible, indicate several alternatives and then point out the reasons you selected the best one
3. *Failing to indicate follow up* – Whenever your answer indicates action on your part, make certain that you will take proper follow-up action to see how successful your recommendations, procedures or actions turn out to be
4. *Taking too long in answering any single question* – Remember to time your answers properly

IX. AFTER THE TEST

Scoring procedures differ in detail among civil service jurisdictions although the general principles are the same. Whether the papers are hand-scored or graded by machine we have described, they are nearly always graded by number. That is, the person who marks the paper knows only the number – never the name – of the applicant. Not until all the papers have been graded will they be matched with names. If other tests, such as training and experience or oral interview ratings have been given, scores will be combined. Different parts of the examination usually have different weights. For example, the written test might count 60 percent of the final grade, and a rating of training and experience 40 percent. In many jurisdictions, veterans will have a certain number of points added to their grades.

After the final grade has been determined, the names are placed in grade order and an eligible list is established. There are various methods for resolving ties between those who get the same final grade – probably the most common is to place first the name of the person whose application was received first. Job offers are made from the eligible list in the order the names appear on it. You will be notified of your grade and your rank as soon as all these computations have been made. This will be done as rapidly as possible.

People who are found to meet the requirements in the announcement are called "eligibles." Their names are put on a list of eligible candidates. An eligible's chances of getting a job depend on how high he stands on this list and how fast agencies are filling jobs from the list.

When a job is to be filled from a list of eligibles, the agency asks for the names of people on the list of eligibles for that job. When the civil service commission receives this request, it sends to the agency the names of the three people highest on this list. Or, if the job to be filled has specialized requirements, the office sends the agency the names of the top three persons who meet these requirements from the general list.

The appointing officer makes a choice from among the three people whose names were sent to him. If the selected person accepts the appointment, the names of the others are put back on the list to be considered for future openings.

That is the rule in hiring from all kinds of eligible lists, whether they are for typist, carpenter, chemist, or something else. For every vacancy, the appointing officer has his choice of any one of the top three eligibles on the list. This explains why the person whose name is on top of the list sometimes does not get an appointment when some of the persons lower on the list do. If the appointing officer chooses the second or third eligible, the No. 1 eligible does not get a job at once, but stays on the list until he is appointed or the list is terminated.

X. HOW TO PASS THE INTERVIEW TEST

The examination for which you applied requires an oral interview test. You have already taken the written test and you are now being called for the interview test – the final part of the formal examination.

You may think that it is not possible to prepare for an interview test and that there are no procedures to follow during an interview. Our purpose is to point out some things you can do in advance that will help you and some good rules to follow and pitfalls to avoid while you are being interviewed.

What is an interview supposed to test?

The written examination is designed to test the technical knowledge and competence of the candidate; the oral is designed to evaluate intangible qualities, not readily measured otherwise, and to establish a list showing the relative fitness of each candidate – as measured against his competitors – for the position sought. Scoring is not on the basis of "right" and "wrong," but on a sliding scale of values ranging from "not passable" to "outstanding." As a matter of fact, it is possible to achieve a relatively low score without a single "incorrect" answer because of evident weakness in the qualities being measured.

Occasionally, an examination may consist entirely of an oral test – either an individual or a group oral. In such cases, information is sought concerning the technical knowledges and abilities of the candidate, since there has been no written examination for this purpose. More commonly, however, an oral test is used to supplement a written examination.

Who conducts interviews?

The composition of oral boards varies among different jurisdictions. In nearly all, a representative of the personnel department serves as chairman. One of the members of the board may be a representative of the department in which the candidate would work. In some cases, "outside experts" are used, and, frequently, a businessman or some other representative of the general public is asked to serve. Labor and management or other special groups may be represented. The aim is to secure the services of experts in the appropriate field.

However the board is composed, it is a good idea (and not at all improper or unethical) to ascertain in advance of the interview who the members are and what groups they represent. When you are introduced to them, you will have some idea of their backgrounds and interests, and at least you will not stutter and stammer over their names.

What should be done before the interview?

While knowledge about the board members is useful and takes some of the surprise element out of the interview, there is other preparation which is more substantive. It *is* possible to prepare for an oral interview – in several ways:

1) Keep a copy of your application and review it carefully before the interview

This may be the only document before the oral board, and the starting point of the interview. Know what education and experience you have listed there, and the sequence and dates of all of it. Sometimes the board will ask you to review the highlights of your experience for them; you should not have to hem and haw doing it.

2) Study the class specification and the examination announcement

Usually, the oral board has one or both of these to guide them. The qualities, characteristics or knowledges required by the position sought are stated in these documents. They offer valuable clues as to the nature of the oral interview. For example, if the job involves supervisory responsibilities, the announcement will usually indicate that knowledge of modern supervisory methods and the qualifications of the candidate as a supervisor will be tested. If so, you can expect such questions, frequently in the form of a hypothetical situation which you are expected to solve. NEVER go into an oral without knowledge of the duties and responsibilities of the job you seek.

3) Think through each qualification required

Try to visualize the kind of questions you would ask if you were a board member. How well could you answer them? Try especially to appraise your own knowledge and background in each area, *measured against the job sought*, and identify any areas in which you are weak. Be critical and realistic – do not flatter yourself.

4) Do some general reading in areas in which you feel you may be weak

For example, if the job involves supervision and your past experience has NOT, some general reading in supervisory methods and practices, particularly in the field of human relations, might be useful. Do NOT study agency procedures or detailed manuals. The oral board will be testing your understanding and capacity, not your memory.

5) Get a good night's sleep and watch your general health and mental attitude

You will want a clear head at the interview. Take care of a cold or any other minor ailment, and of course, no hangovers.

What should be done on the day of the interview?

Now comes the day of the interview itself. Give yourself plenty of time to get there. Plan to arrive somewhat ahead of the scheduled time, particularly if your appointment is in the fore part of the day. If a previous candidate fails to appear, the board might be ready for you a bit early. By early afternoon an oral board is almost invariably behind schedule if there are many candidates, and you may have to wait. Take along a book or magazine to read, or your application to review, but leave any extraneous material in the waiting room when you go in for your interview. In any event, relax and compose yourself.

The matter of dress is important. The board is forming impressions about you – from your experience, your manners, your attitude, and your appearance. Give your personal appearance careful attention. Dress your best, but not your flashiest. Choose conservative, appropriate clothing, and be sure it is immaculate. This is a business interview, and your appearance should indicate that you regard it as such. Besides, being well groomed and properly dressed will help boost your confidence.

Sooner or later, someone will call your name and escort you into the interview room. *This is it.* From here on you are on your own. It is too late for any more preparation. But remember, you asked for this opportunity to prove your fitness, and you are here because your request was granted.

What happens when you go in?

The usual sequence of events will be as follows: The clerk (who is often the board stenographer) will introduce you to the chairman of the oral board, who will introduce you to the other members of the board. Acknowledge the introductions before you sit down. Do not be surprised if you find a microphone facing you or a stenotypist sitting by. Oral interviews are usually recorded in the event of an appeal or other review.

Usually the chairman of the board will open the interview by reviewing the highlights of your education and work experience from your application – primarily for the benefit of the other members of the board, as well as to get the material into the record. Do not interrupt or comment unless there is an error or significant misinterpretation; if that is the case, do not hesitate. But do not quibble about insignificant matters. Also, he will usually ask you some question about your education, experience or your present job – partly to get you to start talking and to establish the interviewing "rapport." He may start the actual questioning, or turn it over to one of the other members. Frequently, each member undertakes the questioning on a particular area, one in which he is perhaps most competent, so you can expect each member to participate in the examination. Because time is limited, you may also expect some rather abrupt switches in the direction the questioning takes, so do not be upset by it. Normally, a board member will not pursue a single line of questioning unless he discovers a particular strength or weakness.

After each member has participated, the chairman will usually ask whether any member has any further questions, then will ask you if you have anything you wish to add. Unless you are expecting this question, it may floor you. Worse, it may start you off on an extended, extemporaneous speech. The board is not usually seeking more information. The question is principally to offer you a last opportunity to present further qualifications or to indicate that you have nothing to add. So, if you feel that a significant qualification or characteristic has been overlooked, it is proper to point it out in a sentence or so. Do not compliment the board on the thoroughness of their examination – they have been sketchy, and you know it. If you wish, merely say, "No thank you, I have nothing further to add." This is a point where you can "talk yourself out" of a good impression or fail to present an important bit of information. Remember, *you close the interview yourself.*

The chairman will then say, "That is all, Mr. _____, thank you." Do not be startled; the interview is over, and quicker than you think. Thank him, gather your belongings and take your leave. Save your sigh of relief for the other side of the door.

How to put your best foot forward

Throughout this entire process, you may feel that the board individually and collectively is trying to pierce your defenses, seek out your hidden weaknesses and embarrass and confuse you. Actually, this is not true. They are obliged to make an appraisal of your qualifications for the job you are seeking, and they want to see you in your best light. Remember, they must interview all candidates and a non-cooperative candidate may become a failure in spite of their best efforts to bring out his qualifications. Here are 15 suggestions that will help you:

1) Be natural – Keep your attitude confident, not cocky

If you are not confident that you can do the job, do not expect the board to be. Do not apologize for your weaknesses, try to bring out your strong points. The board is interested in a positive, not negative, presentation. Cockiness will antagonize any board member and make him wonder if you are covering up a weakness by a false show of strength.

2) Get comfortable, but don't lounge or sprawl

Sit erectly but not stiffly. A careless posture may lead the board to conclude that you are careless in other things, or at least that you are not impressed by the importance of the occasion. Either conclusion is natural, even if incorrect. Do not fuss with your clothing, a pencil or an ashtray. Your hands may occasionally be useful to emphasize a point; do not let them become a point of distraction.

3) Do not wisecrack or make small talk

This is a serious situation, and your attitude should show that you consider it as such. Further, the time of the board is limited – they do not want to waste it, and neither should you.

4) Do not exaggerate your experience or abilities

In the first place, from information in the application or other interviews and sources, the board may know more about you than you think. Secondly, you probably will not get away with it. An experienced board is rather adept at spotting such a situation, so do not take the chance.

5) If you know a board member, do not make a point of it, yet do not hide it

Certainly you are not fooling him, and probably not the other members of the board. Do not try to take advantage of your acquaintanceship – it will probably do you little good.

6) Do not dominate the interview

Let the board do that. They will give you the clues – do not assume that you have to do all the talking. Realize that the board has a number of questions to ask you, and do not try to take up all the interview time by showing off your extensive knowledge of the answer to the first one.

7) Be attentive

You only have 20 minutes or so, and you should keep your attention at its sharpest throughout. When a member is addressing a problem or question to you, give him your undivided attention. Address your reply principally to him, but do not exclude the other board members.

8) Do not interrupt

A board member may be stating a problem for you to analyze. He will ask you a question when the time comes. Let him state the problem, and wait for the question.

9) Make sure you understand the question

Do not try to answer until you are sure what the question is. If it is not clear, restate it in your own words or ask the board member to clarify it for you. However, do not haggle about minor elements.

10) Reply promptly but not hastily

A common entry on oral board rating sheets is "candidate responded readily," or "candidate hesitated in replies." Respond as promptly and quickly as you can, but do not jump to a hasty, ill-considered answer.

11) Do not be peremptory in your answers

A brief answer is proper – but do not fire your answer back. That is a losing game from your point of view. The board member can probably ask questions much faster than you can answer them.

12) Do not try to create the answer you think the board member wants

He is interested in what kind of mind you have and how it works – not in playing games. Furthermore, he can usually spot this practice and will actually grade you down on it.

13) Do not switch sides in your reply merely to agree with a board member

Frequently, a member will take a contrary position merely to draw you out and to see if you are willing and able to defend your point of view. Do not start a debate, yet do not surrender a good position. If a position is worth taking, it is worth defending.

14) Do not be afraid to admit an error in judgment if you are shown to be wrong

The board knows that you are forced to reply without any opportunity for careful consideration. Your answer may be demonstrably wrong. If so, admit it and get on with the interview.

15) Do not dwell at length on your present job

The opening question may relate to your present assignment. Answer the question but do not go into an extended discussion. You are being examined for a *new* job, not your present one. As a matter of fact, try to phrase ALL your answers in terms of the job for which you are being examined.

Basis of Rating

Probably you will forget most of these "do's" and "don'ts" when you walk into the oral interview room. Even remembering them all will not ensure you a passing grade. Perhaps you did not have the qualifications in the first place. But remembering them will help you to put your best foot forward, without treading on the toes of the board members.

Rumor and popular opinion to the contrary notwithstanding, an oral board wants you to make the best appearance possible. They know you are under pressure – but they also want to see how you respond to it as a guide to what your reaction would be under the pressures of the job you seek. They will be influenced by the degree of poise you display, the personal traits you show and the manner in which you respond.

ABOUT THIS BOOK

This book contains tests divided into Examination Sections. Go through each test, answering every question in the margin. We have also attached a sample answer sheet at the back of the book that can be removed and used. At the end of each test look at the answer key and check your answers. On the ones you got wrong, look at the right answer choice and learn. Do not fill in the answers first. Do not memorize the questions and answers, but understand the answer and principles involved. On your test, the questions will likely be different from the samples. Questions are changed and new ones added. If you understand these past questions you should have success with any changes that arise. Tests may consist of several types of questions. We have additional books on each subject should more study be advisable or necessary for you. Finally, the more you study, the better prepared you will be. This book is intended to be the last thing you study before you walk into the examination room. Prior study of relevant texts is also recommended. NLC publishes some of these in our Fundamental Series. Knowledge and good sense are important factors in passing your exam. Good luck also helps. So now study this Passbook, absorb the material contained within and take that knowledge into the examination. Then do your best to pass that exam.

EXAMINATION SECTION

EXAMINATION SECTION
TEST 1

DIRECTIONS: Each question or incomplete statement is followed by several suggested answers or completions. Select the one that BEST answers the question or completes the statement. *PRINT THE LETTER OF THE CORRECT ANSWER IN THE SPACE AT THE RIGHT.*

1. Piles are used in building construction

    A. to provide waterproof construction
    B. to eliminate the need for a cellar
    C. when the building is located on sloping ground
    D. to help support the foundation

2. Of the following, the dominant trade employed in driving precast concrete piles would be

    A. oilers   B. dockbuilders
    C. carpenters   D. concrete workers

3. Upon excavation to subgrade for a pile-supported footing, inspection shows that the soil is inferior to that anticipated.
   Of the following, the proper action for the superintendent representing the contracting agency to take is to

    A. stop the job at once
    B. notify the engineer to redesign the foundation
    C. continue work
    D. excavate to a deeper level

4. Of the following, the type of equipment MOST suitable for making a large, deep excavation in soft earth where truck ramps cannot be used is a

    A. bulldozer
    B. clamshell bucket on a crane
    C. power shovel
    D. backhoe

5. In a pile-driving operation, spudding is used PRIMARILY to

    A. remove a broken pile
    B. increase the length of a pile
    C. compact the soil in the area
    D. get past a subsurface obstruction

6. Of the following, the MOST important information to be recorded for each pile during pile driving is the

    A. number of hammer blows at the final inch
    B. total number of hammer blows
    C. steam pressure and temperature
    D. condition of the ground at the pile location

7. A sidewalk shed

   A. is never permitted
   B. is used when demolishing buildings
   C. is allowed in front of public buildings
   D. must have an open roof

8. Of the following, the FIRST operation in the demolition of a 4-story building adjacent to the property line is the

   A. erection of railings around the stairwells
   B. shoring of adjoining buildings
   C. erection of a sidewalk shed
   D. removal of windows

9. Of the following, the FIRST operation in the demolition of a building is the

   A. shoring of the adjoining buildings
   B. erection of railings around stairwells
   C. removal of windows
   D. venting of the roof

Questions 10-11.

DIRECTIONS: Questions 10 and 11 are to be answered on the basis of the following specification.

Rough grading shall consist of cutting or filling to the elevation herein established with a permissible tolerance of two inches plus or minus. This tolerance shall be so used that, within any area of 100 feet, it will not be necessary for a later contractor performing fine grading to remove excess or bring additional fill to meet the required elevations.

10. From the above specification, it is reasonable to conclude that

    A. the total amount of excavation removed in rough grading should equal the total volume of excavation needed to meet the required elevations
    B. rough grading may end at an elevation 2 inches too high over an area 100' x 100'
    C. rough grading may end at an elevation 2 inches too low over an area 100' x 100'
    D. the contractor performing fine grading will not be permitted to remove excess material

11. Of the following, the BEST reason for specifying the above paragraph is that

    A. a stronger foundation is assured
    B. a savings in concrete will result
    C. by keeping above the water table, a dry foundation is assured
    D. it establishes limits for the rough grading contractor

12. When a structure containing a party wall is demolished, protection for the party wall is specified by the Building Code.
    Of the following items relating to such protection, the one that is NOT specified by the Code is

A. the owner of the building being demolished must pay for protecting the party wall
B. the anchors at the beam ends in the standing wall shall be bent over
C. the party wall shall be shored up and made secure
D. all open beam holes shall be bricked in

13. Of the following, the information of GREATEST significance to be recorded for each pile during pile driving is the

    A. steam pressure and the temperature
    B. condition of the ground at the pile location
    C. number of hammer blows at the last inch
    D. total number of hammer blows

14. Specifications for a building require that machine excavation for foundation footings be within a foot of final subgrade and the remaining excavation be done by hand.
    Of the following, the BEST reason for this requirement is to

    A. prevent cave-ins around the excavation
    B. save the amount of fill needed
    C. prevent disturbing the surrounding excavation
    D. prevent excavation below the subgrade

15. After excavating by a contractor for a footing, the subgrade soil appears to be below the quality shown on the borings.
    Of the following types of footings, the one that would be LEAST affected by this condition is a

    A. spread footing   B. combined footing
    C. footing on piles   D. footing and pier

Questions 16-18.

DIRECTIONS: Questions 16 through 18 are to be answered on the basis of the following specification.

All present walls, cellar floors, foundations, footings, and other existing structural items shall be removed as follows: Within 3 feet of all new building walls, areas and ramp walls, the above work shall be removed to the depth of new construction. Under new footings, the above work shall be entirely removed.

16. From the above specification, it is reasonable to conclude that

    A. present walls must be entirely removed if they are located directly under new walls
    B. old footings may be left in place if they are located within three feet of new building walls
    C. an existing foundation must be completely removed if located under a new footing
    D. the depth of construction may reach a maximum within 3 feet of new walls

17. The above specification MOST likely refers to removal of

    A. walls and footings that were located off line
    B. walls and footings located at incorrect grade

C. walls and footings of demolished buildings
D. defective foundations as determined by test

18. Of the following titles, the one that is MOST appropriate for the section in which the above specification appears is

    A. Work Not In Contract
    B. Removal of City Property
    C. Protection of Excavation
    D. Preparation of Site

19. After excavating to the subgrade of a footing, an examination of the soil reveals that it is of a poorer quality than the soil in that area and at that elevation shown on the soil borings.
    Of the following types of footings, the one that would be LEAST affected by this condition is a

    A. footing on piles
    B. plain concrete footing
    C. combined footing
    D. spread footing

20. A specification on piles states that plumbness must be within 2% of the pile length. If the pile length is 30 feet, the MAXIMUM amount that the pile may be out of plumb is, in inches, MOST NEARLY

    A. 5   B. 6   C. 7   D. 8

KEY (CORRECT ANSWERS)

1.	D	11.	D
2.	B	12.	C
3.	C	13.	C
4.	B	14.	D
5.	D	15.	C
6.	A	16.	C
7.	B	17.	C
8.	C	18.	D
9.	C	19.	A
10.	A	20.	C

EXAMINATION SECTION
TEST 1

DIRECTIONS: Each question or incomplete statement is followed by several suggested answers or completions. Select the one that BEST answers the question or completes the statement. *PRINT THE LETTER OF THE CORRECT ANSWER IN THE SPACE AT THE RIGHT.*

1. When filling an empty aqueduct, the valve should be opened

   A. slowly to prevent damage to the aqueduct
   B. rapidly to fill the line as soon as possible
   C. slowly to prevent rapid lowering of the reservoir level
   D. rapidly so that there are no air locks

   1._____

2. The BEST way of detecting the location of a suspected chlorine leak is by placing a _____ near the suspected leak.

   A. rag, which has been dipped in a strong ammonia water,
   B. match
   C. piece of litmus paper
   D. flow meter

   2._____

3. The term *run-off* refers to the

   A. amount a valve must be turned in order to open it fully
   B. length of time an electric motor continues to turn after the current is shut off
   C. amount of rainfall which flows from the ground surface into the streams and reservoirs
   D. distance the water falls from the intake gate to the turbine

   3._____

4. Algae in reservoirs may be killed by using

   A. zeolite   B. copper sulphate
   C. sodium chloride   D. calcium chloride

   4._____

5. The one of the following types of valves that USUALLY operates without manual control is a(n) _____ valve.

   A. check   B. globe   C. gate   D. angle

   5._____

6. Rate of flow of water through a water treatment plant is USUALLY referred to in terms of

   A. c.f.s.   B. c.f.m.   C. r.p.m.   D. m.g.d.

   6._____

7. In order to make it easier to operate a large valve or gate, pressures on both sides of the valve or gate are balanced by

   A. using weights on each side of the valve or gate
   B. opening a smaller by-pass valve
   C. partially shutting down the water in the upstream line
   D. opening the downstream valve very slowly

   7._____

8. Leaves are removed from the water entering the treatment plant or aqueduct by

   A. skimming   B. coagulating   C. draining   D. screening

   8._____

9. Odors, due to gases in the water, are removed by

   A. surging B. sluicing C. aerating D. clarifying

10. Chlorine residual refers to the

    A. amount of chlorine that must be added to the water
    B. amount of chlorine that remains in the water after a given period
    C. method of adding the chlorine to the water
    D. method of protecting personnel using chlorine from the effects of the chlorine

11. One of the processes that takes place in an Imhoff tank is

    A. oxidation B. flocculation C. digestion D. coagulation

12. As used in a sewage disposal plant, *effluent* refers to the

    A. basic treatment process of sewage
    B. time it takes for complete treatment of sewage
    C. type of control the plant uses for treatment
    D. final liquid coming out of the treatment process

13. A grit chamber operates on the basis that

    A. grit will settle out of slow-moving water
    B. grit will float and can be removed by skimming the surface
    C. increasing the rate of flow of water will leave the grit behind
    D. spraying water into the air will cause the heavier grit to separate from the water

14. The purpose of sedimentation in any sewage treatment process is to

    A. aerate the sewage
    B. increase the chlorine content of the sewage
    C. remove suspended matter from the sewage
    D. kill the bacteria in the sewage

15. The final treatment for sludge before it is disposed of is

    A. drying B. adding chlorine
    C. mixing D. washing

16. The amount of sewage applied to a filter bed is GENERALLY controlled by a

    A. sluice gate B. flow meter
    C. dosing siphon D. regulating valve

17. Methane gas which results from the sewage treatment process is MOST frequently

    A. vented to the outside air to prevent injury to plant personnel
    B. used as a fuel in the plant
    C. combined with other gases to render it harmless
    D. burned in the open air

18. The filtering material in a *filter bed* at a sewage treat-ment plant is USUALLY

    A. activated charcoal B. sand
    C. alum D. ammonium chloride

19. Cleaning sewer lines is USUALLY done by the use of a

    A. catch basin
    B. flushometer
    C. sewer rod
    D. center line

20. One of the ways of locating a leak in a water line is by using a

    A. manometer
    B. sounding rod
    C. poling board
    D. diffusor

21. MOST sewer pipes are made of

    A. cast iron
    B. agricultural tile
    C. brass
    D. copper

22. One of the materials generally used in caulking joints in bell and spigot pipe is

    A. tar   B. litharge   C. red lead   D. oakum

23. Water pipe must be laid at least two feet below the ground surface MAINLY to

    A. prevent freezing
    B. discourage malicious tampering
    C. reduce the pressure required to make the water flow
    D. eliminate possibility of damage to roads in case of water main break

24. When soldering copper gutters, the flux that is GENERALLY used is

    A. sal ammoniac
    B. resin
    C. killed muriatic acid
    D. calcium chloride

25. A good concrete mix for use in the foundations of a small building is

    A. 1:2:5   B. 5:2:1   C. 2:5:1   D. 1:5:2

26. When painting steel, red lead is used MAINLY as a

    A. primer coat so final coat will adhere better
    B. primer coat to protect the steel from rusting
    C. finish coat to protect the steel from the action of the sun and water
    D. second coat to bind the primer and finish coats

27. Studs in frame buildings are USUALLY

    A. 1" x 4"   B. 1" x 6"   C. 2" x 4"   D. 2" x 6"

28. A cement mortar used in brickwork is USUALLY made more workable by adding

    A. phosphate   B. lime   C. calcium   D. grout

Questions 29-32.

DIRECTIONS: The following four questions numbered 29 to 32, inclusive, are to be answered in accordance with the rules of the department of water supply, gas and electricity.

29. The term *water course* refers to

    A. aqueducts only
    B. pipe lines only
    C. natural or artificial streams only
    D. all of the above

30. Where a swimming pool discharges upon or into the ground and the water is not treated, the minimum distance between such discharge and a stream MUST be at least _____ feet.

    A. 50   B. 100   C. 250   D. 450

31. According to the above rules, clothes may

    A. be washed in a spring, if the spring does not feed directly into a reservoir
    B. be washed in a spring if the place where this is being done is at least one mile from a reservoir
    C. be washed in a spring provided a chlorinated soap is used
    D. not be washed in a spring

32. Industrial wastes may

    A. be discharged into a stream provided the stream does not feed directly into a reservoir
    B. be discharged into a stream, provided the point of discharge is at least one mile from a reservoir
    C. be discharged into a stream if the wastes are purified in an approved manner
    D. not be discharged into a stream

33. One method of determining the height of the water in a stream feeding into a reservoir is by means of a

    A. venturi meter   B. flow meter
    C. hook gage   D. strain gage

34. When digging a deep trench, the sides are USUALLY prevented from caving in by using

    A. shoulders   B. blocking   C. pins   D. sheathing

35. The FIRST precaution a worker should take before entering a sewer manhole is to

    A. put on hard-toed shoes
    B. put on safety goggles
    C. check that the next manhole upstream is not obstructed
    D. test the air in the manhole

36. Assume that a fuse blows upon connecting a light load to the circuit. You replace it with the same size fuse, and again the fuse blows.
    The BEST thing to do in this case is to

    A. connect a wire across the fuse so it cannot blow under such a light load
    B. replace the fuse with one having a higher rating
    C. check the wiring of the circuit
    D. place two fuses in series to prevent blowing

37. Of the following material, the one that is BEST for fill as a subgrade for a road is

   A. sand
   B. silt
   C. clay
   D. a mixture of sand, silt, and clay

38. When dealing with leaking chlorine, it is IMPORTANT to remember that chlorine is

   A. highly flammable
   B. made safe by spraying water on it
   C. not corrosive
   D. heavier than air

39. Cast iron pipe is MOST frequently cut with a(n)

   A. hack saw
   B. diamond point chisel
   C. burning torch
   D. abrasive wheel

40. Water hammer in a pipe line is BEST reduced by installing

   A. a pressure regulator
   B. an air chamber
   C. smaller pipes and valves
   D. larger pipes and valves

KEY (CORRECT ANSWERS)

1. A	11. C	21. A	31. D
2. A	12. D	22. D	32. D
3. C	13. A	23. A	33. C
4. B	14. C	24. C	34. D
5. A	15. A	25. A	35. D
6. D	16. C	26. B	36. C
7. B	17. B	27. C	37. D
8. D	18. B	28. B	38. D
9. C	19. C	29. D	39. B
10. B	20. B	30. B	40. B

TEST 2

DIRECTIONS: Each question or incomplete statement is followed by several suggested answers or completions. Select the one that BEST answers the question or completes the statement. *PRINT THE LETTER OF THE CORRECT ANSWER IN SPACE AT THE RIGHT.*

1. When used in conjunction with a centrifugal pump, a foot valve

    A. equalizes the pressure on both sides of the pump
    B. regulates the amount of water flowing through the pump
    C. prevents water in the pump from flowing back down the suction line
    D. adjusts the speed of the pump to the amount of water to be pumped

    1.____

2. Grounding an electric motor is

    A. *good* practice because the motor will operate better
    B. *poor* practice because the motor will not operate as well
    C. *good* practice because it protects against shock hazards
    D. *poor* practice because it increases shock hazards

    2.____

3. The one of the following wrenches that should NOT be used to turn a nut is a _____ wrench.

    A. monkey   B. box   C. stillson   D. socket

    3.____

4. A drill is GENERALLY removed from the chuck of a portable electric drill by using a

    A. drift pin
    B. wedge
    C. centerpunch
    D. key

    4.____

5. The finished surface of a dirt road is MOST frequently maintained with a

    A. blade grader
    B. bulldozer
    C. dragline
    D. carryall

    5.____

6. Frequent stalling of a truck engine is MOST probably due to a

    A. weak battery
    B. low battery water level
    C. leaking oil filter
    D. dirty carburetor

    6.____

7. If the reading of the oil pressure gage on a gasoline motor should suddenly drop to zero, the FIRST thing the operator should do is to

    A. check the filter
    B. inspect the oil lines
    C. tighten the oil pan bolts
    D. stop the motor

    7.____

8. A tractor is to be stored for two months. In order to keep it in BEST condition, it should be

    A. drained of all fuel and oil
    B. lubricated every week
    C. started up periodically and run until warm
    D. steam cleaned and all water drained from the radiator

    8.____

9. Trees suffering from transplanting shock are quickly helped by

    9.____

A. deep watering B. foliage feeding
C. root feeding D. vitamin treatments

10. For MOST rapid healing, trees should be pruned during 10.____

    A. November, December, and January
    B. February, March, and April
    C. May, June, and July
    D. August, September, and October

11. The blades of a lawn mower should be set so that the blades 11.____

    A. firmly touch the bed knife
    B. barely touch the bed knife
    C. clear the bed knife by 1/16 inch
    D. clear the bed knife by 1/8 inch

12. The MAIN reason for mulching is to 12.____

    A. fertilize the soil
    B. prevent erosion
    C. protect plants from the cold
    D. kill insects

13. A compost heap would MOST likely include 13.____

    A. lawn clippings B. sand
    C. stumps of trees D. gravel

14. Of the following statements with regard to *seeding,* the one that is CORRECT is: 14.____

    A. Seeds should be sown on a windy day
    B. The ground should be watered heavily after seeding
    C. Seeding should be done primarily on a bright and sunny day
    D. It is not necessary to carefully apportion the amount of seeds sown

15. Organic matter is often added to soil to better condition it for growing plants. 15.____
    Of the following, the item that is NOT organic matter is

    A. lime B. peat C. manure D. leaf mold

16. Of the following, the BEST way to store coniferous seedlings which cannot be planted 16.____
    for a few days is to

    A. unwrap them and put them in a dark, dry location
    B. place them flat on the ground in a sunny location so they can get plenty of light and air
    C. place them in a trench dug in the earth and cover the root ends with soil
    D. make sure the ball is not loosened and keep in a hothouse

17. Transplanting of seedlings is BEST done in early 17.____

    A. spring B. summer C. autumn D. winter

18. After planting privet hedges, they are frequently cut back to within a few inches of the ground.
    This is USUALLY done to

    A. remove dead parts of the hedge
    B. insure dense growth from the ground up
    C. speed up root development
    D. reduce the possibility of insect damage while the hedge is taking root

19. *Heaving* of pavements in wintertime is USUALLY caused by the

    A. difference of expansion of pavement and subgrade
    B. freezing of water in subgrade
    C. loss of bond between pavement and subgrade
    D. brittleness of pavement

20. Erosion of side slopes caused by the action of water is GREATEST when the soil is

    A. silt   B. clay   C. hardpan   D. silty-clay

21. The MAIN reason for making a crown in a road pavement is to

    A. reduce the amount of paving material necessary
    B. make it easier for cars to go around a curve
    C. drain surface water
    D. increase the strength of the pavement where it is most needed

22. The MAIN reason for paving ditches at the side of a road is to

    A. prevent damage from cars
    B. permit the ditch to carry more water
    C. prevent erosion of the soil in the ditch
    D. block water from getting under the pavement

23. Assume that vitrified clay tile pipe, with open joints, is being used as the underdrain for a roadway.
    This pipe should be laid

    A. directly on the bottom of the trench
    B. on a bed of clay
    C. on a bed of peat
    D. on a bed of gravel

24. A macadam road is one in which the base is GENERALLY made of

    A. asphalt   B. broken stone
    C. concrete   D. stabilized soil

25. To loosen compacted rocky earth road surfaces, the BEST piece of equipment to use is a

    A. disc harrow   B. drag line   C. bulldozer   D. scarifier

26. Oiling of an earth road is BEST done

    A. in the winter before the snow falls
    B. when you expect much rain

C. in the spring during dry weather
D. immediately after snow is cleared from the road

27. Cracks in concrete roads are BEST repaired by filling them with

A. tar B. grout
C. mineral filler D. sand

28. When repairing patches in old asphalt pavements, the edges of the patch should FIRST be painted with

A. the same material used for the patch
B. kerosene
C. asphalt cement
D. asphalt binder

29. The sum of 3 1/4, 5 1/8, 2 1/2, and 3 3/8 is

A. 14 B. 14 1/8 C. 14 1/4 D. 14 3/8

30. Assume that it takes 6 men 8 days to do a particular job.
If you have only 4 men available to do this job and they all work at the same speed, then the number of days it would take to complete the job would be

A. 11 B. 12 C. 13 D. 14

31. The city aims to supply *potable* water. As used in this sentence, the word *potable* means MOST NEARLY

A. clear B. drinkable C. fresh D. adequate

32. Water, after being purified, should not be turbid. As used in this sentence, the word turbid means MOST NEARLY

A. cloudy B. warm C. infected D. hard

33. The flow of water is *impeded* by the silt in the bottom of the stream.
As used in this sentence, the word *impeded* means MOST NEARLY

A. dammed B. hindered C. helped D. dirtied

Questions 34-35.

DIRECTIONS: Questions 34 and 35 are based on the following paragraph.

Repeated burning of the same area should be avoided. Burning should not be done on impervious, shallow, unstable, or highly erodible soils, or on steep slopes - especially in areas subject to heavy rains or rapid snowmelt. When existing vegetation is likely to be killed or seriously weakened by the fire, measures should be taken to assure prompt revegetation of the burned area. Burns should be limited to relatively small proportions of a watershed unit so that the stream channels will be able to carry any increased flows with a minimum of damage.

34. According to the above paragraph, planned burning should be limited to small areas of the watershed because

   A. the fire can be better controlled
   B. existing vegetation will be less likely to be killed
   C. plants will grow quicker in small areas
   D. there will be less likelihood of damaging floods

35. According to the above paragraph, burning usually should be done on soils that

   A. readily absorb moisture
   B. have been burnt before
   C. exist as a thin layer over rock
   D. can be flooded by nearby streams

36. If a foreman does not understand the instructions that are given to him by the district engineer, the BEST thing to do is to

   A. work out the solution to the problem himself
   B. do the job in the way he thinks is best
   C. get one of the other foremen to do the job
   D. ask that the instructions be repeated and clarified

37. The BEST foreman is the one who

   A. can work as fast as the fastest man in the crew
   B. is the most skilled mechanic
   C. can get the most work out of the men
   D. is the strongest man

38. Complimenting a man for good work is

   A. *good* practice since it will give the man an incentive to continue working well
   B. *poor* practice because the other men will become jealous
   C. *good* practice because in the future the foreman will not have to supervise this man
   D. *poor* practice since the man should work well without needing compliments

39. In dealing with his men, it is MOST important that a foreman be

   A. a disciplinarian   B. stern
   C. fair   D. chummy with his men

40. When issuing a violation to a member of the public, it is MOST important that a foreman be

   A. aloof and refuse to discuss the violation
   B. stern, and warn the person to correct the violation immediately
   C. courteous and explain what must be done to correct the violation
   D. friendly and volunteer assistance to correct the violation

KEY (CORRECT ANSWERS)

1. C	11. B	21. C	31. B
2. C	12. C	22. C	32. A
3. C	13. A	23. D	33. B
4. D	14. B	24. B	34. D
5. A	15. A	25. D	35. A
6. D	16. C	26. C	36. D
7. D	17. A	27. A	37. C
8. C	18. B	28. C	38. A
9. B	19. B	29. C	39. C
10. B	20. A	30. B	40. C

EXAMINATION SECTION
TEST 1

DIRECTIONS: Each question or incomplete statement is followed by several suggested answers or completions. Select the one that BEST answers the question or completes the statement. *PRINT THE LETTER OF THE CORRECT ANSWER IN THE SPACE AT THE RIGHT.*

1. Of the following methods of installing pipe in a trench, the one which is MOST acceptable is to

    A. use a flat bottom trench and backfill not tamped
    B. have pipe supported on blocks and backfill tamped
    C. use a flat bottom trench and backfill tamped
    D. have pipe supported on blocks, backfill not tamped

    1.____

2. When cutting a 30" diameter cast iron pipe, it is BEST to use a(n)

    A. cold chisel
    B. diamond point chisel
    C. hardy
    D. ordinary wheel type of cutter

    2.____

3. Of the following materials, the one which is BEST suited for yarning bell and spigot joints on water pipe is

    A. plumber's yarn   B. boatmaker's yarn
    C. tar impregnated oakum   D. sterilized yarn

    3.____

4. A valve that is used between low pressure and high pressure areas in water distribution systems is called a boundary valve.

    A. pressure reducing   B. check
    C. gate   D. globe

    4.____

5. Cast iron pipe is particularly adapted to underground and submerged service because of its

    A. ease in handling and joining
    B. high corrosion-resisting qualities
    C. ability to withstand high pressures
    D. low first cost

    5.____

6. In caulking a pipe joint, excessive *caulking* should be avoided to prevent

    A. *thinning* the lead   B. a second pouring of lead
    C. *misses*   D. bell damage

    6.____

7. The material used to disinfect water pipes before and after laying the pipe is USUALLY

    A. chlordane   B. calcium chloride
    C. chlorine   D. washing soda

    7.____

8. Of the following items, the one that is NOT a component part of a mechanical joint is a(n)

   A. yarn
   B. gland
   C. rubber gasket
   D. socket

9. Of the following causes of water leaks in mains, the one that is LEAST common is

   A. improper caulking
   B. poor backfilling
   C. improper handling of pipe
   D. manufacturing defects in the pipe

10. The BEST type of wrench to use for making up a mechanical joint in cast iron pipe is a _____ wrench.

    A. ratchet   B. monkey   C. strap   D. Stillson

11. The MAIN difference between skeleton sheathing and tight sheathing is that in skeleton sheathing

    A. a greater part of the sheathing is omitted
    B. reinforced laced type of sheathing is used
    C. the rangers and braces are placed differently
    D. no planks are used

12. The width of the trench at each caulking joint, in comparison with the remaining portion of the trench, should generally be

    A. equal to twice the diameter of the pipe to allow for caulking
    B. of sufficient size to allow for caulking
    C. equal to the diameter of the pipe plus 12 inches
    D. equal to the diameter of the pipe plus 1/2 pipe radius

13. Unless otherwise directed, a trench for a water pipe line should USUALLY be excavated to a depth of 4 feet measured from the surface of the roadway to the _____ of the pipe.

    A. center   B. bottom   C. invert   D. top

14. The length of trench excavation for the installation of a 30-inch pipe should NOT exceed _____ feet.

    A. 1500   B. 1300   C. 1100   D. 1000

15. Before laying a new water main, test pits or test trenches may be necessary in order to determine

    A. the amount of materials required
    B. subsurface obstructions
    C. the proper width of excavation
    D. the amount of labor needed

16. The outside circumference of a pipe that has an outside diameter of 11 1/2" is MOST NEARLY

    A. 32"   B. 36"   C. 39"   D. 42"

17. Continuous sheathing is USUALLY used when excavating a trench in   17.____

    A. unstable soil   B. firm earth
    C. stiff clay   D. rock

18. Assume that a pump is pumping water out of an excavated trench at the rate of 30 gallons per minute.   18.____
    The time that is required to pump 2700 gallons of water out of this trench would be MOST NEARLY _____ hour(s).

    A. 4 1/2   B. 3   C. 1 1/2   D. 3/4

19. The size of *rangers* that should be used for trenches dug to a depth of seven (7) feet is APPROXIMATELY   19.____

    A. 1" x 2"   B. 2" x 3"   C. 2" x 4"   D. 4" x 6"

20. The bottom of wood sheathing is USUALLY   20.____

    A. squared on all sides
    B. steel tipped in order to penetrate hard material
    C. capped in order to prevent splintering
    D. bevelled on both one face and one edge

21. The quickest and easiest way of disconnecting a bell and spigot lead joint in a pipe is by   21.____

    A. using a picking chisel at the joint
    B. cracking the bell
    C. melting the lead at the joint with an acetylene torch
    D. using a diamond point chisel

22. A joint runner is USUALLY used as a   22.____

    A. guide for molten lead
    B. scab on sheathing
    C. clamp for two pipes
    D. filler between pavement joints

23. Of the following tools, the one which is NOT usually used for caulking a joint is the   23.____

    A. stub   B. regular
    C. cold chisel   D. diamond joint

24. The type of lead USUALLY used to caulk cast iron pipe joints in water mains is   24.____

    A. lead wool   B. shredded lead
    C. leadite   D. pure soft lead

25. The distance that a *ranger* is USUALLY placed below the surface of a roadway is APPROXIMATELY   25.____

    A. 12"   B. 10"   C. 8"   D. 6"

26. The proper manner to unload cast iron pipe at a trench site which is APPROXIMATELY 300 feet long is to

   A. stack it at convenient locations
   B. stack it in even layers with 4" x 4" stringers between each layer with blocks at each end
   C. lay it along the route with the bell facing in the direction in which the work is to proceed
   D. store it where it will not collect rain water and be damaged in freezing weather

27. Damage to cast iron pipe may sometimes result from rough handling when in transit. A simple method of determining whether the pipe was damaged or not is to

   A. *ring* each length with a hammer
   B. drop the pipe to see if it breaks
   C. hydraulically test the pipe
   D. visually examine the pipe for cracks

28. A blowoff connection in a water distribution main is USUALLY located at the

   A. highest point of the line
   B. lowest point of the line
   C. midway point between two distribution mains
   D. center line of the pipe

29. The proper depth of lead joints for a 4" or 6" cast iron pipe is MOST NEARLY _____ inches.

   A. 3 1/2   B. 3 1/4   C. 3   D. 2 3/8

30. The distance that fire hydrants should be located back from the face of the curb line is MOST NEARLY

   A. 6-10"   B. 12-16"   C. 18-20"   D. 22-26"

31. Your orders to your crew are MOST likely to be followed if you

   A. explain the reasons for these orders
   B. warn that all violators will be punished
   C. promise easy assignments to those who follow these orders best
   D. say that they are for the good of the department

32. In order to be a good supervisor, you should

   A. impress upon your men that you demand perfection in their work at all times
   B. avoid being blamed for your crew's mistakes
   C. impress your superior with your ability
   D. see to it that your men get what they are entitled to

33. In giving instructions to a crew, you should

   A. speak in as loud a tone as possible
   B. speak in a coaxing persuasive manner
   C. speak quietly, clearly, and courteously
   D. always use the word *please* when giving instructions

34. The BEST procedure to follow when a difficult and unusual problem arises involving the laying of a water pipe is to

   A. ask another pipe caulker for his opinion
   B. proceed working in the usual manner
   C. report the situation to the engineer
   D. continue working, making necessary changes yourself

35. Assume that you are in charge of a crew making repairs on a water main. A bystander whom you do not know begins to comment on the way the work is being done. He makes several suggestions which he claims will result in a better job.
    Of the following, you should

   A. hold up the work until you can discuss the suggestions with your superior
   B. listen to him, thank him, and proceed with the work as you have been doing
   C. tell him to go along about his own business since you can do the job without any advice
   D. tell him to take his comments and suggestions to your superior who has the authority to change procedure

36. Assume that a pipe worker earns $16,625 per year. If seventeen percent of his pay is deducted for taxes, social security, and pension, his net weekly pay will be APPROXIMATELY

   A. $319.70   B. $300.80   C. $290.60   D. $265.00

37. If eighteen (18) feet of 4" cast iron pipe weighs approximately 390 pounds, the weight of this pipe per lineal foot will be MOST NEARLY _____ lbs.

   A. 19   B. 21   C. 23   D. 25

38. A one-sixteenth cast iron fitting will change the direction of water APPROXIMATELY

   A. 90°   B. 45°   C. 22 1/2°   D. 11 1/4°

39. The overall length of a standard cast iron bell-and-spigot water pipe is MOST NEARLY

   A. 10' 4 1/2"   B. 11'9"   C. 12' 4 1/2"   D. 20'0"

40. In rock excavations, the minimum depth that rock must be removed from the bottom of the bell of a cast iron pipe to the bottom of a trench should be MOST NEARLY

   A. 3"   B. 4"   C. 6"   D. 9"

KEY (CORRECT ANSWERS)

1. C	11. A	21. C	31. A
2. B	12. B	22. A	32. D
3. D	13. D	23. D	33. C
4. C	14. D	24. D	34. C
5. B	15. B	25. A	35. B
6. D	16. B	26. C	36. D
7. C	17. A	27. A	37. B
8. A	18. C	28. B	38. C
9. D	19. D	29. D	39. C
10. A	20. D	30. C	40. C

TEST 2

DIRECTIONS: Each question or incomplete statement is followed by several suggested answers or completions. Select the one that BEST answers the question or completes the statement. *PRINT THE LETTER OF THE CORRECT ANSWER IN THE SPACE AT THE RIGHT.*

1. If four (4) men are *backfilling* a trench, the proper number of men for *tamping* should usually be NOT LESS than   1.____

    A. 2 B. 4 C. 6 D. 8

2. A subsurface leak in a street main may be located by means of a(n)   2.____

    A. amprobe B. aquaphone
    C. aqueduct D. drill rod

3. The FIRST step in shutting off a water main in a street is to   3.____

    A. close the blowoff and notify the Department of Public Works
    B. close the blowoff and notify the Police Department
    C. notify the householders and the Fire Department
    D. close the head gates and notify the Fire Department

4. Concentric reducers are used for   4.____

    A. maintaining the same center line elevation
    B. keeping the bottom of the pipe at the same level
    C. changing the direction of flow in a pipe
    D. lowering the inverts of the pipe

5. A valve box is generally built with an open bottom so that   5.____

    A. the valve box can rest directly on the pipe
    B. the valve can be removed rapidly
    C. any water seeping into it will drain away
    D. a bottom connection can be made

6. If lead that is being used for caulking is overheated, it will be found that the caulked lead ring from a joint would MOST likely be   6.____

    A. too soft B. porous C. brittle D. flexible

7. A pipe compound used for making up threaded joints USUALLY acts as a filler between the threads and also as a   7.____

    A. hardener B. lubricant
    C. cleanser D. coolant

8. By referring to a concrete mix having a ratio of 1:2:4 is meant that the ingredients are made up of 1 part _____, 2 parts _____, and 4 parts _____.   8.____

    A. cement; sand; gravel B. sand; cement; water
    C. gravel; sand; cement D. sand; cement; gravel

9. The total weight of materials (lead and hemp) used in caulking an 8" bell and spigot joint for water is MOST NEARLY _____ lbs.

   A. 7   B. 10   C. 15   D. 24

10. Assume that a length of cast iron pipe measures 9'8" and three pieces of pipe are to be cut from this pipe, one 2'9", the second 3'2", and the third 1'10".
    The amount of pipe remaining after making these cuts (assuming no waste) is MOST NEARLY

    A. 1'6"   B. 1'9"   C. 1'11"   D. 2'2"

11. Of the following types of valves, the one that is used to permit the flow of water in one direction is the _____ valve.

    A. gate   B. angle   C. globe   D. check

12. Water mains in the city are generally located APPROXIMATELY _____ feet from the _____ line.

    A. four (4); curb
    B. five (5); sewer
    C. six (6); building
    D. nine (9); curb

13. Of the following equipment, the one which a pipe worker is NOT normally required to know how to operate is the

    A. backhoe
    B. air-powered chipping hammers and caulking tools
    C. various types of pipe laying derricks
    D. air-powered pavement breakers and rock drills

14. Assume that, after installing a mechanical joint in a water main, a leak occurs around the joint.
    Of the following, the BEST practice to follow would be to

    A. retighten the bolts
    B. loosen the bolts to expand the rubber gasket
    C. *hammer* home the spigot into the bell
    D. disassemble the joint, clean thoroughly, and reassemble

15. It is a good policy to keep excavated material away from the edge of a trench a distance of AT LEAST

    A. 2 feet   B. 18 inches   C. 1 foot   D. 6 inches

16. Neglecting friction, the height, in feet, to which water can rise having a pressure of 55 pounds per square inch is MOST NEARLY

    A. 120   B. 150   C. 180   D. 210

17. If it takes 3 men 11 days to dig a trench, the number of days it will take 5 men to dig the same trench, assuming all work is done at the same rate of speed, is MOST NEARLY

    A. 6 1/2   B. 7 3/4   C. 8 1/4   D. 8 3/4

18. It is sometimes found that poured lead joints tend to crack open due to shrinkage. This is USUALLY due to

    A. overheating of the lead
    B. impurities in the lead
    C. excessive pressure at the joint
    D. cooling of the lead

19. The BEST material to use for backfilling trenches that are made in rock is USUALLY

    A. tan bark   B. cinders   C. gravel   D. sand

20. For an average pipe repair job, it is the practice to use a gang made up of

    A. one pipe caulker and three laborers
    B. two pipe caulkers and three laborers
    C. one supervisor, two pipe caulkers, and two laborers
    D. three laborers and two helpers

21. Slack in cables or tie rods is USUALLY *taken up* by the use of

    A. drift pins   B. clamps
    C. Crosby clips   D. turnbuckles

22. A pneumatic tool is one that is USUALLY directly operated by means of

    A. gasoline   B. compressed air
    C. oil pressure   D. electricity

23. The BEST thing to do when a pavement breaker becomes jammed in the pavement is to

    A. attempt to work it loose without using another breaker
    B. shut off the air compressor
    C. increase the air supply
    D. use another pavement breaker to cut it loose

24. If a trench is dug 6'0" deep, 2'6" wide, and 8'0" long, the area of the opening, in square feet, is MOST NEARLY

    A. 48   B. 32   C. 20   D. 15

Questions 25-30.

DIRECTIONS: Questions 25 through 30 are to be answered in accordance with the sketch shown on the following page, which represents a portion of a water distribution map and other facilities.

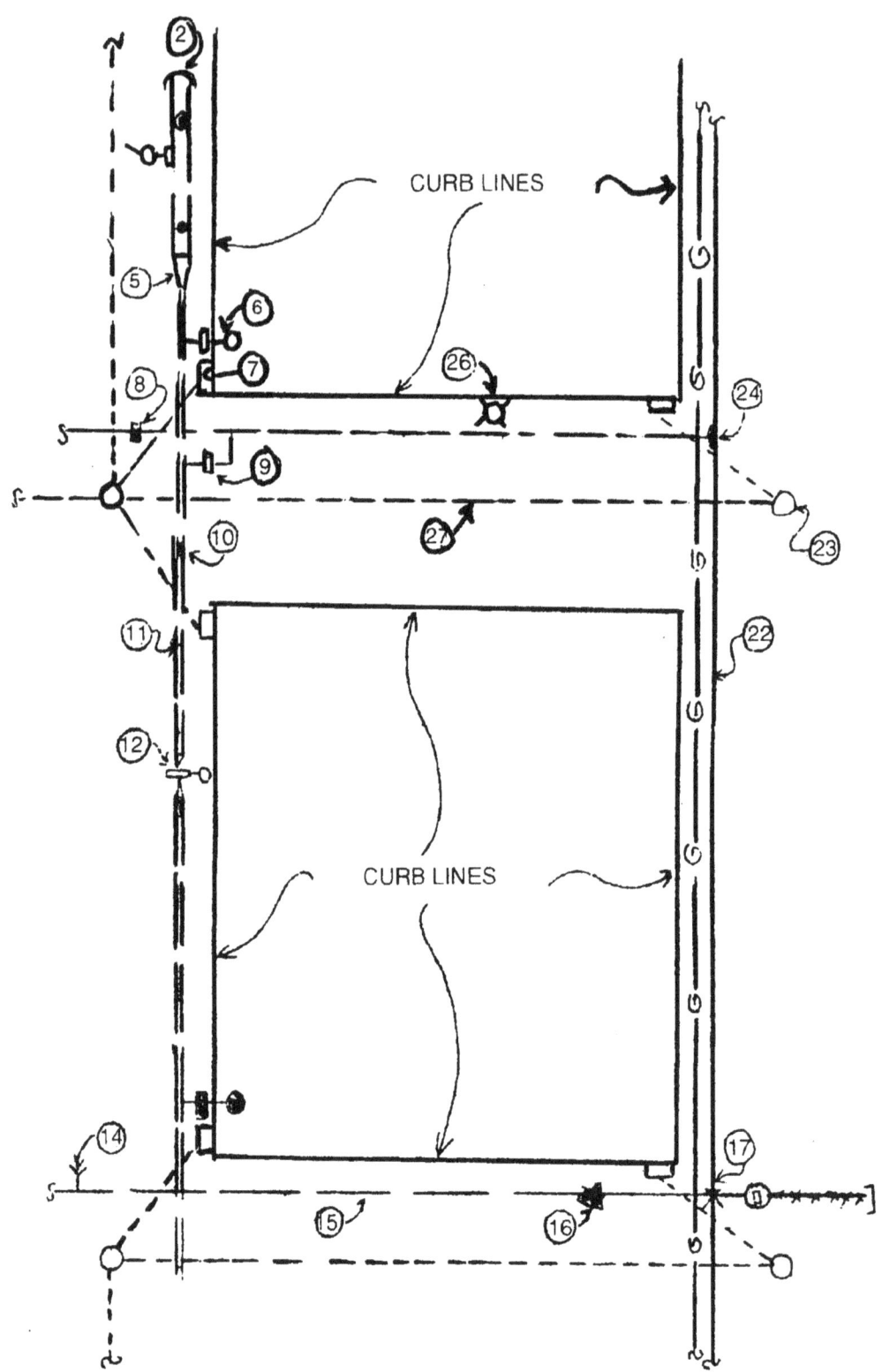

The above sketch represents a portion of a water distribution map and other facilities. To be used in answering questions numbered 25 to 30 inclusive.

25. A hydrant symbol is numbered
    A. 26   B. 14   C. 6   D. 9

26. A cap symbol is numbered
    A. 2   B. 5   C. 9   D. 10

27. Of the following numbered lines, the one which is NOT a water line is numbered
    A. 11   B. 15   C. 22   D. 27

28. A reducer symbol is numbered
    A. 8   B. 16   C. 12   D. 14

29. A catch basin symbol is numbered
    A. 7   B. 10   C. 23   D. 24

30. A valve symbol is numbered
    A. 17   B. 14   C. 10   D. 8

31. Opening a fire hydrant near the high point of a newly installed portion of a water main, prior to testing, is USUALLY done in order to remove
    A. air
    B. obstructions
    C. slime growths
    D. P. mineral deposits

32. Taps, or wet connections to a city main, may be made by
    A. a licensed plumber
    B. the Department of Water Supply, Gas and Electricity
    C. the Department of Public Works
    D. any experienced laborer

33. The supervisor made a ridiculous statement. As used in this sentence, the word ridiculous means MOST NEARLY
    A. incorrect   B. evil   C. unfriendly   D. foolish

34. That pipe caulker is engaged in a hazardous job. As used in this sentence, the word hazardous means MOST NEARLY
    A. inconvenient
    B. dangerous
    C. difficult
    D. demanding

35. Breaks in water distribution mains are front page news for the very reason that they occur infrequently. As used in this sentence, the word infrequently means MOST NEARLY
    A. at regular intervals
    B. often
    C. rarely
    D. unexpectedly

36. Several kinds of self-caulking substitutes for lead have been developed. As used in this sentence, the word substitutes means MOST NEARLY
    A. additives
    B. replacements
    C. hardeners
    D. softeners

37. Cast iron is essentially an alloy of iron and carbon. As used in this sentence, the word essentially means MOST NEARLY

    A. never   B. basically   C. barely   D. sometimes

    37._____

38. A pipe worker sometimes makes a trivial mistake. As used in this sentence, the word trivial means MOST NEARLY

    A. common   B. significant
    C. obvious   D. unimportant

    38._____

39. When water moves through pipe, friction is developed between the water and the inside surface of the pipe. As used in this sentence, the word friction means MOST NEARLY

    A. resistance   B. heat
    C. slippage   D. pressure

    39._____

40. Assume that a piece of cast iron pipe has to be cut to fit between two cast iron bells fixed in place in a trench. Of the following statements, the one which is MOST NEARLY correct is that, if the pipe is cut too

    A. short, the next joint may have to be broken to make up the difference
    B. short, the yarn used for caulking might be pushed through past the end of the pipe
    C. long, the proper amount of caulking lead could not be used at the joints
    D. long, the joint would need a bottom support

    40._____

KEY (CORRECT ANSWERS)

1. B	11. D	21. D	31. A
2. B	12. D	22. B	32. B
3. C	13. A	23. D	33. D
4. A	14. D	24. C	34. B
5. C	15. A	25. C	35. C
6. C	16. A	26. A	36. B
7. B	17. A	27. D	37. B
8. A	18. D	28. B	38. D
9. C	19. D	29. A	39. A
10. C	20. A	30. D	40. B

EXAMINATION SECTION
TEST 1

DIRECTIONS: Each question or incomplete statement is followed by several suggested answers or completions. Select the one that BEST answers the question or completes the statement. *PRINT THE LETTER OF THE CORRECT ANSWER IN THE SPACE AT THE RIGHT.*

Questions 1-9.

DIRECTIONS: Questions 1 to 9 refer to the ferry rack shown below.

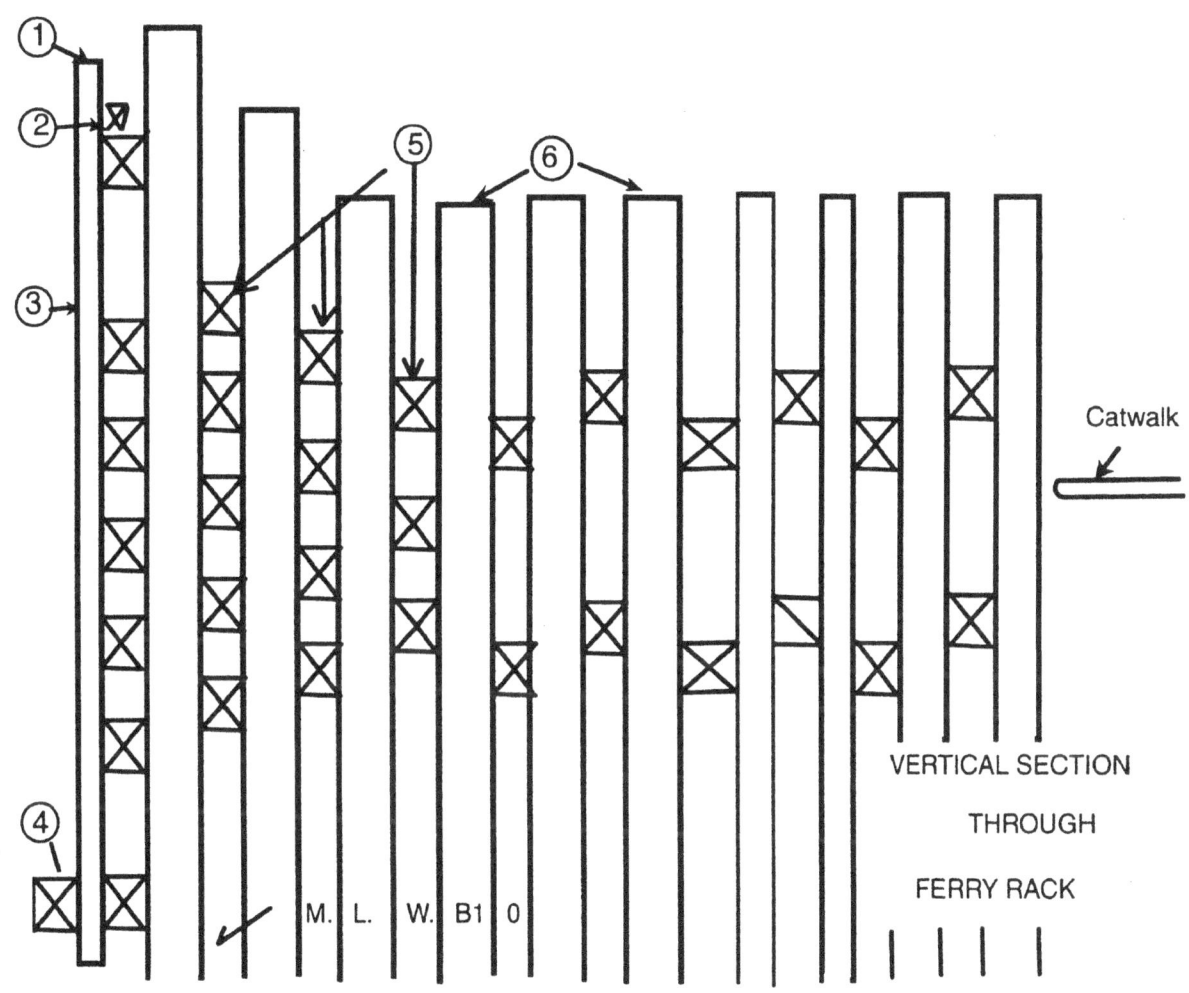

1. The distance point ① should be above M.L.W. is APPROXIMATELY _____ feet. 1._____

   A. 10   B. 20   C. 30   D. 40

2. Member ② is called a 2._____

   A. fender
   C. spacer
   B. ribbon piece
   D. hanging piece

29

2 (#1)

3. Member ③ should be made from   3.____

   A. greenheart   B. pine   C. oak   D. Cyprus

4. Member ④ is called a   4.____

   A. fender   B. ribbon piece
   C. waler   D. hanging piece

5. The size of member ⑤ should be approximately   5.____

   A. 4" x 4"   B. 8" x 8"   C. 10" x 10"   D. 12" x 12"

6. Member ⑥ should be   6.____

   A. greenheart   B. pine   C. oak   D. fir

7. The elevation of the catwalk should be approximately _____ feet.   7.____

   A. 5   B. 10   C. 15   D. 20

8. The wood used for the catwalk should be   8.____

   A. spruce   B. oak   C. greenheart   D. pine

9. To tie members ⑤ and ⑥ together, a dockbuilder should use   9.____

   A. wrought-iron bolts   B. high-strength steel bolts
   C. galvanized iron pins   D. wire rope

10. The size of the head of the 15-pound, double-face wood maul shown below is approximately _____ inches diameter by _____ inches long.   10.____
    A. 4; 10
    B. 8; 10
    C. 12; 15
    D. 14; 16

11. The cross-cut saw shown below would generally have   11.____
    A. 4 cutting teeth alternating with 1 raker tooth
    B. 2 cutting teeth alternating with 2 raker teeth
    C. 4 cutting teeth alternating with 4 raker teeth
    D. alternating raker teeth and cutting teeth

12. The blade of the carpenter's adze shown below has a width of APPROXIMATELY _____ inch(es).
    A. 1
    B. 4
    C. 8
    D. 10

12.____

13. The tool shown below is called a
    A. cant hook
    B. peavy
    C. mandrel
    D. boat hook

13.____

14. The tool shown below is called a
    A. come-along
    B. grapple hook
    C. load binder
    D. tugger

14.____

15. The sketch below shows a method of preventing a rope from unraveling which is called
    A. splicing
    B. whipping
    C. mousing
    D. seizing

15.____

16. The placing of rope yarn on a hook to prevent the load from being detached as shown below is called
    A. splicing
    B. whipping
    C. mousing
    D. seizing

16.____

17. The rope splice shown below is called a(n) _____ splice.
    A. eye
    B. short
    C. net
    D. cut

17.____

18. The tool shown below is a
    A. cant hook
    B. timber-carrying hook
    C. beam dog
    D. girder dog

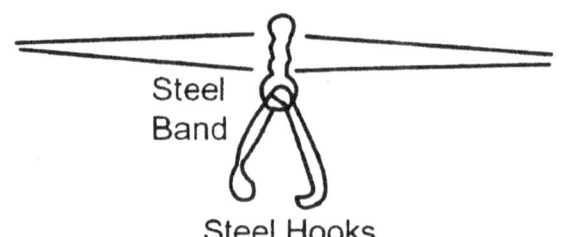

Questions 19-24.

DIRECTIONS: Questions 19 to 24 refer to the common rope knots, bends, and hitches shown below.

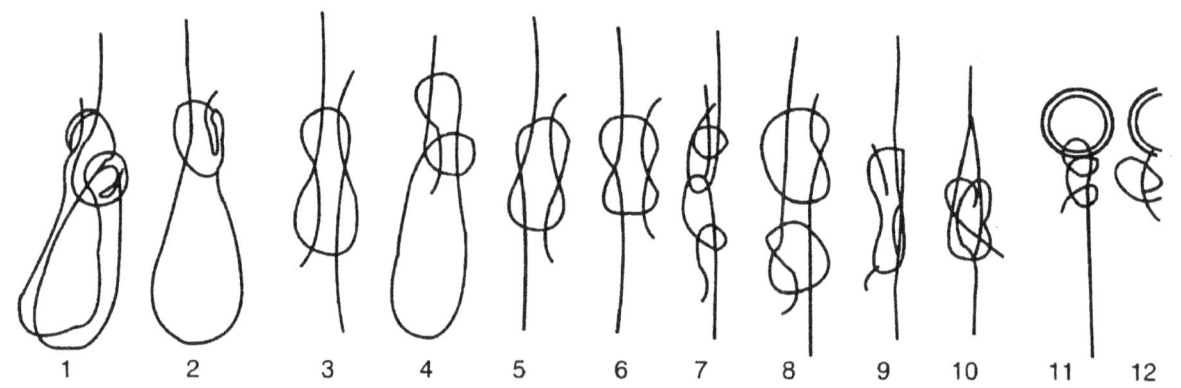

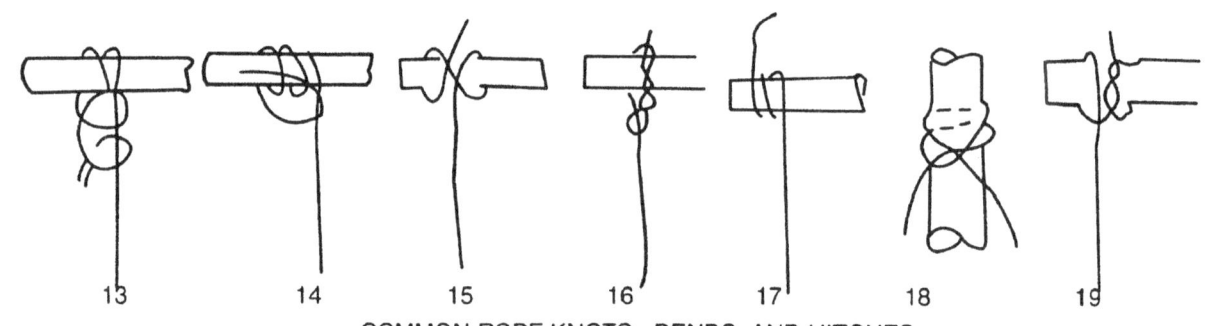

COMMON ROPE KNOTS, BENDS, AND HITCHES

19. A square knot is number
    A. 3   B. 6   C. 9   D. 12

20. A bowline is number
    A. 2   B. 3   C. 4   D. 5

21. Two half hitches are number
    A. 11   B. 12   C. 15   D. 16

22. A timber hitch is number
    A. 13   B. 14   C. 15   D. 16

23. A bowline on a bight is number

    A. 1   B. 2   C. 3   D. 8

24. A clove hitch is number

    A. 7   B. 10   C. 15   D. 18

25. The MOST important safety precaution to take when shipping concrete is to wear

    A. a hard hat
    B. goggles
    C. heavy gloves
    D. a long-sleeved shirt

26. Continuous sheathing is usually used when excavating a trench in

    A. firm earth
    B. stiff clay
    C. rock
    D. sand

27. The number of blows-per-minute of the driving hammer is generally controlled by the

    A. rig-operating engineer
    B. dockbuilder at the throttle
    C. foreman
    D. lead man

28. The ADVANTAGE of plywood over pine boards is that the plywood

    A. is cheaper
    B. never splinters
    C. resists warping
    D. is heavier

29. The practice of momentarily *cracking* the valves of each gas cylinder before connecting the hoses of a cutting outfit is

    A. really of no practical value
    B. a dangerous shortcut due to possible explosion
    C. useful for blowing any dirt out of the valves
    D. a practical means of determining how much gas is left

30. Oil is frequently applied to the inside of forms prior to pouring the concrete in order to

    A. make stripping easier
    B. prolong the life of the forms
    C. make the concrete flow more easily
    D. prevent the forms from absorbing water from the concrete

31. The piece of equipment used to drive the head of a pile below the water surface is known as a(n)

    A. overdrive   B. spud   C. follower   D. extender

32. A structural member has a designation of 6WF12. The *12* in this designation is the

    A. depth of web
    B. width of flange
    C. weight per foot
    D. Brinell hardness number

33. The reason for NOT painting wood ladders is that the paint

    A. would quickly wear off
    B. might hide serious defects
    C. might rub off onto clothing
    D. might make the rungs slippery

34. Although cloth tapes are used for taking measurements in many kinds of work, they should NOT be used when accurate measurements must be obtained because

   A. the numbers soon become worn and thus difficult to read
   B. there are not enough sub-divisions of each inch
   C. the ink runs when wet, thus making the tape difficult to read
   D. small changes in the amount of pull on the tape will make big differences in reading

Questions 35-37.

DIRECTIONS: Questions 35 to 37 refer to the common timber joints shown below.

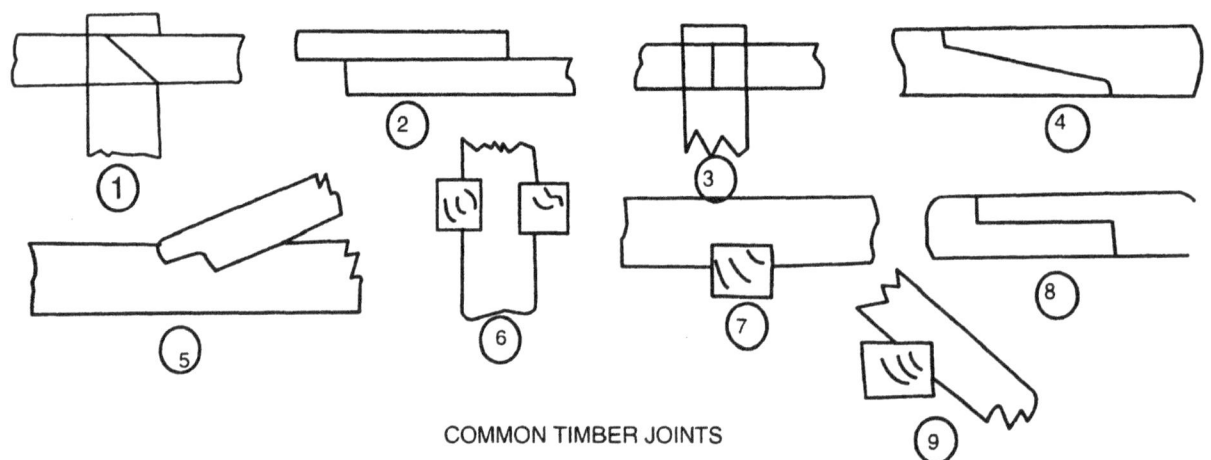

COMMON TIMBER JOINTS

35. A bird's mouth joint is number

   A. 1   B. 4   C. 7   D. 9

36. A scarf joint is number

   A. 2   B. 4   C. 6   D. 8

37. A double-notched joint is number

   A. 5   B. 6   C. 7   D. 9

38. The MOST satisfactory combination of dockbuilding, welding, and cutting, GENERALLY is _____ welding and _____ cutting.

   A. electric; electric   B. electric; gas
   C. gas; gas   D. gas; electric

39. Instructions in first aid are given to some dockbuilders to

    A. reduce the number of accidents
    B. help them understand safety rules
    C. eliminate the need for calling a doctor
    D. prepare them to give emergency aid

40. Wedges are used under vertical shoring timbers MAINLY to

    A. obtain tight shoring
    B. reduce construction noise
    C. lessen needed accuracy in cutting the timber
    D. permit the use of short, less expensive timbers

KEY (CORRECT ANSWERS)

1. B	11. A	21. A	31. C
2. D	12. B	22. D	32. C
3. C	13. B	23. A	33. B
4. B	14. C	24. C	34. D
5. D	15. B	25. B	35. D
6. A	16. C	26. D	36. B
7. B	17. B	27. B	37. B
8. D	18. B	28. C	38. B
9. A	19. B	29. C	39. D
10. B	20. C	30. A	40. A

TEST 2

DIRECTIONS: Each question or incomplete statement is followed by several suggested answers or completions. Select the one that BEST answers the question or completes the statement. *PRINT THE LETTER OF THE CORRECT ANSWER IN THE SPACE AT THE RIGHT.*

1. Shoes which have a sponge rubber sole should NOT be worn around a construction site because such a sole

   A. is not waterproof
   B. is too slippery
   C. is easily punctured
   D. will wear quickly

2. The method of removing a length of wire rope from its reel that should NOT be used is to

   A. mount the reel on a shaft and trunnions and then rotate the reel
   B. mount the reel on a turntable and then rotate the turntable
   C. fix the free end and then roll the reel along the floor
   D. take off the rope from the top side of a reel resting on one side

3. The BEST reason for using a vibrator when placing concrete is to

   A. move the concrete into place
   B. eliminate air trapped in the concrete
   C. prevent segregation in the concrete
   D. increase the amount of air entrained in the concrete

4. Wooden piles are BEST used when they

   A. will be above the permanent ground water level
   B. will be partially submerged in salt water
   C. will be below the permanent ground water level
   D. are partially submerged but not subject to attacks by the Teredo

5. In reinforced concrete work, wire chairs are generally used to

   A. position reinforcing bars
   B. reinforce sharp corners
   C. tie reinforcing bars together
   D. reinforce concrete at shear points

6. A mason's level is placed on a flat surface which appears to be horizontal. The bubble reads 1/16" to the right of center. When the level is placed on the surface with the ends of the level reversed, the bubble again reads 1/16" to the right of center.
   This indicates that

   A. the bubble tube is set properly
   B. the surface is exactly horizontal
   C. the bubble tube is not set properly
   D. it is necessary to test the level on a horizontal surface first

7. MOST specifications prohibit the painting of steel reinforcement bars since

   A. the bars are not exposed to view
   B. concrete would scrape off the paint

C. paint would prevent proper bending of the bars
D. moisture in the concrete would make the paint ineffective

8. The cable which is run out from the pile driver rig to pick up the next pile to be driven is usually fitted with a heavy steel ball located just above the hook.
   The purpose of this ball is to

   A. keep the hook vertical
   B. reduce the whipping of the cable
   C. keep the cable tight on the drum
   D. prevent the hook from being pulled through the pulley

9. The PRINCIPAL reason for making butted joints in long columns on wooden scaffolding is that this results in

   A. lighter timbers
   B. better appearance
   C. less strain on the nail
   D. more resistance to the wood

Questions 10-16.

DIRECTIONS: Questions 10 to 16 refer to the standard signals for hoists shown below.

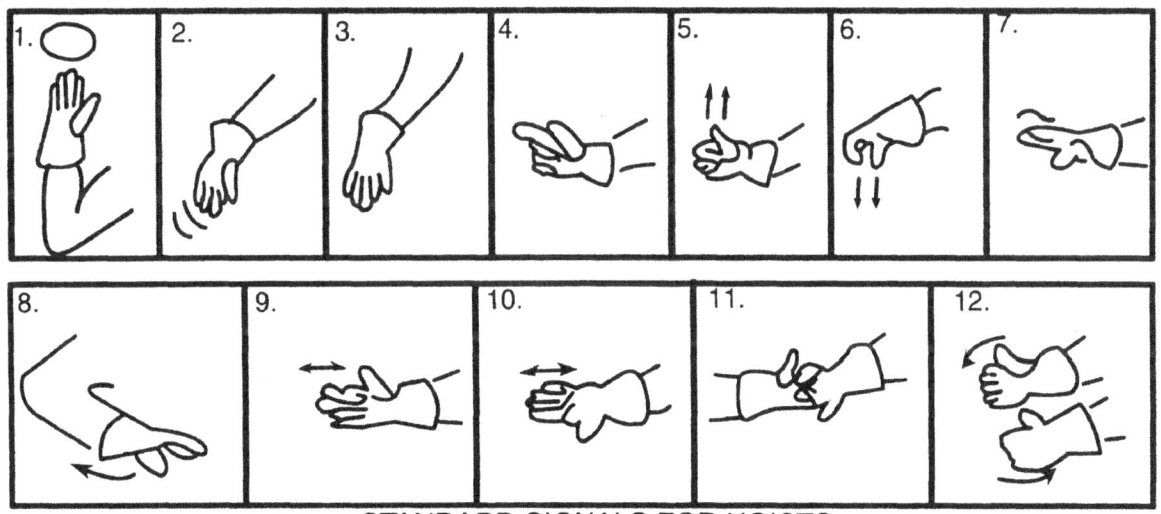

STANDARD SIGNALS FOR HOISTS

10. The proper signal for an emergency stop is number

    A. 1   B. 3   C. 8   D. 11

11. The proper signal for lowering the load is number

    A. 2   B. 3   C. 6   D. 10

12. The proper signal for booming up is number

    A. 1   B. 4   C. 5   D. 8

13. The proper signal for swing is number

    A. 4   B. 7   C. 8   D. 10

14. The proper signal to hoist is number

    A. 1   B. 4   C. 5   D. 12

15. The proper signal to boom down is number

    A. 2   B. 6   C. 10   D. 11

16. The proper signal to dog off everything is number

    A. 3   B. 4   C. 8   D. 11

17. The BEST way for a dockbuilder to avoid accidents is to

    A. refuse any job on which he could get hurt
    B. take a complete course in first aid in a good school
    C. figure out for himself what is the safest way to do the work
    D. learn and obey all safety rules that should be used in his work

18. The term *interlocking* is applied normally to

    A. reinforced concrete sheeting
    B. pre-stressed concrete piling
    C. pipe piling
    D. steel sheeting

19. The device shown below is a
    A. steamboat ratchet
    B. turnbuckle
    C. spool
    D. heel dolly

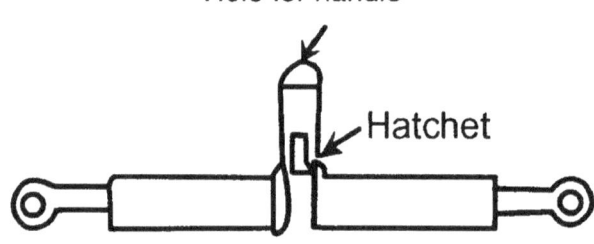

20. The mooring hardware shown is a
    A. cleat
    B. bollard
    C. dolphin
    D. mole

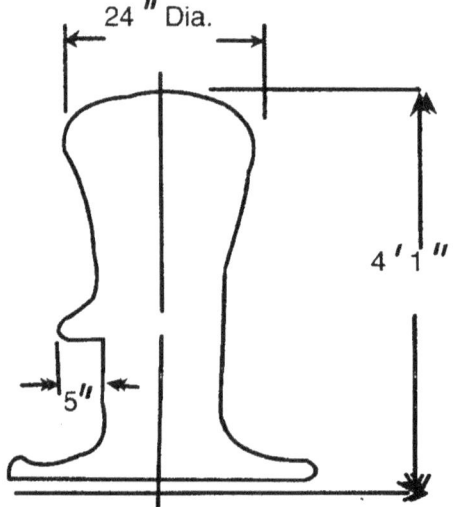

21. The tool shown below is a
    A. timber hook
    B. beam dog
    C. girder dog
    D. tagline hook

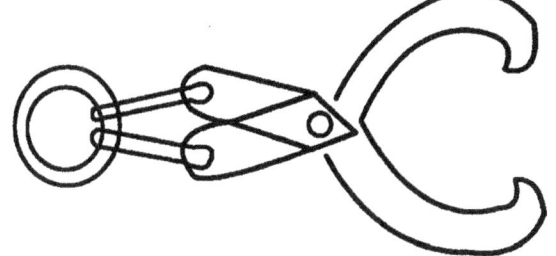

22. The rigging device shown below is a
    A. screw clamp
    B. pin shackle
    C. clevis
    D. thimble

23. The wire-rope clip shown below is called a
    A. Crosby
    B. Loughlin
    C. fist-grip
    D. c-clamp

24. The mooring hardware shown below is a
    A. cleat
    B. bollard
    C. dolphin
    D. mole

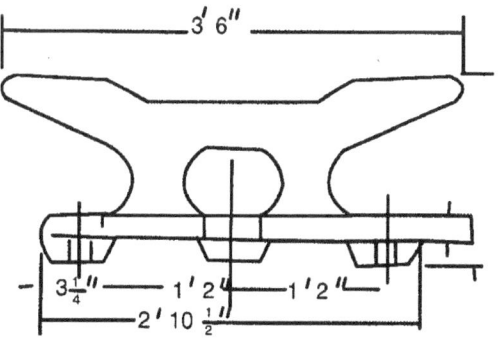

Questions 25-33.

DIRECTIONS: Questions 25 to 33 refer to the typical single pile row of a pier shown below.

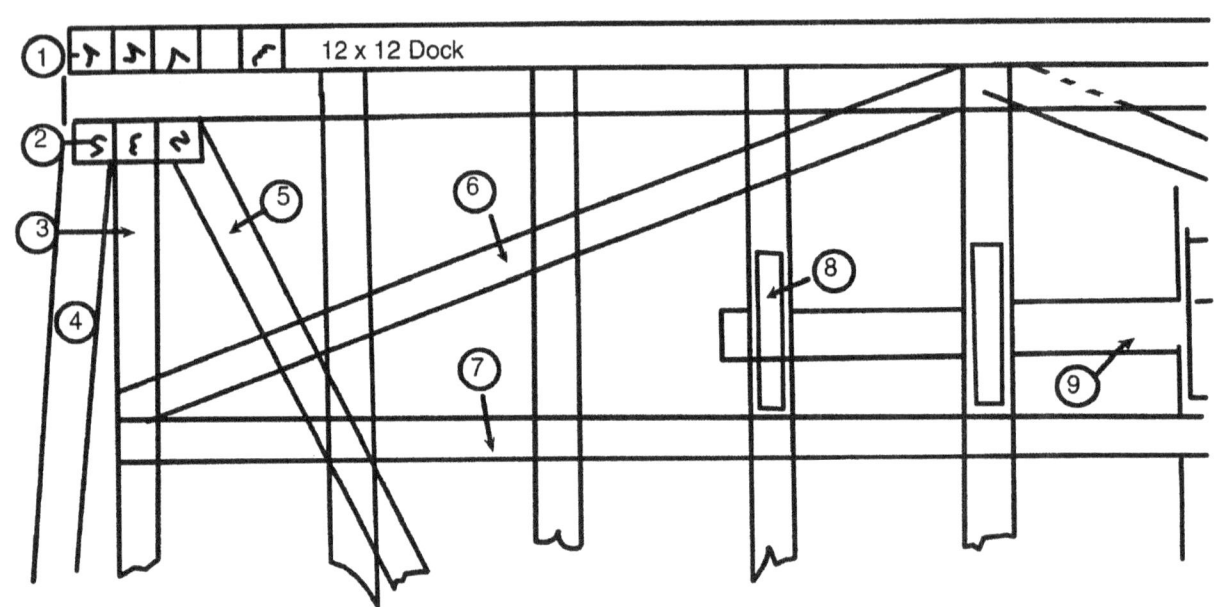

VERTICAL SECTION THROUGH SINGLE FILE ROW

25. Member ① is a

　A. side cap　　　　　　　　　B. fender chock
　C. fender cap　　　　　　　　D. bench cap

26. Member ② is a

　A. side cap　　　　　　　　　B. fender chock
　C. fender cap　　　　　　　　D. bench cap

27. Member ③ is a _____ pile.

　A. fender　　B. line　　C. brace　　D. stiffener

28. Member ④ is a pile.

　A. fender　　B. line　　C. brace　　D. pre-stressed

29. Member ⑤ is a _____ pile.

　A. fender　　B. line　　C. brace　　D. pre-stressed

30. Member ⑥ is a(n)

　A. T brace　　　　　　　　　B. low water brace
　C. brace post　　　　　　　　D. A brace

31. Member (7) is a(n)

    A. T brace
    B. low water brace
    C. brace post
    D. A brace

32. Member (8) is a _____ plate.

    A. fish
    B. tie
    C. lining
    D. support

33. Member (9) is a

    A. side cap
    B. fender chock
    C. fender cap
    D. bench cap

34. One of the strictest safety rules enforced in a gang using a crane is that only one designated man gives the signal to the crane operator, and the rest of the gang follows the signals.
    The ONLY signal that anyone in the gang can properly give is a _____ signal.

    A. boom-up
    B. stop
    C. hoist
    D. swing

35. A pile that is intentionally driven at an angle is called a _____ pile.

    A. bearing
    B. sheet
    C. batter
    D. diagonal

36. If it is necessary for you to work with your hands under a piece of heavy equipment while another dockbuilder lifts one end with a crow bar, you should

    A. wear heavy gloves
    B. work as fast as possible
    C. support the handle of the crow bar on a timber
    D. insert temporary blocks to support the piece

37. On a driving rig, the dockbuilder who centers the head of the pile under the hammer is called the

    A. centerer
    B. monkey
    C. lead man
    D. pointer

38. Of the following, the safety device used on a crane to prevent overtravel is called a(n)

    A. governor
    B. limit switch
    C. overload relay
    D. unloader

39. Creosote is commonly used to

    A. fireproof timber
    B. season wood
    C. preserve wood
    D. make painting easier

40. In dockbuilding, a *skull cracker* should be used for

    A. straightening piles
    B. boring bolt holes
    C. pulling piles
    D. driving sheeting

KEY (CORRECT ANSWERS)

1. C	11. A	21. A	31. B
2. D	12. C	22. B	32. A
3. B	13. A	23. A	33. D
4. C	14. A	24. A	34. B
5. A	15. B	25. C	35. C
6. A	16. D	26. B	36. D
7. C	17. D	27. B	37. B
8. C	18. D	28. A	38. B
9. C	19. A	29. C	39. C
10. C	20. B	30. D	40. C

EXAMINATION SECTION
TEST 1

DIRECTIONS: Each question or incomplete statement is followed by several suggested answers or completions. Select the one that BEST answers the question or completes the statement. *PRINT THE LETTER OF THE CORRECT ANSWER IN THE SPACE AT THE RIGHT.*

1. Assume that a certain file has a safe edge. This is an edge that has
   A. no teeth
   B. the teeth pointing backward
   C. the teeth pointing forward
   D. fine criss-cross teeth

2. The one of the following which is the proper tool for threading a round rod is a
   A. tap   B. countersink   C. counterbore   D. die

3. A rasp is a
   A. type of chisel
   B. type of file cleaner
   C. type of coarse file
   D. kind of plane

4. The one of the following which is the proper tool to use to tighten a round nut which has a series of notches cut in its outer surface is a(n) _____ wrench.
   A. box   B. spanner   C. Stillson   D. monkey

5. Small leaks resulting from poor threads on steel or wrought-iron water pipes will often stop because the leaky threads are in time filled with
   A. sediment   B. stalactite   C. rust   D. soapstone

6. A metal that can be rolled or beaten into very fine sheets is said to be
   A. anodized   B. malleable   C. tempered   D. ferrous

7. To *rod* a sewer pipe means MOST likely to
   A. clean it out by means of rods
   B. keep the pipe clear of debris by placing a grating of rods at the intake
   C. support the sewer pipe with horizontal reinforcing metal rods
   D. shore up the pipe

8. Of the following abrasives, the one which is the LEAST coarse is
   A. No. 2 emery cloth
   B. crocus cloth
   C. No. 1 sandpaper
   D. No. 1/0 sandpaper

9. In order to permit free passage of water in one direction only and prevent a reversal of flow in the pipe, it is necessary to use a _____ valve.
   A. gate   B. check   C. globe   D. needle

10. Assume that a cubic foot of water contains 7 1/2 gallons. The number of gallons of water which could be contained in a rectangular tank 3 feet long, 2 feet wide, and 2 feet deep is MOST NEARLY
    A. 12   B. 45   C. 90   D. 120

11. The weight, in pounds, of a cubic foot of fresh water is MOST NEARLY

A. 8.5 B. 32.4 C. 62.4 D. 98.6

12. The total weight, in pounds, of ten bags of Portland cement is MOST NEARLY _____ pounds.

A. 108 B. 187 C. 940 D. 1,200

13. If a concrete mix is said to be 1:2:4, this would mean that the mix is made up of 1 part by 1

A. volume of cement to 2 parts by volume of sand to 4 parts by volume of coarse aggregate
B. volume of cement to 2 parts by volume of coarse aggregate to 4 parts by volume of sand
C. volume of coarse aggregate to 2 parts by volume of sand to 4 parts by volume of cement
D. weight of cement to 2 parts by weight of coarse aggregate to 4 parts by weight of sand

14. The ratio of the weight of a substance to the weight of an equal volume of water is called the _____ of the substance.

A. specific volume B. specific gravity
C. viscosity D. fractional weight

15. Of the following, the pipe fitting which has four openings which permits connecting a line at right angles to another line is called a(n)

A. side outlet street L B. double elbow
C. tee D. cross

16. To tighten a nut where only a short swing of the wrench handle is possible, it is BEST to use a _____ wrench.

A. ratchet B. hook spanner
C. Stillson D. Bristo

17. Of the following, the proper tool to use to remove the burr from the inside of a pipe is a

A. half round file B. reamer
C. mandrel D. chisel

18. Fittings commonly used with copper pipe should be made of

A. brass B. cast iron
C. malleable iron D. pure tin

19. With respect to pipe, the abbreviation I.P.S. means

A. Internal Pipe Size B. Iron Pipe Size
C. Iron Pipe Shape D. International Pipe Size

20. A Stillson wrench is the proper wrench to use when tightening a

    A. square nut B. hexagonal nut
    C. valve gland nut D. pipe fitting

21. The one of the following which is the proper tool to use for cutting wood along the grain is a _____ saw.

    A. rip B. panel C. cross-cut D. back

22. The one of the following which is the proper tool to use to cut internal screw threads is a

    A. broach B. die C. tap D. stock

23. A center punch is the proper tool used to

    A. cut out the center of a gasket
    B. dent metal prior to drilling
    C. drive nails beneath the surface of the wood
    D. punch a small hole in sheet metal

24. The one of the following knots which can be safely used for tying together the ends of two dry ropes of the same size is a

    A. granny knot B. clove hitch
    C. half hitch D. square knot

25. The PRIMARY purpose of a trap under a plumbing fixture is to

    A. act as a seal against sewer gas
    B. permit cleaning out the drain line
    C. permit the recovery of valuables accidentally dropped into the fixture
    D. permit the making of tests on the drain line

26. The one of the following which contains exactly 10 board feet is a board 10 feet long, _____ inches wide, _____ inch(es) thick.

    A. 24; 1 B. 12; 2 C. 12; 1 D. 10; 1

27. Short pieces of pipe threaded on both ends are called

    A. nipples B. couplings C. bushing D. sleeves

28. The unit of electrical capacitance is the

    A. ampere B. farad C. henry D. cycle

29. As used in the electrical industry, BX means

    A. best grade of electrical wire
    B. type B extension wire
    C. metal greenfield
    D. insulated wires in flexible metal tubing

Questions 30-33.

DIRECTIONS: Questions 30 to 33, inclusive, are to be answered in accordance with the following paragraph.

One of the categories of nuisance is a chemical one and relates to the dissolved oxygen of the watercourse. The presence in sewage and industrial wastes of materials capable of undergoing biochemical oxidation and resulting in reduction of oxygen in the watercourse leads to a partial or complete depletion of this oxygen. This, in turn, leads to the subsequent production of malodorous products of decomposition, to the destruction of aquatic plant life and major fish life and to conditions offensive to sight and smell.

30. The word *malodorous* as used in the above paragraph means MOST NEARLY

    A. fragrant   B. fetid   C. wholesome   D. redolent

31. From the above paragraph, because of pollution, the amount of dissolved oxygen in the waterways is

    A. released   B. multiplied   C. lessened   D. saturated

32. The word *categories* as used in the above paragraph means MOST NEARLY

    A. divisions   B. clubs   C. symbols   D. products

33. The word *offensive* as used in the above paragraph means MOST NEARLY

    A. pliable
    B. complaint
    C. deferential
    D. disagreeable

34. The terminal voltage of 5 dry cells connected in a series is _____ of one(each) cell.

    A. 1/5 the voltage
    B. the same as the voltage
    C. 5 times the voltage
    D. determined by the current

35. If a 15 ampere fuse blows out and blows out again after inserting a new fuse, it is BEST to

    A. replace it with a 10 ampere fustat
    B. replace it with two 10 ampere fuses connected in series
    C. replace it with a 20 ampere fuse
    D. have the circuit checked to find the trouble

36. Ordinary soft solder is a mixture of lead and

    A. sulphur   B. brass   C. zinc   D. tin

37. The electrolyte used in the ordinary flashlight-type dry cell is

    A. calcium chloride
    B. ammonium chloride
    C. manganese dioxide
    D. sulfuric acid

38. An electrical transformer is an electrical device used primarily to 38.____

    A. raise or lower A.C. voltages
    B. change the frequency of alternating current
    C. rectify currents from A.C. to D.C.
    D. change currents from D.C. to A.C.

39. Of the following, the MAIN reason for the grounding of electrical equipment and circuits is to 39.____

    A. save power
    B. increase the voltage
    C. protect personnel from electric shock
    D. prevent serious short circuits

40. In order to properly ground portable electric hand tools, it is USUALLY necessary to use a 40.____

    A. solenoid   B. circuit breaker
    C. fuse   D. three prong plug

41. The current in a simple electrical circuit can be calculated by dividing the voltage by the resistance in ohms. Assume that the resistance of a certain circuit is 60 ohms and its voltage is 120 volts, 60 cycle A.C. The current in this circuit will be MOST NEARLY _____ ampere(s). 41.____

    A. 1/2   B. 2   C. 1   D. 30

42. The one of the following which is the MOST common type of motor that may be used with an A.C. or D.C. source of supply is the _____ motor. 42.____

    A. shunt   B. squirrel cage
    C. compound   D. series

43. The electrolyte in the ordinary storage battery is 43.____

    A. nitric acid   B. sulphuric acid
    C. manganese dioxide   D. ammonium chloride

44. The one of the following terms which is used in expressing the rating of a storage battery is 44.____

    A. ampere-hours   B. amperes
    C. volt-ampere   D. watt-hours

45. The size of the SMALLEST graduation on the ordinary 6-foot folding rule is usually 45.____

    A. 1/8"   B. 1/16"   C. 1/32"   D. 1/64"

46. A given saw has 8 points per inch. This saw is PROBABLY a _____ saw. 46.____

    A. cross-cut   B. hack   C. veneer   D. back

47. Assume that it takes 6 men 8 days to do a certain job. Working at the same same speed, the number of days that it will take 4 men to do this job is

   A. 9   B. 10   C. 12   D. 14

48. The sum of 3 5/8 + 4 1/4 + 6 1/2 + 7 1/8 is

   A. 20 7/8   B. 21 1/4   C. 21 1/2   D. 22 1/8

49. The fraction which is equal to .0625 is

   A. 1/64   B. 3/64   C. 1/16   D. 5/8

50. The volume, in cubic feet, of a rectangular coal bin 8 ft. long by 5 ft. wide by 7 ft. high is MOST NEARLY

   A. 40   B. 56   C. 186   D. 280

KEY (CORRECT ANSWERS)

1. A	11. C	21. A	31. C	41. B
2. D	12. C	22. C	32. A	42. D
3. C	13. A	23. B	33. D	43. B
4. B	14. B	24. D	34. C	44. A
5. C	15. D	25. A	35. D	45. B
6. B	16. A	26. C	36. D	46. A
7. A	17. B	27. A	37. B	47. C
8. B	18. A	28. B	38. A	48. C
9. B	19. B	29. D	39. C	49. C
10. C	20. D	30. B	40. D	50. D

TEST 2

DIRECTIONS: Each question or incomplete statement is followed by several suggested answers or completions. Select the one that BEST answers the question or completes the statement. *PRINT THE LETTER OF THE CORRECT ANSWER IN THE SPACE AT THE RIGHT.*

Questions 1-7

DIRECTIONS: Questions 1 to 7, inclusive, are to be answered in accordance with the following information.

At sea level, the atmosphere can exert a pressure of 14.7 pounds per square inch. This pressure is capable of sustaining a column of water having a height equal to 14.7 pounds, multiplied by 2.304 (the height of water in feet which will exert one pound per square inch pressure). No pump built can produce a perfect vacuum. The atmospheric pressure exerting its force on the surface of the water from which suction is being taken forces the water up through the suction to the pump. From this, it is evident that the maximum height which a water pump of this type can lift water is determined ultimately by the atmospheric pressure. The tightness of the pump and its ability to create a vacuum also have a bearing.

1. The meaning of the word *vacuum* as used in the above article is a
    A. space entirely devoid of matter
    B. sealed tube filled with gas
    C. bottle-shaped vessel with a double wall
    D. cleaning device

2. With reference to the above article, if a pump could produce a perfect vacuum, the MAXIMUM height, in feet, that it could lift water at sea level is MOST NEARLY
    A. 33.9   B. 29.4   C. 23.3   D. 14.7

3. With reference to the above article, a column of water having a height of 4.6 feet at sea level will exert a pressure of MOST NEARLY _____ pound(s) per square inch.
    A. 3   B. 2   C. 1   D. 1/2

4. The word *atmosphere* as used in the above article means
    A. the pull of gravity
    B. perfect vacuum
    C. the whole mass of air surrounding the earth
    D. the weight of water at sea level

5. The word *bearing* as used in the above article means MOST NEARLY
    A. direction   B. connection
    C. divergence   D. convergence

6. The word *evident* as used in the above article means MOST NEARLY 6.____

   A. disconcerting   B. obscure   C. equivocal   D. manifest

7. The word *maximum* as used in the above article means MOST NEARLY 7.____

   A. best   B. median   C. adjacent   D. greatest

8. Assume that a car travels at a constant speed of 36 miles per hour. The speed of this car, in feet per second, is MOST NEARLY (one mile equals 5,280 ft.) 8.____

   A. 3   B. 24.6   C. 52.8   D. 879.8

9. If one-third of a 19-foot length of lumber is cut off, the length of the remaining piece will measure APPROXIMATELY 9.____

   A. 8'8"   B. 9'8"   C. 12'8"   D. 13'8"

10. The circumference of a circle having a diameter of 10" is MOST NEARLY ____ inches. 10.____

    A. 3.14   B. 18.72   C. 24.96   D. 31.4

11. Assume that in the purchase of paint, the seller quotes a discount of 10%. If the price per gallon is $6.35, the actual payment in dollars per gallon is MOST NEARLY 11.____

    A. $5.72   B. $5.95   C. $6.25   D. $6.50

12. On a 1" bolt that has 10 threads per inch, if the nut is turned 6 complete turns, the distance, in inches, that the nut will move along the bolt is MOST NEARLY 12.____

    A. .3   B. .6   C. .9   D. 1

13. Assume that at one end of a 6-inch horizontal line, an 8-inch vertical line is drawn at right angles to the horizontal line. The length, in inches, between the ends of the two lines is MOST NEARLY 13.____

    A. 6   B. 8   C. 10   D. 12

Questions 14-21.

DIRECTIONS: Questions 14 to 21, inclusive, are to be answered in accordance with the following information.

In his 2012 annual report to the Mayor, the Public Works Commissioner stated that the city's basic water pollution control program begun in 1996 and costing $425 million so far would be completed in five or six years at a cost of $275 million more. However, he said, the city must spend an additional $175 million more on its marginal pollution control program to protect present and proposed beaches. Under the basic program, the city will have eliminated the last major discharges of raw sewage into the harbor. Over 800 million gallons, two thirds of the city's spent water each day, is now treated at 12 plants, to which six new plants will be added, enabling the city to treat the estimated 1.8 billion gallons that will be discharged daily in 2030. The department had about $200 million worth of municipal construction under way in 2012, and completed $85.5 millions' worth.

14. According to the above, the city will add _____ new plants. 14._____

    A. 18   B. 12   C. 6   D. 4

15. The amount of municipal construction under way in 2012 was _____ million. 15._____

    A. $85.5   B. $175   C. $200   D. $425

16. It is estimated that in 2030, the city will treat daily _____ gallons. 16._____

    A. 700 million   B. 800 million
    C. 900 million   D. 1.8 billion

17. According to the above article, the total cost of the water pollution program begun in 1996 will be _____ million. 17._____

    A. $275   B. $425   C. $700   D. $815

18. According to the above article, to protect present and proposed beaches, the city must spend an additional _____ million. 18._____

    A. $175   B. $275   C. $425   D. $450

19. The above article concerns the statements of the Commissioner of Public Works in his _____ annual report to the Mayor. 19._____

    A. 1996   B. 2002   C. 2012   D. 2013

20. The word *discharged* as used in the above article means MOST NEARLY 20._____

    A. emitted   B. erased   C. refuted   D. repelled

21. The word *pollution* as used in the above article means MOST NEARLY 21._____

    A. condensation   B. purification
    C. contamination   D. distillation

22. A tool commonly used to cut off the head of a rivet is a 22._____

    A. cold chisel   B. cape chisel   C. band saw   D. file

23. A metal washer is MOST often used with a _____ screw. 23._____

    A. wood   B. lag   C. hand   D. machine

24. A good safety rule to follow is that water should NOT be used to extinguish fires in or around electrical apparatus. Of the following, the PRIMARY reason for this is that water 24._____

    A. will damage the insulation
    B. will corrode the electrical conductors
    C. may cause the circuit fuse to blow
    D. may conduct electric current and cause a shock hazard

25. One should be extremely careful to keep open flames and sparks away from storage batteries when they are being charged because the

   A. sulphate given off during this operation is highly flammable
   B. hydrogen given off during this operation is highly flammable
   C. oxygen given off during this operation is extremely flammable
   D. static electricity of the battery may cause combustion

26. A good safety rule to follow is that an electric hand tool, such as a portable electric drill, should never be lifted or carried by its service cord.
Of the following, the PRIMARY reason for this rule is that the

   A. tool might swing and be damaged by striking some hard object
   B. cord might be pulled off its terminals and become short circuited
   C. tool may slip out of the hand as it is hard to get a good grip on a slick rubber cord
   D. rubber covering of the cord might overstretch

27. When a man is working on a 15-foot ladder with its top placed against a wall, the MAXIMUM safe distance that he may reach out to one side of the ladder is

   A. as far out as he can reach lifting one foot off the rung for balance
   B. as far out as he can reach without bending his body more than 45 from the vertical
   C. one-third the length of the ladder
   D. as far out as his arm's length

28. When NOT in use, oily waste rags should be stored in

   A. water-tight oak barrels
   B. open metal containers
   C. sealed cardboard boxes
   D. self-closing, metal containers

29. Assume that one of your co-workers has suffered an electric shock. Artificial respiration should be started on him immediately if he is

   A. unconscious and breathing
   B. conscious and in a daze
   C. unconscious and not breathing
   D. conscious and badly burned

30. Assume that the top of a 12-foot portable straight ladder is placed against a wall but is not held by a man or fastened in any way. In order to be safe, the ladder should be placed so that the distance from the wall to the foot of the ladder is

   A. not over 3 feet
   B. not over 4 feet
   C. at least 4 feet
   D. at least 5 feet

31. Of the following, the one which is an acceptable method of caring for wooden ladders is to

   A. coat the ladder with clear shellac
   B. paint the ladder with red lead followed by a second coat of the desired color
   C. paint the ladder with a coat of paint of the desired color
   D. apply a sealer coat before painting with a second coat of the desired color

32. The MOST important safety precaution to follow when using an electric drill press is to

    A. wear safety shoes
    B. drill at a slow speed
    C. use plenty of cutting oil
    D. clamp the work firmly

33. The proper method of lifting heavy objects is to stand

    A. far enough away from the load so that, with knees bent, the back is at an angle of 45, then lift by straightening the back
    B. close to the load, with feet solidly placed and slightly apart and knees bent; then lift by straightening the legs, keeping the back as nearly vertical as possible
    C. close to the load, with feet solidly placed and far apart, knees bent; then lift by straightening the legs, keeping the body at an angle of 30°
    D. far away from the load, with knees bent and the back at an angle of 45°, then lift by straightening the knees and slowly straightening the back

34. An oilstone is often made of

    A. silicon   B. carborundum   C. tungsten   D. emery

35. To draw a circle, you should use a(n)

    A. compass   B. caliper   C. awl   D. gage

36. A *mushroomed* head is a common defect of a

    A. rivet
    B. hammer
    C. chisel
    D. screwdriver

37. The tool USUALLY used to drive a lag screw is a(n)

    A. open end wrench
    B. Stillson wrench
    C. screwdriver
    D. Allen wrench

38. It is BEST to lubricate machinery

    A. whenever you feel the oil is running low
    B. only if the machinery needs it
    C. when the machine begins to vibrate
    D. on a regular schedule

39. When repairing machinery that is to be reassembled, punch marks are often placed on parts that are next to each other.
    The reason for this is to

    A. make sure you assemble the pieces in proper order
    B. make it easier to line up the parts in proper position
    C. keep count of the number of pieces that belong to this machine
    D. provide a stop so that parts cannot be assembled too tightly

Questions 40-46.

DIRECTIONS: Questions 40 to 46, inclusive, are to be answered in accordance with the following paragraph.

At 2:30 P.M. on Monday, October 25, Mr. Paul Jones, a newly appointed Sewage Treatment Worker, started on a routine inspectional tour of the settling tanks and other sewage treatment works installations of the plant to which he was assigned. At 2:33 P.M., Mr. Jones discovered a co-worker, Mr. James P. Brown, lying unconscious on the ground. Mr. Jones quickly reported the facts to his immediate superior, Mr. Jack Rota, who immediately telephoned for an ambulance. Mr. Rota then rushed to the site and placed a heavy woolen blanket over the victim. Mr. Brown was taken to the Ave. H hospital by an ambulance driven by Mr. Dave Smith, which arrived at the sewage disposal plant at 3:02 P.M. Patrolman Robert Daly, badge number 12520, had arrived before the ambulance and recorded all the details of the incident, including the statements of Mr. Jones, Mr. Rota, and Mr. Nick Nespola, a Stationary Engineer (Electric), who stated that he saw the victim when he fell to the ground.

40. The time which elapsed between the start of the sewage treatment worker's routine inspection and the arrival of the ambulance was MOST NEARLY _____ minutes.

    A. 3   B. 28   C. 29   D. 32

41. The name of the sewage treatment worker's immediate superior was

    A. James P. Brown   B. Jack Rota
    C. Paul Jones   D. Robert Daly

42. The name of the patrolman was

    A. James P. Brown   B. Jack Rota
    C. Paul Jones   D. Robert Daly

43. Referring to the above, the incident occurred on

    A. Monday, Oct. 25   B. Monday, October 26
    C. Tuesday, Oct. 25   D. Tuesday, October 26

44. The victim was found at exactly

    A. 2:30 A.M.   B. 2:33 P.M.   C. 2:33 A.M.   D. 2:30 P.M.

45. The sewage treatment worker's name was

    A. James P. Brown   B. Jack Rota
    C. Paul Jones   D. Dave Smith

46. The man named Nick Nespola was the

    A. Stationary Engineer (Electric)   B. patrolman
    C. victim   D. ambulance driver

47. When sharpening a tool on a grindstone, the tool is often dipped in water. The MAIN reason for this is to

    A. prevent overheating of the tool
    B. lubricate the grindstone
    C. produce a sharper edge on the tool
    D. anneal the tool

47.____

48. It is BEST to use a screwdriver having a square shank

    A. when clearance is limited
    B. on sheet metal screws
    C. on small screws
    D. where a wrench is to be used to help turn the screwdriver

48.____

49. Brass liners are often placed over the jaws of a bench vise to

    A. grip the work better
    B. prevent damage to the work
    C. protect the vise
    D. make it easier to adjust the work

49.____

50. Other than the bulb, the part of a fluorescent light that must be changed MOST often as it wears is the

    A. switch   B. ballast   C. control   D. starter

50.____

KEY (CORRECT ANSWERS)

1.	A	11.	A	21.	C	31.	A	41.	B
2.	A	12.	B	22.	A	32.	D	42.	D
3.	B	13.	C	23.	D	33.	B	43.	A
4.	C	14.	C	24.	D	34.	B	44.	B
5.	B	15.	C	25.	B	35.	A	45.	C
6.	D	16.	D	26.	B	36.	C	46.	A
7.	D	17.	C	27.	D	37.	A	47.	A
8.	C	18.	A	28.	D	38.	D	48.	D
9.	C	19.	C	29.	C	39.	B	49.	B
10.	D	20.	A	30.	A	40.	D	50.	D

EXAMINATION SECTION
TEST 1

DIRECTIONS: Each question or incomplete statement is followed by several suggested answers or completions. Select the one that BEST answers the question or completes the statement. *PRINT THE LETTER OF THE CORRECT ANSWER IN THE SPACE AT THE RIGHT.*

1. When all of her employees are assigned to perform identical routine tasks, a supervisor would PROBABLY find it most difficult to differentiate among these employees as to the
    A. amount of work each completed
    B. initiative each one shows in doing the work
    C. number of errors in each one's work
    D. number of times each one is absent or late

    1.____

2. The one of the following guiding principles to which a supervisor should give the GREATEST weight when it becomes necessary to discipline an employee is that the
    A. discipline should be of such a nature as to improve the future work of the employee
    B. main benefit gained in disciplining one employee is that all employees are kept from breaking the same rule
    C. morale of all the employees should be improved by the discipline of the one
    D. rules should be applied in a fixed and unchanging manner

    2.____

3. In using praise to encourage employees to do better work, the supervisor should realize that praising an employee too often is not good MAINLY because the
    A. employee will be resented by her fellow employees
    B. employee will begin to think she's doing too much work
    C. praise will lose its value as an incentive
    D. supervisor doesn't have the time to praise an employee frequently

    3.____

4. A supervisor notices that one of her best employees has apparently begun to loaf on the job.
   In this situation, the supervisor should FIRST
    A. allow the employee a period of grace in view of her excellent record
    B. change the employee's job assignment
    C. determine the reason for the change in the employee's behavior
    D. take disciplinary action immediately as she would with any other employee

    4.____

5. A supervisor who wants to get a spirit of friendly cooperation from the employees in her unit is MOST likely to be successful if she
    A. makes no exceptions in strictly enforcing department procedures
    B. shows a cooperative spirit herself
    C. tells them they are the best in the department
    D. treats them to coffee once in a while

    5.____

6. *Accidents do not just happen.*
   In view of this statement, it is important for the supervisor to realize that
   A. accidents are sometimes deliberate
   B. combinations of unavoidable circumstances cause accidents
   C. she must take the blame for each accident
   D. she should train her employees in accident prevention

7. Suppose your superior points out to you several jobs that were poorly done by the employees under your supervision.
   As the supervisor of these employees, you should
   A. accept responsibility for the poor work and take steps to improve the work in the future
   B. blame the employees for shirking on the job while you were busy on other work
   C. defend the employees since up to this time they were all good workers
   D. explain that the poor work was due to circumstances beyond your control

8. If a supervisor discovers a situation which is a possible source of grievance, it would be BEST for her to
   A. be ready to answer the employees when they make a direct complaint
   B. do nothing until the employees make a direct complaint
   C. tell the employees, in order to keep them from making a direct complaint, that nothing can be done
   D. try to remove the cause before the employees make a direct complaint

9. Suppose there is a departmental rule that requires supervisors to prepare reports of unusual incidents by the end of the tour of duty in which the incident occurs.
   The MAIN reason for requiring such prompt reporting is that
   A. a quick decision can be made whether the employee involved was neglectful of her duty
   B. other required reports cannot be made out until this one is turned in
   C. the facts are recorded before they are forgotten or confused by those involved in the incident
   D. the report is submitted before the supervisor required to make the report may possibly leave the department

10. A good practical method to use in determining whether an employee is doing his job properly is to
    A. assume that if he asks no questions, he knows the work
    B. question him directly on details of the job
    C. inspect and follow-up the work which is assigned to him
    D. ask other employees how this employee is making out

11. If an employee continually asks how he should do his work, you should
    A. dismiss him immediately
    B. pretend you do not hear him unless he persists
    C. explain the work carefully but encourage him to use his own judgment
    D. tell him not to ask so many questions

12. You have instructed an employee to complete a job in a certain area.
    To be sure that the employee understands the instructions you have given him, you should
    A. ask him to repeat the instructions to you
    B. check with him after he has done the job
    C. watch him while he is doing the job
    D. repeat the instructions to the employee

13. One of your men disagrees with your evaluation of his work.
    Of the following, the BEST way to handle this situation would be to
    A. explain that you are in a better position to evaluate his work than he is
    B. tell him that since other men are satisfied with your evaluation, he should accept their opinions
    C. explain the basis of your evaluation and discuss it with him
    D. refuse to discuss his complaint in order to maintain discipline

14. Of the following, the on which is NOT a quality of leadership desirable in a supervisor is
    A. intelligence   B. integrity   C. forcefulness   D. partiality

15. Of the following, the one which LEAST characterizes the grapevine is that it
    A. consists of a tremendous amount of rumor, conjecture, information, advice, prediction, and even orders.
    B. seems to rise spontaneously, is largely anonymous, spreads rapidly, and changes in unpredictable directions
    C. can be eliminated without any great effort
    D. commonly fills the gaps left by the regular organizational channels of communication

16. When a superintendent delegates authority to a foreman, of the following, it would be MOST advisable for the superintendent to
    A. set wide limits of such authority to allow the foreman considerable leeway
    B. define fairly closely the limits of the authority delegated to the foreman
    C. wait until the foreman has some experience in the assignment before setting limits to his authority
    D. inform him that it is the foreman's ultimate basic responsibility to get the work done

17. One of the hallmarks of a good supervisor is his ability to use many different methods of obtaining information about the status of work in progress.
    Which one of the following would probably indicate that a supervisor does NOT have this ability?
    A. Holding specified staff meetings at specified intervals
    B. Circulating among his subordinates as often as possible
    C. Holding staff meetings only when absolutely necessary
    D. Asking subordinates to come in and discuss the progress of their work and their problems

18. Of the following, the one which is the LEAST important factor in deciding that additional training is necessary for the men you supervise is that
    A. the quality of work is below standard
    B. supplies are being wasted
    C. too much time is required to do specific jobs
    D. the absentee rate has declined

19. To promote proper safety practices in the operation of power tools and equipment, you should emphasize in meetings with the staff that
    A. every accident can be prevented through proper safety regulations
    B. proper safety practices will probably make future safety meetings unnecessary
    C. when safety rules are followed, tools and equipment will work better
    D. safety rules are based on past experience with the best methods of preventing accidents

20. Employee morale is the way employees feel about each other and their job. To a supervisor, it should be a sign of good morale if the employees
    A. are late for work
    B. complain about their work
    C. willingly do difficult jobs
    D. take a long time to do simple jobs

21. A supervisor who encourages his workers to make suggestions about job improvement shows his workers that he
    A. is not smart enough to improve the job himself
    B. wants them to take part in making improvements
    C. does not take the job seriously
    D. is not a good supervisor

22. Suppose that your supervisor tells you that a procedure which has been followed for years is going to be changed. It is your job to make sure the workers you supervises understand and accept the new procedure.
    What would be the BEST thing for you to do in this situation?
    A. Give a copy of the new procedure to each worker with orders that it must be followed
    B. Explain the new procedure to one worker and have him explain it to the others
    C. Ask your supervisor to explain the new procedure since he has more authority
    D. call your workers together to explain and discuss the new procedure

23. One of the foundations of scientific management of an organization is the proper use of control measures.
    Of the following, the BEST way, in general, to implement control measures is to
    A. develop suitable procedures, systems, and guidelines for the organization
    B. evaluate the actual employees' job performance realistically and reasonably
    C. set standards which are designed to increase productivity
    D. publish a set of rules and insist upon strict compliance with these rules

24. A district superintendent would MOST likely be justified in taking up a matter with his borough superintendent when the problem involved
    A. a dispute among different factions in his district
    B. a section foreman's difficulties with his assistant foreman
    C. his own men and others not under his control
    D. methods of doing the work and the amount of production

25. The superintendent has the authority to recommend disciplinary action. He can BEST use this authority to
    A. demonstrate his authority as a superintendent
    B. improve a man's work
    C. make it less difficult for other superintendents to maintain order
    D. punish the men for wrong-doing

KEY (CORRECT ANSWERS)

1.	B		11.	C
2.	A		12.	A
3.	C		13.	C
4.	C		14.	D
5.	B		15.	C
6.	D		16.	B
7.	A		17.	C
8.	D		18.	D
9.	C		19.	D
10.	C		20.	C

21. B
22. D
23. C
24. B
25. B

TEST 2

DIRECTIONS: Each question or incomplete statement is followed by several suggested answers or completions. Select the one that BEST answers the question or completes the statement. *PRINT THE LETTER OF THE CORRECT ANSWER IN THE SPACE AT THE RIGHT.*

1. From the standpoint of equal opportunity, the MOST critical item that a superintendent should focus on is
   A. assigning only minority workers to supervisory positions
   B. helping minority employees to upgrade their knowledge so they may qualify for higher positions
   C. placing minority workers in job categories above their present level of ability so that they can *sink or swim*
   D. disregarding merit system principles

   1.____

2. After careful deliberation, you have decided that one of your workers should be disciplined.
   It is MOST important that the
   A. discipline be severe for best results
   B. discipline be delayed as long as possible
   C. worker understands why he is being disciplined
   D. other workers be consulted before the discipline is administered

   2.____

3. Of the following, the MOST important qualities of an employee chosen for a supervisory position are
   A. education and intelligence
   B. interest in the objectives and activities of the agency
   C. skill in performing the type of work to be supervised
   D. knowledge of the work and leadership ability

   3.____

4. Of the following, the CHIEF characteristic which distinguishes a good supervisor from a poor supervisor is the good supervisor's
   A. ability to favorably impress others
   B. unwillingness to accept monotony or routine
   C. ability to deal constructively with problem situations
   D. strong drive to overcome opposition

   4.____

5. Of the following, the MAIN disadvantage of on-the-job training is that, generally,
   A. special equipment may be needed
   B. production may be slowed down
   C. the instructor must maintain an individual relationship with the trainee
   D. the on-the-job instructor must be better qualified than the classroom instructor

   5.____

6. If it becomes necessary for you, as a supervisor, to give a subordinate employee confidential information, the MOST effective of the following steps to take is to make sure the information is kept confidential by the employee is to

   6.____

A. tell the employee that the information is confidential and is not to be repeated
B. threaten the employee with disciplinary action if the information is repeated
C. offer the employee a merit increase as an incentive for keeping the information confidential
D. remind the employee at least twice a day that the information is confidential and is not to be repeated

7. Three new men have just been assigned to work under your supervision. Every time you give them an assignment, one of these men asks you several questions.
Of the following, the MOST desirable action for you to take is to
   A. assure him of your confidence in his ability to carry out the assignment correctly without asking so many questions
   B. have all three men listen to your answers to these questions
   C. point out that the other two men do the job without asking so many questions
   D. tell him to see if he can get the answers from other workers before coming to you

8. Two of your subordinates suggest that you recommend a third man for an above-standard service rating because of his superior work.
You should
   A. ask the two subordinates whether the third man knows that they intended to discuss this matter with you
   B. explain to the two subordinates that an above-standard service rating for one man would have a detrimental effect on many of the other men
   C. recommend the man for an above-standard service rating if there is sufficient justification for it
   D. tell the two subordinates that the matter of service ratings is not their concern

9. All of the following are indications of good employee morale EXCEPT
   A. the number of grievances are lowered
   B. labor turnover is decreased
   C. the amount of supervision required is lowered
   D. levels of production are lowered

10. All of the following statements regarding the issuance of direct orders are true EXCEPT
    A. use direct orders only when necessary
    B. make sure that the receiver of the direct order is qualified to carry out the order
    C. issue direct orders in clear, concise words
    D. give direct orders only in writing

11. In order to achieve the BEST results in on-the-job training, supervisors should   11._____
    A. allow frequent coffee breaks during the training period
    B. be in a higher salary range than that of the individuals they are training
    C. have had instructions or experience in conducting such training
    D. have had a minimum of five years' experience in the job

12. Of the following, the LEAST important quality of a good supervisor is   12._____
    A. technical competence
    B. teaching ability
    C. ability to communicate with others
    D. ability to socialize with subordinates

13. One of your usually very hard working, reliable employees brings in a bottle of whiskey to celebrate his birthday during the rest period.   13._____
    Which one of the following actions should you take?
    A. Offer to pay for the cost of the whiskey
    B. Confiscate the bottle
    C. Tell him to celebrate after working hours
    D. Pretend that you have not seen the bottle of whiskey

14. Assume that you find it necessary to discipline two subordinates, Mr. Tate and Mr. Sawyer, for coming to work late on several occasions. Their latenesses have had disruptive effects on the work schedule, and you have given both of them several verbal warnings. Mr. Tate has been in your work unit for many years, and his work has always been satisfactory. Mr. Sawyer is a probationary employee, who has had some problem in learning your procedures. You decide to give Mr. Tate one more warning, in private, for his latenesses.   14._____
    According to good supervisory practice, which one of the following disciplinary actions should you take with regard to Mr. Sawyer?
    A. Give him a reprimand in front of his co-workers, to make a lasting impression
    B. Recommend dismissal since he has not yet completed his probationary period
    C. Give him one more warning, in private, for his latenesses
    D. Recommend a short suspension or payroll deduction to impress upon him the importance of coming to work on time

15. Assume that you have delegated a very important work assignment to Johnson, one of your most experienced subordinates. Prior to completion of the assignment, your superior accidentally discovers that the assignment is being carried out incorrectly, and tells you about it.   15._____
    Which one of the following responses is MOST appropriate for you to give to your superior?
    A. *I take full responsibility, and I will see to it that the assignment is carried out correctly.*
    B. *Johnson has been with us for many years now and should know better.*

C. *It really isn't Johnson's fault, rather it is the fault of the ancient equipment we have to do the job.*
D. *I think you should inform Johnson since he is the one at fault, not I.*

16. Assume that you observe that one of your employees is talking excessively with other employees, quitting early, and taking unusually long rest periods. Despite these abuses, she is one of your most productive employees, and her work is usually of the highest quality.
Of the following, the MOST appropriate action to take with regard to this employee is to
    A. ignore these infractions since she is one of your best workers
    B. ask your superior to reprimand her so that you can remain on the employee's good side
    C. reprimand her since not doing so would lower the morale of the other employees
    D. ask another of your subordinates to mention these infractions to the offending employee and suggest that she stop breaking rules

17. Assume that you have noticed that an employee whose attendance had been quite satisfactory is now showing marked evidence of a consistent pattern of absences.
Of the following, the BEST way to cope with this problem is to
    A. wait several weeks to see whether this pattern continues
    B. meet with the employee to try to find out the reasons for this change
    C. call a staff meeting and discuss the need for good attendance
    D. write a carefully worded warning to the employee

18. It is generally agreed that the successful supervisor must know how to wisely delegate work to her subordinates since she cannot do everything herself. Which one of the following practices is MOST likely to result in ineffective delegation by a supervisor?
    A. Establishment of broad controls to assure feedback about any deviations from plans
    B. Willingness to let subordinates use their own ideas about how to get the job done, where appropriate
    C. Constant observance of employees to see if they are making any mistakes
    D. Granting of enough authority to make possible the accomplishment of the delegated work

19. Suppose that, in accordance with grievance procedures, an employee brings a complaint to you, his immediate supervisor.
In dealing with his complaint, the one of the following which is MOST important for you to do is to
    A. talk to the employee's co-workers to learn whether the complaint is justified
    B. calm the employee by assuring him that you will look into the matter as soon as possible

C. tell your immediate superior about the employee's complaint
D. give the employee an opportunity to tell the full story

20. Holding staff meetings at regular intervals is generally considered to be a good supervisory practice.
Which one of the following subjects is LEAST desirable for discussion at such a meeting?
    A. Revisions in agency personnel policies
    B. Violation of an agency rule by one of the employees present
    C. Problems of waste and breakage in the work area
    D. Complaints of employees about working conditions

21. Suppose that you are informed that your staff is soon to be reduced by one-third due to budget problems.
Which one of the following steps would be LEAST advisable in your effort to maintain a quality service with the smaller number of employees?
    A. Directing employees to speed up operations
    B. Giving employees training or retraining
    C. Rearranging the work area
    D. Revising work methods

22. Of the following which action on the part of the supervisor LEAST likely to contribute to upgrading the skills of her subordinates?
    A. Providing appropriate training to subordinates
    B. Making periodic evaluations of subordinates and discussing the evaluations with the subordinates
    C. Consistently assigning subordinates to those tasks with which they are familiar
    D. Giving increased responsibility to appropriate subordinates

23. Suppose that a new employee on your staff has difficulty in performing his assigned tasks after having been given training.
Of the following courses of action, the one which would be BEST for you, his supervisor, to take FIRST is to
    A. change his work assignment
    B. give him a poor evaluation since he is obviously unable to do the work
    C. give him the training again
    D. have him work with an employee who is more experienced in the tasks for a short while

24. Several times, an employee has reported to work unit for duty because he had been drinking. He refused to get counseling for his emotional problems when this was suggested by his superior. Last week, his supervisor warned him that he would face disciplinary action if he again reported to work unfit for duty because of drinking. Now, the employee has again reported to work in that condition.

Of the following, the BEST action for the supervisor to take now would be to
A. arrange to have the employee transferred to another work location
B. give the employee one more chance by pretending to not notice his condition this time
C. start disciplinary action against the employee
D. warn him that he will face disciplinary action if he reports for work in that condition again

25. An employee has been calling in sick repeatedly, and these absences have disrupted the work schedule.
To try to make sure that the employee use sick leave only on days when he is actually sick, which of the following actions would be the BEST for his supervisor to take?
A. Telephone the employee's home on days when he is out on sick leave
B. Require the employee to obtain a note from a physician explaining the reason for his absence whenever he uses sick leave in the future
C. Require that he get a complete physical examination and have his doctor send a report to the supervisor
D. Warn the employee that he will face disciplinary action the next time he stays out on sick leave

25.____

KEY (CORRECT ANSWERS)

1.	B		11.	C
2.	C		12.	D
3.	D		13.	C
4.	C		14.	C
5.	B		15.	A
6.	A		16.	C
7.	B		17.	B
8.	C		18.	C
9.	D		19.	D
10.	D		20.	B

21. A
22. C
23. D
24. C
25. B

TEST 3

DIRECTIONS: Each question or incomplete statement is followed by several suggested answers or completions. Select the one that BEST answers the question or completes the statement. *PRINT THE LETTER OF THE CORRECT ANSWER IN THE SPACE AT THE RIGHT.*

1. Suppose that, as a supervisor, you have an idea for changing the way a certain task is performed by your staff so that it will be less tedious and get done faster. Of the following, the MOST advisable action for you to take regarding this idea is to
   A. issue a written memorandum explaining the new method and giving reasons why it is to replace the old one
   B. discuss it with your staff to get their reactions and suggestions
   C. set up a training class in the new method for your staff
   D. try it out on an experimental basis on half the staff

   1.____

2. A troubled subordinate privately approaches his supervisor in order to talk about a problem on the job.
   In this situation, the one of the following actions that is NOT desirable on the part of the supervisor is to
   A. ask the subordinate pertinent questions to help develop points further
   B. close his office door during the talk to block noisy distractions
   C. allow sufficient time to complete the discussion with the subordinate
   D. take over the conversation so the employee won't be embarrassed

   2.____

3. Suppose that one of your goals as a supervisor is to foster good working relationships between yourself and your employees, without undermining your supervisory effectiveness by being too friendly.
   Of the following, the BEST way to achieve this goal when dealing with employees' work problems is to
   A. discourage individual personal conferences by using regularly scheduled staff meetings to discuss work problems
   B. try to resolve work problems within a relatively short period of time
   C. insist that employees put all work problems into writing before seeing you
   D. maintain an open-door policy, allowing employees complete freedom of access to you without making appointments to discuss work problems

   3.____

4. An employee under your supervision complains that he is assigned to work late more often than any of the other employees. You check the records and find that this isn't so.
   You should
   A. advise this employee not to worry about what the other employees do but to see that he puts in a full day's work himself
   B. explain to this employee that you get the same complaint from all the other employees
   C. inform this employee that you have checked the records and the complaint is not justified
   D. not assign this employee to work late for a few days in order to keep him satisfied

   4.____

5. An employee has reported late for work several times.
   His supervisor should
   A. give this employee less desirable assignments
   B. overlook the lateness if the employee's work is otherwise exceptional
   C. recommend disciplinary action for habitual lateness
   D. talk the matter over with the employee before doing anything further

6. In choosing a man to be in charge in his absence, the supervisor should select FIRST the employee who
   A. has ability to supervise others
   B. has been longest with the organization
   C. has the nicest appearance and manner
   D. is most skilled in his assigned duties

7. An employee under your supervision comes to you to complain about a decision you have made in assigning the men. He is excited and angry. You think what he is complaining about is not important, but it seems very important to him.
   The BEST way for you to handle this is to
   A. let him talk until *he gets it off his chest* and then explain the reasons for your decision
   B. refuse to talk to him until he has cooled off
   C. show him at once how unimportant the matter is and how ridiculous his arguments are
   D. tell him to take it up with your superior if he disagrees with your decision

8. Suppose that a new employee has been appointed and assigned to your supervision.
   When this man reports for work, it would be BEST for you to
   A. ask him questions about different problems connected with his line of work and see if he answers them correctly
   B. check him carefully while he carries out some routine assignment that you give him
   C. explain to him the general nature of the work he will be required to do
   D. make a careful study of his previous work record before coming to your department

9. *The competent supervisor will be friendly with the employees under his supervision but will avoid close familiarity.*
   This statement is justified MAINLY because
   A. a friendly attitude on the part of the supervisor toward the employee is likely to cause suspicion on the part of the employee
   B. a supervisor can handle his employees better if he doesn't know their personal problems
   C. close familiarity may interfere with the discipline needed for good supervisor-subordinate relationships
   D. familiarity with the employees may be a sign of lack of ability on the part of the supervisor

10. An employee disagrees with the instructions that you, his supervisor, have given him for carrying out a certain assignment.
    The BEST action for you to take is to tell this employee that
    A. he can do what he wants but you will hold him responsible for failure
    B. orders must be carried out or morale will fall apart
    C. this job has been done in this way for many years with great success
    D. you will be glad to listen to his objections and to his suggestions for improvement

11. As a supervisor, it is LEAST important for you to use a new employee's probationary period for the purpose of
    A. carefully checking how he performs the work you assign him
    B. determining whether he can perform the duties of his job efficiently
    C. preparing him for promotion to a higher position
    D. showing him how to carry out his assigned duties properly

12. Suppose you have just given an employee under your supervision instructions on how to carry out a certain assignment.
    The BEST way to check that he has understood your instructions is to
    A. ask him to repeat your instructions word for word
    B. check the progress of his work the first chance you get
    C. invite him to ask questions if he has any doubts
    D. question him briefly about the main points of the assignment

13. Suppose you find it necessary to change a procedure that the men under your supervision have been following for a long time.
    A good way to get their cooperation for this change would be to
    A. bring them together to talk over the new procedure and explain the reasons for its adoption
    B. explain to the men that if most of them still don't approve of the change after giving it a fair try you will consider giving it up
    C. give them a few weeks' notice of the proposed change in procedure
    D. not enforce the new procedure strictly at the beginning

14. An order can be given by a supervisor in such a way as to make the employee want to obey it.
    According to this statement, it is MOST reasonable to suppose that
    A. a person will be glad to obey an order if he realizes that he must
    B. if an order is given properly, it will be obeyed more willingly
    C. it is easier to obey an order than to give one correctly
    D. supervisors should inspire confidence by their actions as well as by their words

15. If one of the men you supervise disagrees with how you rate his work, the BEST way for you to handle this is to
    A. advise him to appeal to your superior about it
    B. decline to discuss the matter with him in order to keep discipline
    C. explain why you rate him the way you do and talk it over with him
    D. tell him that you are better qualified to rate his work than he is

16. A supervisor should be familiar with the experience and abilities of the employees under his supervision MAINLY because
    A. each employee's work is highly important and requires a person of outstanding ability
    B. it will help him to know which employees are best fitted for certain assignments
    C. nearly all men have the same basic ability to do any job equally well
    D. superior background shortly shows itself in superior work quality, regardless of assignment

17. The competent supervisor will try to develop respect rather than fear in his subordinates.
    This statement is justified MAINLY because
    A. fear is always present and, for best results, respect must be developed to offset it
    B. it is generally easier to develop respect in the men than it is to develop fear
    C. men who respect their supervisor are more likely to give more than the required minimum amount and quality of work
    D. respect is based on the individual, and fear is based on the organization as a whole

18. If one of the employees you supervise does outstanding work, you should
    A. explain to him how his work can still be improved so that he will not become self-satisfied
    B. mildly criticize the other men for not doing as good a job as this man
    C. praise him for his work so that he will know it is appreciated
    D. say nothing or he might become conceited

19. A supervisor can BEST help establish good morale among his employees if he
    A. confides in them about his personal problems in order to encourage them to confide in him
    B. encourages them to become friendly with him but discourages social engagements with them
    C. points out to them the advantages of having a cooperative spirit in the department
    D. sticks to the same rules that he expects them to follow

20. The one of the following situations which would seem to indicate poor scheduling of work by the supervisor is
    A. everybody seeming to be very busy at the same time
    B. re-assignment of a man to other work because of breakdown of a piece of equipment
    C. two employees on vacation at the same time
    D. two operators waiting to use the same equipment at the same time

KEY (CORRECT ANSWERS)

1.	B	11.	C
2.	D	12.	D
3.	B	13.	A
4.	C	14.	B
5.	D	15.	C
6.	A	16.	B
7.	A	17.	C
8.	C	18.	C
9.	C	19.	D
10.	D	20.	D

EXAMINATION SECTION
TEST 1

DIRECTIONS: Each question or incomplete statement is followed by several suggested answers or completions. Select the one that BEST answers the question or completes the statement. *PRINT THE LETTER OF THE CORRECT ANSWER IN THE SPACE AT THE RIGHT.*

1. The BEST technique for a superintendent to use to gain and keep the respect of his subordinates is to

   A. approve and commend all work done
   B. be scrupulously fair in dealing with all subordinates
   C. offer specific criticism at each phase of each job
   D. use contests to motivate speed up of work

   1.____

2. The MOST important of the following qualities for a good superintendent to have is

   A. a dignified appearance to set a standard for his men to follow
   B. neatness of dress so that his subordinates will have a model to follow if promoted
   C. the ability to handle men
   D. skill in writing reports which are to be forwarded to higher echelons

   2.____

3. In making decisions, a new superintendent who wishes to impress his subordinates should make these decisions

   A. after consulting his subordinates for their ideas
   B. as rapidly as possible, changing them if they are wrong
   C. only after studying all the information related to the matter
   D. promptly and stick to them even if an error is made

   3.____

4. After a superintendent has submitted his service ratings of the work of his subordinates, one of them whose work has not been satisfactory complains to the superintendent that his rating was unjustified.
   For the superintendent to avoid discussing the rating but to point out two or three specific instances where the employee's work is below standard is

   A. *desirable;* an employee should be told what parts of his work are unsatisfactory
   B. *undesirable;* once a rating has been submitted, there is no point in discussing it
   C. *desirable;* entering into a general argument is bad for the discipline of the department
   D. *undesirable;* it would have been better to have explained how the rating was arrived at

   4.____

5. A new employee who has shown himself capable of doing superior work during the first month of his probationary period falls below this standard during the second month. For the supervisor to wait until the end of the probationary period and then recommend that the man be dropped if his work is still unsatisfactory is

   A. *undesirable;* he should have been discharged when his work became unsatisfactory
   B. *desirable;* there is no place in the department for unsatisfactory employees
   C. *undesirable;* the supervisor should immediately attempt to determine the cause of the unsatisfactory performance
   D. *desirable;* the employee is entitled to a chance to prove himself

   5.____

6. The one which is NOT a principle of leadership is:

    A. Know your job, yourself, and your men
    B. Be sure that a task is understood, supervised, and accomplished
    C. See responsibility and develop a sense of responsibility in your men
    D. Use every effort to shift responsibility to lower echelons

7. A superintendent starting a safety campaign should be aware that

    A. accidents are more likely to occur to the same few people in an organization
    B. accidents occur equally to all kinds of people
    C. people who worry are usually more careful and, therefore, have a lower accident rate
    D. the physical and emotional condition of a person has no effect on his accident potential

8. At a staff meeting of foremen, it was said, *The most important job you foremen have is to get across to your subordinates the desirability of achieving our department's goals and the importance of the jobs they are performing toward reaching our objectives.*
    The adoption of this point of view would tend to create a department

    A. in which less supervision is required of the work of the average employee
    B. having more clearly defined lines of authority
    C. in which most employees would be capable of taking over a supervisory position when necessary
    D. in which supervisors would tend to neglect their primary mission of getting the assigned work completed efficiently

9. A comment made by an employee about a training course was, *We never know how we are getting along in that course.* The error in training methods to which such a criticism points is

    A. insufficient participation by the students in the course
    B. failure to develop a feeling of need for the material being presented in the class
    C. no attempt is being made to connect the new material being presented with what is presently in use in a department
    D. no goals have been set for the students participating

10. When a superintendent first assumes command of an area, which one of the following tasks should have the LOWEST priority?

    A. Making an effort to meet and know his men
    B. Ascertaining the problem areas
    C. Developing a good rapport with his subordinate officers
    D. Studying the organization of his area with a view to specific reorganization

11. Which of the following steps would be BEST for a superintendent to take if he is to obtain maximum gains in the productivity of his group?

    A. Formulate a specific plan that is complete and relatively inflexible
    B. Leave his own program fairly open but plan for the most effective use of his manpower
    C. Study all of the factors in the work situation and arrange them in order of priority
    D. Consider the solution to problems only when they occur

12. Assume that, as superintendent, your policy is to consult your subordinates for assistance in formulating decisions, when feasible.
    Of the following, the benefit MOST likely to result from this policy is that

    A. your subordinates will become more knowledgeable in other aspects of the work
    B. your decisions will have greater acceptance than when made alone
    C. there will be more *right* decisions made
    D. your workload will be considerably lessened

13. Assume that you are a newly-appointed superintendent, and a report has been submitted to you by one of your foremen, which contains an extensive amount of daily productivity data. On the basis of your knowledge, you seriously question some of the data.
    Which of the following actions would probably be MOST advisable for you to take FIRST?

    A. Accept the report since the foreman has apparently done extensive work to obtain the data
    B. Request that copies of the source material for the report be given to you
    C. Return the report to the foreman for his signature
    D. Question the veracity of the writer

14. Assume that one of your foremen, who is otherwise capable, consistently submits badly written reports.
    To improve his ability to write reports, it would be MOST advisable to

    A. carefully go over his reports with him, indicating their weaknesses and making suggestions for improvement
    B. provide him with some textbooks on report writing and give him a deadline to complete reading them
    C. insist that each report be rewritten until it is acceptable
    D. have another foreman collaborate with him in writing his reports

15. Assume that, as superintendent, you have been requested to write a lengthy report for your supervisor. You decide to include a summary of the report and its findings.
    The summary should be useful MAINLY because

    A. it will pinpoint your conclusions and recommendations
    B. it probably includes as much as the rest of the report
    C. the subject of the report is probably routine in nature
    D. the summary may include material not mentioned previously

16. When a superintendent finds it necessary to let a man know that he is dissatisfied with his level of performance, which of the following tactics would *usually* prove MOST effective in improving his performance?

    A. The superintendent should *chew the man out* in order to prevent the mistakes from recurring.
    B. Once criticism has been made, the superintendent should be sure to continuously remind the man of the seriousness of the mistakes.
    C. When making his criticism, the superintendent should guard against referring to any work that was well done since this would reduce the effect of his criticism.
    D. The superintendent should focus his criticism on the mistakes being made and should avoid downgrading the subordinate personally.

17. While training a group of new men, a superintendent notices that one of them is not paying attention.
Of the following, the MOST appropriate method for the superintendent to use in order to properly sustain attention and maintain discipline would *generally* be for him to

    A. reprimand the new man immediately in front of the group
    B. call a break period and then privately find out why this man is not paying attention
    C. ask the man to leave the training area until he has a chance to speak to him
    D. ignore the man's behavior since the man will be the one who will suffer later on

18. Several weeks after you begin your job as superintendent, you realize that although your working days seem busy, you are not accomplishing as much as you would like.
Of the following, the BEST solution to your problem would be to

    A. figure out how much time you spend on various activities and, from this, adjust your time schedule as needed
    B. accept the fact that you were not ready for the promotion and request that you be placed in your former position
    C. realize that there is a limit to how much any man can accomplish and be satisfied with what you already do
    D. eliminate the routine paperwork to allow time for more pressing work

19. One factor which may be considered in determining the best span of control for a supervisor over his immediate subordinates is the position of the supervisor in the structure of the organization.
It is usually considered MOST desirable that the number of subordinates immediately supervised by a higher echelon supervisor _____ the number supervised by lower level supervisors.

    A. have no relation at all to
    B. be roughly the same as
    C. be larger than
    D. be smaller than

20. Suppose that a superintendent wishes to hold a subordinate strictly accountable for carrying out an order.
Of the following, the BEST course of action for the superintendent to adopt is to

    A. be sure that at least one other officer is present when the order is given to the subordinate
    B. give the order, explain the order, and have the subordinate repeat the order to be sure there is no misunderstanding
    C. issue a direct and complete order in writing to the subordinate
    D. tell the subordinate what is to be done and then relate the job to be done to appropriate department regulations

21. Proper planning of his work by a superintendent will NOT generally result in the

    A. apportionment of time to each aspect of his job in accord with its relative importance
    B. delegation of fewer tasks to subordinates
    C. determination of the best way of doing a job
    D. handling of all details involved in coordinating his work with a minimum of effort

22. Suppose that one of the clerks in your office discovers what appears to be an incorrect figure on a weekly statistical report submitted by one of the sections in your control.
The MOST appropriate action for you as a superintendent to take is to

    A. tell the clerk to use his best judgment and insert what he believes is the correct figure
    B. return the report to the section with a memo stating that the report is incorrect
    C. call the foreman of the section and ask him to check the accuracy of the questionable figure
    D. send your clerk to the section and have him double-check the original data with the section clerk

23. A superintendent observes that reports reaching him from foremen and assistant foremen tend to emphasize the favorable and play down the unfavorable aspects of conditions existing in the sections.
The MOST valid conclusion to draw from this, of the following, is that the

    A. subordinates are influenced by a normal tendency to put themselves and their work in the best light
    B. subordinates are willing to take a chance that their somewhat optimistic reports will not be checked too carefully
    C. superintendent has been, perhaps subconsciously, indirectly suggesting to his subordinates that he would prefer to receive good, rather than bad, news
    D. superintendent has been motivated to accept such reports since he is interested more in getting work done than in getting meticulous reports

24. If a superintendent realizes that his foremen frequently write reports which require considerable revision before they can be forwarded, the superintendent would BEST improve future reports prepared by these foremen by

    A. assigning a skilled officer to rewrite these reports
    B. discussing with the foremen needed revisions in their reports
    C. emphasizing the importance of reports and report writing
    D. sending back the worst reports for rewriting without comment, thus letting the officers learn by doing

25. Many reports are sent to the office of a superintendent conveying information about the performance of the men and equipment in the section.
The BEST reason for the superintendent to regularly analyze the information in these reports is to

    A. discover the sections which are not meeting departmental work standards
    B. account for the time he is required to spend in direct field supervision of his force
    C. establish objective measures for disciplinary action
    D. help him train his subordinate supervisors to establish better non-official relationships with the men

26. A superintendent at his first meeting with a new foreman senses an attitude of hostility. Of the following, it would be BEST for him to

   A. firmly assert his authority in order to nip a potentially troublesome situation in the bud
   B. make a quick check with this foreman's previous superintendent to *get a line* on the man
   C. say nothing at this time about the foreman's attitude but try to learn the reasons for it if it continues
   D. tell the foreman that he finds his attitude very unreasonable

27. In delegating authority to a foreman, a superintendent should ORDINARILY

   A. define the limits of the delegated authority as precisely and as specifically as possible
   B. evaluate the *effectiveness potential* of the foreman to determine whether or not to set predetermined limits
   C. make no attempt to define the limits of such authority until the foreman himself discovers from practical experience what the limits should be
   D. depend on the temperament of the foreman to set his own reasonable limits

28. A serious error has been discovered by a senior superintendent in work done under your supervision as a superintendent.
    Your BEST response would be:

   A. *I am very sorry but you must admit I cannot check every detail of this complex job.*
   B. *I am sorry it happened, and I'm really surprised that Foreman Smith would make such a mistake.*
   C. *I'll look into it and do all I can to prevent a recurrence.*
   D. *No matter what I tell these officers, they don't get it. We need a real training program.*

29. As a result of examination, you receive an appointment as superintendent.
    Of the following, the FIRST thing you should do is to

   A. analyze the duties and responsibilities of your new position
   B. carefully observe the procedures of experienced superintendents
   C. develop your skills in human relations
   D. read recognized texts on specific practices in your area

30. The PRINCIPAL argument in favor of filling top positions in the department by promotion rather than by open competitive examinations is that this procedure

   A. assures that candidates will be given due credit for experience
   B. assures that capable men will get the jobs
   C. encourages a career service within the department
   D. increases public interest in the examination

KEY (CORRECT ANSWERS)

1.	B	16.	D
2.	C	17.	B
3.	C	18.	A
4.	D	19.	D
5.	C	20.	C
6.	D	21.	B
7.	A	22.	C
8.	A	23.	A
9.	D	24.	B
10.	D	25.	A
11.	C	26.	C
12.	B	27.	A
13.	B	28.	C
14.	A	29.	A
15.	A	30.	C

TEST 2

DIRECTIONS: Each question or incomplete statement is followed by several suggested answers or completions. Select the one that BEST answers the question or completes the statement. *PRINT THE LETTER OF THE CORRECT ANSWER IN THE SPACE AT THE RIGHT.*

1. The MOST important factor in the success of the department training program is

    A. adequate training center facilities
    B. an adequate supply of study material on department practices
    C. coordination with training programs of other large related departments
    D. officers who know common procedures and can instruct men

2. The more complex an organization and the more highly specialized the division of work, the GREATER the need for

    A. coordinating authority
    B. clearer division of supervisory responsibility
    C. performance standards
    D. strict discipline

3. The MOST important of the following factors for a superintendent to consider when setting up a work schedule for a job modification is the

    A. cost of manpower to perform the job
    B. availability of men and helpers to do the job
    C. cost of the equipment that will be used on this job
    D. quality of the equipment that will be used on this job

4. A supervisor requests his foreman to submit a written report to him by a certain date. After starting work on this assignment, the foreman determines that he cannot meet the deadline if he is to do a complete and thorough job on this report.
In this case, the foreman should

    A. inform his supervisor of the situation
    B. work to the deadline and then ask for an extension
    C. meet the deadline even if he has to submit an inadequate report
    D. ask another foreman for assistance

5. Of the following, the BEST way to begin criticism of a report written by a subordinate is:

    A. If you keep on like this, you'll never learn how to write
    B. This is partly right; now take it back and fix it up
    C. This is pretty good, but I think we can improve it
    D. You know you can do better than this

6. A superintendent is called upon to administer an order with which he does not agree. He has reason to believe his men do not agree with it either.
In discussing the order with them, he should express

    A. his belief that the order will undoubtedly be changed later
    B. such reasons as he may know that support the order
    C. that he has unsuccessfully taken the matter up with his superiors
    D. that he is basically in accord with their disapproval of the order

7. One of the factors making it difficult for officers to introduce new methods which will alter procedures that have been in existence for some time is the tendency of people to

   A. change likes and dislikes rapidly
   B. dislike change
   C. dislike experts
   D. like old ideas because they are old

8. In comparison with the number of men under a supervisor in other agencies, the number of men under a superintendent might seem excessive.
   However, a factor which makes such conclusion ERRONEOUS is the

   A. command nature of the superintendent's authority
   B. large amount of authority delegated to the superintendent
   C. small number of men under his supervisor to whom the superintendent reports
   D. uniformity of the work supervised by the superintendent

9. The need in departmental administration is for foremen to project their thinking to a higher level, for superintendents to see the problems of the department.
   This statement describes the need for employees who

   A. consider their jobs as inferior to those of a higher level
   B. plan operations on a broader basis than their own districts
   C. understand their jobs as part of the larger job of the department
   D. do their jobs as well as they possibly can

10. The one of the following which is NOT a sound procedure for a superintendent to follow is to

    A. create a feeling of warmth between himself and his men
    B. ignore petty grievances until they work themselves out
    C. instill confidence and security among subordinates
    D. take prompt action on a decision once it is made

11. Which of the following acts by a superintendent would be MOST subject to criticism on the basis of principles underlying good supervision?
    He

    A. allows a man who has shown a talent for such things a large measure of initiative in devising new methods of doing the work
    B. asks his men to give him their opinions as to methods of doing the work but, in some cases, does not accept these opinions as a basis for change
    C. gives no definite answer on being told by one man of his difficulties in working with another but tells him he will look into the matter
    D. tries to avoid disappointing either side by giving an answer that is not decisive but to some extent satisfactory to both, when asked to settle a matter by men who differ as to a proper procedure

12. Use of competition between squads or gangs in an accident-reduction program is

    A. *desirable;* it gives men an incentive
    B. *desirable;* all have an opportunity
    C. *undesirable;* it may arouse ill-feeling
    D. *undesirable;* prizes are expensive

13. With respect to delegation of authority, a superintendent should be guided by the principle that he should

    A. delegate as much authority as he effectively can
    B. discourage his men from consulting him on section matters
    C. keep all authority centralized in himself
    D. personally confirm all decisions made by his men

14. A superintendent is faced with the problem of a conflict in authority between two foremen.
    The FINAL step he should take in handling this problem is to

    A. consider the effect his orders will have on the subordinates
    B. find out what rules have been applied to similar situations
    C. issue the orders which designate the action to be taken
    D. point out to the foremen the importance of harmonious working relationships

15. In explaining new work procedures to his foremen, a superintendent should place LEAST emphasis on

    A. how the new procedures are to be carried out
    B. what is to be accomplished by the new procedures
    C. when the new procedures are to be started
    D. who ordered the change to the new procedures

16. A supervisor asks his superintendent for a report on the capabilities of a new piece of equipment. The superintendent asks a foreman to turn in the report; and the foreman, in turn, assigns the job to an assistant foreman. The assistant foreman makes the investigation and writes the report. The report goes up through channels to the supervisor and turns out to be full of inaccuracies.
    Who is to be held responsible for the inaccurate report?
    The

    A. assistant foreman *only*
    B. superintendent *only*
    C. foreman and assistant foreman *only*
    D. superintendent, foreman, and assistant foreman

17. The one of the following which is MOST likely to have the MOST lasting good effect on a man's morale is

    A. a good social and recreational program
    B. a suggestion system with cash awards for good ideas
    C. liberal rest periods and coffee breaks
    D. recognition by his superiors of his efforts

18. Suppose your supervisor tells you he is contemplating a certain assignment for one of your section foremen. You consider this a wrong assignment for a good man.
    You should

    A. say nothing since this is a matter to be handled by your superior
    B. speak to the foreman advising him to refuse the assignment
    C. suggest the assignment of another foreman fitted for the job
    D. tell the supervisor you can't spare this man

19. In rating a man's work, a superintendent should be MOST aware that

    A. a man's home environment should be taken into consideration when this has affected the quality of his work
    B. a man's rating should not be influenced by his previous rating
    C. a new man should be rated on the same basis as senior employees
    D. the job classification grade of the man should not be considered

20. The one of the following which is an ADVANTAGE of the employee service rating system is that

    A. an above-average rating will bring the employee an added increment
    B. employees receive formal notification of their rating immediately after the end of the rating year
    C. evaluation of supervisors' ratings by department personnel boards contributes to application of more uniform rating standards
    D. ratings are assigned on a proportional basis which insures that not too many higher ratings are given out

21. In a section, there are usually some assignments that are disliked by the men. To assign men to these jobs as a disciplinary measure after a rule violation is UNDESIRABLE because

    A. severity of the punishment should be related to the seriousness of the offense, such assignments being reserved for the most serious offenses
    B. such assignments should be based on more valid factors such as the requirements of the job and the needs and abilities of the men
    C. the men assigned are sure to do a poor job
    D. the number of violations exceeds the number of such assignments, resulting in inequity

22. Department policy with respect to permitting men to receive presents from private citizens on their routes should be

    A. not to allow it
    B. to allow it at Christmas
    C. to allow if if other city departments follow the practice
    D. to allow if it the superintendent authorizes it

23. As an organizational unit of the department, the function of the sanitary education unit is BEST described as

    A. coordinating   B. housekeeping   C. preventative   D. regulatory

24. The employees' suggestion award program, in addition to bringing forth new ideas, is of MOST value to the department in terms of

    A. developing a competitive spirit among employees and groups
    B. fostering in individual employees a sense of participation
    C. giving an objective basis for employee evaluation and training
    D. keeping lower level supervisors alert and *on their toes*

25. A survey in the sanitation department showed for the first time that a substantial number of streets previously classified as *fair* were now classified as *dirty*.
The LEAST probable reason for this change is the

    A. abundance of heavy litter
    B. shifts in population
    C. very hot summer
    D. winter of heavy snow

26. Leadership is the ability to act in a manner designed to secure cooperation on behalf of an established purpose. Which one of the following indicates that a superintendent is exercising leadership in the manner defined here?

    A. He delegates full authority and responsibility to his foremen to settle grievances at the section level.
    B. He explains to his subordinates the reasons for any changes in established procedures.
    C. He gives none of the men in his command a below-standard performance evaluation.
    D. His area has the lowest accident rate in the borough.

27. Of the following, the MAIN goal of a superintendent in a safety program should be to

    A. stress safety as an important factor in producing more work
    B. make department employees recognize the physical hazards of the job
    C. lessen the dissatisfaction of older employees with what they consider to be restrictive safety practices
    D. produce a safety-conscious work environment in which the men themselves try to achieve safer work methods

28. For a superintendent to permit his subordinates to participate in making decisions is usually desirable, when practicable, MAINLY because

    A. better decisions may be arrived at
    B. it will eliminate grievances in the long run
    C. subordinates acquire more prestige as a result of participating in decision making
    D. such decisions become virtually self-executing

29. A newly-appointed superintendent made a special effort to learn the names of all the officers and men in his command and to address them by name whenever possible.
GENERALLY speaking, such a procedure is considered

    A. *good;* since people like to feel they are being thought of as individuals
    B. *poor;* since the men are apt to feel they will be under excessive supervision
    C. *good;* since the officers and men will realize that exceptionally good work will be recognized and rewarded
    D. *poor;* since the subordinates will suspect ulterior motives are influencing the superintendent

30. The principle of administration that the responsibility of higher officers for the acts of subordinates MUST be absolute means that

     A. discretionary authority should not be delegated
     B. each and every subordinate bears the fullest measure of self-responsibility and self-control
     C. each superior officer is held responsible for the acts of his subordinates
     D. officers at the same echelon in the organization cannot escape responsibility for each other's acts

KEY (CORRECT ANSWERS)

1.	D	16.	D
2.	A	17.	D
3.	B	18.	C
4.	A	19.	B
5.	C	20.	C
6.	B	21.	B
7.	B	22.	A
8.	D	23.	C
9.	C	24.	B
10.	B	25.	A
11.	D	26.	B
12.	A	27.	D
13.	A	28.	A
14.	C	29.	A
15.	D	30.	C

WORK SCHEDULING

EXAMINATION SECTION
TEST 1

DIRECTIONS: Each question or incomplete statement is followed by several suggested answers or completions. Select the one that BEST answers the question or completes the statement. *PRINT THE LETTER OF THE CORRECT ANSWER IN THE SPACE AT THE RIGHT.*

Questions 1-6.

DIRECTIONS: Questions 1 through 6 are to be answered SOLELY on the basis of the information given in the ELEVATOR OPERATORS' WORK SCHEDULE shown below.

ELEVATOR OPERATORS' WORK SCHEDULE				
Operator	Hours of Work	A.M. Relief Period	Lunch Hour	P.M. Relief Period
Anderson	8:30-4:30	10:20-10:30	12:00-1:00	2:20-2:30
Carter	8:00-4:00	10:10-10:20	11:45-12:45	2:30-2:40
Daniels	9:00-5:00	10:20-10:30	12:30-1:30	3:15-3:25
Grand	9:30-5:30	11:30-11:40	1:00-2:00	4:05-4:15
Jones	7:45-3:45	9:45-9:55	11:30-12:30	2:05-2:15
Lewis	9:45-5:45	11:40-11:50	1:15-2:15	4:20-4:30
Nance	8:45-4:45	10:50-11:00	12:30-1:30	3:05-3:15
Perkins	8:00-4:00	10:00-10:10	12:00-1:00	2:40-2:50
Russo	7:45-3:45	9:30-9:40	11:30-12:30	2:10-2:20
Smith	9:45-5:45	11:45-11:55	1:15-2:15	4:05-4:15

1. The two operators who are on P.M. relief at the SAME time are

   A. Anderson and Daniels B. Carter and Perkins
   C. Jones and Russo   D. Grand and Smith

   1._____

2. Of the following, the two operators who have the SAME lunch hour are

   A. Anderson and Perkins B. Daniels and Russo
   C. Grand and Smith   D. Nance and Russo

   2._____

3. At 12:15, the number of operators on their lunch hour is

   A. 3   B. 4   C. 5   D. 6

   3._____

4. The operator who has an A.M. relief period right after Perkins and a P.M. relief period right before Perkins is

   A. Russo   B. Nance   C. Daniels   D. Carter

   4._____

5. The number of operators who are scheduled to be working at 4:40 is

   A. 5   B. 6   C. 7   D. 8

   5._____

87

6. According to the schedule, it is MOST correct to say that
   A. no operator has a relief period during the time that another operator has a lunch hour
   B. each operator has to wait an identical amount of time between the end of lunch and the beginning of P.M. relief period
   C. no operator has a relief period before 9:45 or after 4:00
   D. each operator is allowed a total of 1 hour and 20 minutes for lunch hour and relief periods

6._____

KEY (CORRECT ANSWERS)

1. D
2. A
3. C
4. D
5. A
6. D

TEST 2

DIRECTIONS: Each question or incomplete statement is followed by several suggested answers or completions. Select the one that BEST answers the question or completes the statement. *PRINT THE LETTER OF THE CORRECT ANSWER IN THE SPACE AT THE RIGHT.*

Questions 1-7.

DIRECTIONS: Questions 1 through 7 are to be answered SOLELY on the basis of the time sheet and instructions given below.

The following time sheet indicates the times that seven laundry workers arrived and left each day for the week of August 23. The times they arrived for work are shown under the heading IN, and the times they left are shown under the heading OUT. The letter (P) indicates time which was used for personal business. Time used for this purpose is charged to annual leave. Lunch time is one-half hour from noon to 12:30 P.M. and is not accounted for on this time record.

The employees on this shift are scheduled to work from 8:00 A.M. to 4:00 P.M. Lateness is charged to annual leave. Reporting after 8:00 A.M. is considered late.

	MON.		TUES.		WED.		THURS.		FRI.	
	AM IN	PM OUT	AM IN	PM OUT	AM IN	PM OUT	AM IN	PM OUT	AM IN	PM OUT
Baxter	7:50	4:01	7:49	4:07	8:00	4:07	8:20	4:00	7:42	4:03
Gardner	8:02	4:00	8:20	4:00	8:05	3:30(P)	8:00	4:03	8:00	4:07
Clements	8:00	4:04	8:03	4:01	7:59	4:00	7:54	4:06	7:59	4:00
Tompkins	7:56	4:00	Annual leave		8:00	4:07	7:59	4:00	8:00	4:01
Wagner	8:04	4:03	7:40	4:00	7:53	4:04	8:00	4:09	7:53	4:00
Patterson	8:00	2:30(P)	8:15	4:04	Sick leave		7:45	4:00	7:59	4:04
Cunningham	7:43	4:02	7:50	4:00	7:59	4:02	8:00	4:10	8:00	4:00

1. Which one of the following laundry workers did NOT have any time charged to annual leave or sick leave during the week?   1._____

   A. Gardner   B. Clements   C. Tompkins   D. Cunningham

2. On which day did ALL the laundry workers arrive on time?   2._____

   A. Monday   B. Wednesday   C. Thursday   D. Friday

3. Which of the following laundry workers used time to take care of personal business?   3._____

   A. Baxter and Clements   B. Patterson and Cunningham
   C. Gardner and Patterson   D. Wagner and Tompkins

4. How many laundry workers were late on Monday?   4._____

   A. 1   B. 2   C. 3   D. 4

5. Which one of the following laundry workers arrived late on three of the five days?   5._____

   A. Baxter   B. Gardner   C. Wagner   D. Patterson

6. The percentage of laundry workers reporting to work late on Tuesday is MOST NEARLY   6._____

   A. 15%   B. 25%   C. 45%   D. 50%

7. The percentage of laundry workers that were absent for an entire day during the week is   7._____
   MOST NEARLY

   A. 6%   B. 9%   C. 15%   D. 30%

KEY (CORRECT ANSWERS)

1. D
2. D
3. C
4. B
5. B
6. C
7. D

TEST 3

Questions 1-9.

DIRECTIONS: Questions 1 through 9 are to be answered SOLELY on the basis of the following information and timesheet given below.

The following is a foreman's timesheet for his crew for one week. The hours worked each day or the reason the man was off on that day are shown on the sheet. *R* means rest day. *A* means annual leave. *S* means sick leave. Where a man worked only part of a day, both the number of hours worked and the number of hours taken off are entered. The reason for absence is entered in parentheses next to the number of hours taken off.

Name	Saturday	Sunday	Monday	Tuesday	Wednesday	Thursday	Friday
Smith	R	R	7	7	7	3 4(A)	7
Jones	R	7	7	7	7	7	R
Green	R	R	7	7	S	S	S
White	R	R	7	7	A	7	7
Doe	7	7	7	7	7	R	R
Brown	R	R	A	7	7	7	7
Black	R	R	S	7	7	7	7
Reed	R	R	7	7	7	7	S
Roe	R	R	A	7	7	7	7
Lane	7	R	R	7	7	A	S

1. The caretaker who worked EXACTLY 21 hours during the week is

   A. Lane B. Roe C. Smith D. White

2. The TOTAL number of hours worked by all caretakers during the week is

   A. 268 B. 276 C. 280 D. 288

3. The two days of the week on which MOST caretakers were off are

   A. Thursday and Friday
   B. Friday and Saturday
   C. Saturday and Sunday
   D. Sunday and Monday

4. The day on which three caretakers were off on sick leave is

   A. Monday B. Friday C. Saturday D. Sunday

5. The two workers who took LEAST time off during the week are

   A. Doe and Reed
   B. Jones and Doe
   C. Reed and Smith
   D. Smith and Jones

6. The caretaker who worked the LEAST number of hours during the week is

   A. Brown B. Green C. Lane D. Roe

7. The caretakers who did NOT work on Thursday are

   A. Doe, White, and Smith
   B. Green, Doe, and Lane
   C. Green, Doe, and Smith
   D. Green, Lane, and Smith

8. The day on which one caretaker worked ONLY 3 hours is 8._____
   A. Friday B. Saturday C. Thursday D. Wednesday

9. The day on which ALL caretakers worked is 9._____
   A. Monday B. Thursday C. Tuesday D. Wednesday

KEY (CORRECT ANSWERS)

1. A
2. B
3. C
4. B
5. B

6. B
7. B
8. C
9. C

TEST 4

Questions 1-6.

DIRECTIONS: Questions 1 through 6 are to be answered SOLELY on the basis of the table below which shows the initial requests made by staff for vacation. It is to be used with the RULES AND GUIDELINES to make the decisions and judgments called for in each of the questions.

VACATION REQUESTS FOR THE ONE YEAR PERIOD FROM MAY 1, YEAR X THROUGH APRIL 30, YEAR Y				
Name	Work Assignment	Date Appointed	Accumulated Annual Leave Days	Vacation Periods Requested
DeMarco	MVO	Mar. 2003	25	May 3-21; Oct. 25-Nov. 5
Moore	Dispatcher	Dec. 1997	32	May 24-June 4; July 12-16
Kingston	MVO	Apr. 2007	28	May 24-June 11; Feb. 7-25
Green	MVO	June 2006	26	June 7-18; Sept. 6-24
Robinson	MVO	July 2008	30	June 28-July 9; Nov. 15-26
Reilly	MVO	Oct. 2009	23	July 5-9; Jan. 31-Mar. 3
Stevens	MVO	Sept. 1996	31	July 5-23; Oct. 4-29
Costello	MVO	Sept. 1998	31	July 5-30; Oct. 4-22
Maloney	Dispatcher	Aug. 1992	35	July 5-Aug. 6; Nov. 1-5
Hughes	Director	Feb. 1990	38	July 26-Sept. 3
Lord	MVO	Jan. 2010	20	Aug. 9-27; Feb. 7-25
Diaz	MVO	Dec. 2009	28	Aug. 9-Sept. 10
Krimsky	MVO	May 2006	22	Oct. 18-22: Nov. 22-Dec. 10

RULES AND GUIDELINES

1. The two Dispatchers cannot be on vacation at the same time, nor can a Dispatcher be on vacation at the same time as the Director.

2. For the period June 1 through September 30, not more than three MVO's can be on vacation at the same time.

3. For the period October 1 through May 31, not more than two MVO's at a time can be on vacation.

4. In cases where the same vacation time is requested by too many employees for all of them to be given the time under the rules, the requests of those who have worked the longest will be granted.

5. No employee may take more leave days than the number of annual leave days accumulated and shown in the table.

6. All vacation periods shown in the table and described in the questions below begin on a Monday and end on a Friday.

7. Employees work a five-day week (Monday through Friday). They are off weekends and holidays with no charges to leave balances. When a holiday falls on a Saturday or Sunday, employees are given the following Monday off without charge to annual leave.

8. Holidays:
May 31	October 25	January 1
July 4	November 2	February 12
September 6	November 25	February 21
October 11	December 25	February 21

9. An employee shall be given any part of his initial requests that is permissible under the above rules and shall have first right to it despite any further adjustment of schedule.

---

1. Until adjustments in the vacation schedule can be made, the vacation dates that can be approved for Krimsky are

   A. Oct. 18-22; Nov. 22-Dec. 10
   B. Oct. 18-22; Nov. 29-Dec. 10
   C. Oct. 18-22 *only*
   D. Nov. 22-Dec. 10 *only*

2. Until adjustments in the vacation schedule can be made, the vacation dates that can be approved for Maloney are

   A. July 5-Aug. 6; Nov. 1-5
   B. July 5-23; Nov. 1-5
   C. July 5-9; Nov. 1-5
   D. Nov. 1-5 *only*

3. According to the table, Lord wants a vacation in August and another in February. Until adjustments in the vacation schedule can be made, he can be allowed to take _____ of the August vacation and _____ of the February vacation.

   A. all; none
   B. all; almost half
   C. almost all; almost half
   D. almost half; all

4. Costello cannot be given all the vacation he has requested because

   A. the MVO's who have more seniority than he has have requested time he wishes
   B. he does not have enough accumulated annual leave
   C. a dispatcher is applying for vacation at the same time as Costello
   D. there are five people who want vacation in July

5. According to the table, how many leave days will DeMarco be charged for his vacation from October 25 through November 5?

   A. 10   B. 9   C. 8   D. 7

6. How many leave days will Moore use if he uses the requested vacation allowable to him under the rules?

   A. 9   B. 10   C. 14   D. 15

KEY (CORRECT ANSWERS)

1. D
2. B
3. A
4. B
5. C
6. A

TEST 5

Questions 1-8.

DIRECTIONS: Questions 1 through 8 are to be answered SOLELY on the basis of Charts I, II, III, and IV. Assume that you are the supervisor of Operators R, S, T, U, V, W, and X, and it is your responsibility to schedule their lunch hours.

The charts each represent a possible scheduling of lunch hours during a lunch period from 11:30 - 2:00. An operator-hour is one hour of time spent by one operator. Each box on the chart represents one half-hour. The boxes marked L represent the time when each operator is scheduled to have her lunch hour. For example, in Chart I, next to Operator R, the boxes for 11:30 - 12:00 and 12:00 -12:30 are marked L. This means that Operator R is scheduled to have her lunch hour from 11:30 to 12:30.

I

	11:30-12:00	12:00-12:30	12:30-1:00	1:00-1:30	1:30-2:00
R	L	L			
S		L	L		
T		L	L		
U			L	L	
V			L	L	
W				L	L
X				L	L

II

	11:30-12:00	12:00-12:30	12:30-1:00	1:00-1:30	1:30-2:00
R				L	L
S		L	L		
T	L	L			
U		L	L		
V				L	L
W				L	L
X		L	L		

III

	11:30-12:00	12:00-12:30	12:30-1:00	1:00-1:30	1:30-2:00
R	L	L			
S				L	L
T	L	L			
U			L	L	
V	L	L			
W				L	L
X				L	L

IV

	11:30-12:00	12:00-12:30	12:30-1:00	1:00-1:30	1:30-2:00
R	L	L			
S	L	L			
T		L	L		
U			L	L	
V				L	L
W				L	L
X			L	L	

1. If, under the schedule represented in Chart II, Operator R has her lunch hour changed to 12:30-1:30, that leaves how many operator-hours of phone coverage from 1:00-2:00?

   A. 2   B. 2 1/2   C. 3   D. 4 1/2

2. If Operator S asks you whether she and Operator T may have the same lunch hour, you could accommodate her by using the schedule in Chart

   A. I   B. II   C. III   D. IV

3. From past experience you know that the part of the lunch period when the phones are busiest is from 12:30-1:30. Which chart shows the BEST phone coverage from 12:30 to 1:30?

   A. I   B. II   C. III   D. IV

4. At least three operators have the same lunch hour according to Chart(s)

   A. II and III   B. II and IV
   C. III only   D. IV only

5. Which chart would provide the POOREST phone coverage during the period 12:00-1:30, based on total number of operator-hours from 12:00 to 1:30? 5.____

   A. I   B. II   C. III   D. IV

6. Which chart would make it possible for U, W, and X to have the same lunch hour? 6.____

   A. I   B. II   C. III   D. IV

7. The portion of the lunch period during which the telephones are least busy is 11:30-12:30. 7.____
   Which chart is MOST likely to have been designed with that fact in mind?

   A. I   B. II   C. III   D. IV

8. Assume that you have decided to use Chart IV to schedule your operators' lunch hours on a specific day. Operator T asks you if she can have her lunch hour changed to 1:00-2:00. 8.____
   If you grant her request, how many operators will be working during the period 12:00 to 12:30?

   A. 1   B. 2   C. 4   D. 5

KEY (CORRECT ANSWERS)

1. D
2. A
3. B
4. A
5. A

6. C
7. C
8. D

TEST 6

Questions 1-13.

DIRECTIONS: Questions 1 through 13 consist of a statement. You are to indicate whether the statement is TRUE (T) or FALSE (F). *PRINT THE LETTER OF THE CORRECT ANSWER IN THE SPACE AT THE RIGHT.* Questions 1 through 13 are to be answered SOLELY on the basis of the information given in the table below.

DEPARTMENT OF FERRIES ATTENDANTS WORK ASSIGNMENT - JULY 2003					
Name	Year Employed	Ferry Assigned	Hours of Work	Lunch Period	Days Off
Adams	1999	Hudson	7 AM - 3 PM	11-12	Fri. and Sat.
Baker	1992	Monroe	7 AM - 3 PM	11-12	Sun. and Mon.
Gunn	1995	Troy	8 AM - 4 PM	12-1	Fri. and Sat.
Hahn	1989	Erie	9 AM - 5 PM	1-2	Sat. and Sun.
King	1998	Albany	7 AM - 3 PM	11-12	Sun. and Mon.
Nash	1993	Hudson	11 AM - 7 PM	3-4	Sun. and Mon.
Olive	2003	Fulton	10 AM - 6 PM	2-3	Sat. and Sun.
Queen	2002	Albany	11 AM - 7 PM	3-4	Fri. and Sat.
Rose	1990	Troy	11 AM - 7 PM	3-4	Sun. and Mon.
Smith	1991	Monroe	10 AM - 6 PM	2-3	Fri. and Sat.

1. The chart shows that there are only five (5) ferries being used.   1.____

2. The attendant who has been working the LONGEST time is Rose.   2.____

3. The Troy has one more attendant assigned to it than the Erie.   3.____

4. Two (2) attendants are assigned to work from 10 P.M. to 6 A.M.   4.____

5. According to the chart, no more than one attendant was hired in any year.   5.____

6. The NEWEST employee is Olive.   6.____

7. There are as many attendants on the 7 to 3 shift as on the 11 to 7 shift.   7.____

8. MOST of the attendants have their lunch either between 12 and 1 or 2 and 3.   8.____

9. All the employees work four (4) hours before they go to lunch.   9.____

10. On the Hudson, Adams goes to lunch when Nash reports to work.   10.____

11. All the attendants who work on the 7 to 3 shift are off on Saturday and Sunday.   11.____

12. All the attendants have either a Saturday or Sunday as one of their days off.   12.____

13. At least two (2) attendants are assigned to each ferry.   13.____

KEY (CORRECT ANSWERS)

1. F	6. T	11. F
2. F	7. T	12. T
3. T	8. F	13. F
4. F	9. T	
5. T	10. T	

PREPARING WRITTEN MATERIAL
EXAMINATION SECTION
TEST 1

DIRECTIONS: Each of Questions 1 through 5 consists of a sentence which may or may not be an example of good formal English usage. Examine each sentence, considering grammar, punctuation, spelling, capitalization, and awkwardness. Then choose the correct statement about it from the four options below it. If the English usage in the sentence given is better than any of the changes suggested in options B, C, or D, pick option A. (Do not pick an option that will change the meaning of the sentence.) *PRINT THE LETTER OF THE CORRECT ANSWER IN THE SPACE AT THE RIGHT.*

1. I don't know who could possibly of broken it. 1.____
   A. This is an example of good formal English usage.
   B. The word "who" should be replaced by the word "whom."
   C. The word "of" should be replaced by the word "have."
   D. The word "broken" should be replaced by the word "broke."

2. Telephoning is easier than to write. 2.____
   A. This is an example of good formal English usage.
   B. The word "telephoning" should be spelled "telephoneing."
   C. The word "than" should be replaced by the word "then."
   D. The words "to write" should be replaced by the word "writing."

3. The two operators who have been assigned to these consoles are on vacation. 3.____
   A. This is an example of good formal English usage.
   B. A comma should be placed after the word "operators."
   C. The word "who" should be replaced by the word "whom."
   D. The word "are" should be replaced by the word "is."

4. You were suppose to teach me how to operate a plugboard. 4.____
   A. This is an example of good formal English usage.
   B. The word "were" should be replaced by the word "was."
   C. The word "suppose" should be replaced by the word "supposed."
   D. The word "teach" should be replaced by the word "learn."

5. If you had taken my advice; you would have spoken with him. 5.____
   A. This is an example of good formal English usage.
   B. The word "advice" should be spelled "advise."
   C. The words "had taken" should be replaced by the word "take."
   D. The semicolon should be changed to a comma.

KEY (CORRECT ANSWERS)

1. C
2. D
3. A
4. C
5. D

TEST 2

DIRECTIONS: Select the correct answer. *PRINT THE LETTER OF THE CORRECT ANSWER IN THE SPACE AT THE RIGHT.*

1. The one of the following sentences which is MOST acceptable from the viewpoint of correct grammatical usage is:
   A. I do not know which action will have worser results.
   B. He should of known better.
   C. Both the officer on the scene, and his immediate supervisor, is charged with the responsibility.
   D. An officer must have initiative because his supervisor will not always be available to answer questions.

   1.____

2. The one of the following sentences which is MOST acceptable from the viewpoint of correct grammatical usage is:
   A. Of all the officers available, the better one for the job will be picked.
   B. Strict orders were given to all the officers, except he.
   C. Study of the law will enable you to perform your duties more efficiently.
   D. It seems to me that you was wrong in failing to search the two men.

   2.____

3. The one of the following sentences which does NOT contain a misspelled word is:
   A. The duties you will perform are similar to the duties of a patrolman.
   B. Officers must be constantly alert to sieze the initiative.
   C. Officers in this organization are not entitled to special privileges.
   D. Any changes in procedure will be announced publically.

   3.____

4. The one of the following sentences which does NOT contain a misspelled word is:
   A. It will be to your advantage to keep your firearm in good working condition.
   B. There are approximately fourty men on sick leave.
   C. Your first duty will be to pursuade the person to obey the law.
   D. Fires often begin in flameable material kept in lockers.

   4.____

5. The one of the following sentences which does NOT contain a misspelled word is:
   A. Offices are not required to perform technical maintainance.
   B. He violated the regulations on two occasions.
   C. Every employee will be held responable for errors.
   D. This was his nineth absence in a year.

   5.____

KEY (CORRECT ANSWERS)

1. D
2. C
3. C
4. A
5. B

TEST 3

DIRECTIONS: Select the correct answer. *PRINT THE LETTER OF THE CORRECT ANSWER IN THE SPACE AT THE RIGHT.*

1. You are answering a letter that was written on the letterhead of the ABC Company and signed by James H. Wood, Treasurer.
   What is usually considered to be the correct salutation to use in your reply?
   A. Dear ABC Company:
   B. Dear Sirs:
   C. Dear Mr. Wood:
   D. Dear Mr. Treasurer:

   1.____

2. Assume that one of your duties is to handle routine letters of inquiry from the public.
   The one of the following which is usually considered to be MOST desirable in replying to such a letter is a
   A. detailed answer handwritten on the original letter of inquiry
   B. phone call, since you can cover details more easily over the phone than in a letter
   C. short letter giving the specific information requested
   D. long letter discussing all possible aspects of the question raised

   2.____

3. The CHIEF reason for dividing a letter into paragraphs is to
   A. make the message clear to the reader by starting a new paragraph for each new topic
   B. make a short letter occupy as much of the page as possible
   C. keep the reader's attention by providing a pause from time to time
   D. make the letter look neat and businesslike

   3.____

4. Your superior has asked you to send an e-mail from your agency to a government agency in another city. He has written out the message and has indicated the name of the government agency.
   When you dictate the message to your secretary, which of the following items that your superior has NOT mentioned must you be sure to include?
   A. Today's date
   B. The full address of the government agency
   C. A polite opening such as "Dear Sirs"
   D. A final sentence such as "We would appreciate hearing from your agency in reply as soon as is convenient for you"

   4.____

5. The one of the following sentences which is grammatically preferable to the others is:
   A. Our engineers will go over your blueprints so that you may have no problems in construction.
   B. For a long time he had been arguing that we, not he, are to blame for the confusion.
   C. I worked on this automobile for two hours and still cannot find out what is wrong with it.
   D. Accustomed to all kinds of hardships, fatigue seldom bothers veteran policemen.

   5.____

KEY (CORRECT ANSWERS)

1. C
2. C
3. A
4. B
5. A

TEST 4

DIRECTIONS: Select the correct answer. *PRINT THE LETTER OF THE CORRECT ANSWER IN THE SPACE AT THE RIGHT.*

1. Suppose that an applicant for a job as snow laborer presents a letter from a former employer stating: "John Smith has a pleasing manner and never got into an argument with his fellow employees. He was never late or absent." This letter
    A. indicates that with some training Smith will make a good snow gang boss
    B. presents no definite evidence of Smith's ability to do snow work
    C. proves definitely that Smith has never done any snow work before
    D. proves definitely that Smith will do better than average work as a snow laborer

    1.____

2. Suppose you must write a letter to a local organization in your section refusing a request in connection with collection of their refuse.
    You should start the letter by
    A. explaining in detail the consideration you gave the request
    B. praising the organization for its service to the community
    C. quoting the regulation which forbids granting the request
    D. stating your regret that the request cannot be granted

    2.____

3. Suppose a citizen writes in for information as to whether or not he may sweep refuse into the gutter. A Sanitation officer answers as follows:
    Dear Sir:
       No person is permitted to litter, sweep, throw or cast, or direct, suffer or permit any person under his control to litter, sweep, throw or cast any ashes, garbage, paper, dust, or other rubbish or refuse into any public street or place, vacant lot, air shaft, areaway, backyard or court.
                                  Very truly yours,
                                  John Doe
    This letter is *poorly* written CHIEFLY because
    A. the opening is not indented   B. the thought is not clear
    C. the tone is too formal and cold   D. there are too many commas used

    3.____

4. A section of a disciplinary report written by a Sanitation officer states: "It is requested that subject Sanitation man be advised that his future activities be directed towards reducing his recurrent tardiness else disciplinary action will be initiated which may result in summary discharge."
    This section of the report is *poorly* written MAINLY because
    A. at least one word is misspelled   B. it is not simply expressed
    C. more than one idea is expressed   D. the purpose is not stated

    4.____

5. A section of a disciplinary report written by an officer states: "He comes in late. He takes too much time for lunch. He is lazy. I recommend his services be dispensed with."
    This section of the report is *poorly* written MAINLY because
    A. it ends with a preposition   B. it is not well organized
    C. no supporting facts are stated   D. the sentences are too simple

    5.____

KEY (CORRECT ANSWERS)

1. B
2. D
3. C
4. B
5. C

PREPARING WRITTEN MATERIAL

PARAGRAPH REARRANGEMENT
COMMENTARY

The sentences that follow are in scrambled order. You are to rearrange them in proper order and indicate the letter choice containing the correct answer at the space at the right.

Each group of sentences in this section is actually a paragraph presented in scrambled order. Each sentence in the group has a place in that paragraph; no sentence is to be left out. You are to read each group of sentences and decide upon the best order in which to put the sentences so as to form a well-organized paragraph.

The questions in this section measure the ability to solve a problem when all the facts relevant to its solution are not given.

More specifically, certain positions of responsibility and authority require the employee to discover connection between events sometimes, apparently, unrelated. In order to do this, the employee will find it necessary to correctly infer that unspecified events have probably occurred or are likely to occur. This ability becomes especially important when action must be taken on incomplete information.

Accordingly, these questions require competitors to choose among several suggested alternatives, each of which presents a different sequential arrangement of the events. Competitors must choose the MOST logical of the suggested sequences.

In order to do so, they may be required to draw on general knowledge to infer missing concepts or events that are essential to sequencing the given events. Competitors should be careful to infer only what is essential to the sequence. The plausibility of the wrong alternatives will always require the inclusion of unlikely events or of additional chains of events which are NOT essential to sequencing the given events.

It's very important to remember that you are looking for the best of the four possible choices, and that the best choice of all may not even be one of the answers you're given to choose from.

There is no one right way to solve these problems. Many people have found it helpful to first write out the order of the sentences, as they would have arranged them, on their scrap paper before looking at the possible answers. If their optimum answer is there, this can save them some time. If it isn't, this method can still give insight into solving the problem. Others find it most helpful to just go through each of the possible choices, contrasting each as they go along. You should use whatever method feels comfortable and works for you.

While most of these types of questions are not that difficult, we've added a higher percentage of the difficult type, just to give you more practice. Usually there are only one or two questions on this section that contain such subtle distinctions that you're unable to answer confidently. And you then may find yourself stuck deciding between two possible choices, neither of which you're sure about.

PREPARING WRITTEN MATERIAL
PARAGRAPH REARRANGEMENT

EXAMINATION SECTION
TEST 1

DIRECTIONS: The sentences listed below are part of a meaningful paragraph, but they are not given in their proper order. You are to decide what would be the BEST order to put sentences to form a well-organized paragraph. Each sentence has a place in the paragraph; there are no extra sentences. *PRINT THE LETTER OF THE CORRECT ANSWER IN THE SPACE AT THE RIGHT.*

Questions 1-3.

DIRECTIONS: Questions 1 through 3 are to be answered on the basis of the following paragraph.

The CDC estimates that food-borne pathogens cause approximately 48 million illnesses, 3,000 deaths, and 128,000 hospitalizations in the United States each year. Contamination with disease-causing microbes called pathogens is usually due to improper food handling or storage. Other causes of food-borne diseases are toxic chemicals or other harmful substances in food and beverages. Food-borne diseases are illnesses caused when people consume contaminated food or beverages. More than 250 food-borne illnesses have been described, according to the United States Centers for Disease Control and Prevention (CDC).

1. When the five sentences are arranged in proper order, the paragraph starts with the sentence that begins:
   A. "Food-borne diseases..."
   B. "More than 250..."
   C. "Other causes of..."
   D. The CDC estimates..."

1.____

2. If the above paragraph were correctly organized, which of the following transition words would be appropriate to place at the beginning of the sentence that starts "The CDC estimates..."?
   A. With that said
   B. However
   C. To start off
   D. Ultimately

2.____

3. When the above paragraph is properly arranged, it ends with the words:
   A. "...Disease Control and Prevention (CDC).
   B. "...improper food handling or storage."
   C. "...United States each year."
   D. "...in food and beverages."

3.____

Questions 4-7.

DIRECTIONS: Questions 4 through 7 are to be answered on the basis of the following passage.

111

Her father, Abraham Quintanilla, who worked in the shipping department of a chemical plant and later opened a restaurant, had fronted a moderately successful band called Los Dinos ("The Guys") as a young man. Among them, her murder evoked an outpouring of grief comparable to that experienced by other Americans after the deaths of such major cultural figures as President John F. Kennedy. Selena had become an icon in the Hispanic community.

Selena Quintanilla was born in Lake Jackson, Texas, near Houston, on April 16, 1971. She had turned into a beloved figure to whom Mexican-Americans attached their aspirations and their feelings about their cultural identities. The violent death of beloved Tejano vocalist Selena on Mach 31, 1995 brought to an end more than just a promising musical career.

4. When arranged properly, the paragraph's opening sentence should start with: 4._____
   A. "Among them…" B. "The violent death…"
   C. "Her father, Abraham…" D. "Selena had become…"

5. In the second sentence listed above, "them" refers to 5._____
   A. Selena and her fans B. other non-Mexican Americans
   C. Selena and John F. Kennedy D. Mexican-Americans

6. After correctly organizing the paragraph, the author decides to split it into two separate paragraphs. Which of the following would begin the newly made second paragraph? 6._____
   A. "Selena had become…" B. "Selena Quintanilla was…"
   C. "The violent death…" D. "Her father, Abraham…"

7. When correctly organized, the final sentence of the paragraph should end end with the words: 7._____
   A. "…as a young man." B. "…on April 16, 1971."
   C. "…in the Hispanic community." D. "…a promising music career."

Questions 8-10.

DIRECTIONS: Questions 8 through 10 are to be answered on the basis of the following paragraph.

Whether Death takes the form of a decrepit old man, a grim reaper, or a ferryman, his visit is almost never welcome by the poor mortal who finds him at the door. Such is not the case in "Because I Could Not Stop for Death." Knowing that the woman has been keeping herself too busy in her daily life to remember Death, he "kindly" comes by to get her. Perhaps Dickinson's most famous work, "Because I Could Not Stop for Death" is generally considered to be one of the great masterpieces of American poetry. Here, Death is a gentleman, perhaps handsome and well-groomed, who makes a call at the home of a naïve young woman. The poem begins with a comment upon Death's politeness, although he surprises the woman with his visit. While most people would try to bar the door once they recognized his identity, this woman gives the impression that she is quite flattered to find herself in even this gentleman's favor. Death is personified, or described in terms of human characteristics, throughout literature. Figuratively speaking, this poem is about one woman's "date with death." Dickinson uses the personification of Death as a metaphor throughout the poem.

8. Which of the following sentence beginnings indicate the opening sentence of this paragraph?
   A. "Perhaps Dickinson's most…"
   B. "The poem begins with…"
   C. "Death is personified…"
   D. "Whether Death takes…"

   8._____

9. To whom does "his" refer to in the sentence that starts "While most people would…"?
   A. A gentleman
   B. Death
   C. People trying to avoid death
   D. Ms. Dickinson

   9._____

10. If the paragraph were correctly organized, the second to last sentence would end with:
    A. "…gentleman's favor."
    B. "…a naive young woman."
    C. "…of American poetry."
    D. "…throughout literature."

    10._____

Questions 11-13.

DIRECTIONS: Questions 11 through 13 are to be answered on the basis of the following paragraph.

Reformers such as Jacob Riis, author of *The Children of the Tenements* (1903), and George Creel, who with the assistance of Denver's juvenile court judge, Ben Lindsey, wrote *Children in Bondage* (1913), helped broaden awareness of the conditions under which many of the nation's poor children were reared. At the same time, changes were taking place in the way the childhood years were perceived. More and more Americans began to regard children as a national resource that deserved society's protection and guidance. In sharp contrast to these images of child workers worn down by the toil of their labor were the children of the middle class, who led quite different lives and whose progress was measured not in industrial output, but in ways increasingly seen as being vital to their development as productive citizens. Exhibitions of photographs of children employed in all sorts of economic pursuits, including those considered among the most dangerous and grueling, proved equally successful in pricking the public's conscience. When the United States was a nation of farms, shops, and small mills, the use of children to supplement a family's income was so common that it attracted little notice and even less concern. The nation's rapid and dramatic transformation into an industrialized society, however, changed the environment in which children labored and the conditions to which they were exposed.

11. When organized correctly, the third sentence in the above paragraph would start:
    A. "The nation's rapid…"
    B. "In sharp contrast…"
    C. "At the same time…"
    D. "Exhibitions of photographs…"

    11._____

12. If the author wanted to change the beginning of the topic sentence for this paragraph to "In the past," they would need to change which of the following?
    A. "Reformers such as…"
    B. "Exhibitions of photographs…"
    C. "More and more Americans…"
    D. "When the United States…"

    12._____

13. If the above paragraph was organized correctly, its ending words of the last sentence would be:

    13._____

A. "...as productive citizens."
B. "...and even less concern."
C. "...in pricking the public's conscience."
D. "...poor children were reared."

Questions 14-16.

DIRECTIONS: Questions 14 through 16 are to be answered on the basis of the following paragraph.

Here we outline a unique bivariate flood hazard assessment framework that accounts for the interactions between a primary oceanic flooding hazard, coastal water level, and fluvial flooding hazards. Common flood hazard assessment practices typically focus on one flood driver at a time and ignore potential compounding impacts. The results show that, in a warming climate, future sea level rise not only increases the failure probability, but also exacerbates the compounding effects of flood drivers. Using the notion of "failure probability," we also assess coastal flood hazard under different future sea level rise scenarios. Population and assets in coastal regions are threatened by both oceanic and fluvial flooding hazards.

14. When the sentences above are organized correctly, the paragraph starts with the sentence that begins:
    A. "The results show..."
    B. "Here we outline..."
    C. "Population and assets..."
    D. "Using the notion..."

14._____

15. If the author wanted to add the phrase "To sum up" to the above paragraph, he would insert it in front of the sentence that begins:
    A. "Using the notion..."
    B. "Common flood hazard..."
    C. "Here we outline..."
    D. "The results show..."

15._____

16. Assuming the paragraph were organized correctly, the second to last sentence would end:
    A. "...of flood drivers."
    B. "...level rise scenarios."
    C. "...fluvial flooding hazards."
    D. "...compounding impacts."

16._____

Questions 17-19.

DIRECTIONS: Questions 17 through 19 are to be answered on the basis of the following paragraph.

The adhesive stuck to a pig heart even when the surface was coated in blood, the team reported in the July 28 Science. Li, who did the research while at Harvard University, and colleagues also tested the glue in live rats with liver lacerations. A solution might be found under wet leaves on a forest floor, recent research suggests. For surgeons closing internal incisions, that's more than an annoyance. The right glue could hold wounds together as effectively as stitches and staples with less damage to the surrounding soft tissue, enabling safer surgical procedures. It stopped the rats' bleeding, and the animals didn't appear to suffer any bad reaction from the adhesive. Finding a great glue is a sticky task — especially if you want to attach to something as slick as the inside of the human body. Jianyu Li of McGill University in Montreal and colleagues have created a surgical glue that mimics the chemical recipe of goopy slime that slugs exude when they're startled. Using the glue to plug a hole in the pig heart worked so well that the heart still held in liquid after being inflated and deflated tens of thousands of times. Even the strongest human-made adhesives don't work well on wet surfaces like tissues and organs.

17. The above paragraph, when organized correctly, should begin with the words: 17._____
    A. "Finding a great..." B. "Using the glue..."
    C. "The adhesive stuck..." D. "It stopped the rats..."

18. If the author wanted to split the paragraph into two separate paragraphs, the 18._____
    first sentence of the second paragraph would begin:
    A. "For surgeons closing..." B. "Even the strongest..."
    C. "A solution might be..." D. "Jianyu Li of McGill..."

19. If the above paragraph were organized correctly, the final sentence would 19._____
    end with:
    A. "...recent research suggests." B. "...from the adhesive."
    C. "...like tissues and organs." D. "...thousands of times."

Questions 20-22.

DIRECTIONS: Questions 20 to 22 are to be answered on the basis of the following paragraph.

The signal from the spacecraft is gone, and within the next 45 seconds, so will be the spacecraft," Cassini project manager Earl Maize announced from the mission control center at NASA's Jet Propulsion Lab. The signal that Cassini had reached its destination arrived at Earth at 4:54 A.M., and cut out about a minute later as the spacecraft lost its battle with Saturn's atmosphere. I'm going to call this the end of mission. Project manager, off the net." With that, the mission control team erupted in applause, hugs and some tears. This has been an incredible mission, an incredible spacecraft, and you're all an incredible team. The spacecraft entered Saturn's atmosphere at about 3:31 A.M. PDT on September 15 and immediately began running through all of its stabilizing procedures to try to keep itself upright. Cassini went down fighting. After 20 years in space and 13 years orbiting Saturn, the veteran spacecraft spent its last 90 seconds or so firing its thrusters as hard as it could to keep sending Saturnian secrets back to Earth for as long as possible.

20. In the above paragraph, who does "you all" refer to in the sentence that begins 20._____
    "Congratulations"?
    A. All Americans B. Cassini
    C. Earl Maize D. The mission control team

21. If the sentence were organized correctly, the fourth sentence's last words 21._____
    would be:
    A. "...as long as possible." B. "...this amazing accomplishment."
    C. "...Saturn's atmosphere." D. "...off the net."

22. When organized correctly, the final sentence would end with the following: 22._____
    A. "...and some tears." B. "...went down fighting."
    C. "...Jet Propulsion Lab." D. "...keep itself upright."

Questions 23-25.

DIRECTIONS: Questions 23 through 25 are to be answered on the basis of the following paragraph.

As the first African-American woman to carry mail, she stood out on the trail — and became a Wild West legend. Born Mary Fields in around 1832, Fields was born into slavery, and like many other enslaved people, her exact date of birth is not known. Rumor had it that she'd fending off an angry pack of wolves with her rifle, had "the temperament of a grizzly bear," and was not above a gunfight. Bandits beware: In 1890s Montana, would-be mail thieves didn't stand a chance against Stagecoach Mary. Even the place of her birth is questionable, though historians have pinpointed Hickman County, Tennessee as the most likely location. At the time, slaves were treated like pieces of property; their numbers were recorded in record books, their names were not. But how much of Stagecoach Mary's story is myth? The hard-drinking, quick-shooting mail carrier sported two guns, men's clothing, and a bad attitude.

23. Who does "she'd" refer to in the sentence that begins "Rumor had it..."?
 A. An anonymous African-American
 B. Hickman County
 C. A mail thief
 D. Stagecoach Mary

24. If the author were interested in splitting this paragraph into two separate paragraphs, the topic sentence of the second paragraph would begin:
 A. "At the time…"
 B. "Born Mary Fields…"
 C. "Bandits beware…"
 D. "As the first…"

25. When organized correctly, the final sentence of the paragraph would end with the words:
 A. "…their names were not."
 B. "…above a gunfight."
 C. "…against Stagecoach Mary."
 D. "…a Wild West legend."

KEY (CORRECT ANSWERS)

1.	A	11.	C
2.	D	12.	D
3.	C	13.	A
4.	B	14.	C
5.	D	15.	D
6.	B	16.	B
7.	A	17.	A
8.	C	18.	C
9.	B	19.	B
10.	A	20.	D

21. C
22. A
23. D
24. B
25. A

TEST 2

DIRECTIONS: Each question or incomplete statement is followed by several suggested answers or completions. Select the one that BEST answers the question or completes the statement. *PRINT THE LETTER OF THE CORRECT ANSWER IN THE SPACE AT THE RIGHT.*

Questions 1-3.

DIRECTIONS: Questions 1 through 3 are to be answered on the basis of the following paragraph.

The majority of people who develop these issues are athletes who participate in popular high-impact sports, especially football. Although most people who suffer a concussion experience initial bouts of dizziness, nausea, and drowsiness, these symptoms often disappear after a few days. Although both new sports regulations and improvements in helmet technology can help protect players, the sports media and fans alike bear some of the responsibility for reducing the incidence of these devastating injuries. These psychological problems can include depression, anxiety, memory loss, inability to concentrate, and aggression. In extreme cases, people suffering from CTE have even committed suicide or homicide. The long-term effects of concussions, however, are less understood and far more severe. Recent studies suggest that people who suffer multiple concussions are at a significant risk for developing chronic traumatic encephalopathy (CTE), a degenerative brain disorder that causes a variety of dangerous mental and emotional problems to arise weeks, months, or even years after the initial injury. Chronic Traumatic Encephalopathy Concussions are brain injuries that occur when a person receives a blow to the head, face, or neck.

1. When organized correctly, the first sentence of the paragraph begins with: 1.____
   A. "Recent studies suggest…"   B. "The long-term effects…"
   C. "Although both new…"   D. "Chronic Traumatic…"

2. Upon ordering the paragraph correctly, the author wishes to substitute for a 2.____
   word in sentence four that means "progressive irreversible deterioration."
   Which word does the author wish to replace?
   A. Anxiety   B. Degenerative
   C. Responsibility   D. Devastating

3. If put in the right order, the paragraph's last words would be: 3.____
   A. "…to the head, face, or neck."
   B. "…committed suicide or homicide."
   C. "…these devastating injuries."
   D. "…far more severe."

2 (#2)

Questions 4-8.

DIRECTIONS: Questions 4 through 8 are to be answered on the basis of the following paragraph.

These controversies were settled by the 1977 treaty, which provided for a twenty-two-year period of U.S. withdrawal and turnover of the canal to Panama. For its first 85 years the canal was operate exclusively by the United States government as an international maritime passage, according to the 1903 Hay-Buneau-Varilla Treaty and the 1977 Carter-Torrijos Treaty that replaced it. Panamanian and other critics pointed out that the United States took unfair advantage of the newly independent republic (separated from Colombia in 1903, with the help of the United States) to impose conditions for near-sovereign ownership; complained that it exceeded its original concession by creating a strategic military complex with fourteen bases and numerous intelligence sites; and asserted that it created a virtual state within a state by establishing public agencies and enterprises in the 500-plus square miles of territory it controlled in the Canal Zone. One of the world's great engineering projects, the canal was controversial because of the method by which the United States gained the concession (by negotiating a treaty with a French shareholder temporarily representing Panama) and its operation of the utility with regard to the interests of Panama. Built between 1904 and 1914, the canal shortened maritime voyages considerably. The Panama Canal is a 51-mile ship canal with six pairs of locks that crosses the Isthmus of Panama and allows vessels to transit between the Caribbean Sea and the Pacific Ocean. Under the latter treaty, the canal was turned over in 1999 to the Republic of Panama, which has operated it ever since.

4. When organized correctly, the sentence AFTERs the topic sentence should begin:
   A. "Built between 1904…"   B. "The Panama Canal…"
   C. "These controversies…"   D. "Panamanian and other…"

5. If the author ordered the sentences correctly, one sentence that provides evidence of controversy surrounding the Panama Canal would be Sentence
   A. 7   B. 5   C. 1   D. 2

6. When correctly ordered, the last words of the paragraph would be:
   A. "…the canal to Panama."   B. "…in the Canal Zone."
   C. "…and the Pacific Ocean."   D. "…to the interests of Panama."

7. What "latter treaty" is the sentence that begins "Under the latter treaty…" referring to in the paragraph?
   A. The Treaty of Panama   B. The Hay-Buneau-Varilla Treaty
   C. The Carter-Torrijos Treaty   D. Both B and C

8. When organized correctly, the sentence that ends "…in the Canal Zone" would be preceded by the sentence that begins:
   A. "The Panama Canal…"   B. "These controversies were…"
   C. "For its first…"   D. "One of the world's great…"

Questions 9-11.

DIRECTIONS: Questions 9 through 11 are to be answered on the basis of the following paragraph.

Such incidents revolved around many issues, including, among others, job security, wages, occupational safety, and, especially, the eight-hour day. The Haymarket Riot of 1886 grew out of a long string of circumstances that eventually culminated in an unfortunate incident. Not only were skilled craftsmen seeing their professions disappear in the face of machines operated by unskilled labor, but the length of hours in the workday lengthened and could range from ten to twelve and even longer in some specific instances. It was this last issue that was particularly important as the Industrial Revolution truly swept over America. Regardless of who might have been at fault in a labor struggle, each moment of violent upheaval had serious consequences. During the post-Civil War era, there were periods of labor upheaval both in Chicago and across the nation. Each of these topics played an important role in labor unrest as the climate in the country between workers and the state reached fever pitch. At issue were several key points: the continued growth of the Industrial Revolution and its impact on society, the movement for the eight-hour workday, worker dissatisfaction, suppression of labor activities by various government authorities, and the growth of radicalism in the United States.

9. If the author were to put the paragraph in the correct order, the third sentence would begin with the words:
   A. "Each of these…"
   B. "It was this last…"
   C. "Not only were skilled…"
   D. "The Haymarket Riot…"

10. The author has determined that one paragraph is too long, so they wish to split it into two paragraphs and change the start of the new paragraph to "Dating back to". The sentence that the author would need to alter slightly currently begins:
    A. "The Haymarket Riot…"
    B. "Each of these topics…"
    C. "During the post-Civil…"
    D. "Not only were…"

11. When organized correctly, the last sentence of the paragraph would end with the words:
    A. "…an unfortunate incident."
    B. "…some specific instances."
    C. "…in the United States."
    D. "…across the nation."

Questions 12-14.

DIRECTIONS: Questions 12 through 14 are to be answered on the basis of the following paragraph.

Using an experimental design, they find no evidence that the use of Twitter improves students' learning. The authors assess students across three different institutions to see if the use of Twitter improves learning outcomes relative to a traditional Learning Management System. Ever since Becker and Watts (1996) found that economic educators rely heavily on "chalk and talk" as a primary teaching method, economic educators have been seeking new ways to engage students and improve learning outcomes. Recently, the use of social media as a pedagogical tool in economics has received increasing interest.

12. When organized correctly, the paragraph would begin with the words: 12.____
    A. "Using an..."   B. "Recently, the..."
    C. "The authors..."   D. "Ever since..."

13. In the sentence that begins "Using an experimental...", to whom does "they" refer? 13.____
    A. Social media users   B. Becker and Watts
    C. Economic educators   D. Different institutions

14. If the author wanted to start the last sentence with "With that said...", they would be adding it to the sentence that currently starts: 14.____
    A. "Using an..."   B. "The authors..."
    C. "Recently, the..."   D. "Ever since..."

Questions 15-17.

DIRECTIONS: Questions 15 through 17 are to be answered on the basis of the following paragraph.

Teaching the topic of genetics in relationship to ancestry and race generates many questions, and requires a teaching strategy that encourages perspective-based exploration and discussion. We have developed a set of dialogues for discussing the complex science of genetics, ancestry, and race that is contextualized in real human interactions and that contends with the social and ethical implications of this science. This article provides some brief historical and scientific context for these dialogues, describes their development, and relates how we have used them in different ways to engage diverse groups of science learners. The dialogue series can be incorporated into classroom or informal science education settings. After listening to or performing the dialogues and participating in a discussion, students will: (1) recognize misunderstandings about the relationship between DNA and race; (2) describe how DNA testing services assign geographic ancestry; (3) explain how scientific findings have been used historically to promote institutionalized racism and the role personal biases can play in science; (4) identify situations in their own life that have affected their understanding of genetics and race; and (5) discuss the potential consequences of the racialization of medicine as well as other fallacies about the connection of science and race.

15. If the author organized the above paragraph correctly, the fourth sentence would end with the words: 15.____
    A. "...connection of science and race."
    B. "...implications of this science."
    C. "...exploration and discussion."
    D. "...science education settings."

16. The author wishes to split the paragraph into two distinct paragraphs. When organized, the last sentence of the first paragraph would begin: 16.____
    A. "We have developed..."   B. "This article proves..."
    C. "The dialogue series..." D. "Teaching the topic..."

17. When organized correctly, the last sentence would begin with the words: 17._____
    A. "After listening to..." B. "Teaching the topic..."
    C. "We have developed..." D. "This article provides..."

Questions 18-20.

DIRECTIONS: Questions 18 through 20 are to be answered on the basis of the following paragraph.

For example, Canadian Immigration officers have the power to deny persons with OWI convictions from crossing the border into Canada. Individuals who have been acquitted of an OWI can still be stopped at the border and denied entry. Some restrictions, however, are not known to individuals that have been charged with an OWI. In fact, if you have been arrested or convicted for driving under the influence of drugs or alcohol, regardless of whether it was a felony or a misdemeanor, you may be criminally inadmissible to Canada or denied entry. In order to receive an eTA, individuals have to disclose their criminal convictions, which may bar them from entering Canada. The restrictions imposed by an OWI conviction can be quite burdensome. Even if you will not be driving in Canada, you can still be denied entry. This stringent border patrol comes as a surprise to many U.S. citizens. Canadian Immigration Officials have introduced a new entry requirement, known as an Electronic Travel Authorization (eTA).

18. When organized correctly, the topic sentence of the paragraph would begin with 18._____
    the words:
    A. "This stringent border..." B. "In fact, if..."
    C. "Canadian Immigration Officials..." D. "The restrictions imposed..."

19. Once properly ordered, it would make the most sense to insert the words 19._____
    "With that being the case..." in front of the sentence that currently begins:
    A. "The restrictions imposed..." B. "For example..."
    C. "Canadian Immigration Officials..." D. "Even if you will..."

20. If the author were to put the paragraph in correct order, the second to last 20._____
    sentence would end with the words:
    A. "...border into Canada." B. "...from entering Canada."
    C. "...to many U.S. citizens." D. "...to Canada or denied entry."

Questions 21-25.

DIRECTIONS: Questions 21 through 25 are to be answered on the basis of the following paragraph.

Many instructors at the college level require that you use scholarly articles as sources when writing a research paper. Scholarly or peer-reviewed articles are written by experts in academic or professional fields. They are excellent sources for finding out what has been studied or researched on a topic as well as to find bibliographies that point to other relevant sources of information. Peer-reviewed journals require that articles are read and evaluated by experts in the field before they are accepted for publication. Although most scholarly articles are refereed or peer reviewed, some are not. Generally, instructors are happy with either peer-reviewed or scholarly articles, but if your article HAS to be peer-reviewed, you will need to find that information in the front of the journal, or use Ulrich's Periodicals Directory (Reference Z6941 U5) located behind the Reference Desk on the 2nd floor of the library. Look up your title and look for the Document Type: Journal, Academic/Scholarly. Articles that are peer-reviewed will have an arrow to the left of the title.

21. When organized correctly, the introductory sentence would begin with the words:
    A. "They are excellent..."
    B. "Peer-reviewed journals..."
    C. "Many instructors at..."
    D. "Look up your..."

    21.____

22. In the sentence that begins "They are", to what/whom does "They" refer?
    A. Scholarly articles
    B. Instructors
    C. Peers
    D. Library directory

    22.____

23. If the author were interested in splitting up the paragraph into two separate paragraphs, the topic sentence of the second paragraph would begin:
    A. "Many instructors at..."
    B. "Peer-reviewed journals..."
    C. "Generally instructors are..."
    D. "Scholarly or peer-reviewed..."

    23.____

24. When organized correctly, the third sentence of the paragraph would end with the words:
    A. "...a research paper."
    B. "...of the title."
    C. "...of the library."
    D. "...sources of information."

    24.____

25. If the author were to organize the paragraph correctly, the paragraph would end with the words:
    A. "...some are not."
    B. "...a research paper."
    C. "...or professional fields."
    D. "...of the title."

    25.____

KEY (CORRECT ANSWERS)

1. D
2. B
3. C
4. A
5. B

6. A
7. C
8. D
9. A
10. C

11. B
12. D
13. B
14. A
15. D

16. C
17. A
18. D
19. C
20. B

21. C
22. A
23. B
24. D
25. D

PHILOSOPHY, PRINCIPLES, PRACTICES, AND TECHNICS OF SUPERVISION, ADMINISTRATION, MANAGEMENT, AND ORGANIZATION

TABLE OF CONTENTS

	Page
MEANING OF SUPERVISION	1
THE OLD AND THE NEW SUPERVISION	1
THE EIGHT (8) BASIC PRINCIPLES OF THE NEW SUPERVISION	1
I. Principle of Responsibility	1
II. Principle of Authority	2
III. Principle of Self-Growth	2
IV. Principle of Individual Worth	2
V. Principle of Creative Leadership	2
VI. Principle of Success and Failure	2
VII. Principle of Science	3
VIII. Principle of Cooperation	3
WHAT IS ADMINISTRATION?	3
I. Practices Commonly Classed as "Supervisory"	3
II. Practices Commonly Classed as "Administrative"	3
III. Practices Commonly Classed as Both "Supervisory" and "Administrative"	4
RESPONSIBILITIES OF THE SUPERVISOR	4
COMPETENCIES OF THE SUPERVISOR	4
THE PROFESSIONAL SUPERVISOR-EMPLOYEE RELATIONSHIP	4
MINI-TEXT IN SUPERVISION, ADMINISTRATION, MANAGEMENT, AND ORGANIZATION	5
I. Brief Highlights	5
A. Levels of Management	6
B. What the Supervisor Must Learn	6
C. A Definition of Supervision	6
D. Elements of the Team Concept	6
E. Principles of Organization	6
F. The Four Important Parts of Every Job	7
G. Principles of Delegation	7
H. Principles of Effective Communications	7
I. Principles of Work Improvement	7
J. Areas of Job Improvement	7
K. Seven Key Points in Making Improvements	8

	L.	Corrective Techniques for Job Improvement	8
	M.	A Planning Checklist	8
	N.	Five Characteristics of Good Directions	9
	O.	Types of Directions	9
	P.	Controls	9
	Q.	Orienting the New Employee	9
	R.	Checklist for Orienting New Employees	9
	S.	Principles of Learning	10
	T.	Causes of Poor Performance	10
	U.	Four Major Steps in On-the-Job Instructions	10
	V.	Employees Want Five Things	10
	W.	Some Don'ts in Regard to Praise	11
	X.	How to Gain Your Workers' Confidence	11
	Y.	Sources of Employee Problems	11
	Z.	The Supervisor's Key to Discipline	11
	AA.	Five Important Processes of Management	12
	BB.	When the Supervisor Fails to Plan	12
	CC.	Fourteen General Principles of Management	12
	DD.	Change	12
II.	Brief Topical Summaries		13
	A.	Who/What is the Supervisor?	13
	B.	The Sociology of Work	13
	C.	Principles and Practices of Supervision	14
	D.	Dynamic Leadership	14
	E.	Processes for Solving Problems	15
	F.	Training for Results	15
	G.	Health, Safety, and Accident Prevention	16
	H.	Equal Employment Opportunity	16
	I.	Improving Communications	16
	J.	Self-Development	17
	K.	Teaching and Training	17
		1. The Teaching Process	17
		a. Preparation	17
		b. Presentation	18
		c. Summary	18
		d. Application	18
		e. Evaluation	18
		2. Teaching Methods	18
		a. Lecture	18
		b. Discussion	18
		c. Demonstration	19
		d. Performance	19
		e. Which Method to Use	19

PHILOSOPHY, PRINCIPLES, PRACTICES, AND TECHNICS
OF
SUPERVISION, ADMINISTRATION, MANAGEMENT, AND ORGANIZATION

MEANING OF SUPERVISION

The extension of the democratic philosophy has been accompanied by an extension in the scope of supervision. Modern leaders and supervisors no longer think of supervision in the narrow sense of being confined chiefly to visiting employees, supplying materials, or rating the staff. They regard supervision as being intimately related to all the concerned agencies of society, they speak of the supervisor's function in terms of "growth," rather than the "improvement" of employees.

This modern concept of supervision may be defined as follows: Supervision is leadership and the development of leadership within groups which are cooperatively engaged in inspection, research, training, guidance, and evaluation.

THE OLD AND THE NEW SUPERVISION

TRADITIONAL
1. Inspection
2. Focused on the employee
3. Visitation
4. Random and haphazard
5. Imposed and authoritarian
6. One person usually

MODERN
1. Study and analysis
2. Focused on aims, materials, methods, supervisors, employees, environment
3. Demonstrations, intervisitation, workshops, directed reading, bulletins, etc.
4. Definitely organized and planned (scientific)
5. Cooperative and democratic
6. Many persons involved (creative)

THE EIGHT (8) BASIC PRINCIPLES OF THE NEW SUPERVISION

I. Principle of Responsibility
   Authority to act and responsibility for acting must be joined.
   A. If you give responsibility, give authority.
   B. Define employee duties clearly.
   C. Protect employees from criticism by others.
   D. Recognize the rights as well as obligations of employees.
   E. Achieve the aims of a democratic society insofar as it is possible within the area of your work.
   F. Establish a situation favorable to training and learning.
   G. Accept ultimate responsibility for everything done in your section, unit, office, division, department.
   H. Good administration and good supervision are inseparable.

II. Principle of Authority
The success of the supervisor is measured by the extent to which the power of authority is not used.
   A. Exercise simplicity and informality in supervision
   B. Use the simplest machinery of supervision
   C. If it is good for the organization as a whole, it is probably justified.
   D. Seldom be arbitrary or authoritative.
   E. Do not base your work on the power of position or of personality.
   F. Permit and encourage the free expression of opinions.

III. Principle of Self-Growth
The success of the supervisor is measured by the extent to which, and the speed with which, he is no longer needed.
   A. Base criticism on principles, not on specifics.
   B. Point out higher activities to employees.
   C. Train for self-thinking by employees to meet new situations.
   D. Stimulate initiative, self-reliance, and individual responsibility
   E. Concentrate on stimulating the growth of employees rather than on removing defects.

IV. Principle of Individual Worth
Respect for the individual is a paramount consideration in supervision.
   A. Be human and sympathetic in dealing with employees.
   B. Don't nag about things to be done.
   C. Recognize the individual differences among employees and seek opportunities to permit best expression of each personality.

V. Principle of Creative Leadership
The best supervision is that which is not apparent to the employee.
   A. Stimulate, don't drive employees to creative action.
   B. Emphasize doing good things.
   C. Encourage employees to do what they do best.
   D. Do not be too greatly concerned with details of subject or method.
   E. Do not be concerned exclusively with immediate problems and activities.
   F. Reveal higher activities and make them both desired and maximally possible.
   G. Determine procedures in the light of each situation but see that these are derived from a sound basic philosophy.
   H. Aid, inspire, and lead so as to liberate the creative spirit latent in all good employees.

VI. Principle of Success and Failure
There are no unsuccessful employees, only unsuccessful supervisors who have failed to give proper leadership.
   A. Adapt suggestions to the capacities, attitudes, and prejudices of employees.
   B. Be gradual, be progressive, be persistent.
   C. Help the employee find the general principle; have the employee apply his own problem to the general principle.
   D. Give adequate appreciation for good work and honest effort.
   E. Anticipate employee difficulties and help to prevent them.
   F. Encourage employees to do the desirable things they will do anyway.
   G. Judge your supervision by the results it secures.

VII. Principle of Science
Successful supervision is scientific, objective, and experimental. It is based on facts, not on prejudices.
- A. Be cumulative in results.
- B. Never divorce your suggestions from the goals of training.
- C. Don't be impatient of results.
- D. Keep all matters on a professional, not a personal, level.
- E. Do not be concerned exclusively with immediate problems and activities.
- F. Use objective means of determining achievement and rating where possible.

VIII. Principle of Cooperation
Supervision is a cooperative enterprise between supervisor and employee.
- A. Begin with conditions as they are.
- B. Ask opinions of all involved when formulating policies.
- C. Organization is as good as its weakest link.
- D. Let employees help to determine policies and department programs.
- E. Be approachable and accessible—physically and mentally.
- F. Develop pleasant social relationships.

WHAT IS ADMINISTRATION

Administration is concerned with providing the environment, the material facilities, and the operational procedures that will promote the maximum growth and development of supervisors and employees. (Organization is an aspect and a concomitant of administration.)

There is no sharp line of demarcation between supervision and administration; these functions are intimately interrelated and, often, overlapping. They are complementary activities.

I. Practices Commonly Classed as "Supervisory"
- A. Conducting employees' conferences
- B. Visiting sections, units, offices, divisions, departments
- C. Arranging for demonstrations
- D. Examining plans
- E. Suggesting professional reading
- F. Interpreting bulletins
- G. Recommending in-service training courses
- H. Encouraging experimentation
- I. Appraising employee morale
- J. Providing for intervisitation

II. Practices Commonly Classified as "Administrative"
- A. Management of the office
- B. Arrangement of schedules for extra duties
- C. Assignment of rooms or areas
- D. Distribution of supplies
- E. Keeping records and reports
- F. Care of audio-visual materials
- G. Keeping inventory records
- H. Checking record cards and books

I. Programming special activities
J. Checking on the attendance and punctuality of employees

III. Practices Commonly Classified as Both "Supervisory" and "Administrative"
A. Program construction
B. Testing or evaluating outcomes
C. Personnel accounting
D. Ordering instructional materials

RESPONSIBILITIES OF THE SUPERVISOR

A person employed in a supervisory capacity must constantly be able to improve his own efficiency and ability. He represent the employer to the employees and only continuous self-examination can make him a capable supervisor.

Leadership and training are the supervisor's responsibility. An efficient working unit is one in which the employees work with the supervisor. It is his job to bring out the best in his employees. He must always be relaxed, courteous, and calm in his association with his employees. Their feelings are important, and a harsh attitude does not develop the most efficient employees.

COMPETENCES OF THE SUPERVISOR

I. Complete knowledge of the duties and responsibilities of his position.
II. To be able to organize a job, plan ahead, and carry through.
III. To have self-confidence and initiative.
IV. To be able to handle the unexpected situation and make quick decisions.
V. To be able to properly train subordinates in the positions they are best suited for.
VI. To be able to keep good human relations among his subordinates.
VII. To be able to keep good human relations between his subordinates and himself and to earn their respect and trust.

THE PROFESSIONAL SUPERVISOR-EMPLOYEE RELATIONSHIP

There are two kinds of efficiency: one kind is only apparent and is produced in organizations through the exercise of mere discipline; this is but a simulation of the second, or true, efficiency which springs from spontaneous cooperation. If you are a manager, no matter how great or small your responsibility, it is your job, in the final analysis, to create and develop this involuntary cooperation among the people whom you supervise. For, no matter how powerful a combination of money, machines, and materials a company may have, this is a dead and sterile thing without a team of willing, thinking, and articulate people to guide it.

The following 21 points are presented as indicative of the exemplary basic relationship that should exist between supervisor and employee:

1. Each person wants to be liked and respected by his fellow employee and wants to be treated with consideration and respect by his superior.
2. The most competent employee will make an error. However, in a unit where good relations exist between the supervisor and his employees, tenseness and fear do not exist. Thus, errors are not hidden or covered up, and the efficiency of a unit is not impaired.

3. Subordinates resent rules, regulations, or orders that are unreasonable or unexplained.
4. Subordinates are quick to resent unfairness, harshness, injustices, and favoritism.
5. An employee will accept responsibility if he knows that he will be complimented for a job well done, and not too harshly chastised for failure; that his supervisor will check the cause of the failure, and, if it was the supervisor's fault, he will assume the blame therefore. If it was the employee's fault, his supervisor will explain the correct method or means of handling the responsibility.
6. An employee wants to receive credit for a suggestion he has made, that is used. If a suggestion cannot be used, the employee is entitled to an explanation. The supervisor should not say "no" and close the subject.
7. Fear and worry slow up a worker's ability. Poor working environment can impair his physical and mental health. A good supervisor avoids forceful methods, threats, and arguments to get a job done.
8. A forceful supervisor is able to train his employees individually and as a team, and is able to motivate them in the proper channels.
9. A mature supervisor is able to properly evaluate his subordinates and to keep them happy and satisfied.
10. A sensitive supervisor will never patronize his subordinates.
11. A worthy supervisor will respect his employees' confidences.
12. Definite and clear-cut responsibilities should be assigned to each executive.
13. Responsibility should always be coupled with corresponding authority.
14. No change should be made in the scope or responsibilities of a position without a definite understanding to that effect on the part of all persons concerned.
15. No executive or employee, occupying a single position in the organization, should be subject to definite orders from more than one source.
16. Orders should never be given to subordinates over the head of a responsible executive. Rather than do this, the officer in question should be supplanted.
17. Criticisms of subordinates should, whoever possible, be made privately, and in no case should a subordinate be criticized in the presence of executives or employees of equal or lower rank.
18. No dispute or difference between executives or employees as to authority or responsibilities should be considered too trivial for prompt and careful adjudication.
19. Promotions, wage changes, and disciplinary action should always be approved by the executive immediately superior to the one directly responsible.
20. No executive or employee should ever be required, or expected, to be at the same time an assistant to, and critic of, another.
21. Any executive whose work is subject to regular inspection should, wherever practicable, be given the assistance and facilities necessary to enable him to maintain an independent check of the quality of his work.

MINI-TEXT IN SUPERVISION, ADMINISTRATION, MANAGEMENT, AND ORGANIZATION

I. Brief Highlights

Listed concisely and sequentially are major headings and important data in the field for quick recall and review.

A. Levels of Management
Any organization of some size has several levels of management. In terms of a ladder, the levels are:

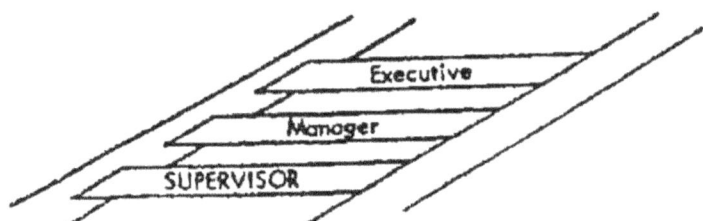

The first level is very important because it is the beginning point of management leadership.

B. What the Supervisor Must Learn
A supervisor must learn to:
1. Deal with people and their differences
2. Get the job done through people
3. Recognize the problems when they exist
4. Overcome obstacles to good performance
5. Evaluate the performance of people
6. Check his own performance in terms of accomplishment

C. A Definition of Supervisor
The term supervisor means any individual having authority, in the interests of the employer, to hire, transfer, suspend, lay-off, recall, promote, discharge, assign, reward, or discipline other employees or responsibility to direct them, or to adjust their grievances, or effectively to recommend such action, if, in connection with the foregoing, exercise of such authority is not of a merely routine or clerical nature but requires the use of independent judgment.

D. Elements of the Team Concept
What is involved in teamwork? The component parts are:
1. Members
2. A leader
3. Goals
4. Plans
5. Cooperation
6. Spirit

E. Principles of Organization
1. A team member must know what his job is.
2. Be sure that the nature and scope of a job are understood.
3. Authority and responsibility should be carefully spelled out.
4. A supervisor should be permitted to make the maximum number of decisions affecting his employees.
5. Employees should report to only one supervisor.
6. A supervisor should direct only as many employees as he can handle effectively.
7. An organization plan should be flexible.

8. Inspection and performance of work should be separate.
9. Organizational problems should receive immediate attention.
10. Assign work in line with ability and experience.

F. The Four Important Parts of Every Job
1. Inherent in every job is the *accountability* for results.
2. A second set of factors in every job is *responsibilities*.
3. Along with duties and responsibilities one must have the *authority* to act within certain limits without obtaining permission to proceed.
4. No job exists in a vacuum. The supervisor is surrounded by key *relationships*.

G. Principles of Delegation
Where work is delegated for the first time, the supervisor should think in terms of these questions:
1. Who is best qualified to do this?
2. Can an employee improve his abilities by doing this?
3. How long should an employee spend on this?
4. Are there any special problems for which he will need guidance?
5. How broad a delegation can I make?

H. Principles of Effective Communications
1. Determine the media.
2. To whom directed?
3. Identification and source authority.
4. Is communication understood?

I. Principles of Work Improvement
1. Most people usually do only the work which is assigned to them.
2. Workers are likely to fit assigned work into the time available to perform it.
3. A good workload usually stimulates output.
4. People usually do their best work when they know that results will be reviewed or inspected.
5. Employees usually feel that someone else is responsible for conditions of work, workplace layout, job methods, type of tools/equipment, and other such factors.
6. Employees are usually defensive about their job security.
7. Employees have natural resistance to change.
8. Employees can support or destroy a supervisor.
9. A supervisor usually earns the respect of his people through his personal example of diligence and efficiency.

J. Areas of Job Improvement
The areas of job improvement are quite numerous, but the most common ones which a supervisor can identify and utilize are:
1. Departmental layout
2. Flow of work
3. Workplace layout
4. Utilization of manpower
5. Work methods
6. Materials handling

7. Utilization
8. Motion economy

K. Seven Key Points in Making Improvements
1. Select the job to be improved
2. Study how it is being done now
3. Question the present method
4. Determine actions to be taken
5. Chart proposed method
6. Get approval and apply
7. Solicit worker participation

I. Corrective Techniques of Job Improvement
Specific Problems
1. Size of workload
2. Inability to meet schedules
3. Strain and fatigue
4. Improper use of men and skills
5. Waste, poor quality, unsafe conditions
6. Bottleneck conditions that hinder output
7. Poor utilization of equipment and machine
8. Efficiency and productivity of labor

General Improvement
1. Departmental layout
2. Flow of work
3. Work plan layout
4. Utilization of manpower
5. Work methods
6. Materials handling
7. Utilization of equipment
8. Motion economy

Corrective Techniques
1. Study with scale model
2. Flow chart study
3. Motion analysis
4. Comparison of units produced to standard allowance
5. Methods analysis
6. Flow chart and equipment study
7. Down time vs. running time
8. Motion analysis

M. A Planning Checklist
1. Objectives
2. Controls
3. Delegations
4. Communications
5. Resources
6. Manpower

7. Equipment
8. Supplies and materials
9. Utilization of time
10. Safety
11. Money
12. Work
13. Timing of improvements

N. Five Characteristics of Good Directions
In order to get results, directions must be:
1. Possible of accomplishment
2. Agreeable with worker interests
3. Related to mission
4. Planned and complete
5. Unmistakably clear

O. Types of Directions
1. Demands or direct orders
2. Requests
3. Suggestion or implication
4. volunteering

P. Controls
A typical listing of the overall areas in which the supervisor should establish controls might be:
1. Manpower
2. Materials
3. Quality of work
4. Quantity of work
5. Time
6. Space
7. Money
8. Methods

Q. Orienting the New Employee
1. Prepare for him
2. Welcome the new employee
3. Orientation for the job
4. Follow-up

R. Checklist for Orienting New Employees   Yes   No
1. Do you appreciate the feelings of new employees when they first report for work? ___ ___
2. Are you aware of the fact that the new employee must make a big adjustment to his job? ___ ___
3. Have you given him good reasons for liking the job and the organization? ___ ___
4. Have you prepared for his first day on the job? ___ ___
5. Did you welcome him cordially and make him feel needed? ___ ___

	Yes	No
6. Did you establish rapport with him so that he feels free to talk and discuss matters with you?	___	___
7. Did you explain his job to him and his relationship to you?	___	___
8. Does he know that his work will be evaluated periodically on a basis that is fair and objective?	___	___
9. Did you introduce him to his fellow workers in such a way that they are likely to accept him?	___	___
10. Does he know what employee benefits he will receive?	___	___
11. Does he understand the importance of being on the job and what to do if he must leave his duty station?	___	___
12. Has he been impressed with the importance of accident prevention and safe practice?	___	___
13. Does he generally know his way around the department?	___	___
14. Is he under the guidance of a sponsor who will teach the right way of doing things?	___	___
15. Do you plan to follow-up so that he will continue to adjust successfully to his job?	___	___

S. Principles of Learning
   1. Motivation
   2. Demonstration or explanation
   3. Practice

T. Causes of Poor Performance
   1. Improper training for job
   2. Wrong tools
   3. Inadequate directions
   4. Lack of supervisory follow-up
   5. Poor communications
   6. Lack of standards of performance
   7. Wrong work habits
   8. Low morale
   9. Other

U. Four Major Steps in On-The-Job Instruction
   1. Prepare the worker
   2. Present the operation
   3. Tryout performance
   4. Follow-up

V. Employees Want Five Things
   1. Security
   2. Opportunity
   3. Recognition
   4. Inclusion
   5. Expression

W. Some Don'ts in Regard to Praise
1. Don't praise a person for something he hasn't done.
2. Don't praise a person unless you can be sincere.
3. Don't be sparing in praise just because your superior withholds it from you.
4. Don't let too much time elapse between good performance and recognition of it

X. How to Gain Your Workers' Confidence
Methods of developing confidence include such things as:
1. Knowing the interests, habits, hobbies of employees
2. Admitting your own inadequacies
3. Sharing and telling of confidence in others
4. Supporting people when they are in trouble
5. Delegating matters that can be well handled
6. Being frank and straightforward about problems and working conditions
7. Encouraging others to bring their problems to you
8. Taking action on problems which impede worker progress

Y. Sources of Employee Problems
On-the-job causes might be such things as:
1. A feeling that favoritism is exercised in assignments
2. Assignment of overtime
3. An undue amount of supervision
4. Changing methods or systems
5. Stealing of ideas or trade secrets
6. Lack of interest in job
7. Threat of reduction in force
8. Ignorance or lack of communications
9. Poor equipment
10. Lack of knowing how supervisor feels toward employee
11. Shift assignments

Off-the-job problems might have to do with:
1. Health
2. Finances
3. Housing
4. Family

Z. The Supervisor's Key to Discipline
There are several key points about discipline which the supervisor should keep in mind:
1. Job discipline is one of the disciplines of life and is directed by the supervisor.
2. It is more important to correct an employee fault than to fix blame for it.
3. Employee performance is affected by problems both on the job and off.
4. Sudden or abrupt changes in behavior can be indications of important employee problems.
5. Problems should be dealt with as soon as possible after they are identified.
6. The attitude of the supervisor may have more to do with solving problems than the techniques of problem solving.
7. Correction of employee behavior should be resorted to only after the supervisor is sure that training or counseling will not be helpful.

8. Be sure to document your disciplinary actions.
9. Make sure that you are disciplining on the basis of facts rather than personal feelings.
10. Take each disciplinary step in order, being careful not to make snap judgments, or decisions based on impatience.

AA. Five Important Processes of Management
1. Planning
2. Organizing
3. Scheduling
4. Controlling
5. Motivating

BB. When the Supervisor Fails to Plan
1. Supervisor creates impression of not knowing his job
2. May lead to excessive overtime
3. Job runs itself—supervisor lacks control
4. Deadlines and appointments missed
5. Parts of the work go undone
6. Work interrupted by emergencies
7. Sets a bad example
8. Uneven workload creates peaks and valleys
9. Too much time on minor details at expense of more important tasks

CC. Fourteen General Principles of Management
1. Division of work
2. Authority and responsibility
3. Discipline
4. Unity of command
5. Unity of direction
6. Subordination of individual interest to general interest
7. Remuneration of personnel
8. Centralization
9. Scalar chain
10. Order
11. Equity
12. Stability of tenure of personnel
13. Initiative
14. Esprit de corps

DD. Change

Bringing about change is perhaps attempted more often, and yet less well understood, than anything else the supervisor does. How do people generally react to change? (People tend to resist change that is imposed upon them by other individuals or circumstances.

Change is characteristic of every situation. It is a part of every real endeavor where the efforts of people are concerned.

1. Why do people resist change?
   People may resist change because of:
   a. Fear of the unknown
   b. Implied criticism
   c. Unpleasant experiences in the past
   d. Fear of loss of status
   e. Threat to the ego
   f. Fear of loss of economic stability

2. How can we best overcome the resistance to change?
   In initiating change, take these steps:
   a. Get ready to sell
   b. Identify sources of help
   c. Anticipate objections
   d. Sell benefits
   e. Listen in depth
   f. Follow up

II. Brief Topical Summaries

   A. Who/What is the Supervisor?
      1. The supervisor is often called the "highest level employee and the lowest level manager."
      2. A supervisor is a member of both management and the work group. He acts as a bridge between the two.
      3. Most problems in supervision are in the area of human relations, or people problems.
      4. Employees expect: Respect, opportunity to learn and to advance, and a sense of belonging, and so forth.
      5. Supervisors are responsible for directing people and organizing work. Planning is of paramount importance.
      6. A position description is a set of duties and responsibilities inherent to a given position.
      7. It is important to keep the position description up-to-date and to provide each employee with his own copy.

   B. The Sociology of Work
      1. People are alike in many ways; however, each individual is unique.
      2. The supervisor is challenged in getting to know employee differences. Acquiring skills in evaluating individuals is an asset.
      3. Maintaining meaningful working relationships in the organization is of great importance.
      4. The supervisor has an obligation to help individuals to develop to their fullest potential.
      5. Job rotation on a planned basis helps to build versatility and to maintain interest and enthusiasm in work groups.
      6. Cross training (job rotation) provides backup skills.

7. The supervisor can help reduce tension by maintaining a sense of humor, providing guidance to employees, and by making reasonable and timely decisions. Employees respond favorably to working under reasonably predictable circumstances.
8. Change is characteristic of all managerial behavior. The supervisor must adjust to changes in procedures, new methods, technological changes, and to a number of new and sometimes challenging situations.
9. To overcome the natural tendency for people to resist change, the supervisor should become more skillful in initiating change.

C. Principles and Practices of Supervision
1. Employees should be required to answer to only one superior.
2. A supervisor can effectively direct only a limited number of employees, depending upon the complexity, variety, and proximity of the jobs involved.
3. The organizational chart presents the organization in graphic form. It reflects lines of authority and responsibility as well as interrelationships of units within the organization.
4. Distribution of work can be improved through an analysis using the "Work Distribution Chart."
5. The "Work Distribution Chart" reflects the division of work within a unit in understandable form.
6. When related tasks are given to an employee, he has a better chance of increasing his skills through training.
7. The individual who is given the responsibility for tasks must also be given the appropriate authority to insure adequate results.
8. The supervisor should delegate repetitive, routine work. Preparation of recurring reports, maintaining leave and attendance records are some examples.
9. Good discipline is essential to good task performance. Discipline is reflected in the actions of employees on the job in the absence of supervision.
10. Disciplinary action may have to be taken when the positive aspects of discipline have failed. Reprimand, warning, and suspension are examples of disciplinary action.
11. If a situation calls for a reprimand, be sure it is deserved and remember it is to be done in private.

D. Dynamic Leadership
1. A style is a personal method or manner of exerting influence.
2. Authoritarian leaders often see themselves as the source of power and authority.
3. The democratic leader often perceives the group as the source of authority and power.
4. Supervisors tend to do better when using the pattern of leadership that is most natural for them.
5. Social scientists suggest that the effective supervisor use the leadership style that best fits the problem or circumstances involved.
6. All four styles—telling, selling, consulting, joining—have their place. Using one does not preclude using the other at another time.

7. The theory X point of view assumes that the average person dislikes work, will avoid it whenever possible, and must be coerced to achieve organizational objectives.
8. The theory Y point of view assumes that the average person considers work to be a natural as play, and, when the individual is committed, he requires little supervision or direction to accomplish desired objectives.
9. The leader's basic assumptions concerning human behavior and human nature affect his actions, decisions, and other managerial practices.
10. Dissatisfaction among employees is often present, but difficult to isolate. The supervisor should seek to weaken dissatisfaction by keeping promises, being sincere and considerate, keeping employees informed, and so forth.
11. Constructive suggestions should be encouraged during the natural progress of the work.

E. Processes for Solving Problems
1. People find their daily tasks more meaningful and satisfying when they can improve them.
2. The causes of problems, or the key factors, are often hidden in the background. Ability to solve problems often involves the ability to isolate them from their backgrounds. There is some substance to the cliché that some persons "can't see the forest for the trees."
3. New procedures are often developed from old ones. Problems should be broken down into manageable parts. New ideas can be adapted from old one.
4. People think differently in problem-solving situations. Using a logical, patterned approach is often useful. One approach found to be useful includes these steps:
    a. Define the problem
    b. Establish objectives
    c. Get the facts
    d. Weigh and decide
    e. Take action
    f. Evaluate action

F. Training for Results
1. Participants respond best when they feel training is important to them.
2. The supervisor has responsibility for the training and development of those who report to him.
3. When training is delegated to others, great care must be exercised to insure the trainer has knowledge, aptitude, and interest for his work as a trainer.
4. Training (learning) of some type goes on continually. The most successful supervisor makes certain the learning contributes in a productive manner to operational goals.
5. New employees are particularly susceptible to training. Older employees facing new job situations require specific training, as well as having need for development and growth opportunities.
6. Training needs require continuous monitoring.
7. The training officer of an agency is a professional with a responsibility to assist supervisors in solving training problems.

8. Many of the self-development steps important to the supervisor's own growth are equally important to the development of peers and subordinates. Knowledge of these is important when the supervisor consults with others on development and growth opportunities.

G. Health, Safety, and Accident Prevention
 1. Management-minded supervisors take appropriate measures to assist employees in maintaining health and in assuring safe practices in the work environment.
 2. Effective safety training and practices help to avoid injury and accidents.
 3. Safety should be a management goal. All infractions of safety which are observed should be corrected without exception.
 4. Employees' safety attitude, training and instruction, provision of safe tools and equipment, supervision, and leadership are considered highly important factors which contribute to safety and which can be influenced directly by supervisors.
 5. When accidents do occur, they should be investigated promptly for very important reasons, including the fact that information which is gained can be used to prevent accidents in the future.

H. Equal Employment Opportunity
 1. The supervisor should endeavor to treat all employees fairly, without regard to religion, race, sex, or national origin.
 2. Groups tend to reflect the attitude of the leader. Prejudice can be detected even in very subtle form. Supervisors must strive to create a feeling of mutual respect and confidence in every employee.
 3. Complete utilization of all human resources is a national goal. Equitable consideration should be accorded women in the work force, minority-group members, the physically and mentally handicapped, and the older employee. The important question is: "Who can do the job?"
 4. Training opportunities, recognition for performance, overtime assignments, promotional opportunities, and all other personnel actions are to be handled on an equitable basis.

I. Improving Communications
 1. Communications is achieving understanding between the sender and the receiver of a message. It also means sharing information—the creation of understanding.
 2. Communication is basic to all human activity. Words are means of conveying meanings; however, real meanings are in people.
 3. There are very practical differences in the effectiveness of one-way, impersonal, and two-way communications. Words spoken face-to-face are better understood. Telephone conversations are effective, but lack the rapport of person-to-person exchanges. The whole person communicates.
 4. Cooperation and communication in an organization go hand in hand. When there is a mutual respect between people, spelling out rules and procedures for communicating is unnecessary.
 5. There are several barriers to effective communications. These include failure to listen with respect and understanding, lack of skill in feedback, and misinterpreting the meanings of words used by the speaker. It is also common

practice to listen to what we want to hear, and tune out things we do not want to hear.
6. Communication is management's chief problem. The supervisor should accept the challenge to communicate more effectively and to improve interagency and intra-agency communications.
7. The supervisor may often plan for and conduct meetings. The planning phase is critical and may determine the success or the failure of a meeting.
8. Speaking before groups usually requires extra effort. Stage fright may never disappear completely, but it can be controlled.

J. Self-Development
1. Every employee is responsible for his own self-development.
2. Toastmaster and toastmistress clubs offer opportunities to improve skills in oral communications.
3. Planning for one's own self-development is of vital importance. Supervisors know their own strengths and limitations better than anyone else.
4. Many opportunities are open to aid the supervisor in his developmental efforts, including job assignments; training opportunities, both governmental and non-governmental—to include universities and professional conferences and seminars.
5. Programmed instruction offers a means of studying at one's own rate.
6. Where difficulties may arise from a supervisor's being away from his work for training, he may participate in televised home study or correspondence courses to meet his self-development needs.

K. Teaching and Training
1. The Teaching Process
Teaching is encouraging and guiding the learning activities of students toward established goals. In most cases this process consists of five steps: preparation, presentation, summarization, evaluation, and application.

   a. Preparation
   Preparation is two-fold in nature; that of the supervisor and the employee. Preparation by the supervisor is absolutely essential to success. He must know what, when, where, how, and whom he will teach. Some of the factors that should be considered are:
   1) The objectives
   2) The materials needed
   3) The methods to be used
   4) Employee participation
   5) Employee interest
   6) Training aids
   7) Evaluation
   8) Summarization

   Employee preparation consists in preparing the employee to receive the material. Probably the most important single factor in the preparation of the employee is arousing and maintaining his interest. He must know the objectives of the training, why he is there, how the material can be used, and its importance to him.

b. Presentation
In presentation, have a carefully designed plan and follow it. The plan should be accurate and complete, yet flexible enough to meet situations as they arise. The method of presentation will be determined by the particular situation and objectives.

c. Summary
A summary should be made at the end of every training unit and program. In addition, there may be internal summaries depending on the nature of the material being taught. The important thing is that the trainee must always be able to understand how each part of the new material relates to the whole.

d. Application
The supervisor must arrange work so the employee will be given a chance to apply new knowledge or skills while the material is still clear in his mind and interest is high. The trainee does not really know whether he has learned the material until he has been given a chance to apply it. If the material is not applied, it loses most of its value.

e. Evaluation
The purpose of all training is to promote learning. To determine whether the training has been a success or failure, the supervisor must evaluate this learning.
In the broadest sense, evaluation includes all the devices, methods, skills, and techniques used by the supervisor to keep himself and the employees informed as to their progress toward the objectives they are pursuing. The extent to which the employee has mastered the knowledge, skills, and abilities, or changed his attitudes, as determined by the program objectives, is the extent to which instruction has succeeded or failed.
Evaluation should not be confined to the end of the lesson, day, or program but should be used continuously. We shall note later the way this relates to the rest of the teaching process.

2. Teaching Methods
A teaching method is a pattern of identifiable student and instructor activity used in presenting training material.
All supervisors are faced with the problem of deciding which method should be used at a given time.

a. Lecture
The lecture is direct oral presentation of material by the supervisor. The present trend is to place less emphasis on the trainer's activity and more on that of the trainee.

b. Discussion
Teaching by discussion or conference involves using questions and other techniques to arouse interest and focus attention upon certain areas, and by doing so creating a learning situation. This can be one of the most

valuable methods because it gives the employees an opportunity to express their ideas and pool their knowledge.

c. Demonstration
The demonstration is used to teach how something works or how to do something. It can be used to show a principle or what the results of a series of actions will be. A well-staged demonstration is particularly effective because it shows proper methods of performance in a realistic manner.

d. Performance
Performance is one of the most fundamental of all learning techniques or teaching methods. The trainee may be able to tell how a specific operation should be performed but he cannot be sure he knows how to perform the operation until he has done so.
As with all methods, there are certain advantages and disadvantages to each method.

e. Which Method to Use
Moreover, there are other methods and techniques of teaching. It is difficult to use any method without other methods entering into it. In any learning situation, a combination of methods is usually more effective than any one method alone.

Finally, evaluation must be integrated into the other aspects of the teaching-learning process.

It must be used in the motivation of the trainees; it must be used to assist in developing understanding during the training; and it must be related to employee application of the results of training.

This is distinctly the role of the supervisor.

TIMBER PILE WHARVES

Section I. INSTALLATION OF PILES

1. Introduction

Wharves are used for loading and unloading ships. This chapter describes how a carpenter constructs a timber pile wharf used in loading and unloading ships. Section I discusses the layout, straightening, and bracing of piles for pile wharf construction. Section II deals with the construction of the wharf superstructure and the installation of docking hardware.

2. Wharf Structures

Wharf is an overall term which applies to any waterfront structure designed to make it possible for vessels to lie alongside for loading and unloading. Figure 1 shows the most common types of structures of this kind. The term wharf is confined in practice to the T-type and U-type marginal wharves. The other structures shown are all called piers, with the exception of the quay. A quay is a constructed landing place made toward the sea or at the side of a harbor for convenience of loading and unloading. All the structures shown in figure 1 may consist of fill supported by bulkheads. A marginal wharf or a pier usually consists of a timber, steel, or superstructure, supported by a series of timber, steel, or concrete pile bents.

3. Construction Features

To be sure that a wharf can absorb the normal wear and tear, three types of piles are used for wharf construction: bearing pile, fender pile, and mooring pile.

a. Bearing piles support the wharf or pier framework and decking. The piles should be straight and measure at least 6 inches across the top, 18 inches across the butt (bottom), and from 60 to 80 feet in length. The length varies according to the depth of the water and condition of the bottom. These bearing piles should be spaced from 6 to 10 feet apart, center to center, in one direction and 5 feet apart, center to center, in the other direction.

b. The force of a moving ship coming in direct contact with bearing piles is enough to collapse a wharf if the pilings are not protected. To furnish this protection and absorb the initial shock, fender piles are placed about 2 1/4 feet out from the centerline of the outside row of bearing piles. These piles are placed about 18 feet apart and along the sides where the ships dock.

c. The third type of piles, mooring, is placed in line with the outside row of bearing piles, spaced approximately 30 feet apart, and braced along the outside row of bearing piles. These piles usually extend about 4 feet above the floor, or deck, of the platform. The 4-foot extension provides ample space to secure mooring lines.

d. Timber piling must be treated with creosote or some other preservative compound to protect it from fungi and marine borer attacks.

4. Special Tools

Since all of the heavy timbers used to build waterfront structures cannot be manhandled, special tools are used to move and place these timbers. They are known as logger's tools and consist of peavys, cant hooks, timber carriers, and pike poles (fig. 2). The peavy and cant hook are lever type tools and are primarily used to roll timbers. Timber carriers are considered two-man tools; they are primarily used to pick up and/or carry timbers. Pike poles are used to hold or steady timbers while they are being placed. Although the crane cannot be considered a special tool, it is included here because it is used to raise and lower heavy timbers. Normally, two men are assigned to the crane: the operator and the helper. The helper drives the crane carrier (truck), hooks and unhooks loads, and signals the operator when to lift and lower the load and where to position the load. Standard signals are used for these purposes. After the heavy timbers have been moved and placed, the carpenter's level is used to level them properly.

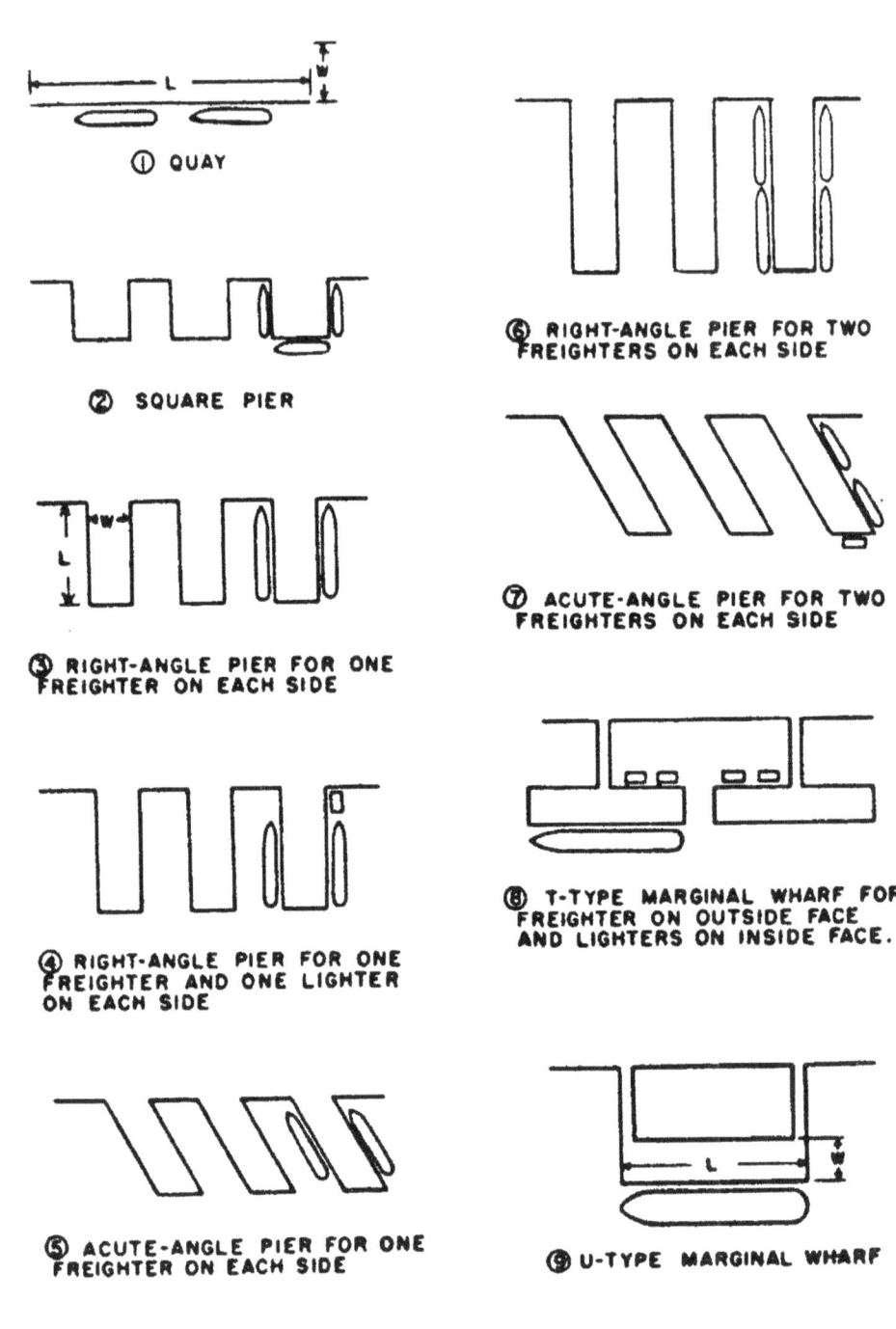

Figure 1. Common types of wharfage structures.

5. Straightening, Cutting, Capping, and Bracing Piles

The equipment is operated by a special crew, but the carpenter is present during the pile-driving to direct the alinement of the piles.

a. Straightening Piles. Piles should be straightened as soon as any misalinement is noticed during the driving. The accuracy of alinement to be sought for the finished job depends on various factors, but if a pile is more than a few inches out of its plumb line, an effort should be made to true it up. The greater the penetration along the wrong line the more difficult to get the pile back into plumb. The following are ways to realine a pile:

(1) By the use of pull from block and tackle

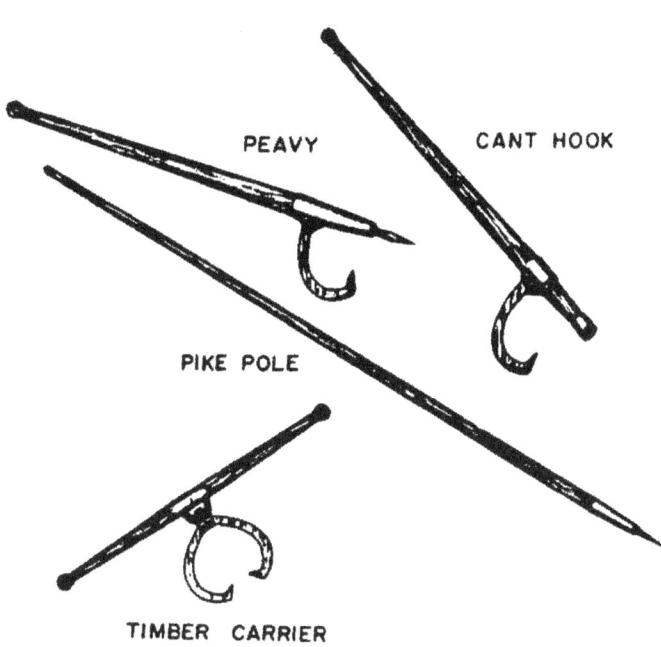

Figure 2. Logger's tools.

(fig. 3) with the impact of the hammer jarring the pile back into line.

(2) By the use of a jet (fig. 4), either alone or in conjunction with the above.

(3) When all the piles in a bent have been driven they may be pulled into proper spacing and alinement by using a block and tackle and an alining frame as shown in figure 5.

b. *Templates.* When a floating piledriver is used, a frame (template) for positioning piles may be fastened to the hull. A floating template (fig. 6) is sometimes used for positioning the piles in each bent. The spacing of battens is such that the center line between them is along the line desired for each pile, and the battens are placed far enough apart so that as the pile is driven the larger-diameter butt end will not bind on the template and carry it under water. A chain or collar permits the template to rise and fall with the tide. If the ends of the battens are hinged and brought up vertically, the template may be withdrawn from between

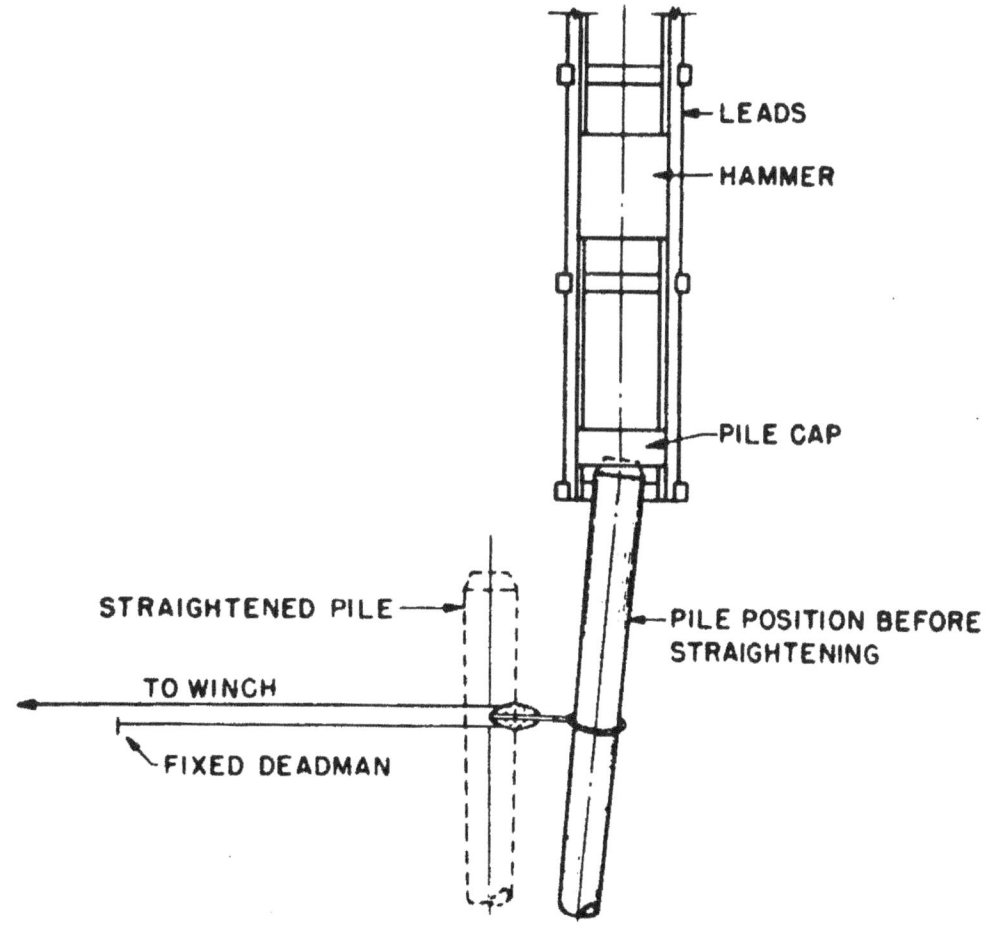

Figure 3. *Realining pile by pull from block and tackle.*

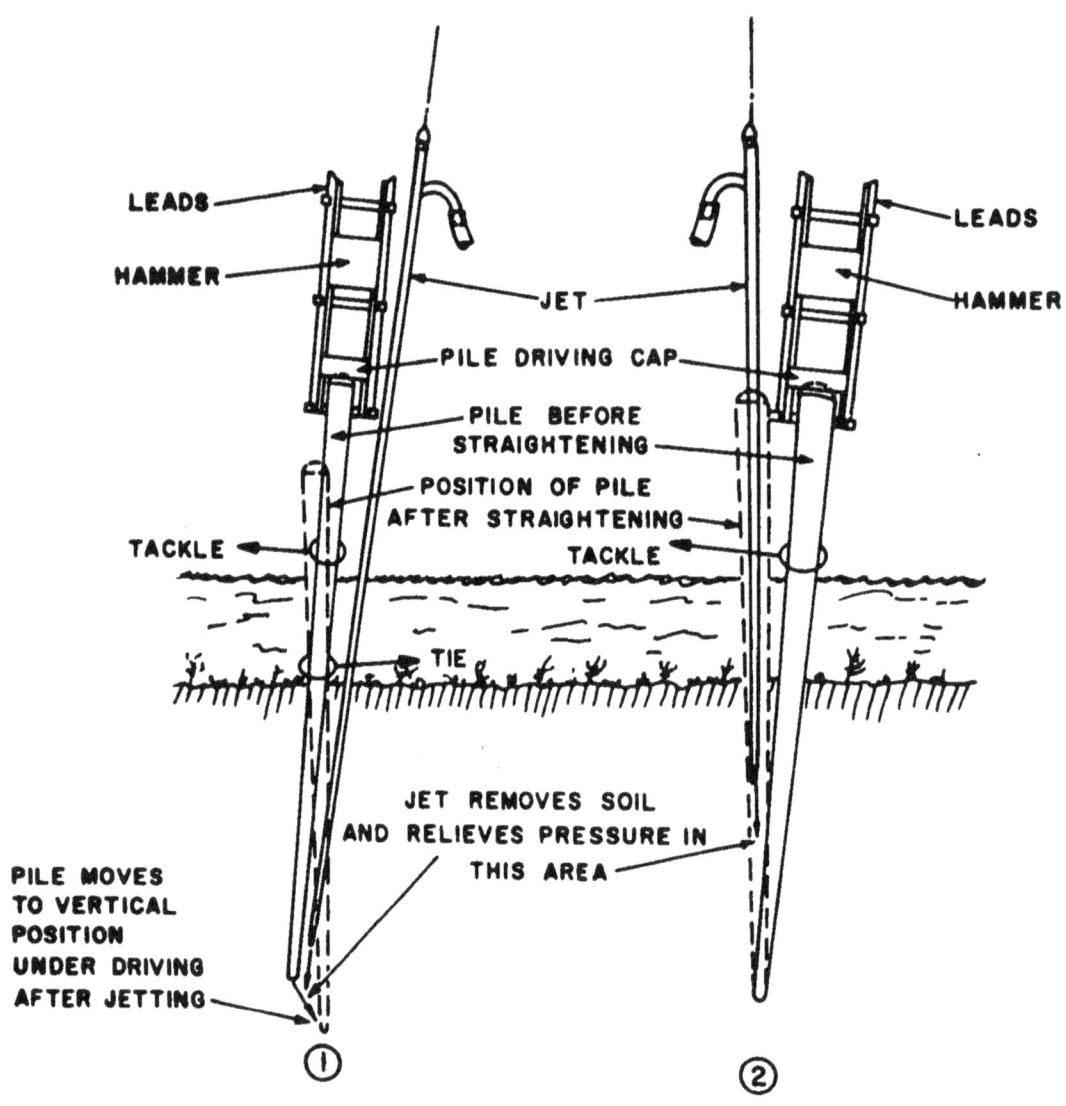

Figure 4. Realining pile by jetting.

the bents and floated into position for the next bent. Several templates may be used for a bent, or a single template is moved for use with the next group if the pile spacing is uniform. The position of the piles is controlled as follows:

(1) After each bent has been driven, a line is run back from each pile in the outer bent to the corresponding pile several bents shoreward.

(2) The alinement and longitudinal spacing of the outshore bent is verified.

(3) Any deviation in position by previously driven piles is made up when the template is positioned for the next bent. Piles which are slightly out of position may later be pulled into place as described in *a* above.

6. Cutting Piles

The lengths of pile selected for a structure should be such that after driving to the desired penetration the butts are 2 or 3 feet higher than the desired finished elevation. Since the pile capping should bear evenly on every pile in the bent, the cutting-off should be carried out accurately. The best way is to nail sawing guides across all piles in the bent (fig. 7).

7. Capping Timber Piles

Caps are large timbers which are placed on top of the timber bearing piles to support the superstructure. The following are ways of fastening pile capping:

a. After the piles have been cut, the cap is put in place, a hole for a driftpin is bored through the cap into the top of each pile, and the driftpins driven into it.

b. At a joint between pile cap timbers, a splice scab (fig. 8) is bolted across the joint to each side of the pile cap.

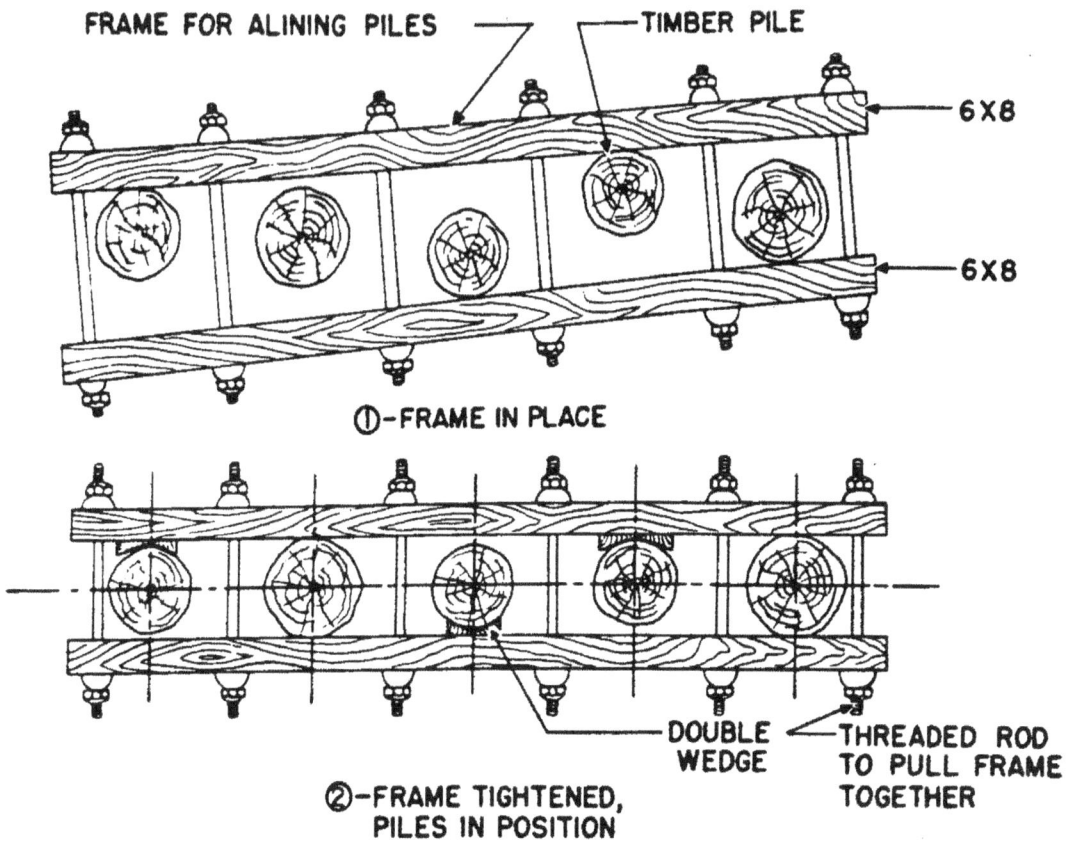

Figure 5. Alining frame for pile bent.

c. The working platform, the alining cables, or the spacing frame may then be removed, since the driftpins will hold the piles in the proper relative positions.

8. Bracing Piles
Bents are braced as follows:

a. Diagonal timbers are bolted to each pile with the bracing running in one direction on one side of the bent and the opposite direction of the other side (fig. 8).

b. If the piles in a bent differ considerable in diameter at the point of bracing, the large ones may be flattened down with an adze (dapped), or the smaller ones blocked out with filler pieces, or the flexibility of the braces made use of to pull them tight against each of the piles (fig. 9).

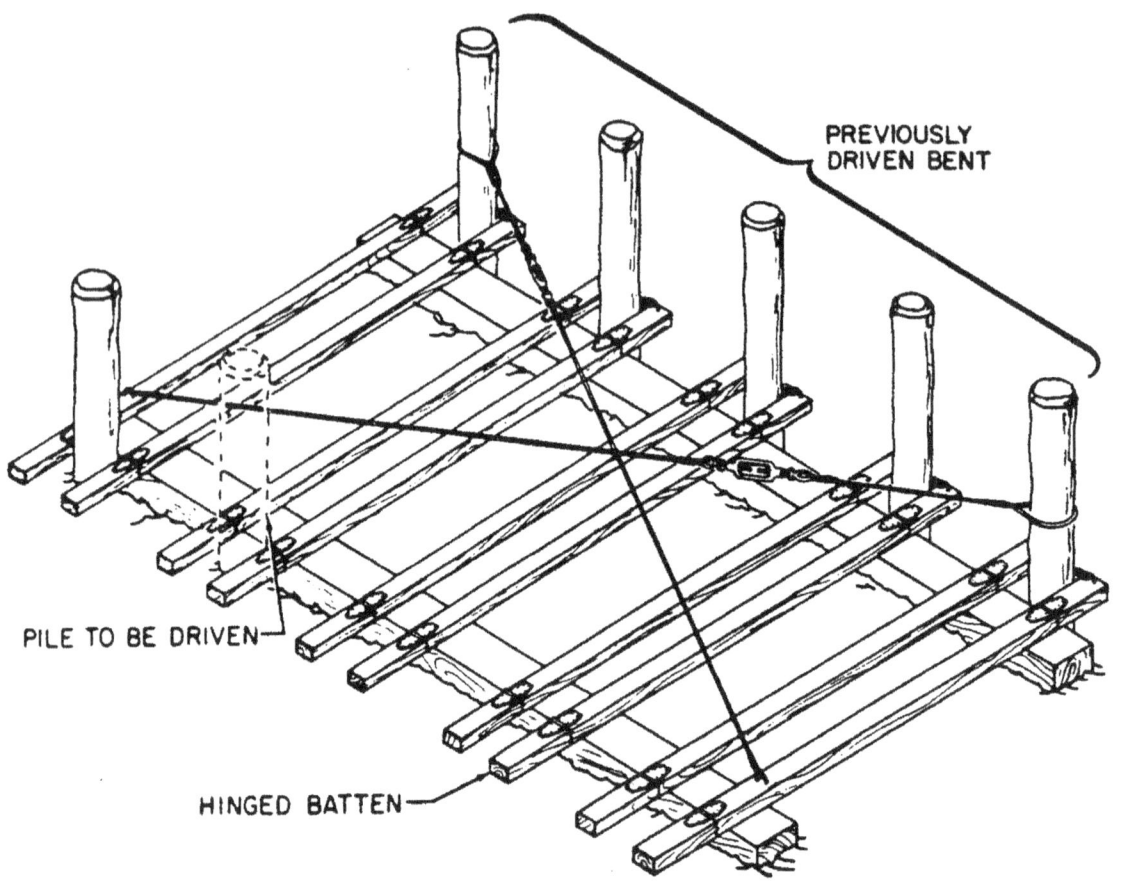

Figure 6. Floating template.

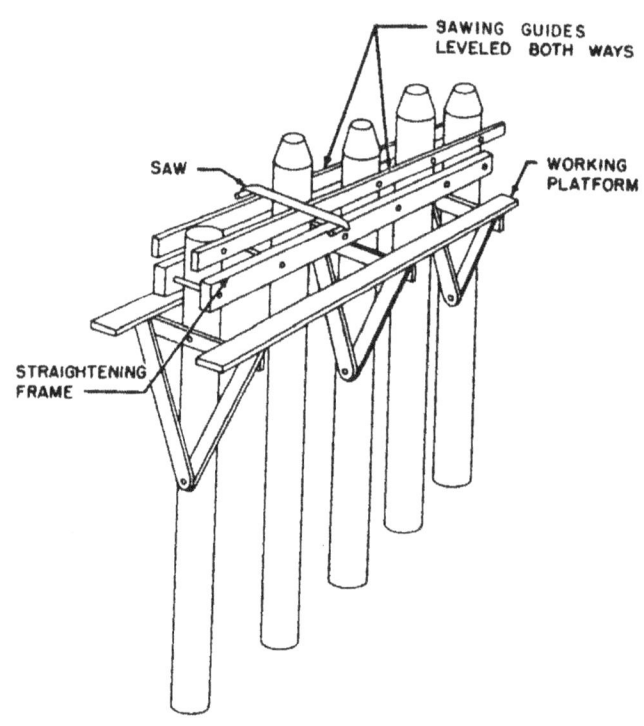

Figure 7. Cutting pile to finish elevation.

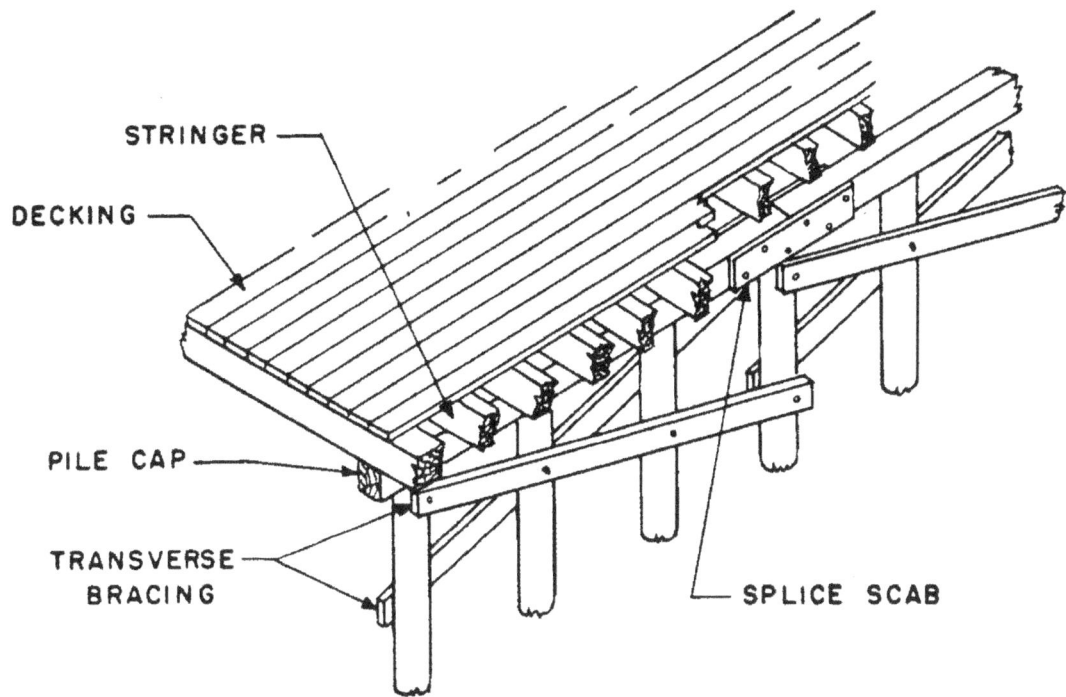

Figure 8. Typical pile bent.

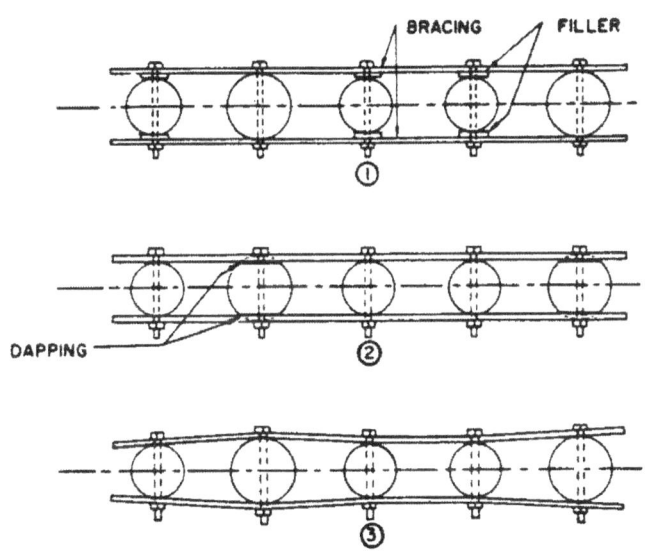

Figure 9. Transverse bracing for piles of differing sizes.

Section II. WHARF SUPERSTRUCTURE

9. General

After the timber pile bents have been alined, braced, and capped, the construction of the wharf superstructure is begun. The building of the superstructure consists of the installation of stringers, the decking, the curb or stringpiece, the erection of the fender systems, and the installation and bracing of dock hardware.

10. Erection of Stringers

The positions of the stringers are measured off from the centerline of the wharf. The stringers are toenailed to the pile caps with two 3/8- by 10-inch spikes at each bearing point. The ends of the stringers have overlap to provide complete bearing on the pile caps. Spacer blocks (fig. 10) between stringers are toenailed with two 60d nails.

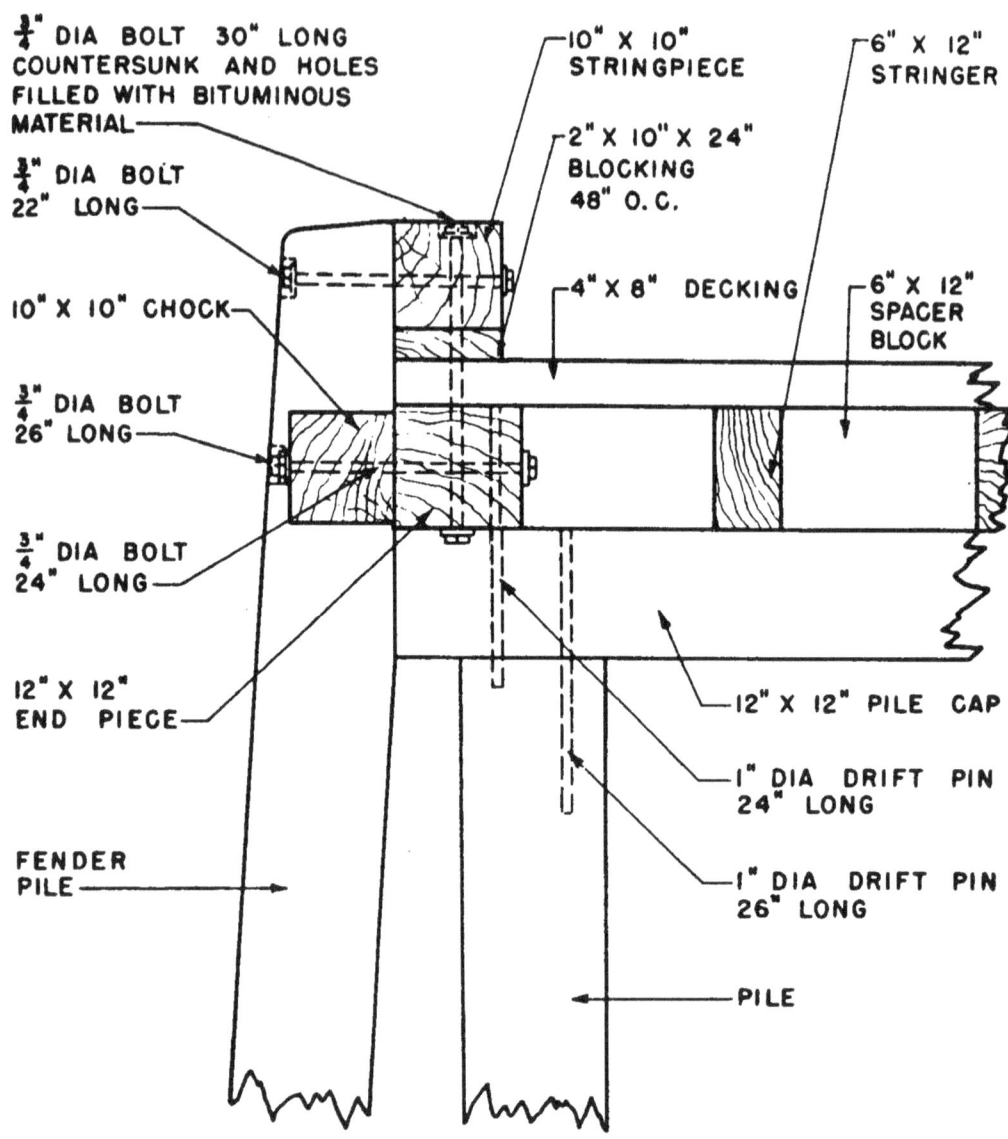

Figure 10. Wharf-edge cross-section, timber-pile wharf.

11. Decking

Standard decking consists of 4- by 8-inch planks (fig. 10) which are spiked to each stringer with two 5/16- by 7-inch spikes, and set with 1/4-inch spacing. Openings between planks greater than 1/4 inch may be used in areas which are subject to heavy rains.

12. Stringpiece

The stringpiece, or curb, is placed on 2- by 10-inch blocking, 24 inches in length spaced on 48-inch centers along the edge of the deck (fig. 10). Stringpiece bolts are countersunk and the hole sealed with bituminous material.

a. When the stringpiece is parallel to the direction of the wharf stringers, the stringpiece is bolted through the blocking, the decking, and the stringer end piece (fig. 10).

b. When the stringpiece is perpendicular to the direction of the stringer, it is bolted through the blocking, the decking, alternate stringers, and pile cap.

13. Fender Piles and Chocks

a. Use of Timber. For theater of operations construction, timber is the most suitable material for use as wharf fenders. Fender piles serve the following purposes:

(1) They cushion a wharf from impact of ships and protect the outer row of bearing piles from damage.

(2) They protect the hulls of craft from undue abrasion.

154

(3) The 3- or 4-foot extension of a fender pile above the deck level of a wharf supplements wharf mooring hardware but is not used for warping a ship into or out of the berth.

b. Ease of Replacement. Since fender piles are not part of the structural support of the wharf, they are easier to replace than bearing piles.

c. Methods of Protecting Fender Piles. To lengthen the life of fender piles, various protective devices are used.

(1) A heavy timber wearing ribbon which may easily be replaced is sometimes installed along a line of fender piles at the elevation which receives the heaviest abrasion.

(2) Floating logs or camels are used.

(3) Rope wrappings, particularly on corner fenders, are used.

d. Fender Piles for Quays. Structures which are almost completely rigid, such as solid-fill quays, sometimes have their fender piles backed up with heavy springs to provide a combination of yielding and resistance.

e. Installation. Fender piles are driven at a slight batter, usually 1 to 12 along the outside edge of all rows of bearing piles, except on the extreme inshore wharf sections. Every third fender pile may extend 3 to 4 feet above the curb. The others are cut off flush with the top of the curb.

f. Chocks and Wales.

(1) Chocks are timber braces placed between fender piles, at the level of the stringpiece or pile cap, to hold them in position and give them lateral stability. The ends of the chocks should be firmly seated against the piles.

(a) *Timber pile wharves.* Each chock is fastened with two bolts through the stringer endpiece or pile cap.

(b) *Steel pile wharves.* Each chock is bolted to 12- by 12-inch blocks driftpinned to the ends of the stringers or bolted to the ends of the wharf pile cap.

(2) Wales (horizontal beams) are used at mean low water elevation when tidal currents are swift or tidal variations are great to add rigidity to the line of fender piles. A 12- by 12-inch continuous longitudinal timber wale is fastened to the back fender of each pile with bolts. Timber chocks are placed between fender piles and bolted to the line wales.

14. Pile Clusters and Corner Fenders

Pile clusters, whether at the faces or corners of wharves or acting as isolated dolphins (para 16), must combine beam strength, rigidity, and stability against horizontal stresses of the component piles. Therefore, the individual piles which make up the cluster must be joined so that the cluster acts as a unit.

a. Mooring Piles.

(1) Mooring piles are clusters of three or more piles used to supplement or replace wharf mooring hardware. The top of the cluster is lashed together as described in paragraph 16b.

(2) They are placed at intervals along the face of a wharf when bollards and other items of mooring hardware are not available. A maximum of three piles of each cluster extend 3 feet or more above the wharf deck (fig. 11).

b. Corner Fenders. Corner fenders are provided so that a ship may use the corner to pivot in warping in and out of the berth. Corner fenders are piles driven in clusters at the exposed corners, bolted and lashed together. The wharf structure at the corners is strongly reinforced with layers of diagonal planking laid one across the other, and this reinforcing is backed up with diagonal batter piles. The standard corner-fender cluster is made up of 10 piles battered for adequate spacing at the points. Timber connectors may be used in conjunction with the bolts to tie the piles more firmly into a single rigid member. To avoid undue abrasion to the hulls of ships, and to the outside pile surfaces, heavy rope mats may be lashed to the clusters at the level of contact. To supplement mooring hardware, the corner piles extend 3 to 4 feet above deck level.

Figure 11. Pile cluster at face of timber pile wharf.

(1) *Deck reinforcing on wood pile wharves.* Before setting stringers, wooden piles battered inward are driven to support a cap set diagonally across each corner and bolted to the bottom face of the other caps. Another piece of cap timber is set to act as a strut between the fender cluster and the diagonal cap. The space between the cluster and the diagonal cap is then floored over with two layers of plank each 6 inches thick, laid diagonally (and transversely to each other) to fill the thickness between the cap timbers. To complete the reinforcing, stringers are set close and spiked together over the outer half of each corner panel.

(2) *Steel pile wharves.* In steel pile marginal wharves and piers with corner fenders the deck in each corner panel is similarly reinforced with timber. Wood piles battered inward carry a diagonal cap timber bolted to the bottom flanges of the steel pile caps. The diagonal cap is strutted against the fender cluster, the diagonal layers of plank are applied, and the stringers are set close and spiked together, as described above for wood pile wharves.

15. Floating Log Fenders (Camels)

a. Floating logs are used to absorb part of the impact shock when a ship is berthed and protect the surface of fender piles while the ship is tied up. The simplest type of fender logs is a single line of floating logs. Each log is secured by two or more lengths of 1/2-inch galvanized chain fastened to 3/4-inch eyebolts in the fender log and the wharf pile. Some arrangement such as loose steel collars around the wharf piles is provided to permit the floating logs to rise and fall with the tide.

b. Floating clusters or logs or strongly constructed rafts are called camels. In addition to absorbing impact shock, and protecting fender piles from the sliding friction of a ship moving in the berth, camels may be required to breast a ship off the face of the wharf into deeper water than exists at the face of the wharf.

16. Construction of Pile Mooring Dolphins

a. Dolphins are isolated clusters of piles to which a ship may be moored. The center of the cluster called a king pile may be a single pile or a cluster driven vertically and wrapped as to act as a unit. The other piles are driven in one or more concentric rings around the king pile, each battered towards the center. The king pile normally is left somewhat longer than the others for use as a mooring post (fig. 12).

b. The king pile when composed of a cluster is wrapped with at least six turns of 1-inch diameter galvanized wire rope stapled to each pile at every turn.

c. Two wrappings of the same type as described above are used for the pile cluster. One wrapping is located near the top of the cluster. The second wrapping is located about 2/3 the distance above mean low water.

d. To further assure that the cluster will act as a unit, the piles are chocked and bolted together approximately 2 feet above mean low water.

17. Mooring Hardware

Ships tie up to wharves with lines fastened to mooring fittings such as bollards, corner mooring posts, and cleats.

a. Bollards. Bollards, single or double-bitt, are steel or cast iron posts (fig. 13) to which large ships tie up. The prevent ships' lines from riding up off the post, they may have waist diameters smaller than top diameters, caps, or projecting, rounded horns. Double-bitt bollards are also known as double steamship bitts or simply as double bitts. Bollard bodies may be hollow for filling with concrete after installation. They are usually designed to take line pulls of about 35 tons.

b. Corner Mooring Posts. Corner mooring posts (fig. 14), which are larger than bollards, are sometimes located at the outshore corners of a pier, wharf, or quay. They are used to bring the ship into the pier or to warp the ship around the corner of the pier or around a turning dolphin as well as for securing lines. Corner mooring posts usually are designed to take line pulls of up to 50 tons.

c. Cleats. Cleats (fig. 15) are generally cast iron, shaped with arms extending horizontally from a relatively low body. The base may be open or closed. They are used for securing smaller ships, tugs, and workboats.

d. Chocks. Open or closed chocks (fig. 16), generally made of cast iron, are used for directing lines and for snubbing lines when working a ship into or out of her berth. The closed chock must be used when there is a change in the vertical as well as the horizontal direction of the line.

e. Pad Eyes. Pad eyes (fig. 17) are metal rings mounted vertically on a plate and intended to receive a ship's line spliced with thimble and shackle. They are used for securing only small craft.

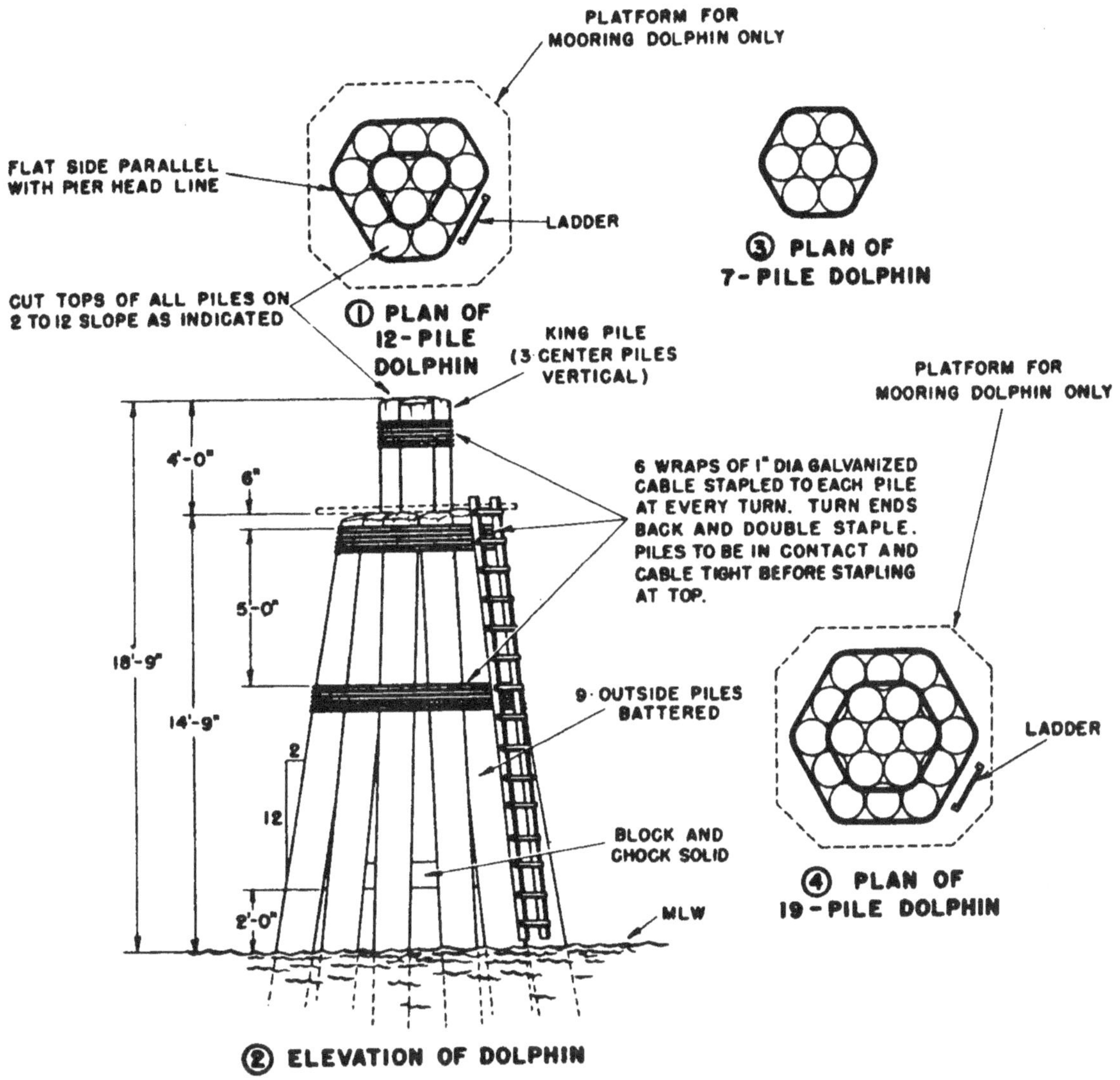

Figure 12. Timber pile dolphins.

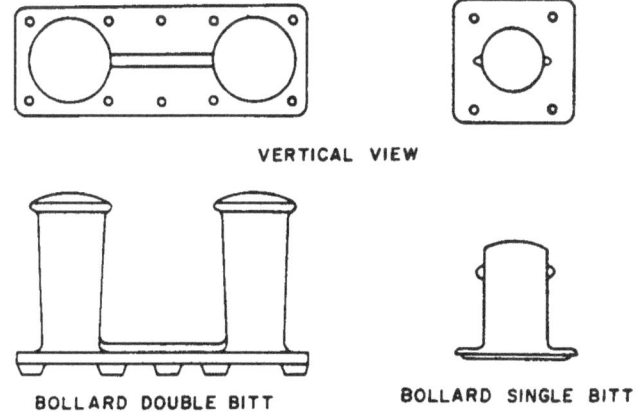

Figure 13. Bollards.

18. Installation of Wharf Hardware

a. Stringer Reinforcement. Proper installation requires that the vertical and horizontal stress on any structural unit on which mooring hardware is attached be transferred to a considerable extent to the wharf structure. This is done by increasing the number and size of stringers under the hardware installation and by providing an anchorage for mooring hardware bolts that will transfer the stress through the pile cap of one or more bents to several piles. The number and size of stringers are increased at the location of major items of hardware. When base widths of hardware are less than 24 inches, but greater than 12 inches, at least two 12- by 12-inch stringers are needed; for base widths less than 36 inches, but greater than 24 inches, three 12-inch stringers; and so forth. Stringers are laid close together and spiked to each other and at each bearing point. Mooring hardware bolts pass through stringers, filler blocks, and anchorage timbers.

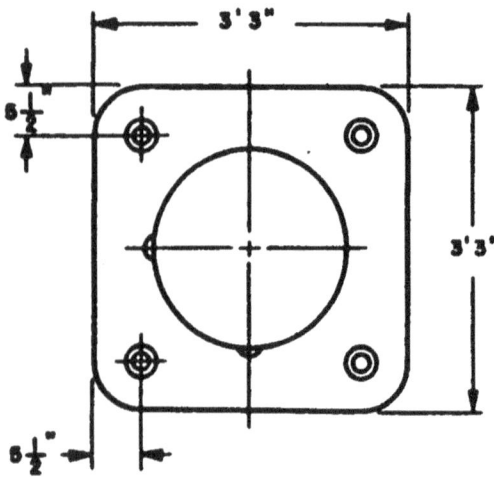

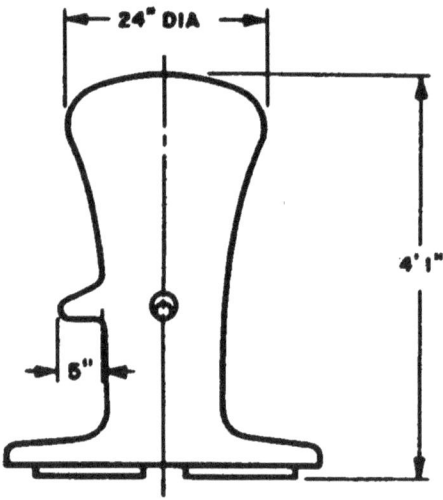

Figure 14. Corner mooring post.

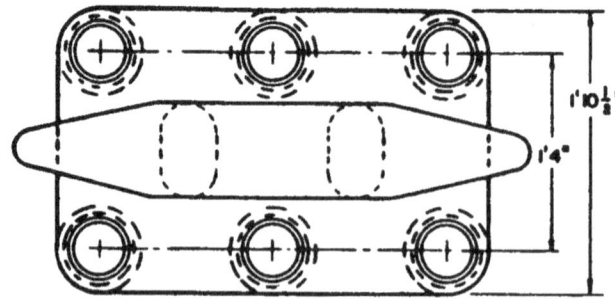

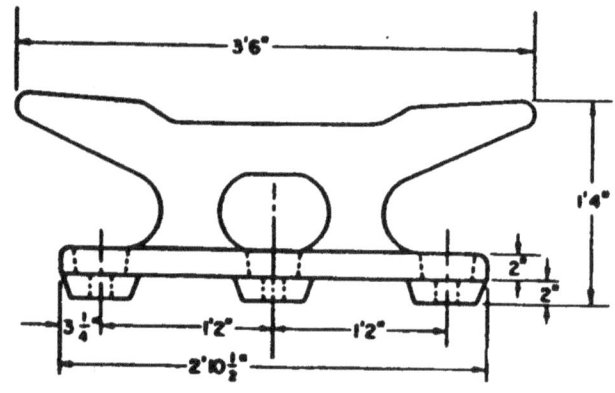

Figure 15. Open wide-base cleat.

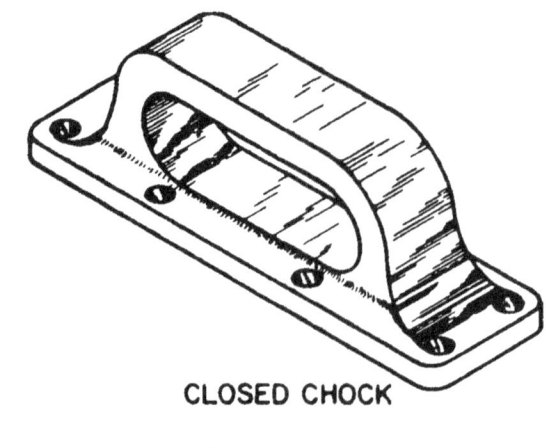

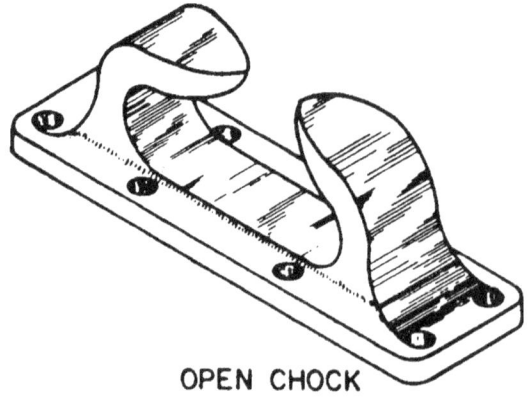

Figure 16. Chocks.

b. *Standard Installations.* The standard wharf structures have mooring hardware as follows:

(1) Pier, 90 x 500 feet—six, large double-bitt bollards on each side on 100-foot centers and five 42-inch cleats on each side centered between bollards.

(2) Offshore marginal wharf, 60 x 500 feet—six large, double-bitt bollards and five 42-inch cleats spaced as above on the outshore side only.

(3) Lighterage quay, 35 x 500 feet—eleven 42-inch cleats on 50-foot centers.

c. *Nonstandard Installations.*

(1) For nonstandard wharf structures, mooring hardware should be installed in numbers, types, and spacing approximating that of standard wharves.

(2) When cleats and pad eyes are not available, every third fender pile must be installed to

ware are placed clear of cranes and traffic, and as close to the curb as possible. Where onshore mooring anchors are used, they should be located so the lines will not have to be moved for traffic.

19. Anchorages for Hardware

a. Location Between Pile Bents. The provide an anchorage for heavy items of mooring hardware located between pile bents, a timber grillwork of 12- by 12-inch timbers is bolted underneath the pile cap (fig. 18). Each of the four piles directly affected by the upward pull on the grillwork is strapped to the pile cap with 3- by 3/8-inch steel strapping. The straps are spiked to piles and pile caps. Filler blocks of 12- by 12-inch timbers are centered to receive the mooring hardward bolts.

b. Location at Pile Bent. Mooring hardware is also located directly over the outside bearing pile of a bent (fig. 19). Mooring hardware with 22- to 26-inch bolt centers is anchored as follows:

(1) Two 12- by 12-inch by approximately 20-foot long timbers are bolted to both sides of three piles of the bent and under the pile cap over which the hardware is located. The batter

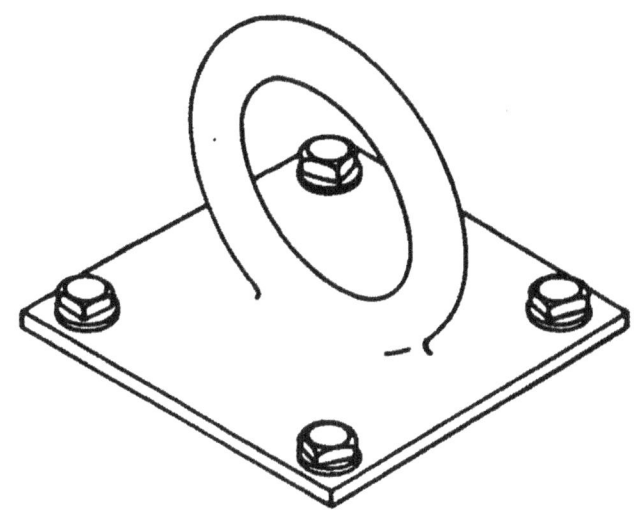

Figure 17. Pad eye.

extend 3 to 4 feet above the wharf deck. Fender pile extensions may be used to steady a ship in the berth, but not to winch a ship into position.

(3) On berths located near enough to the shore, bollards or mooring posts may be located on shore.

d. Location. Bollards and other mooring hard-

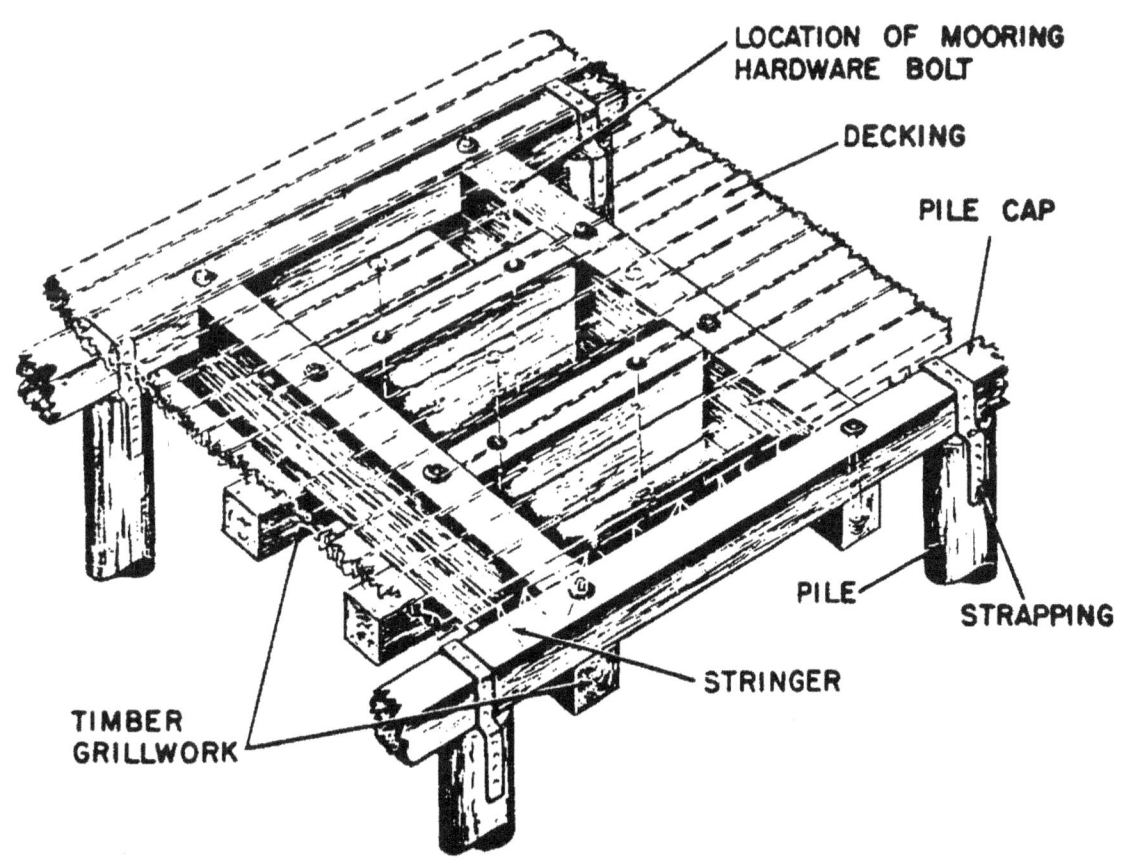

Figure 18. Timber grillwork for hardware anchorage.

pile and batter pile cap shown in figure 19 may be omitted when the wharf design does not need additional lateral stability.

(2) Twelve- by twelve-inch filler timbers approximately 4 feet long are bolted to the wharf pile cap under the hardware bolt location.

(3) Each of the three piles which is directly affected by the upward pull on the grillwork is strapped to the pile cap with steel strapping as described in *a* above.

(4) Items of mooring hardware with bolt centers greater than 26 inches require timber wider than 12 inches, doubling the number of timbers, or locating the hardware between bents using timber grillwork anchorage described in *a* above.

c. Bracing. The wharf structure is longitudinally braced at the location of bollard installations. Diagonal bracing is done from just below the pile caps to approximately low water level at the location of each bollard. The cross bracing is bolted to each pile.

d. Installation of Light Items. Light items of mooring hardware, with bolt centers less than 8 inches, such as cleats, chocks, and pad eyes, are bolted through the stringpiece, blocking, decking, and stringer end piece.

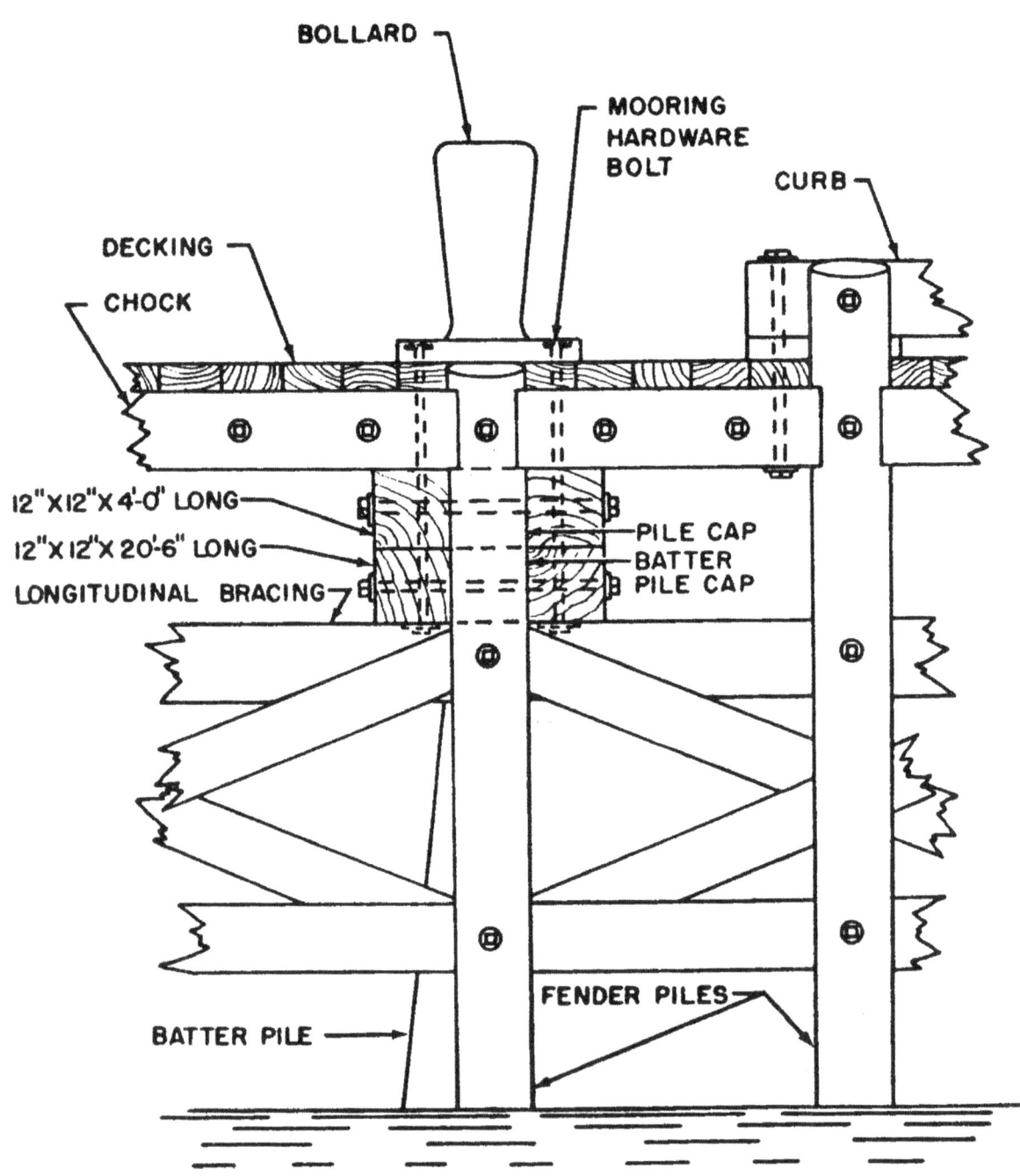

Figure 19. Mooring hardware located over bearing pile.

§ 50.1
# NAVIGATION AND USE OF THE BARGE CANAL SYSTEM

Barge Canal System

PART
- 50 General Provisions
- 51 Navigational Rules
- 52 Special Rules for Pleasure Boats
- 53 Terminal Use
- 54 Fees and Charges for Salvage Work and for Use of Dry Docks
- 55 Dimension Requirements and Mileage Data
- 56 Revocable Permits
- 507 Transportation of Hazardous Materials

PART 50
GENERAL PROVISIONS
(Statutory authority: Canal Law, §§ 10, 86)

Sec.
- 50.1 Definitions
- 50.2 Canal free
- 50.3 The navigation season
- 50.4 Unauthorized operation of locks
- 50.5 Propelling float against gate
- 50.6 Police powers
- 50.7 Canal officials not to be freight agents
- 50.8 Misconduct; taking of gratuities

Sec.
- 50.9 Prohibiting movement of explosives
- 50.10 Seizure of obstruction
- 50.11 Swimming, diving, fishing and hunting at canal structures
- 50.12 Hunting and fishing permits not authorized
- 50.13 Aircraft on canal waters

Historical Note
Part (§ 50.1) added, filed Nov. 9, 1962; repealed, new (§§ 50.1-50.13) filed Mar. 29, 1974 eff. Apr. 1, 1974.

Section 50.1 Definitions. The following terms when used in this Chapter, unless otherwise expressly stated or unless the context or subject matter requires otherwise, shall have the following meanings:

(a) *Commissioner of Transportation* shall mean the duly appointed administrative head of the State Department of Transportation who shall be hereinafter referred to as the commissioner.

(b) *Regional director* shall mean the administrative head of a designated area constituting a region of the State Department of Transportation.

(c) *Canal system* or *barge canal system* shall each mean all the canals and canal terminals of the State as hereinafter defined.

(d) *Canals* or *canal* shall mean the channel and adjacent State-owned banks of the inland waterways of the State constructed, improved, or designated by authority of the Legislature as canals and shall include canalized rivers and lakes, canal water supply reservoirs, canal water supply feeder channels and all appertaining structures including locks, dams, bridges, etc., necessary for the proper maintenance and operation of the canals.

(e) *Canal terminal* or *barge canal terminal* shall each mean the facilities which have been constructed or acquired under authority of the Legislature in connection with the canal system for loading, unloading, and/or temporarily storing commodities transported upon the canals and shall include docks, dock walls, bulkheads, wharves, piers, slips, basins, harbors, buildings, equipment, tracks and roadways together with the lands now owned or as may hereafter be acquired by the State for the proper maintenance and operation of the canal terminals.

(f) *Erie Canal* shall mean the portion of the canal system connecting the Hudson River at Waterford with the Niagara River at Tonawanda.

§ 50.2

(g) *Oswego Canal* shall mean the portion of the canal system connecting the Erie Canal at Three Rivers with Lake Ontario at Oswego.

(h) *Champlain Canal* shall mean the portion of the canal system connecting the easterly end of the Erie Canal at Waterford with Lake Champlain at Whitehall.

(i) *Cayuga and Seneca Canals* shall mean the portions of the canal system connecting the Erie Canal at a point near Montezuma with Cayuga and Seneca Lakes and through Cayuga Lake and Cayuga inlet to the southerly side of State Street in the city of Ithaca and through Seneca Lake with Montour Falls.

(j) *Canal lands* shall mean all lands and waters forming a part of the canal system, title to which was originally vested in the State, acquired by the State or which may in the future be acquired by the State for canal purposes.

(k) *Permit* shall mean a revocable agreement granting temporary occupancy or use of lands, facilities, or structures of the canal system.

(l) *Float* shall mean every boat, vessel, raft or floating thing navigated on the canals or moved thereupon under the direction of some person having the charge thereof.

(m) *Master* shall mean every person having for the time, the charge, control or direction of any float.

(n) *Person* shall mean an individual, partnership, corporation or association.

(o) *Mooring* applies to the making fast of a float to a structure. This may be by direct attachment to the structure or through other floats.

(p) *Dockage* applies to the charges which are established for the mooring of a vessel at a terminal.

(q) *Wharfage* applies to the charges which are established for the privilege of moving commodities from or into floats while moored at a terminal.

(r) *Storage* applies to the temporary occupancy, by commodities, of space on a canal terminal. Storage carries no responsibility by the State for damage or loss of commodities.

(s) *Canal freight* applies to commodities moved or to be moved via the New York State canals.

(t) *Day* means a period of 24 hours or fraction thereof.

(u) *Area occupied* will include driveways, passageways, etc., which are monopolized by the commodity to the exclusion of other shippers.

(v) *Outgoing canal freight* shall mean freight delivered on a canal terminal for transportation on the canal system.

(w) *Incoming canal freight* shall mean freight delivered on a canal terminal after transportation on the canal system.

(x) *Owner* of a vessel, operating on the canals, is the person so declared and filed with the United States Treasury Department (Bureau of Customs), and who is also required to file proper certificate of registry with the commissioner's office.

Historical Note

Sec. added, filed Nov. 9, 1962; repealed, new filed Oct. 10, 1966; amds. filed: June 13, 1967; Jan. 24, 1972; Mar. 23, 1972; repealed new filed Mar. 29, 1974 eff. Apr. 1, 1974.

50.2 Canal free. Navigation on the State canals is free except for mooring, dockage, wharfage, storage, or use of canal equipment or facilities for which a permit is required and charges are established in this Chapter. The acceptance of fees or gratuities of any kind by lock officials or other canal employees is forbidden.

Historical Note

Sec. added, filed Mar. 29, 1974 eff. Apr. 1, 1974.

CHAPTER II BARGE CANAL SYSTEM § 50.8

50.3 The navigation season. The opening of the navigation season depends upon natural conditions. Notice of official opening and closing dates will be announced by the commissioner annually. For general information, such dates in recent years, have been April 5 to April 20, as the time of opening, and from November 15 to November 30 as the usual closing dates for the various types of vessels.

Historical Note
Sec. added, filed Mar. 29, 1974 eff. Apr. 1, 1974.

50.4 Unauthorized operation of locks. Neither the lock gates, valves, paddles, capstans, nor any part of the machinery on or connected with a lock, shall be operated by any person other than the duly appointed lock officials; nor shall any mechanical part of any lock be handled or interfered with by any other person. Any person violating this section shall be subject to a penalty of not to exceed $100 for each offense.

Historical Note
Sec. added, filed Mar. 29, 1974 eff. Apr. 1, 1974.

50.5 Propelling float against gate. Any person who propels a float to or against any lock gate, or, being in control of such float, permits it to be propelled against any lock gate, buffer beam or other structure, for the purpose of opening, closing or otherwise operating the same, shall be deemed guilty of violating the foregoing section and shall be subject to the penalty therefor.

Historical Note
Sec. added, filed Mar. 29, 1974 eff. Apr. 1, 1974.

50.6 Police powers. The commissioner and any officer or responsible employee in the Department of Transportation in charge of canal structures or forces thereof, upon whom any duty in connection with the canal system may devolve, has all the authority of a peace officer with a warrant, to arrest any person engaged in the commission of a crime affecting the canal system or its operation, or any person whom he has reasonable cause to believe has committed such a crime; and shall forthwith take the person so arrested before any magistrate of the county within which the crime is committed, to be dealt with according to law.

Historical Note
Sec. added, filed Mar. 29, 1974 eff. Apr. 1, 1974.

50.7 Canal officials not to be freight agents. No collector of canal statistics, clerk, nor any canal official or employee shall act as agent for shippers, boat owners, or freighting firms engaged in canal commerce, or receive directly or indirectly any compensation from any shipper, boat owner, firm, or any person for procuring freight on freight boats. Such information as may be available as to freight to be shipped or as to freight boats will be furnished by the department to all applicants without charge of any kind.

Historical Note
Sec. added, filed Mar. 29, 1974 eff. Apr. 1, 1974.

50.8 Misconduct; taking of gratuities. Any person employed on the canal locks or any other post on the canal who shall report for duty in an intoxicated condition, or who becomes intoxicated while on duty, or who is absent from his business during working hours without permission, or who shall demand or receive, under any pretense or any form or manner whatsoever, any gratuity, valuable thing or

§ 50.9   TITLE 17 TRANSPORTATION

what is commonly known as "scale money" from boatmen or others, or who unlawfully takes or receives any merchandise or other articles from floats navigated on the canals shall be subject to dismissal.

Historical Note
Sec. added, filed Mar. 29, 1974 eff. Apr. 1, 1974.

50.9 Prohibiting the movement of explosives. The movement of explosives through the New York State canals is prohibited. The term *explosives* as used in this Chapter includes liquid nitro-glycerine, dynamite, nitrocellulose fireworks, black powder, smokeless powder, fulminate, ammunition, bombs, fuses, squibs and other articles of like nature.

Historical Note
Sec. added, filed Mar. 29, 1974 eff. Apr. 1, 1974.

50.10 Seizure of obstruction. The commissioner may cause to be seized and removed any object, article, float or sunken thing found within the limits of the canal system not under the care or charge of any person. He shall sell, or offer for sale all seized objects, articles, floats or sunken things either before or after their removal, as he deems essential for maintenance of the canal system. The sale shall be at public auction after giving 10 days' written notice of such proposed sale conspicuously posted at two public places in the city or town where such object, article, float or sunken thing is found unless before the time of such sale the owner thereof appears and claims same and pays to the commissioner the cost and expense which has been incurred by him in connection with the seizure, removal and proposed sale. The owner thereof shall be liable for the cost and expense of such seizure, removal and sale of the said object, article, float or sunken thing which cost and expense may be recovered by the Attorney-General in an appropriate action or proceeding brought in the name of the people of the State in any court of competent jurisdiction. The avails of such sale shall be accounted for by the commissioner to the Department of Taxation and Finance which may, on the application of the owner and upon due proof of ownership, pay over such proceeds to him after deducting all costs, expenses and reasonable charges of the seizure, removal and sale thereof. Whenever, in the opinion of the commissioner, the navigation or operation of any part of the canal system is interrupted or endangered, the commissioner may cause to be cut up, destroyed or otherwise removed, any object, article, float or sunken thing in or partly in the waters of the canal system which may, in his judgment, be causing such interruption or damage. The commissioner may enter into an agreement with the owner or owners of any property so cut up, destroyed, or otherwise removed, covering the amount of damage sustained. Such agreement when approved by the Attorney-General shall become an obligation of the State and paid from moneys available therefor. In case no agreement is consummated, the amount of damages sustained may be determined as provided in section 120 of the Canal Law.

Historical Note
Sec. added, filed Mar. 29, 1974 eff. Apr. 1, 1974.

50.11 Swimming, diving, fishing and hunting at canal structures. Swimming, diving or fishing in the lock chambers or from the lock walls or any other canal structure is prohibited. Hunting on, at or near canal locks or any other canal structure is prohibited. Any person violating this section shall be subject to a penalty of not to exceed $25 for each offense.

Historical Note
Sec. added, filed Mar. 29, 1974 eff. Apr. 1, 1974.

CHAPTER II BARGE CANAL SYSTEM § 51.2

50.12 Hunting and fishing permits not authorized. No gate tender or other canal employee has any authority or shall be allowed to grant any person, hunting permits or permits to fish in any of the canals of the State or in the State reservoirs. (See § 50.11 of this Part.)

Historical Note
Sec. added, filed Mar. 29, 1974 eff. Apr. 1, 1974.

50.13 Aircraft on canal waters. The taking off from or landing upon the surface of waters of the canal system by aricraft is prohibited, except under conditions specified in a revocable permit or when a landing and subsequent take-off is necessary under actual distress conditions. Any person violating this section shall be subject to a penalty of not to exceed $100 for each offense. (See § 56.3 of this Title.)

Historical Note
Sec. added, filed Mar. 29, 1974 eff. Apr. 1, 1974.

PART 51

NAVIGATIONAL RULES

(Statutory authority: Canal Law, §§ 10, 86)

Sec.		Sec.	
51.1	Equipment	51.16	Assistance to floats
51.2	Floats in bad condition	51.17	Speed on canals
51.3	Tank vessels; certificate of inspection	51.18	Speed when passing
		51.19	When passing dredge, etc.
51.4	Canal officers may examine floats	51.20	Preference of floats in passing
51.5	Dimensions and design of floats	51.21	Locks
51.6	Draft markings on floats	51.22	Signaling lift bridges
51.7	Number of units in tow	51.23	Warning signal approaching bends
51.8	Formation of tows	51.24	When traffic congested
51.9	Propulsion of barge by pushing	51.25	Sailing rules
51.10	Mooring	51.26	Aids to navigation
51.11	Lights on moored floats	51.27	Bill of lading
51.12	Obstruction of navigation	51.28	Clearance
51.13	Pollution of canal waters or deposit of rubbish on canal lands	51.29	Registration
		51.30	Non-navigation season storage of floats
51.14	When canal levels are drawn		
51.15	Buoys and lights displaced		

Historical Note
Part added, filed July 5, 1963; repealed, new filed: Jan. 10, 1969; May 6, 1970; July 1, 1971; July 6, 1973; Jan. 11, 1974; Mar. 29, 1974 eff. Apr. 1, 1974.

Section 51.1 Equipment. Every float navigated on the canal shall be properly manned. Each float shall be equipped with proper bow and stern lines, hand rope fenders to prevent the corners of the float from breaking concrete of the lock and approach walls, and suitable lights for night operation. Fenders and/or bumpers made from automobile or truck tires are not permitted.

Historical Note
Sec. added, filed July 5, 1963; repealed, new filed: Jan. 10, 1969; May 6, 1970; July 1, 1971; July 6, 1973; Mar. 29, 1974 eff. Apr. 1, 1974.

51.2 Floats in bad condition. Any float which is in such condition as, in the opinion of the commissioner or his representative, may jeopardize the canal structures, or is likely to become a source of damage or of delay to navigation, shall be prohibited from proceeding into any canal. If such a float is already in the canal, it shall be prohibited from proceeding farther therein. Should there be any refusal or failure on the part of any person in charge of the float to obey such prohibition, such person and also the owner shall be subject to a penalty of not to exceed $100.

Historical Note

Sec. added, filed July 5, 1963; amd. filed Jan. 24, 1967; repealed, new filed; Jan. 10, 1969; May 6, 1970; July 1, 1971; amd. filed July 3, 1972; repealed, new filed July 6, 1973; Mar. 29, 1974 eff. Apr. 1, 1974.

51.3 Tank vessels; certificate of inspection. All tank vessels intended to enter the canals must comply with the general rules and regulations for tank vessels, as prescribed and amended by the commandant of the United States Coast Guard, governing merchant tank vessels that have on board any inflammable or combustible liquid cargo in bulk. Tank vessels are defined in said regulations as "any vessel especially constructed or converted to carry liquid bulk cargo in tanks". Tank vessels which have not been granted a certificate of inspection are prohibited from entering the canals.

Historical Note

Sec. added, filed July 5, 1963; amd. filed Jan 24, 1967; repealed, new filed: Jan. 10, 1969; May 6, 1970; amd. filed Jan. 7, 1971; repealed, new filed, July 1, 1971; amd. filed July 3, 1972; repealed, new filed: July 6, 1973; Mar. 29, 1974 eff. Apr. 1, 1974.

51.4 Canal officers may examine floats. The commissioner or his representative shall, at all times, have full power to stop any float at any point on the canal, and to board and remain on such float, as long as he may deem necessary for the purpose of examining the same; and every facility shall be afforded him for obtaining such information as he may desire. Any person obstructing such officer in the execution of his duty, shall, at the discretion of the commissioner, subject the owner of the float to a penalty of not to exceed $100 for each offense.

Historical Note

Sec. added, filed July 5, 1963; repealed, new filed: Jan. 10, 1969; May 6, 1970; July 1, 1971; amd. filed July 3, 1972; repealed, new filed: July 6, 1973; Mar. 29, 1974 eff. Apr. 1, 1974.

51.5 Dimensions and design of floats. (a) The maximum dimensions of a float (barge and tug coupled together, or motor-vessel, or bow-thruster barge) which may enter the locks of the canal system are 300 feet long and 43½ feet wide.

(b) The maximum height above water of floats navigated on the canal system shall not exceed the vertical overhead clearance of canal structures.

(c) All floats passing through the locks must be so designed as not to damage the locks and shall be free from projections or sharp corners that may scar the walls or otherwise injure the lock structure.

(d) Any float not conforming to the provisions of this section may be refused passage through the locks.

(e) The owner of any float navigating the canal in violation of the provisions of this section shall be subject to a penalty of not to exceed $100.

Historical Note

Sec. added, filed July 5, 1963; repealed, new filed: Jan. 10, 1969; May 6, 1970; July 1, 1971; amd. filed July 3, 1972; repealed, new filed: July 6, 1973; Mar. 29, 1974 eff. Apr. 1, 1974.

51.6 Draft markings on floats. All floats of every nature operating on the canal, normally drawing over six feet, shall be plainly marked both fore and aft on each side, showing the actual draft of the float at all times. The marking shall be of such color paint as to be visible at all times 100 feet away. The figures shall be not less than four inches in height and the draft markings shall be at the bottom of each such figure. All draft markings shall show feet and half feet of draft.

Historical Note

Sec. added, filed May 6, 1970; repealed, new filed July 1, 1971; amd. filed July 3, 1972; repealed, new filed: July 6, 1973; Mar. 29, 1974 eff. Apr. 1, 1974.

CHAPTER II BARGE CANAL SYSTEM § 51.9

51.7 Number of units in tow. Without special permission of the commissioner, no fleet shall consist of more units than may be passed through a lock in two lockings.

Historical Note
Sec. added, filed May 6, 1970; repealed, new filed July 1, 1971; amd. filed July 3, 1972; repealed, new filed: July 6, 1973; Mar. 29, 1974 eff. Apr. 1, 1974.

51.8 Formation of tows. Fleet formation of two loaded barges abreast is permitted in the canalized river and lake sections. Such formation shall not be used in other sections without the written permission of the commissioner. Where difficulty is experienced in holding light fleets within the buoyed channels, the commissioner or his representative may order such formation and devices for control as in his judgment will best protect the buoys. Failure to comply with such orders will subject the master of the towing tug to a penalty of not to exceed $100.

Historical Note
Sec. added, filed May 6, 1970; repealed, new filed: July 1, 1971; July 6, 1973; Mar. 29, 1974 eff. Apr. 1, 1974.

51.9 Propulsion of barge by pushing. (a) No barge may be pushed in canal waters, unless:

(1) The construction and make-up of the fleet is such that the steersman has an unobstructed view of the full outline of the deck at the bow of the forward barge and of the water surface 400 feet in advance of its bow, or,

(2) When under way, there is at all times on the deck of the first pushed barge a deckhand to signal directions to the steersman.

(3) When entering or leaving a lock, deckhands shall be stationed at the forward end of the first pushed barge to signal directions to the steersman and to handle fenders as required.

(4) When under way, between the hours of sunset and sunrise, there shall be displayed a white light on the center bow, a red light on the port bow and a green light on the starboard bow of the barge. The colored lights shall be located within 20 feet of the port and starboard bow points of square-bowed barges, and at the most forward point of the straight-line side adjacent to the quarter deck on rounded bow barges. They shall be placed at such an elevation above the deck of the barge as to be visible to an approaching vessel under all loading conditions of the barge. The white light shall be carried on the bow of the barge on a line midway between the port and starboard lights, and not to exceed two feet abaft the extreme forward end of the barge. These lights shall be visible on a dark night with a clear atmosphere at a distance of at least two miles. They shall be provided with globes not less than six inches in diameter and not less than five inches high in the clear. They shall be so screened as to be visible as follows: The white light through 20 points of the compass, from dead ahead to two points abaft the beam on both port and starboard sides; the red light through 10 points of the compass, from dead ahead to two points abaft the beam on the port side; and the green light through 10 points of the compass, from dead ahead to two points abaft the beam on the starboard side.

(b) Neglect to observe the above subdivision, or violation of its provisions, shall subject the master of the propelling unit to a penalty of not to exceed $100 for each offense.

(c) The following illustrates the placing of lights on *pushed barges* as required by this section of the rules and regulations governing navigation on New York State canals:

§ 51.10   TITLE 17 TRANSPORTATION

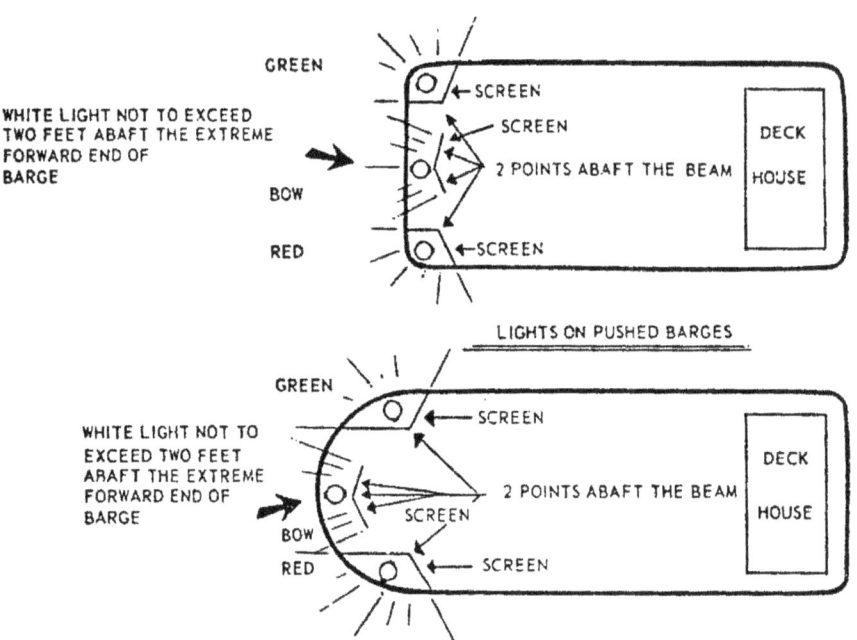

LIGHTS ON PUSHED BARGES

(d) All floats navigating the canals shall comply with the provisions of the *Pilot Rules for Inland Waters,** as published and amended by the U. S. Coast Guard, relative to lights to be carried on floats, except as otherwise provided herein.

Historical Note

Sec. added, filed May 6, 1970; amd. filed Jan. 7, 1971; repealed, new filed: July 1, 1971; July 6, 1973; Mar. 29, 1974 eff. Apr. 1, 1974.

51.10 Mooring. (a) Each float moored in the canal shall be made fast to secure moorings, at bow and stern, with good and sufficient lines so as to prevent such float from breaking away under the ordinary strain caused by passing floats, current, etc.

(b) No float shall be moored or anchored in the canal channel at any point where its presence will interfere with navigation, and no float shall be moored or anchored at any point in the canal for a period in excess of 24 hours without the written consent of the commissioner or his representative.

(c) No float shall be moored at any State-maintained dock or terminal in excess of 48 hours in any calendar month, without first obtaining an official permit. (See § 56.1 of this Title.)

(d) No mooring is permitted in the "Waterford Flight" between the foot of lock E-2 and guard gate no. 2.

(e) Should a float moored at the Waterford Canal terminal remain at such terminal for a period in excess of 24 hours there may be assessed against the registered owner of such float a dockage charge of not to exceed five dollars for each day such float remains at the terminal beyond the first 24 hours.

(f) No float shall tie by or be moored at the head or foot of any lock except with the consent of the lock official in charge of such lock, and all directions given by him shall be complied with by the captain or master of such float.

(g) The use of ladders in the lock chambers for mooring purposes is forbidden and no float shall be tied or fastened to the same. Every float while in a lock shall be moored to the proper snubbing posts by bow and stern lines.

---

* [Not filed with the Department of State.]

CHAPTER II BARGE CANAL SYSTEM   § 51.14

(h) No float shall moor to or attach a line to any buoy, light or channel marker in the canals.

(i) In cities or villages no float shall be moored in the canal for a longer period than is reasonably necessary for the discharge or taking aboard of its cargo without the written permission of the commissioner or his local representative.

(j) Violation of this section shall subject the owner or person in charge of the offending float to a penalty of not to exceed $100.

Historical Note

Sec. added, filed May 6, 1970; repealed, new filed July 1, 1971; amd. filed July 3, 1972; repealed, new filed: July 6, 1973; Mar. 29, 1974 eff. Apr. 1, 1974.

51.11 Lights on moored floats. (a) Barges, scows or canal boats moored within or along the edge of the canal channel at night shall display:

(1) If moored on the starboard side of the canal (starboard side proceeding from Waterford), a red light shall be placed on the outside of the bow of the forward float and on the outside of the stern of the rear float.

(2) If moored on the port side of the canal (port side proceeding from Waterford), a white light shall be placed on the outside of the bow of the forward float and the outside of the stern of the rear float.

(3) These lights shall be so placed as to be plainly visible to approaching floats.

(b) Failure to comply with this section, or violation of its provisions, shall subject the owner or person in charge of the offending float to a penalty of not to exceed $100.

Historical Note

Sec. added, filed May 6, 1970; repealed, new filed July 1, 1971; amd. filed July 3, 1972; repealed, new filed: July 6, 1973; Mar. 29, 1974 eff. Apr. 1, 1974.

51.12 Obstruction of navigation. The master of any float who obstructs navigation of the canal by improper mooring, management or conduct of a float or any person who obstructs navigation of a canal by placing any object in the waters of the canal or by placing any obstruction upon the bank thereof shall, at the discretion of the commissioner, be subject to a penalty of not to exceed $100 for each such obstruction. (See also, Canal Law, § 83, as amended.)

Historical Note

Sec. added, filed July 1, 1971; amd. filed July 3, 1972; repealed, new filed: July 6, 1973; Mar. 29, 1974 eff. Apr. 1, 1974.

51.13 Pollution of canal waters or deposit of rubbish on canal lands. (a) No rubbish, debris, carcass, dead animal, putrid substance, filth or sewage of any kind, shall be thrown, dumped, deposited, placed or discharged into any canals of this State, or into any basin, reservoir or feeder connected therewith. Nor shall there be pumped or otherwise discharged from the bilge of any float, boat or carrier, bilge water containing any oil, molasses, chemical or refuse in the canal. Any person violating this subdivision shall be subject to damages to the amount as will compensate the State for the expenses involved in restoring such waters to its useful condition to meet the needs of canal navigation.

(b) No rubbish, debris, carcass, dead animal, putrid substance, filth or sewage of any kind shall be thrown, dumped, deposited, placed or discharged on any canal lands. Any person violating this subdivision shall be subject to a penalty of not to exceed $100 for each offense.

Historical Note

Sec. added, filed Mar. 29, 1974 eff. Apr. 1, 1974.

51.14 When canal levels are drawn. In case of any damage to the canals necessitating the drawing of water from any canal level, all floats which may be upon such level shall be moved to such points as the commissioner or his representative shall direct. The master of a float who fails or refuses to comply with such direction from the commissioner or his representative shall be subject to a penalty of not to exceed $100.

Historical Note
Sec. added, filed Mar. 29, 1974 eff. Apr. 1, 1974.

51.15 Buoys and lights displaced. When a buoy or light is struck by a float or whenever a buoy or light is noticed to be out of position its light out or otherwise in bad order, or whenever some other hazardous physical condition is observed or encountered, the master of the float having knowledge of such condition shall report the matter to the lock official at the next lock through which the float passes with a written statement as to the location of the displaced buoy, extinguished light or other improper condition and the time when the accident occurred, or the condition reported was noticed. Forms for such report may be obtained from the lock official.

Historical Note
Sec. added, filed Mar. 29, 1974 eff. Apr. 1, 1974.

51.16 Assistance to floats. (a) In case any float grounds, sinks or otherwise obstructs navigation on the canal, the commissioner may cause the same to be salvaged, destroyed or removed, subject to the provisions of section 83 of the Canal Law.

(b) The following policy has been adopted by the department in connection with the use of State equipment and personnel in assisting canal floats meeting with mishap on the canal:

(1) Where a float is in the channel and in danger of obstructing navigation, or there is danger of loss of life or serious property damage, the assistance will be as prompt and thorough as possible. The department's first duty is to keep navigation open.

(2) Where a float is sunk entirely outside of the channel and there is no immediate prospect of such float coming into the channel, State equipment will ordinarily not be used in salvage work. However, in special circumstances, the regional director may make an exception to this rule. Where the use of State equipment is requested to assist in the removal of wrecks which do not interfere with navigation, the request may be granted when, in the discretion of the regional director, the equipment may be spared. In instances of this character, a fee established by this Chapter will be charged. Before starting work of this character, a guarantee in the form of a certified check for the estimated cost of the work is to be delivered by the owner, master or their representative, to the appropriate regional director.

Historical Note
Sec. added, filed Mar. 29, 1974 eff. Apr. 1, 1974.

51.17 Speed on canals. In the canal channels the speed limit of floats shall not exceed six miles per hour, except in canalized rivers and lakes. In canalized rivers and lakes the limit of speed shall depend upon the conditions of traffic. So far as may be practicable, the rates of speed will be indicated for the various sections at each lock and in no event shall such rates of speed be exceeded. Any person violating this section shall be subject to a penalty of not to exceed $100 for each offense and the float involved in the violation may be refused passage through any lock or lift bridge on the canal system for a period of not less than three hours and not more than 24 hours by the lock or bridge official at which the float first appears following such violation.

Historical Note
Sec. added, filed Mar. 29, 1974 eff. Apr. 1, 1974.

CHAPTER II BARGE CANAL SYSTEM § 51.21

51.18 Speed when passing. Every float, when passing any float underway or while passing a moored float, shall slow down to a speed and exercise proper control which will prevent damage to said floats. Any person violating this section shall be subject to a penalty of not to exceed $100 for each offense.

Historical Note
Sec. added, filed Mar. 29, 1974 eff. Apr. 1, 1974.

51.19 When passing dredge, etc. When two floats, going in opposite directions, shall approach each other in the vicinity of a float which is stationary or moving at a slow rate of speed, in such manner that they would, if both should continue their headway, meet by the side of such third float, the float which shall be going in the same direction as the intermediate float is going, or is headed, shall stop until the float going in the opposite direction has passed. In canalized rivers where the above contingency may occur, however, should conditions of current exist, the float which is proceeding with the current shall have the right of way past the stationary or slow-moving float and the float which is proceeding against the current shall wait until the float proceeding with the current has passed. The float proceeding with the current shall indicate to the approaching float its intention to proceed. Any person violating this section shall be subject to a penalty of not to exceed $100 for each offense.

Historical Note
Sec. added, filed Mar. 29, 1974 eff. Apr. 1, 1974.

51.20 Preference of floats in passing. (a) Floats in passing shall be governed by the whistle signals as prescribed in the *Pilot Rules for Inland Waters** of the U. S. Coast Guard, as published and amended.

(b) In any channel every float shall, when it is safe and practicable, keep to that side of the fairway or mid-channel which lies on the starboard side of such float.

(c) When floats are approaching a lock on the same level the overtaking float shall not attempt to pass the overtaken float within a distance of 1,000 feet of a lock toward which the floats are progressing.

(d) Any person violating this section shall be subject to a penalty of not to exceed $100 for each offense.

Historical Note
Sec. added, filed Mar. 29, 1974 eff. Apr. 1, 1974.

51.21 Locks. (a) *Passage.* (1) When a float is approaching a lock, the signal to the lock operator of the desire of the float to pass through the lock shall consist of three distinct blasts or soundings of the whistle, horn or other signaling device. Answering signals from the lock will be given by means of colored signal lights. Green will indicate that the lock is ready and the float may advance. Red will indicate that the float must wait for the lock to be made ready.

(2) A float approaching a lock which is not ready to receive it shall come to a full stop at a safe distance from the lock and wait the signal of the lock official to approach. If the lock is ready to receive the float, the float shall slow down at a proper distance from the lock to avoid hitting or otherwise damaging the lock gates.

(3) If no light is shown, the float shall stop and stay in place or tie up immediately to the approach wall. If a signal of six flashes of either red or green is given, the float shall come to an immediate stop and await further instructions.

(4) A float which shall arrive at any lock and which shall not employ the

*[Not filed with the Department of State.]

§ 51.22   TITLE 17 TRANSPORTATION

first opportunity of passing through same, shall lose its preference if there is any other float ready to pass through the lock.

(5) No owner or master shall unnecessarily or unreasonably delay, hinder or detain his entry into, passage through, or exit from a lock or the passage through a lock of any other float awaiting locking. Such floats may be ordered removed from the lock and the owner thereof shall pay all expenses involved in towing or removing the float from the lock.

(6) Crew members shall use fenders as required to prevent damage to the lock structure. Floats leaving the lock shall navigate at a reduced speed until the stern of such float has reached a point of at least 150 feet beyond the lock chamber.

(7) Every float shall comply strictly with directions or orders of the lock official as to management of the float while awaiting locking, during locking or on entering or leaving a lock.

(8) Operators of double-locking tows, eastbound, are required to have the power unit remain on the upper level at Lockport until the first locking is complete. When westbound, the power unit shall enter the lock with the first locking of its double-locking tow, so as to provide power on the upper level for the floats comprising the first locking. Double-locking tows are not allowed in either direction through the Waterford flight of locks without special permission of the commissioner or his representative.

(b) *Floats under control.* Floats shall, at all times, enter each lock squarely and under proper control at a speed that is consistent with navigation safety under the weather and water conditions prevailing in the vicinity of the lock to prevent any damage to the lock structure or its equipment. All specified and required navigation and safety measures shall be executed by the float personnel to bring the float safely into the lock and to insure a full stop in the lock chamber without touching, hitting or damaging lock gates or any other vulnerable part of the lock structure or its equipment. Lines shall be put out from the float to retard its final drift speed, bring it to a stop and hold it safely in the lock during locking operation.

(c) *Penalties.* Any person violating this section shall be subject to a penalty of not to exceed $100 for each offense and the float involved in the violation may be refused passage through the lock for a period of not less than three hours and not more than 24 hours.

Historical Note
Sec. added, filed Mar. 29, 1974 eff. Apr. 1, 1974.

51.22 Signaling lift bridges. When a float is approaching any lift bridge, the signal to the lift bridge operator of the desire of the float to pass under the bridge, consisting of three short distinct blasts or soundings of the whistle or horn or other signaling device, must be given at least 1,000 feet from the bridge in order that the operator may have ample time to clear his bridge of traffic and raise same for the passage of the float. Answering signals from lift bridges will be given by means of colored lights, horn, whistle or bell, dependent upon the type of installation provided at the particular bridge. Six rapid signal indications from the lift bridge will mean that the float shall come to an immediate stop and await further instructions.

Historical Note
Sec. added, filed Mar. 29, 1974 eff. Apr. 1, 1974.

51.23 Warning signal approaching bends. Every power unit when nearing a short bend in the channel where, from the height of the banks or other cause, a float approaching from the opposite direction cannot be seen, shall sound a long distinct signal at least one-half mile from such point. This signal shall be answered

CHAPTER II BARGE CANAL SYSTEM § 51.27

by a similar signal by any float that may be approaching in the oposite direction. Any person violating this section shall be subject to a penalty of not to exceed $100 for each offense.

Historical Note
Sec. filed Mar. 29, 1974 eff. Apr. 1, 1974.

51.24 When traffic congested. In case of a delay to navigation causing a congestion of floats at any point, the floats shall take such places as shall be assigned to them by the commissioner or his representative and they shall be passed through the lock or allowed to proceed along the canal in such order as in the judgment of the commissioner, or his authorized representative, shall be deemed best for the interests of general navigation. In all such cases, detained floats must comply strictly with the directions of the commissioner or his representative. Failure or refusal to comply with such directions will subject the owner or master to a penalty of not to exceed $100.

Historical Note
Sec. filed Mar. 29, 1974 eff. Apr. 1, 1974.

51.25 Sailing rules. All floats navigating the canals shall comply with the provisions of the *Pilot Rules for Inland Waters*,* as published and amended by the U. S. Coast Guard, relative to the rules for floats passing each other, as to lights on floats and other matters consistent with the proper use of the canal, except as otherwise provided in this Chapter. Any person violating this section shall be subject to a penalty of not to exceed $100 for each offense.

Historical Note
Sec. filed Mar. 29, 1974 eff. Apr. 1, 1974.

51.26 Aids to navigation. (a) Red buoys and red lights are located on the starboard side of the canal channel when entering canals at the Waterford entrance, while white buoys and white lights are located on the port side of the canal channel from the same entrance.

(b) The safe navigation of the canals requires a familiarity with the channels. Navigation charts outlining the canal channels, with the exception of the western stretch from Lyons to the Niagara River, may be purchased from the Distribution Division (C-44), National Ocean Survey, Riverdale, Maryland 20840 by these numbers:

Chart No.	Area
14786	Champlain Canal, Erie Canal east of Lyons, Oswego Canal, and the Cayuga and Seneca Canal.
14788	Lock 22 to Lock 23, including Oneida Lake.
14791	Cayuga and Seneca Lakes.

(c) Charts of the Hudson River below Troy, Lake Champlain, the Great Lakes, and the U.S. coastal waters may be purchased from the same source.

Historical Note
Sec. filed Mar. 29, 1974; amd. filed Oct. 26, 1976 eff. immediately.

51.27 Bill of lading. (a) Every master of a float conveying property on the canal shall exhibit to the first collector of canal statistics, or, if there be no collector, the State employee designated to perform such duties, a bill of lading or manifest of the property carried, signed by himself and by the consignor thereof, containing:

---
* [Not filed with the Department of State.]

§ 51.28   TITLE 17 TRANSPORTATION

(1) The name of each port from which any portion of such property was taken on board and of the port or ports to which it is destined. (See map and profile cross section in Appendix A-1, *infra*.)

(2) A statement of the names, description and weight in net tons of each class of articles comprising the cargo. Movement of explosives on the canal is prohibited. (See § 50.9 of this Title.)

(b) No clearance of a float and cargo shall be granted or issued by any collector of canal statistics or employee acting in that capacity except upon the exhibit to him of a bill of lading or manifest containing the above particulars.

(c) If, during the passage for which a float is cleared, other articles are taken on board, the master shall procure a bill of lading or manifest for such additional articles. If a float enters the canal without a cargo, or following the discharge of a cargo within the canal should take on board property for conveyance to another port, the master shall procure and exhibit to the first lock official or collector of canal statistics by whose office the float passes, a bill of lading or manifest as provided in subdivision (a) of this section.

(d) Every master must familiarize himself with the contents of the cargo, so that he can, if required, verify his bill of lading or manifest by his oath.

(e) Any master who refuses to comply with any provision of this section shall be subject to a penalty of not to exceed $100 for each offense.

Historical Note
Sec. filed Mar. 29, 1974 eff. Apr. 1, 1974.

51.28 Clearance. (a) Every commercial float shall have a clearance. Clearances may be obtained at the first lock on the canal system through which the float may pass after taking cargo aboard. Clearance shall be refused for floats not properly registered in accordance with this Chapter. No float may proceed beyond the place for which it has clearance or unload any article before its arrival there. Property transferred from one float to another shall in all cases be recleared.

(b) The clearance of every float shall be exhibited to any lock official requesting to examine it. Unless the clearance has on it the signature of the official designated to issue clearances, the lock official shall not permit the float to pass.

(c) A float whose clearance is lost may be detained until it is recleared or until the master has procured a duplicate clearance from the lock office where clearance is claimed to have been issued.

(d) Clearance may be refused for a float against whose registered owner there is an unpaid penalty involving such float assessed under this Chapter, or against whose registered owner there is an unpaid bill rendered by the commissioner for assistance to such float, or for repairing damage to State property caused by such float.

(e) Clearance for any float, or further passage of any float already in the canal, may be denied when, in the opinion of the commissioner or his representative, its condition or equipment does not comply with this Chapter or the crew of which has navigated the float in a careless, reckless or inefficient manner.

Historical Note
Sec. filed Mar. 29, 1974 eff. Apr. 1, 1974.

51.29 Registration. (a) The owner shall obtain a New York State certificate of registry for each commercial float before it may be navigated on the canals. Certificate of registry may be obtained from the commissioner upon the filing of a properly executed application for registration.

CHAPTER II BARGE CANAL SYSTEM   § 52.1

(b) If the owner of the commercial float is a company or corporation, the title of the official signing the application shall appear thereon.

(c) Upon approval by the commissioner of the application for registration, a State registry number will be assigned for the float and a certificate of registry will be issued.

(d) A new certificate of registry must be obtained for a float, previously registered, whose ownership, name, or hailing place has since been changed. In case of change in ownership a new certificate of registry will not be issued until a certificate of change in ownership signed by both parties to such transaction, or a certified copy of the bill of sale, has been filed in the office of the commissioner. In case of change in name or hailing place, a new certificate of registry will not be issued until the consent of the commissioner, in writing, to such change has been obtained.

(e) The name and State registry number of each float, with the hailing place as it is registered, shall be painted in letters at least four inches in height on some conspicuous and prominent part of the outside of the float. The markings shall be of such color paint as to be visible at all times 100 feet away.

(f) The penalty for a violation of this section shall be not less than $50 nor more than $100.

Historical Note
Sec. added, filed Mar. 29, 1974 eff. Apr. 1, 1974.

51.30 Non-navigation season storage of floats. (a) No float of any kind shall be placed or stored in any lock chamber during the closed or winter season without written consent of the commissioner or his representative.

(b) The owner, master or captain of any float desiring to keep or store the same in any basin, harbor, or part of the canal channel during the closed or winter season shall submit to the commissioner or his representative, a description of the proposed place of storage and obtain his written approval thereof before the close of the navigation season. (See § 53.10 of this Title for mooring at terminals during closed season.)

Historical Note
Sec. added, filed Mar. 29, 1974 eff. Apr. 1, 1974.

PART 52

SPECIAL RULES FOR PLEASURE BOATS

(Statutory authority: Canal Law, §§ 10, 86)

Sec.
52.1 Special regulations for pleasure boats
52.2 Houseboats

Sec.
52.3 Locking of canoes or rowboats

Historical Note
Part (§§ 52.1-52.3) added, filed Mar. 29, 1974 eff. Apr. 1, 1974.

Section 52.1 Special regulations for pleasure boats. In addition to the regulations governing general traffic on the canals, the following special regulations apply to pleasure boats:

(a) Pleasure boats will not be permitted to enter or navigate any of the canals when, in the judgment of the commissioner or his representative, they may become a source of danger or of delay to navigation.

(b) Pleasure boats shall be operated in such a manner on the canal as not to interfere with the use of such waters by commercial floats.

(c) During any period of low water, the locks will be operated for pleasure boats at such hours and at such intervals as will, in the judgment of the commissioner or his representative, conserve the water supply for the locking of freight carriers.

(d) During the summer months or periods of heavy pleasure boat traffic on the canals the locks may be operated for pleasure boats on a definite time schedule as established by the commissioner.

(e) Pleasure boats are required to come to a stop at each lift or swing bridge, and said bridge will then be operated with due regard to street traffic and public convenience.

(f) Pleasure boats will not be permitted to cruise back and forth on the canal in cities where doing so will compel the operation of lift or swing bridges, resulting in interference with street traffic.

(g) Sections 51.17 through 51.20 of this Title, in regard to speed and passing regulations, shall be complied with at all times by all pleasure boats, whether powered either by inboard or outboard motors.

(h) Any person violating any of these rules and regulations shall be subject to a penalty of not to exceed $100 for each offense and the float involved in the violation may be refused passage through any lock or lift bridge on the canal system for a period of not less than three hours and not more than 24 hours by the lock or bridge official at which the float first appears following such violation.

Historical Note
Sec. added, filed Mar. 29, 1974 eff. Apr. 1, 1974.

52.2 Houseboats. Floats commonly known as houseboats shall observe strictly the provisions of section 51.10 of this Title relative to the mooring of floats.

Historical Note
Sec. added, filed Mar. 29, 1974 eff. Apr. 1, 1974.

52.3 Locking of canoes or rowboats. The lock official may require the removal of all persons and perishable property from canoes or rowboats during locking, if in his judgment, the locking would be dangerous to them.

Historical Note
Sec. added, filed Mar. 29, 1974 eff. Apr. 1, 1974.

CHAPTER II BARGE CANAL SYSTEM § 53.3

PART 53

TERMINAL USE

(Statutory authority: Canal Law, §§ 10, 86)

Sec.	Sec.
53.1 Points for float receipt and discharge of cargoes	53.6 Charges for non-canal business if authorized
53.2 Payment of charges	53.7 Special storage provisions at all terminals
53.3 Dockage and wharfage for canal floats	53.8 Stevedoring
54.4 Storage charges for canal frieght at all barge canal terminals	53.9 Abandoned property
	53.10 Mooring facilities during closed season
53.5 Storage rates for canal freight	53.11 Refusal to obey directions

Historical Note

Part (§§ 53.1-53.11) added, filed Mar. 29, 1974 eff. Apr. 1, 1974.

Section 53.1 Points for float receipt and discharge of cargoes. Terminals are provided for the receipt and discharge of canal freight at the principal points of shipment. The loading, unloading or storage of commodities at points on the canal system other than these terminals shall not be allowed without the written permission of the commissioner.

Historical Note

Sec. added, filed Mar. 29, 1974 eff. Apr. 1, 1974.

53.2 Payment of charges. All charges, fees and penalties in connection with the use of a canal terminal or terminal facilities shall be paid promptly to the commissioner or his duly authorized representative. In case of delay in payment of any charge, fee or penalty, the commissioner may withhold clearance for a float or floats registered under the name of the defaulting person.

Historical Note

Sec. added, filed Mar. 29, 1974 eff. Apr. 1, 1974.

53.3 Dockage and wharfage for canal floats. (a) There are no docking or wharfage charges for canal floats while receiving or discharging canal freight.

(b) *Charges for use of cranes or derricks.* The following is a schedule of charges for the use of cranes or derricks, including operator, fuel and oil:

(1) For canal freight only, the charge for a crane or derrick of the rated capacity of over 3,000 pounds shall be five dollars per hour, with a minimum charge of $10.

(2) For canal freight only, the charge for a crane or derrick of the rated capacity of 3,000 pounds or less shall be four dollars per hour, with a minimum charge of eight dollars.

(3) Should the handling of non-canal freight be authorized, the charge for any crane or derrick will be seven dollars per hour, with a minimum charge of $14. Additional charges will be made when special services are furnished.

(4) For any crane requiring transportation to the point of operation there will be a charge made for such transportation. Cranes ordinarily operate on an eight-hour per day basis. Special arrangements will be necessary for service beyond the eight-hour period.

Historical Note

Sec. added, filed Mar. 29, 1974 eff. Apr. 1, 1974.

53.4 Storage charges for canal freight at all barge canal terminals. (a) Outgoing canal freight delivered on any canal terminal *during the non-navigation season* will be allowed a free storage period from February 15 to 15 days after the official opening of the canal. Regular storage rates will be charged for each 10-day period, or fraction thereof, elapsing before and after such free period, during which such freight remains on the terminal.

(b) Outgoing canal freight delivered on any canal terminal *during the navigation season* will be allowed a free storage period of 20 days. Regular storage rates will be charged for each 10-day period, or fraction thereof, elapsing after such free period.

(c) (1) Incoming canal freight delivered on any canal terminal *during the navigation season* will be allowed no definite free time storage. If such freight is entirely removed from the canal terminal within 20 days from delivery, no storage charge will be made.

(2) If any part of such freight remains on the canal terminal after 20 days, a storage charge at the regular rate for one 10-day period will be made against the entire cargo. This charge will cover the first 20 days of occupancy of the canal terminal. Thereafter the regular storage rates will apply for each 10-day period, or fraction thereof, on such amount of freight as remains on the terminal at the commencement of each 10-day period. All of the terminals shall be cleared of such storage by February 1, unless special permission is granted covering an extension of such storage period.

(d) Any freight delivered to and placed on a canal terminal ostensibly for shipment via canal system which may, after such delivery, be diverted for shipment by other means than by canal, will be subject to double regular storage charges for each 10-day period, or fraction thereof, elapsed from date of delivery on the terminal to time of its removal therefrom.

Historical Note
Sec. added, filed Mar. 29, 1974 eff. Apr. 1, 1974.

53.5 Storage rates for canal freight. (a) *Outdoor storage at all terminals.* Outdoor storage charges shall be at the rate of one-quarter cent per hundredweight for each 10-day period, or fraction thereof, that freight remains on the canal terminal, in accordance with section 53.4 of this Part.

(b) *Storage, materials, supplies or equipment.* Any materials, supplies or equipment maintained or stored on a canal terminal will be subject to a storage charge for each 10-day period of occupancy at the rate specified under subdivision (a) of this section.

(c) *Alternate method of determining storage charges.* When, in the opinion of the commissioner, it is not feasible to determine the weight of any commodity subject to storage charges under this Part, the charge shall be based on the area occupied with one square foot of such area to be considered as representing 200 pounds. The basis of storage charges shall be determined by the commissioner's representative, which shall be by weight, as far as practicable. Such representative shall also determine the manner of storing all such commodities.

Historical Note
Sec. added, filed Mar. 29, 1974 eff. Apr. 1, 1974.

CHAPTER II BARGE CANAL SYSTEM § 53.9

53.6 Charges for non-canal business if authorized. Non-canal business at the canal terminals, authorized under a revocable permit issued by the commissioner or his representative, shall be at the following rates:

(a) *Dockage.* For canal boats, barges, lighters and tugs, the charge for dockage will be one cent per lineal foot per day, or fraction thereof, with a minimum charge of one dollar. For non-canal commercial floats, the charge will be based on the registered net tonnage at a rate of one cent per net registered ton per day, or fraction thereof. For other floats two days' free mooring time will be allowed, after which dockage charges will be made at the rate of 25 cents per foot of overall length per month, or fraction thereof, payments to be made monthly, in advance; the maximum sum to be paid per year not to exceed the fee for four months' occupancy. The rates for dockage for the season when the canal is closed for navigation will be quoted by the commissioner upon application.

(b) *Wharfage.* Wharfage shall be based on a ton of 2,000 pounds at a rate of 20 cents per ton for dock wharfage, or as rates may be established for specific commodities by the commissioner.

(c) *Shipside wharfage.* The rate for shipside wharfage shall be one half of that for dock wharfage.

(d) *Top wharfage.* Materials that are unloaded directly from floats to railroad cars or trucks, or materials loaded directly from railroad cars or trucks to floats, shall be handled as topside wharfage for which the charge shall be five cents less per ton of 2,000 pounds than for materials that are stored on State property to compensate the shipper for the loss of 48-hour free storage period allowed for dock wharfage.

(e) *Storage.* Commodities on which a wharfage charge is paid will be entitled to 48 hours free storage on a canal terminal. Storage charges accrue from the expiration of the 48-hour free period at the rate of one-quarter cent per hundredweight for each 10-day period, or fraction thereof, that freight remains on the terminal beyond the 48-hour free period.

Historical Note
Sec. added, filed Mar. 29, 1974 eff. Apr. 1, 1974.

53.7 Special storage provisions at all terminals. The commissioner may issue special permits when, in his opinion, the circumstances are such that the general regulations are impractical of application. Such permits will be issued under terms and upon conditions to be determined by him. (See § 56.1 of this Title.)

Historical Note
Sec. added, filed Mar. 29, 1974 eff. Apr. 1, 1974.

53.8 Stevedoring. The State will not provide stevedoring or handling service, nor provide insurance. All freight storage is at the owner's risk and expense.

Historical Note
Sec. added, filed Mar. 29, 1974 eff. Apr. 1, 1974.

53.9 Abandoned property. In case of any commodity or property of any name or nature stored or left at any canal terminal, or in any storehouse connected therewith, beyond the period authorized, or in the case of the abandonment of such commodity or other property by its owner, the commissioner may notify the owner of such left or abandoned commodity or property, if the name and address of such owner be known to him, to remove the same forthwith. But if the name and

§ 53.10 TITLE 17 TRANSPORTATION

address of such owner be not known or he fails to comply promptly with the notice of removal, the commissioner may cause such commodity or property to be removed from the canal terminal site at the owner's risk, cost and expense, and the cost and expense incurred in such removal may be recovered by the Attorney-General in an appropriate action or proceeding instituted in the name of the people of the State of New York in any court of competent jurisdiction.

Historical Note
Sec. added, filed Mar. 29, 1974 eff. Apr. 1, 1974.

53.10 Mooring facilities during closed season. (a) On November 16 of each year, and continuing for a period of not more than one year thereafter, floats registered for canal traffic, which have actually transported freight on the canal system at some time during the navigation season then being brought to a close, including tugs which have supplied motive power to such floats, will be afforded free mooring facilities at the canal terminals under a revocable permit insofar as space is available. Space to be occupied will be assigned by the commissioner or his representative. (See § 56.1 of this Title.)

(b) Preference will be given to loaded over light floats and the master of any float or floats may be called upon to shift such float or floats from time to time to a different berth, or to another terminal, when in the opinion of the commissioner or his representative, such change of berth is desirable. When adequate space for loaded floats is not available, the light floats may be required to vacate the terminal. If such order for change of berth or to vacate a berth is not accomplished promptly, the shift may be made by the commissioner and the cost of such shift will become a charge against the float and its owner. Floats registered for canal traffic, but which do not come within the provisions of the preceding subdivision, may be allowed to moor at the canal terminals under a revocable permit and at a mooring rate of one cent per running foot per day.

(c) Floats used in the repair of the active canal floats described in the above subdivisions may be assigned mooring facilities when, in the discretion of the commissioner, space is available and at a mooring rate of one cent per running foot per day.

Historical Note
Sec. added, filed Mar. 29, 1974 eff. Apr. 1, 1974.

53.11 Refusal to obey directions. (a) In case the master of a float moored at any terminal fails or refuses to obey this Part, or in case the commissioner or his representative is unable, after reasonable inquiry and effort, to communicate with the master of such float, the commissioner or his representative may cause the float to be moved away from said terminal, or from place to place at the said terminal, when the proper enforcement of this Part so requires, or as may be necessary to relieve congestion. The cost and expense incurred in moving the offending or obstructing float shall be chargeable to the owner of said float or the person having the same under charter.

(b) The owner of a float or the master who fails or refuses to obey any of this Part, including any directions given him or them by the commissioner or his representative pursuant to this Part, shall be subject to a penalty of not to exceed $100 per day for each and every day's failure, or refusal to comply therewith.

Historical Note
Sec. added, filed Mar. 29, 1974 eff. Apr. 1, 1974.

CHAPTER II BARGE CANAL SYSTEM § 54.1

PART 54

FEES AND CHARGES FOR SALVAGE WORK AND FOR USE OF DRY DOCKS

(Statutory authority: Canal Law, §§ 10, 86)

Sec.
54.1 Salvage work

Sec.
54.2 Use of dry docks

Historical Note

Part (§§ 54.1-54.2) filed Mar. 29, 1974 eff. Apr. 1, 1974.

Section 54.1 Salvage work. (a) The following rates will be charged for the use of State equipment:

(1)	Tug	$35.00 per hour
(2)	Tender tug	20.00 per hour
(3)	Buoy boat (with operator and supplies)	9.00 per hour
(4)	Derrick boat (without propulsion)	35.00 per hour
(5)	Derrick boat (self-propelled)	50.00 per hour
(6)	Self-propelled scow (with operator, deck hand and supplies)	15.00 per hour
(7)	Steel flat scow (150 ton) (without personnel or equipment)	35.00 per day or fraction thereof
(8)	Steel flat scow (450 ton) (without personnel or equipment)	45.00 per day or fraction thereof
(9)	Dump scow (without personnel or equipment)	50.00 per day or fraction thereof
(10)	Dipper-dredge	55.00 per hour
(11)	Hydraulic dredge	60.00 per hour
(12)	Gasoline pump (with operator and accessories, but gasoline and oil to be furnished by the user)	8.00 per hour

(b) The basis for applying daily rates will include the entire period from the time when such equipment is taken from its headquarters or its normal station location to the time that such equipment is returned thereto. The basis for applying hourly rates will be the actual hours that the equipment is worked or operated, including transit time for movement of such equipment from its normal station location and its return thereto.

(c) Use of equipment and personnel will be limited to salvage work on floats sunk in the canal channel or those in danger of obstructing navigation.

(1) Regional director will determine with the director of waterways maintenance subdivision as to necessity for use of State equipment; if same is to be used he will advise the Office of Management and Finance.

(2) Regional director will determine what personnel and equipment will be needed and probable length of service.

(i) Regional director will bill owner or person responsible for estimated cost of assistance at established rates and make request for immediate payment.

(ii) Copies to the director of waterways maintenance subdivision and the Office of Management and Finance.

(3) State equipment will be operated as directed by the person in charge of salvage operations but the State shall assume no responsibility therefor.

(4) On completion of work and return to department location, regional

director will prepare revised invoice in quadruplicate, and disperse all copies as follows:

  (i) Owner.
  (ii) Director of waterways maintenance subdivision.
  (iii) Office of Management and Finance. This copy to show payroll and voucher reference on detail sheet.
  (iv) Regional director.

(d) *Reimbursement for damages to canal structures.* (1) Regional director estimates the cost of the work and submits original estimate invoice as follows:

  (i) Owner—with request for payment of 75 percent.
  (ii) Director of waterways maintenance subdivision.
  (iii) Office of Management and Finance.
  (iv) Regional director retains copy.

(2) Regional director prepares revised invoice when work is completed. If final invoice exceeds the 75 percent, request is made by the regional director for the difference, if it is less than 75 percent, refund is made by the Office of Management and Finance. The regional director disperses invoices as follows:

  (i) Owner.
  (ii) Director of waterways maintenance subdivision.
  (iii) Office of Management and Finance.
  (iv) Regional director retains copy.

Historical Note
Sec. filed Mar. 29, 1974; Oct. 26, 1976 eff. immediately. Amended (c)(4).

54.2 Use of dry docks. (a) The following rates will be charged for the use of State-owned dry docks:

  (1) Minimum charge for docking for any type of float will be $100 for 24 hours or portion thereof.
  (2) Charge for lay docking for any type of float will be $50 for 24 hours or portion thereof.

(b) *Invoices.* To be submitted in regular manner.

  (1) Credit may be extended to regular operators on canal.
  (2) Other transactions shall be on a cash basis.

(c) *State's services.* Shall consist of labor required for receiving and discharging float from dock. No labor shall be available for repair work.

(d) *Payrolls.* Time will be submitted on regular payrolls at approved rates. Distribution shall show time and amount in receiving or discharging float and reference to invoice number.

Historical Note
Sec. filed Mar. 29, 1974 eff. Apr. 1, 1974.

PART 55

DIMENSION REQUIREMENTS AND MILEAGE DATA

(Statutory authority: Canal Law, §§ 10, 86)

Sec.
55.1 Floats
55.2 Channel
55.3 Bridges
55.4 Locks

Sec.
55.5 Mileage
55.6 Distance between certain points on canals and connecting waters

Historical Note
Part (§§ 55.1-55.6) filed Mar. 29, 1974 eff. Apr. 1, 1974.

CHAPTER II BARGE CANAL SYSTEM

Section 55.1 Floats. See section 51.5 of this Title for maximum dimensions of floats permitted to navigate the canals.

Historical Note
Sec. filed Mar. 29, 1974 eff. Apr. 1, 1974.

55.2 Channel. (a) *Waterford to Oswego route.*

Minimum bottom width, land line, earth section	104 ft.
Width of channel, water surface, land line, earth section	160 ft.
Minimum bottom width, land line, rock section	120 ft.
Bottom width of channel in canalized rivers, generally	200 ft.
Depth	14 ft.

(b) *All other routes.*

Minimum bottom width, land line, earth section	75 ft.
Width of channel, water surface, land line, earth section	123 ft.
Minimum bottom width, land line, rock section	94 ft.
Bottom width of channel in canalized rivers, generally	200 ft.
Depth	12 ft.

Historical Note
Sec. added, filed Mar. 29, 1974 eff. Apr. 1, 1974.

55.3 Bridges.

Limiting clearances under bridges:

Erie Canal, Waterford to Three Rivers Point, and the Oswego Canal	20 ft.
Erie Canal, Three Rivers Point to Tonawanda, Cayuga and Seneca Canal, and the Champlain Canal	15½ ft.

Historical Note
Sec. filed Mar. 29, 1974; amd. filed Oct. 26, 1976 eff. immediately.

55.4 Locks. Built of concrete, operated by electricity:

Average time of locking	20 min.
Length between lock gates	328 ft.
Available length inside lock chambers	300 ft.
Width of lock chambers (minimum 44.45 ft.)	45 ft.
Depth of water on lock sills:	
Waterford to Oswego route	13 ft.
All other routes	12 ft.
Number	57

Historical Note
Sec. filed Mar. 29, 1974 eff. Apr. 1, 1974.

55.5 Mileage.

Erie Canal, Waterford to Tonawanda	338 miles
Oswego Canal, Three Rivers Point to Oswego	24 miles
Cayuga and Seneca Canal, junction with the Erie Canal Canal to Ithaca and Watkins Glen, including Cayuga and Seneca Lakes and the spur to Montour Falls	92 miles
Champlain Canal, Waterford to Whitehall	60 miles
Canal harbors at Utica, Syracuse and Rochester	10 miles
Total canal mileage	524 miles

Historical Note
Sec. filed Mar. 29, 1974; amd. filed Oct. 26, 1976 eff. immediately.

§ 55.6 Distance between certain points on canals and connecting waters.

New York City, Pier 6, East River to Waterford	154 miles
Tonawanda to Buffalo	12 miles
Lockport to Tonawanda	18 miles
Waterford to Three Rivers Point	160 miles
Junction, Erie and Cayuga and Seneca Canals, to Lock 1, C. and S.	4 miles
Junction, Lock 1, Cayuga and Seneca Canal, to Lock 4, C. and S.	8 miles
Whitehall to Rouses Point	110 miles
Albany to Whitehall	70 miles
Waterford to Oswego	184 miles

Historical Note
Sec. filed Mar. 29, 1974 eff. Apr. 1, 1974.

PART 56

REVOCABLE PERMITS

(Statutory authority: Canal Law, §§ 10, 86)

Sec.		Sec.	
56.1	Granting revocable permits	56.3	Permits for aircraft on canal waters
56.2	Occupancy and use of canal lands or waters		

Historical Note
Part (§§ 56.1-56.3) filed Mar. 29, 1974 eff. Apr. 1, 1974.

Section 56.1 Granting revocable permits. The commissioner or his representative may, in his discretion, issue revocable permits granting certain limited privileges whenever the same can be done without detriment to canal navigation or damage to the canal banks or other structures thereof. He shall prescribe the terms and conditions by which such revocable permits may be issued for the temporary use of canal lands or facilities and for the diversion of canal waters for sanitary, farm purposes or industrial use. An application for a revocable permit may be obtained from the Commissioner of Transportation, State Campus, Albany, New York 12232, or any regional office.

Historical Note
Sec. filed Mar. 29, 1974 eff. Apr. 1, 1974.

56.2 Occupancy and use of canal lands or waters. (a) Canal lands or waters may not be occupied or used except under the terms and conditions prescribed in a revocable permit issued by the commissioner or his representative.

(b) Any person violating this section shall be subject to a penalty of not to exceed $100 for each offense.

Historical Note
Sec. filed Mar. 29, 1974 eff. Apr. 1, 1974.

56.3 Permits for aircraft on canal waters. The commissioner or his representative may, under certain limited and special conditions, issue revocable permits granting the taking off from or landing upon the surface waters of the canal system by aircraft whenever, in his judgment, the same can be done without detriment to canal navigation or without endangering the life or property of others. (See § 50.13 of this Title.)

Historical Note
Sec. filed Mar. 29, 1974 eff. Apr. 1, 1974.

PART 507

TRANSPORTATION OF HAZARDOUS MATERIALS

(Statutory authority: Transportation Law, § 14 - f)

Sec.		Sec.	
507.1	General	507.4	Transportation of hazardous materials
507.2	Application	507.5	Cooperative Agreements
507.3	Definitions	507.6	Exemptions

Historical Note

Part (507) added, filed Feb.11, 1977 eff. Apr. 1, 1977

Section 507.1 General. (a) Section 14-f of the Transportation Law authorizes the Commissioner of Transportation to make rules and regulations governing transportation of hazardous materials by all modes and provides that these rules shall be no less protective to public safety than the rules and regulations promulgated by the Federal government with respect to the transportation of hazardous materials and that, with respect to the transportation of radioactive materials, these rules shall not be construed to abrogate or effect the provisions of any other Federal or State statute or local ordinance, regulation or resolution which are more restrictive than or which supersede these rules.

(b) Federal law governing the transportation of hazardous materials (section 112 of the Federal Hazardous Materials Transportation Act, title I of Pub. L. 93-633) provides for Federal preemption in the area of hazardous materials transportation. It states that any requirement of the State or political subdivision thereof which is inconsistent with Federal law or regulations in the field is preempted. It affords a procedure whereby State requirements may be determined by the U.S. Secretary of Transportation to be not preempted if the State requirement affords an equal or greater level of protection to the public than the Federal requirements and does not unreasonably burden the commerce.

507.2 Application. (a) Every carrier, whether by highway, by rail, by water or by air, engaged in the transportation of hazardous materials within this State shall be subject to the rules and regulations contained in this Part.

(b) No person shall offer or accept a hazardous material for transportation within this State unless that material is properly classed, described, packaged, clearly marked, clearly labeled, and in the condition for shipment as required by this Part.

(c) No person shall offer or accept a hazardous material for transportation unless that material is handled and transported in accordance with this Part.

507.3 Definitions. For the purposes of this Part, the following definitions shall apply: (a) *Hazardous materials* shall mean those materials listed in the table of hazardous materials contained in section 172.101 of title 49 of the Code of Federal Regulations, revised as of October 1, 1976, and including any amendments or additions thereto.

(b) *Transports or transportation* shall mean any movement of property by highway, by rail, by water and by air and any loading, unloading or storage incidental thereto.

(c) *Commerce* shall mean trade, traffic, commerce or transportation within the jurisdiction of New York State which affects trade, traffic, commerce or transportation within the State.

(d) *Person* shall mean an individual, firm, co-partnership, corporation, company, association or joint-stock association, and includes any trustee, receiver, assignee or personal representative thereof.

(e) *Serious harm* shall mean death, serious illness, or severe personal injury.

507.4 Transportation of hazardous materials. (a) To promote the uniform enforcement of law and to minimize the dangers to life and property incident to the transportation of hazardous materials by all modes of transportation, all carriers and persons engaged in the transportation of hazardous materials that are subject to this Part shall classify, describe, package, mark, label and prepare all hazardous materials which are defined and listed in section 172.101 of chapter I of title 49 of the Code of Federal Regulations and any amendments or additions thereto in accordance with the regulations promulgated by the Materials Transportation Bureau of the United States Department of Transportation contained in parts 170-189 of title 49 of the Code of Federal Regulations, revised as of October 1, 1976, and any amendment or addition thereto, which regulations are hereby adopted in toto, defining these articles and stating the precautions that must be observed by the carrier in handling them while in transit.

(b) All carriers and persons engaged in the transportation of hazardous materials shall afford to authorized employees of the Department of Transportation and the Division of State Police and the Federal Highway Administration reasonable opportunity to enter vehicles or any place where hazardous materials are offered into commerce for the purpose of inspection to determine compliance with the provisions of this Part.

507.5 Cooperative agreements. (a) The cooperative agreement entered into on August 16, 1968 between the New York State Public Service Commission and the Federal Highway Administration accepting the provisions then identified as sections 277c.4, 277c.5, 277c.6 and 277c.7 of title 49 of the Code of Federal Regulations with regard to the exchange of information between the agencies, requests for assistance, joint investigation, inspection and examination and joint administrative activities relating to the enforcement of safety and hazardous materials laws and regulations shall continue to remain in full force and effect.

(b) The Division of State Police shall refer all violations of this Part to the Department of Transportation, Traffic and Safety Division, 1220 Washington Avenue, Albany, New York, 12232 on a form supplied for such purpose by the Department of Transportation.

507.6 Exemptions. With respect to the transportation of radioactive materials nothing in this Part shall be construed to abrogate or effect the provisions of any Federal or State statute or local ordinance, regulation or resolution which are more restrictive than or which supersede the provisions of this Part.

APPENDIX A-1

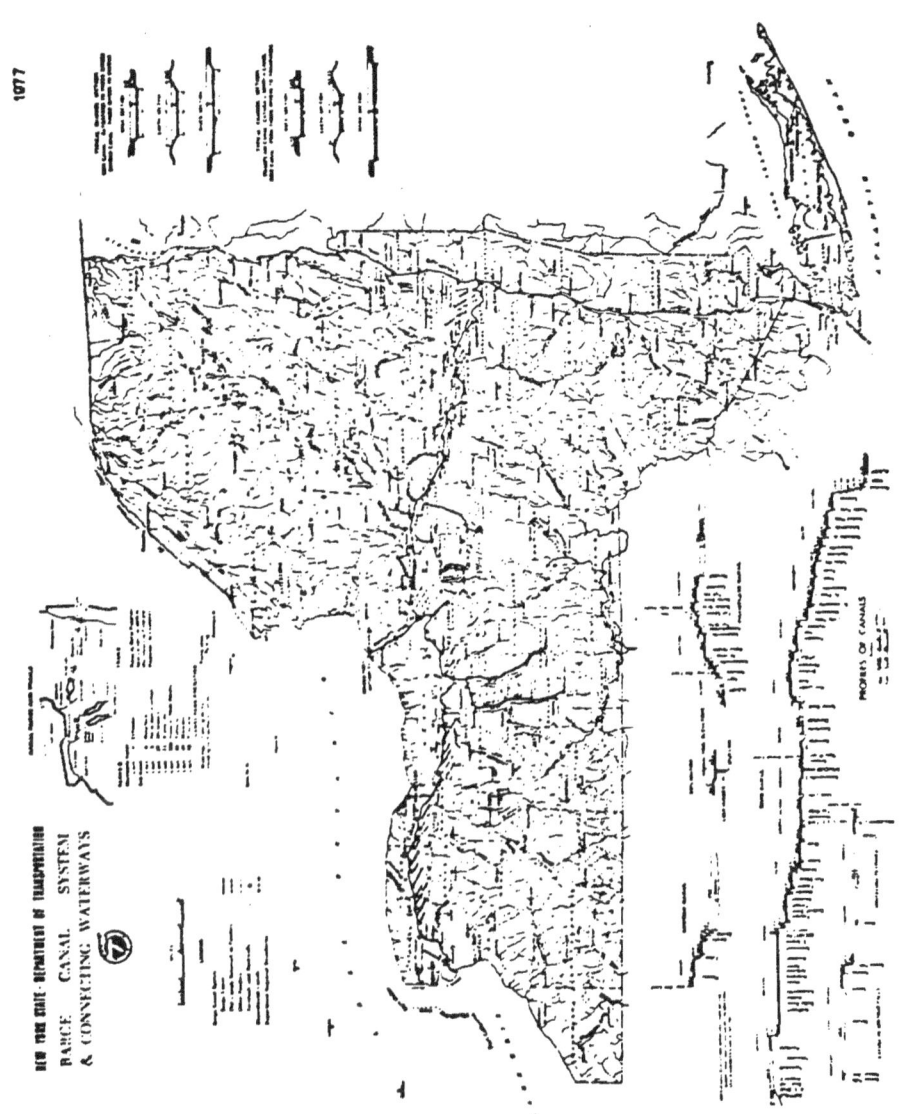

APPENDIX A-2
TABLE OF LOCKS
ERIE CANAL

Lock No.	Nearest Town	Miles from Troy dam	Elevation of water surface Above lock	Elevation of water surface Below lock	Lift of lock in feet
U. S.	Troy		15.20	1.25	13.95
2	Waterford	3	48.75	15.20	33.55
3	Waterford	3	83.25	48.75	34.50
4	Waterford	4	117.75	83.25	34.50
5	Waterford	4	151.00	117.75	33.25
6	Crescent	7	184.00	151.00	33.00
7	Vischer Ferry	15	211.00	184.00	27.00
8	Scotia	26	225.00	211.00	14.00
9	Rotterdam	31	240.00	225.00	15.00
10	Cranesville	37	255.00	240.00	15.00
11	Amsterdam	41	267.00	255.00	12.00
12	Tribes Hill	46	278.00	267.00	11.00
13	Yosts	56	286.00	278.00	8.00
14	Canajoharie	64	294.00	286.00	8.00
15	Fort Plain	67	302.00	294.00	8.00
16	St. Johnsville	73	322.50	302.00	20.50
17	Little Falls	81	363.00	322.50	40.50
18	Jacksonburg	85	383.00	363.00	20.00
19	Frankfort	98	404.00	383.00	21.00
U. H. L.	Utica	105	404.00	397.50	6.50
20	Whitesboro	108	420.00	404.00	16.00
21	New London	126	420.00	395.00	25.00
22	New London	127	395.00	369.90	25.10
23	Brewerton	156	369.90	363.00	6.90
24	Baldwinsville	175	374.00	363.00	11.00
25	May's Point	205	380.00	374.00	6.00
26	Clyde	211	386.00	380.00	6.00
27	Lyons	223	398.50	386.00	12.50
28-A	Lyons	224	418.00	398.50	19.50
28-B	Newark	228	430.00	418.00	12.00
29	Palmyra	238	446.00	430.00	16.00
30	Macedon	241	462.40	446.00	16.40
32	Pittsford	258	487.50	462.40	25.10
33	Rochester	259	512.60	487.50	25.10
34	Lockport	322	539.50	514.90	24.60
35	Lockport	322	564.00	539.50	24.50

CHAMPLAIN CANAL

Lock No.	Nearest Town	Miles from Troy dam	Above lock	Below lock	Lift
1	Waterford	5.8	29.5	15.2	14.3
2	Mechanicville	9.7	48.0	29.5	18.5
3	Mechanicville	12.3	67.5	48.0	19.5
4	Stillwater	15.0	83.5	67.5	16.0
5	Northumberland	28.5	102.5	83.5	19.0
6	Fort Miller	33.0	119.0	102.5	16.5
7	Fort Edward	39.3	129.0	119.0	10.0
8	Fort Edward	41.3	140.0	129.0	11.0
9	Smith's Basin	47.0	140.0	124.0	16.0
11	Comstock	56.2	124.0	112.0	12.0
12	Whitehall	62.8	112.0	96.5	15.5

OSWEGO CANAL

Lock No.	Nearest Town	Miles	Above lock	Below lock	Lift
1	Phoenix	165.0	363.0	352.8	10.2
2	Fulton	175.0	352.8	335.0	17.8
3	Fulton	175.5	335.0	308.0	27.0
5	Minetto	181.5	308.0	290.0	18.0
6	High Dam	185.0	290.0	270.0	20.0
7	Oswego	185.5	270.0	255.8	14.2
8	Oswego	186.0	255.8	245.0	10.8

CAYUGA AND SENECA CANAL

Lock No.	Nearest Town	Miles	Above lock	Below lock	Lift
1	Cayuga	208.0	381.5	374.0	7.5
2	Seneca Falls	212.0	406.0	381.5	24.5
3	Seneca Falls	212.0	430.5	406.0	24.5
4	Waterloo	217.0	445.0	430.5	14.5

1903 TR 10-31-76

APPENDIX A-3

DISTANCE TABLES OF POINTS

Along Hudson River and Erie Canal Between New York City and Buffalo

	Place to place	From New York	From Buffalo
New York City, piers 5 and 6, East River		0.00	504.72
Yonkers	18.00	18.00	486.72
Dobbs Ferry	5.80	23.80	480.92
Tarrytown	4.50	28.30	476.42
Nyack	.90	29.20	475.52
Ossining	4.60	33.80	470.92
Haverstraw	4.00	37.80	466.92
Peekskill	7.10	44.90	459.82
West Point	7.40	52.30	452.42
Cold Spring	2.60	54.90	449.82
Cornwall Landing	2.60	57.50	447.22
Newburgh	3.60	61.10	443.62
Fishkill	.30	61.40	443.32
New Hamburg	6.40	67.80	436.92
Poughkeepsie	7.90	75.70	429.02
Kingston, on side line 1.2 miles long	16.40	92.10	415.02
Rhinecliff	15.30	91.00	413.72
Saugerties	10.50	101.50	403.22
Catskill	10.60	112.10	392.62
Athens	4.10	116.20	388.52
Hudson	.20	116.40	388.32
Coxsackie	6.90	123.30	381.42
New Baltimore	6.40	129.70	375.02
Coeymans	2.00	131.70	373.02
Castleton	4.00	135.70	369.02
Albany (North Ferry Street)	9.10	144.80	359.92
Troy terminal	5.10	149.90	354.82
Troy, Federal Lock	2.03	151.93	352.79
Waterford junction, Erie and Champlain Canals	2.45	154.38	350.34
Waterford terminal	.12	154.50	350.22
Lock No. 2, Erie Canal	.70	155.20	349.52
Lock No. 3, Erie Canal	.28	155.48	349.24
Lock No. 4, Erie Canal	.62	156.10	348.62
Lock No. 5, Erie Canal	.16	156.26	348.46
Lock No. 6, Erie Canal	.28	156.54	348.18
Guard gate No. 2, Erie Canal	.63	157.17	347.55
Crescent terminal	1.33	158.50	346.22
Dunsbach Ferry	2.39	160.89	343.83
Vischer Ferry	5.01	165.90	338.82
Lock No. 7, Vischer Ferry	1.47	167.37	337.35
Rexford	3.83	171.20	333.52
Lock No. 8, Scotia	7.00	178.20	326.52
Rotterdam Junction (west)	4.40	182.60	322.12
Lock No. 9, Rotterdam	.42	183.02	321.70
Hoffman's (north shore) / Pattersonville (south shore)	1.38	184.40 / 184.40	320.32
Cranesville	4.40	188.80	315.92
Lock No. 10, Cranesville	.38	189.18	315.54
Amsterdam terminal	2.72	191.90	312.82
Lock No. 11, Amsterdam	1.33	193.23	311.49
Lock No. 12, Tribes Hill	4.57	197.80	306.92
Fultonville (south shore) / Fonda (north shore)	5.10	202.90 / 202.90	301.82
Lock No. 13, Yosts	4.58	207.48	297.24
Yosts (north shore)	.80	208.28	296.44
Sprakers	3.42	211.70	293.02
Canajoharie terminal / Palatine Bridge (north shore)	3.10	214.80 / 214.80	289.92
Lock No. 14, Canajoharie	.58	215.38	289.34
Nelliston (north shore)	2.92	218.30	286.42
Lock No. 15, Fort Plain	.43	218.73	285.99

1905 TR 10-31-76

APPENDIX A-3

DISTANCE TABLES OF POINTS

Along Hudson River and Erie Canal Between New York City and Buffalo

(continued)

	Place to place	From New York	From Buffalo
St. Johnsville terminal	5.25	223.98	280.74
Lock No. 16, St. Johnsville	1.46	225.44	279.28
Mindenville bridge	.26	225.70	279.02
Guard gate No. 3, Indian Castle	3.10	228.80	275.92
Lock No. 17, Little Falls	4.41	233.21	271.51
Guard gate No. 4, Little Falls	.89	234.10	270.62
Little Falls terminal	.30	234.40	270.32
Lock No. 18, Jacksonburg	3.00	237.40	267.32
Guard gate No. 5, Mohawk	4.13	241.53	263.19
Herkimer terminal	.17	241.70	263.02
Ilion terminal	1.80	243.50	261.22
Frankfort terminal	2.90	246.40	258.32
Lock No. 19, Frankfort	3.00	249.40	255.32
Utica, harbor lock	7.20	256.60	248.12
Utica terminal (side line)	.70	257.30	248.82
Whitesboro bridge	2.20	258.80	245.92
Lock No. 20, Whitesboro	.88	259.68	245.04
Oriskany bridge	2.42	262.10	242.62
Guard gate No. 6, Erie Canal	4.20	266.30	238.42
Rome terminal	3.00	269.30	235.42
Guard gate No. 7, Erie Canal	.15	269.45	235.27
New London dry dock	6.41	275.86	228.86
Lock No. 21, New London	2.04	277.90	226.82
Lock No. 22, New London	1.35	279.25	225.47
Sylvan Beach (north side)	4.35	283.60	221.12
Cleveland	8.50	292.10	212.62
Fort Brewerton (north shore)	12.70	304.80	199.92
Fort Brewerton (north shore)	21.20	304.80	199.92
Brewerton terminal	.20	305.00	199.72
Lock No. 23, Brewerton	2.90	307.90	196.82
Oak Orchard bridge	2.90	310.80	193.92
Three Rivers Point junction, Erie and Oswego Canals	3.81	314.61	190.11
Three Rivers Point dock	.09	314.70	190.02
West Junction	.20	314.90	189.82
Belgium bridge	1.80	316.70	188.02
Cold Spring bridge, east junction Syracuse branch	4.70	321.40	183.32
Long Branch dock	.95	322.35	183.77
Lake entrance, side line	.45	322.80	184.22
Liverpool	2.00	324.80	186.22
Syracuse terminal	3.40	328.20	189.62
West Junction, Syracuse branch	.50	321.90	182.82
Lock No. 24, Baldwinsville	4.75	326.65	178.07
State ditch bridge	8.80	335.45	169.27
Jones Point, Cross Lake entrance	1.73	337.18	167.54
Jordan bridge	2.12	339.30	165.42
Bontas bridge	1.87	341.17	163.55
Weedsport terminal	2.03	343.20	161.52
Port Byron (free bridge)	4.10	347.30	157.42
Fox Ridge bridge	3.50	350.80	153.92
Montezuma (aqueduct)	4.58	355.38	149.34
East junction, Cayuga and Seneca Canal	.52	355.90	148.82
West junction, Cayuga and Seneca Canal	.30	356.20	148.52
Lock No. 25, May's Point	1.20	357.40	147.32
Lock No. 26, Clyde	5.84	363.24	141.48
Clyde viaduct	2.36	365.60	139.12
Lyons terminal	9.60	375.20	129.52
Lock No. 27, Lyons	.10	375.30	129.42
Lock No. 28-A, Lyons	1.27	376.57	128.15

APPENDIX A-3

DISTANCE TABLES OF POINTS

Along Hudson River and Erie Canal Between New York City and Buffalo

(continued)

	Place to place	From New York	From Buffalo
County House	1.08	377.65	127.07
Lock No. 28-B, Newark	2.85	380.50	124.22
Newark terminal	.40	380.90	123.82
Port Gibson	3.40	384.30	120.42
Guard gate No. 8, Erie Canal	1.68	385.98	118.74
Lock No. 29, Palmyra	4.22	390.20	114.52
Lock No. 30, Macedon	3.00	393.20	111.52
Wayneport	3.00	396.20	108.52
Fairport terminal	} 4.63	{ 400.83	} 103.89
Fairport lift bridge		400.83	
Guard Gate No. 9, Erie Canal	3.27	404.10	100.62
Bushnell's Basin bridge (Marsh Road)	.64	404.74	99.98
Guard gate No. 10, Erie Canal	1.76	406.50	98.22
Pittsford terminal	1.20	407.70	97.02
Lock No. 32, Pittsford	1.60	409.30	95.42
Lock No. 33, Rochester	1.30	410.60	94.12
Guard lock, east	3.60	414.20	90.52
Center of river	.50	414.70	90.02
Guard lock, west	.50	415.20	89.52
South Greece	6.60	421.80	82.92
Guard gate No. 11, Erie Canal	2.30	424.10	80.62
Spencerport terminal	} 1.30	{ 425.40	} 79.32
Spencerport lift bridge		425.40	
Adams basin dock	} 2.90	{ 428.30	} 76.42
Adams basin lift bridge		428.30	
Brockport lift bridge (Park Avenue)	4.61	432.91	71.81
Brockport lift bridge (Main Street)	.19	433.10	71.62
Guard gate No. 12, Erie Canal	.90	434.00	70.72
Holley terminal	} 3.70	{ 437.70	{ 67.02
Holley lift bridge		437.70	
Guard gate No. 13, Erie Canal	.63	438.33	66.39
Hulberton lift bridge	2.37	440.70	64.02
Albion lift bridge (Ingersoll Street)	6.40	447.10	57.62
Albion lift bridge (Main Street)	.20	447.30	57.42
Guard gate No. 14, Erie Canal	1.10	448.40	56.32
Eagle Harbor lift bridge	2.20	450.60	54.12
Knowlesville lift bridge	3.00	453.60	51.12
Guard gate No. 15, Erie Canal	3.20	456.80	47.92
Medina terminal	1.00	457.80	46.92
Medina lift bridge	.40	458.20	46.52
Guard gate No. 16, Erie Canal	3.21	461.41	43.31
Middleport lift bridge	1.49	462.90	41.82
Guard gate No. 17, Erie Canal	4.90	467.80	36.92
Gasport lift bridge	.40	468.20	36.52
Lockport lift bridge (Adams Street)	5.77	473.97	30.75
Lockport lift bridge (Exchange Street)	.23	474.20	30.52
Lockport lower terminal	.10	474.30	30.42
Locks No. 34 and 35, Lockport	.50	474.80	29.92
Lockport upper terminal	.50	475.30	29.42
Guard gate No. 18, Erie Canal	4.00	479.30	25.42
Pendleton bridge	2.20	481.50	23.22
Martinsville	6.40	487.90	16.82
Tonawanda terminal	} 4.40	{ 492.30	} 12.42
North Tonawanda terminal		492.30	
Port of Buffalo	12.42	504.72	0.00

1907 TR 10-31-76

APPENDIX A-3

DISTANCE TABLES OF POINTS

Oswego Canal

	Place to place	From New York	From Oswego
Three Rivers Point junction, Erie and Oswego Canals		314.61	23.79
Phoenix lift bridge	2.29	316.90	21.50
Lock No. 1, Phoenix	.10	317.00	21.40
Hinmansville bridge	3.20	320.20	18.20
Lock No. 2, Fulton	6.30	326.50	11.90
Fulton terminal	.20	326.70	11.70
Lock No. 3, Fulton	.35	327.05	11.35
Battle Island cut	3.50	330.55	7.85
Lock No. 5, Minetto	2.95	333.50	4.90
Lock No. 6, High Dam	3.30	336.80	1.60
Lock No. 7, Oswego	.36	337.16	1.24
Lock No. 8, Oswego	.54	337.70	0.70
Oswego terminal	.30	338.00	0.40
Oswego lake terminal	.40	338.40	0.00

Champlain Canal

	Place to place	From New York	From Canadian Line
Troy, Federal Lock		151.93	174.57
Waterford junction, Erie and Champlain Canals	2.45	154.38	172.12
Waterford bridge	.54	154.92	171.58
Lock No. 1, Waterford	2.88	157.80	168.70
Lock No. 2, Mechanicville	3.90	161.70	164.80
Mechanicville terminal	1.90	163.60	162.90
Lock No. 3, Mechanicville	.63	164.23	162.27
Lock No. 4, Stillwater	1.83	166.06	160.44
Stillwater bridge	.42	166.48	160.02
Bemis Heights	2.82	169.30	157.20
Lock No. 5, Northumberland	11.06	180.36	146.14
Thomson terminal	1.04	181.40	145.10
Northumberland bridge	.10	181.50	145.00
Lock No. 6, Fort Miller	2.50	184.00	142.50
Guard gate (Crocker's Reef)	2.07	186.07	140.43
Lock No. 7, Fort Edward	5.17	191.24	135.26
Fort Edward terminal, side line	1.00	192.34	136.26
Lock No. 8, Fort Edward	2.06	193.30	133.20
Dunham Basin bridge	1.70	195.00	131.50
Lock No. 9, Smith's Basin	4.10	199.10	127.40
Smith's Basin bridge	.44	199.54	126.96
Fort Ann bridge	3.76	203.30	123.20
Comstock bridge	3.94	207.24	119.26
Lock No. 11, Comstock	.96	208.20	118.30
Whitehall terminal	6.30	214.50	112.00
Lock No. 12, Whitehall	.29	214.79	111.71
Ticonderoga	22.31	237.10	89.40
Crown Point	8.30	245.40	81.10
Port Henry	8.10	253.50	73.00
Essex	21.00	274.50	52.00
Burlington	11.00	285.50	41.00
Port Kent	3.00	288.50	38.00
Plattsburgh	12.00	300.50	26.00
Rouses Point	24.50	325.00	1.50
Canadian line	1.50	326.50	0.00

1908 TR 10-31-76

APPENDIX A-3

DISTANCE TABLES OF POINTS

Cayuga and Seneca Canal

	Place to place	From New York	From Buffalo
Albany (North Ferry Street)		144.80	359.92
Lock No. 2, Erie Canal	10.40	155.20	349.52
East junction, Erie and Cayuga and Seneca Canals	200.70	355.90	148.82
West junction, Erie and Cayuga and Seneca Canals	.30	356.20	148.52
Lock No. 1, Cayuga	4.07	359.97	152.59
Ithaca	37.83	397.80	190.42
Lock No. 1, Cayuga		359.97	152.59
Seneca Falls	4.38	364.35	156.97
Waterloo	3.71	368.06	160.68
Geneva	6.94	375.00	167.62
Watkins Glen	32.80	407.80	200.42
Montour Falls (Ayer Street)	2.50	410.30	202.92

Distances, Albany to Montreal by Way of Hudson River, Lake Champlain and Richelieu and St. Lawrence Rivers (*approximate distances*)

	Place to place	Total distances
Albany		
Whitehall	70	70
Rouses Point	110	180
St. John's (Chambly Canal entrance)	25	205
Chambly	12	217
St. Ours Lock	32	249
Sorel	14	263
Montreal	46	309

1909 TR 10-31-76

APPENDIX A-5
NEW YORK STATE BARGE CANAL TERMINALS
THEIR LOCATIONS AND FACILITIES

Location of terminal	Dock wall		Type of building		Facilities	
	Length	Height	Frame	Brick	Cranes	Derricks
*Adams Basin	530	3	None	None	None	None
Albion	400	2½	30 x 50	None	None	None
Amsterdam	500	9	None	None	None	None
Baldwinsville	800 and 570	5	None	None	None	None
Brewerton	570	5½	None	None	None	None
Brockport	1200	3	None	None	None	None
Canajoharie	410	6	None	None	None	None
Cleveland	240	6	None	None	None	None
Crescent	150	6	None	None	None	None
Fairport	650	3	None	None	None	None
Fonda	600	6	None	None	None	7-T Steel (El.)
Fort Edward:						
Hudson River	640	6	None	None	None	None
*Lock No. 7	300	4½	None	None	None	None
Frankfort	300	6	None	None	None	None
Fulton	800	6	None	None	None	None
*Gasport	800	2½	None	None	None	None
Herkimer	500	6	16 x 100	None	None	None
Holley	300	3	16 x 30	None	None	None
Ilion	670	6	16 x 60	None	None	None
*Knowlesville	960	2½	None	None	None	None
Little Falls	500	6	32 x 150	None	None	None
Lockport:						
Upper	725	9	30 x 100	None	None	None
Lower	1720	2	32 x 100	None	None	None
Lyons	300	6½	None	None	None	None
Mechanicville	430	6	None	None	None	None
Medina	490	6	24 x 70	None	None	None
Middleport	1000	2	None	None	None	None
Newark	650	6	None	None	None	None
North Tonawanda	800	5½	None	None	None	None
Oswego	594	8	None	None	None	None

1913 TR 10-31-76

APPENDIX A-5
NEW YORK STATE BARGE CANAL TERMINALS
THEIR LOCATIONS AND FACILITIES (continued)

Location of terminal	Dock wall		Type of building			Facilities	
	Length	Height	Frame	Brick		Cranes	Derricks
Palmyra	570	4	None	None		None	None
Pittsford	400	6	None	None		None	None
Plattsburgh, Pier	200 x 400	6½	None	None		None	None
Port Henry, Pier	75 x 500	6½	None	None		None	None
Rome	910	6	32 x 200	None		None	None
Rouses Point	75	3½	None	None		None	None
St. Johnsville	340	6	None	None		None	None
Seneca Falls	1915	3½	None	None		None	None
Spencerport	270	3	None	None		None	None
Sylvan Beach	1910	5	None	None		None	None
Syracuse, North Dock	365	7	None	None		None	None
North Pier, North	335	7	None	None		None	None
North Pier, South	365	7	None	None		None	None
South Dock	735	7	None	None		None	None
South Pier, North	335	7	None	None		None	None
South Pier, South	365	7	None	None		None	None
Thomson	230	6	None	None		None	None
*Three Rivers	350	8½	None	None		None	None
Tonawanda	940	6½	32 x 80	None		None	None
Troy	960	15	30 x 100, 16 x 50	None		None	None
Utica	1160	7	32 x 200	None		7-T Loco. (St.)	None
*Waterloo	100	3½	None	None		None	None
Waterford	1150	8½	None	None		None	None
Weedsport	150	6	None	None		None	None
Whitehall	470	5	None	None		None	None

*These locations have not been established as terminals, but they have vertical walls where floats may tie up for purpose of discharging or taking on cargo.

1914 TR 10-31-76

CHAPTER II BARGE CANAL SYSTEM § 50.6

50.6 Prohibited activities. The activities and uses enumerated in this section shall be absolutely prohibited on any canal system land:

(a) Alms. No person shall solicit alms or contributions.

(b) Pollution of waters. No person shall in any manner cause to be placed in waters or into any storm sewer, drain or stream flowing into such waters any sewage, garbage, trash, litter, debris, waste material or any nauseous or offensive matter.

(c) Littering. No person shall in any manner cause any rubbish, garbage, refuse, organic or inorganic waste, diseased or dead animal, or other offensive matter or any abandoned property or material to be placed or left in or on any property, except in receptacles provided for that purpose.

(d) Injury to property. No person shall make an excavation on or injure, destroy, deface, remove, fill in, tamper with or cut any real or personal property, tree or other plant life.

(e) Disorderly conduct. No person shall do any of the following:

(1) Disobey a lawful order of any officer or employee of the Department of Transportation or any sign erected by or at the direction of the Department of Transportation;

(2) Throw stones or other objects or missiles which may inflict bodily injury or damage to property;

(3) Obstruct vehicular or pedestrian traffic;

(4) Climb upon any wall, fence, structure or monument;

(5) Throw away or discard any lighted match, cigar, cigarette, charcoal or other burning object other than in a receptacle provided for that purpose;

(6) Operate any vehicle, equipment in such a manner as to endanger other persons or property or in such a manner so as to create an unreasonable noise or disturbance;

(7) Commit an act which may result in injury to any person or damage to real or personal property or create a hazardous or offensive condition by any act which serves no legitimate purpose;

(8) Operate a snowmobile, motorbike or any other motorized vehicle;

(9) Dumping of garbage or refuse;

(10) Horseback riding, and

(11) Carrying of firearms.

(f) Property closed to public. No person shall enter or remain upon any property or within any structure during such hours, seasonal or indefinite periods that such property or structure has been designated as closed by a sign or by an employee of the Department of Transportation.

(g) Use of established ways. No person shall use other than trails, overlooks, roads and other ways established and provided for public use by the Department of Transportation. No liability shall attach to the State, its officers, employees or agents for injuries to persons resulting from the use of other than such established trails, overlooks, roads or ways. /1/r

Historical Note
Sec. repealed, filed June 1, 1981
eff. June 1, 1981.

con'td from 33   TR 3-31-74

BASIC FUNDAMENTALS OF HYDRAULICS AND ELECTRICITY

TABLE OF CONTENTS

	Page
INTRODUCTION	1
HYDRAULICS	1
HYDRAULIC RADIUS	5
ELECTRICITY	18

BASIC FUNDAMENTALS OF HYDRAULICS AND ELECTRICITY

There are similarities between fluids and electricity which help us to understand the fundamental of both. For example, we have the following units of measurement:

	Fluid	Electricity
Pressure	pounds per square inch (psi) or feet of water	electromotive force (emf) E or volts
Flow	gallons per minute (gpm) or cubic feet per second (cfs)	amperes (amp)
Resistance to flow	head loss feet of fluid or psi	resistance (ohms)
Quantity	gallons or cubic feet (gal) or (cf)	kilowatt hours (KWH)

Hydraulics

This is the name given to that branch of science which deals with fluids at rest and in motion. The former is sometimes spoken of as hydrostatics and the latter as hydrodynamics. We are concerned here mainly with water at rest and in motion. Many of the same principles apply to air and gases.

Consideration will be given to water moving or flowing through pipes, channels and pumps and ways of measuring the quantity flowing in a given time. We must be careful of units, the basic ones being:

Length in feet	ft
Area in square feet	sq ft or ft^2
Rate: gallons per minute	gpm.
million gallons per day	mgd
cu ft per second	cfs or sec ft
Weight: 1 gallon of water	8.34 lb
1 cu ft water	62.4 lb
Speed or velocity of flow in feet per second	ft/sec

Head. The precise meaning of the term *head* is the amount of energy possessed by a unit quantity of water at its given location. Ordinarily, the energy is expressed in *foot-pounds*, and the unit quantity of water considered is one pound. The head, then, is expressed in foot-pounds of energy per pound of water, or,

$$\frac{ft \times lb}{lb} = ft$$

Thus, all heads can be expressed in feet. Water may contain energy due to (a) its elevation, (b) its pressure, or (c) its velocity. These energies are called elevation (or static) head, pressure head, and velocity head, respectively. In addition, operators often have occasion to refer to *pump head,* which is the energy required for a pump to move one pound of water, and to *friction head,* which is the energy lost due to friction within the fluid and against the walls of the pipe or channel.

Elevation (or static) head. Elevations must be expressed as the vertical distance from some base level, or reference plane, such as mean sea level, the surface of the ground, or some other arbitrarily chosen level.
Then, for example, water that is 100 ft above the reference plane, has 100 ft-lbs of energy, and its elevation head is 100 ft.

Pressure head. Pressures are expressed in terms of force per unit area, such as pounds per square inch or pounds per square foot. One square foot contains 144 square inches. Therefore, a pressure of 1 lb/in^2 = 144 lb/ft^2, since every square inch is subjected to a force of one pound.
To calculate the energy per pound of water, we must consider the number of pounds of water in a unit volume, which is called the "density" of the water. The density of water is 62.4 lb/ft^3. Then if the pressure of the water is 1 lb/in^2 (often written 1 psi), the "pressure head" is

$$\frac{144 \; lb/ft^2}{62.4 \; lb/ft^3} = 2.3 ft$$

or
1 psi = 2.3 ft pressure head

By the same kind of calculation, a water pressure of 40 psi equals

$$\frac{40 \times 144 \; lb/ft^2}{62.4 lb/ft^2} = 92.3 \, ft \; \text{pressure head}$$

or
40 X 2.3 = 92.3 ft pressure head

Velocity head. The energy of motion is called kinetic energy, and is calculated by the relationship

$$\text{Energy} = \frac{mv^2}{2g}$$

where m represents the mass of the moving object, v its velocity, and g the force which gravity exerts on a mass of one pound.

In everyday speech, we are accustomed to expressing both force and mass in pounds. However, this causes confusion when energy calculations are attempted, because the force exerted by gravity is not numerically equal to the mass in pounds. That is to say, force and mass cannot properly be expressed in the same units.

One way of avoiding this difficulty is to speak of the force of gravity in terms of the acceleration it produces when it acts upon a unit mass. One of the fundamental laws of physics is that force equals mass times acceleration. Thus, the force on a unit mass of one pound is numerically equal to the acceleration.

Acceleration is the rate at which velocity changes. If an automobile goes from zero miles per hour to sixty miles per hour in two minutes, we can say that its average change of speed was thirty miles per hour in each minute, or thirty miles per hour per minute. Likewise, if water moving ten feet per second speeds up to fifteen feet per second, and the time required for the change of speed is one second, we could say that it accelerated five feet per second per second. Accelerations are often expressed in feet per second. The units can then be written ft/sec. This is equivalent to writing $\frac{ft}{sec \times sec}$ or $\frac{ft}{sec^2}$

When gravity acts upon a free-falling body, it produces an acceleration of 32.2 ft/sec^2. This value of g can be used in the equation for calculating velocity head. If we consider, for example one pound of water moving with a velocity of 10 ft/sec, its velocity head is calculated as follows:

$$\text{Energy} = \frac{1 \text{ lb} \times 10 \text{ ft/sec} \times 10 \text{ ft/sec}}{2 \times 32.2 \text{ ft/sec}^2} = 1.5 \text{ ft-lb}$$

$$\text{Velocity head} = \frac{1.5 \text{ ft-lb}}{1 \text{ lb}} = 1.5 \text{ ft}$$

In the first of these two equations we multiplied by the weight of the water. In the second we divided by the weight of the water. Since these two operations cancel each other, the velocity head can be calculated by leaving out the weight in the first place:

$$\text{Velocity head} = \frac{v^2}{2g}$$

Friction head. Friction head equals the loss of energy due to friction within the liquid and friction against the walls of the pipe or channel. When we are dealing with water, the friction within the liquid is relatively small, and most of the energy is lost due to friction against the walls. Therefore, the friction loss depends mostly upon the characteristics of the material of which the pipe or channel is made and its surface smoothness. The usual procedure for estimating friction head losses is to use a table in an engineering handbook which gives directly the friction loss per foot of a particular kind of pipe or channel.

Pump head. The pump head equals the ft-lb of energy given to each pound of water passing through the pump.

Pumping. Pumps are used to move liquids to a higher level or to increase the rate of flow. Figure (1) and Figure (2) show two typical pumping conditions. To understand these figures it is necessary to know that in a liquid at rest the pressure at any point is equal to the weight of the liquid above the point, plus the weight of the atmosphere above the surface of the liquid. Both, must be expressed in the same units.

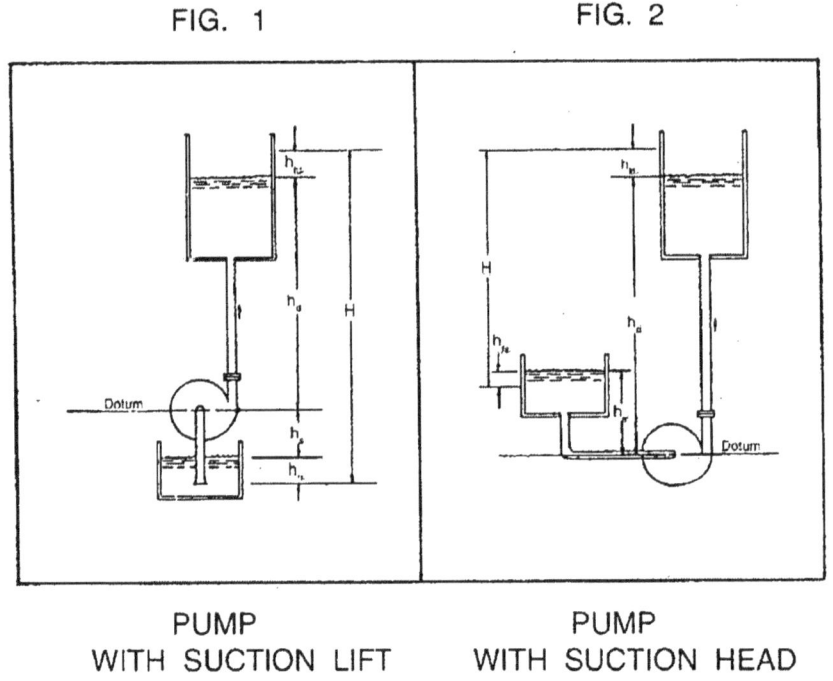

PUMP WITH SUCTION LIFT   PUMP WITH SUCTION HEAD

These units are usually pounds per square inch (psi) or feet of water. Since most pumping problems involve difference in pressure, the atmospheric pressure may be neglected and gauge pressures (psig) or height in feet may be used. Total head in feet at a point can be expressed as the height of a column of water whose weight would produce a certain pressure at that point. Psi X 2.31 = head in feet.

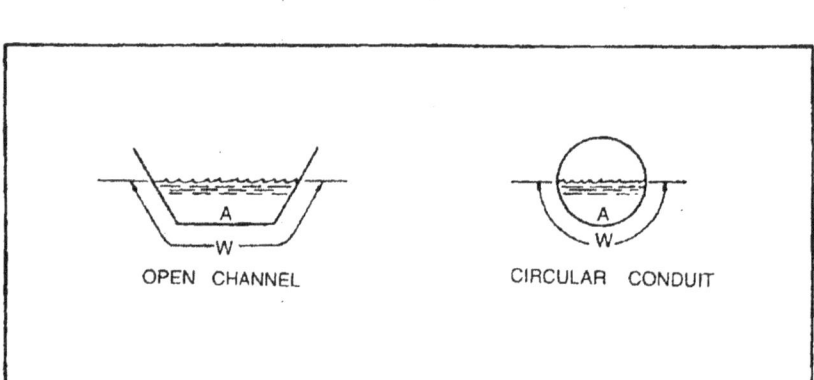

OPEN CHANNEL   CIRCULAR CONDUIT

HYDRAULIC RADIUS

For Figure 1— Pump operating with a suction lift:

$$H = h_d + h_s + h_{fd} + h_{fa} + \frac{V_d^2}{2g} \frac{V_s^2}{2g}$$

For Figure 2 — Pump operating with suction head:

$$H = h_d + h_s + h_{fd} + h_{fa} + \frac{V_d^2}{2g} \frac{V_s^2}{2g}$$

Where —
- H = Total head in feet (formerly called total dynamic head) at which the pump operates.
- h_d = Static discharge head in feet, or the vertical distance between the pump datum and liquid surface in the receiving tank. The pump datum is at the center line for horizontal pumps and at the entrance eye of the impeller for vertical pumps.
- $h.$ = Static suction head or lift in feet or vertical distance between pump datum and liquid surface in the suction well.
- h_{fd} = Friction head in discharge in feet or the head necessary to overcome friction in valves, fittings, etc. in the discharge piping.
- h_{fs} = Friction head in suction in feet
- g = 32.2 ft/sec^2 = Acceleration due to gravity.

$\frac{V_d^2}{2g}$ and $\frac{V_s^2}{2g}$ discharge nozzle and suction nozzle of the pump. When the nozzles are of the same diameter these values are equal and cancel out. Velocity head represents energy which the pump must deliver to the liquid but which is not measured by a pressure gage. It is the head required to give to the liquid the velocity "V" in feet per second.

The relationship between the volume of water flowing per unit of time, the velocity of the moving water and the size of pipe or channel through which the flow takes place may be expressed by the equation:

$$Q = AV$$

Where
- Q = rate of flow or volume per unit time (usually expressed as cubic ft/sec (cfs)
- A = Area through which water is flowing, measured at right angles in the direction of flow (usually expressed in sq ft)
- V = Average velocity of flow or distance traveled per unit of time (usually expressed as ft/sec)

There are three general types of problems using the equation $Q = AV$. These are as follows:

1. The water in an open channel has been observed to flow a distance of 180 feet in 2 minutes. The dimensions of the channel are 2 feet wide and 18 inches deep. Compute the rate of flow

$$V = \frac{180}{2 \text{ min}} = \frac{90 \text{ ft}}{\text{min}} = \frac{1.5 \text{ ft}}{\text{sec}}$$

$$A = 2 \text{ ft} \times 18 \text{ in} \times \frac{\text{ft}}{12 \text{ in}} = 3.0 \text{ sq ft}$$

then

$$Q = AV = 3.0 \text{ sq ft} \times \frac{1.5 \text{ ft}}{\text{sec}} = 4.5 \text{ cfs}$$

2. A meter shows water flowing through a 12 inch diameter pipe at the rate of 2 mgd. To determine the velocity of the water

$$Q = \frac{2,000,000 \text{ gal}}{\text{day}} \times \frac{\text{cu ft}}{7.5 \text{ gal}} \times \frac{\text{day}}{24 \text{ hr}} \times \frac{\text{hr}}{60 \text{ min}} \times \frac{\text{min}}{60 \text{ sec}} = 3.08 \text{ cfs}$$

$$A = \pi r^2 = 3.1416 \times 6 \text{ in} \times 6 \text{ in} \times \frac{\text{sq ft}}{144 \text{ sq ft}} = 0.79 \text{ sq ft}$$

then $V = Q/A = \frac{3.08 \text{ cu ft}}{0.79 \text{ sq ft} \times \text{sec}} = 3.9 \frac{\text{ft}}{\text{sec}}$

3. Baffles are to be placed in a coagulation tank so that the velocity of flow between baffles is 0.3 ft/sec. The depth of flow in the tank is 8 feet and the rate of flow through the tank is 2 mgd. Find the distance, w between baffles.

$$Q = 2 \text{ mgd} \times 1.55 \frac{\text{cfs}}{\text{mgd}} = 3.08 \text{ cfs}$$

V=0.3 ft/sec
let the distance between baffles equal w

then $A = 8 \times w = \frac{Q}{V} = 3.08 \frac{\text{cu ft}}{\text{sec}} \times \frac{\text{sec}}{0.3 \text{ ft}}$

$$W = \frac{3.08 \text{ cu ft/sec}}{8 \text{ ft} \times 0.3 \text{ ft/sec}} = 1.28 \text{ ft}$$

Pipe Friction. The h_{fd} and h_{fs} in the preceding paragraphs are those portions of the total head necessary to overcome friction between the fluid and the walls of the suction and discharge piping. The values of these terms depend upon the length of the pipeline, its diameter, the velocity of the flowing liquid and the condition of the internal walls of the pipe, usually called the roughness factor. These influences are expressed in the formula

h_f = Friction head = $f \dfrac{L}{d} \dfrac{V^2}{2g}$

Where f = roughness factor
L = length of pipe
d = diameter
$\dfrac{V^2}{2g}$ = velocity head

Tables are available for the value of f, which varies with both V and d in this formula. The value of f is fractional, varying from .04 for small V and d to .01 for large values of V and d. Another formula derived from this basic one expresses the roughness factor as a whole number known as the C value in the Hazen & Williams formula. Tables and a special slide rule have been developed for solving pipe problems by this formula. The value of C varies from 140 for very smooth large pipe to a low of 40 or less for badly corroded or dirty pipe. See Figure 4 (Flow Chart for value "C" equals 100)

FIG. 4

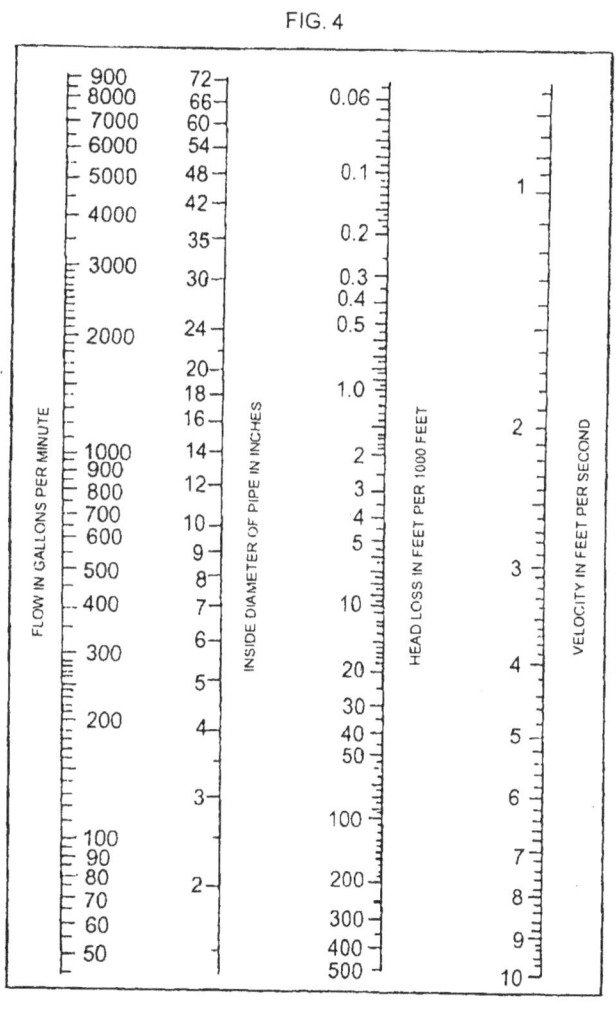

FLOW CHART
"C" 100
Based on the Hazen-Williams Formula

FIG. 5

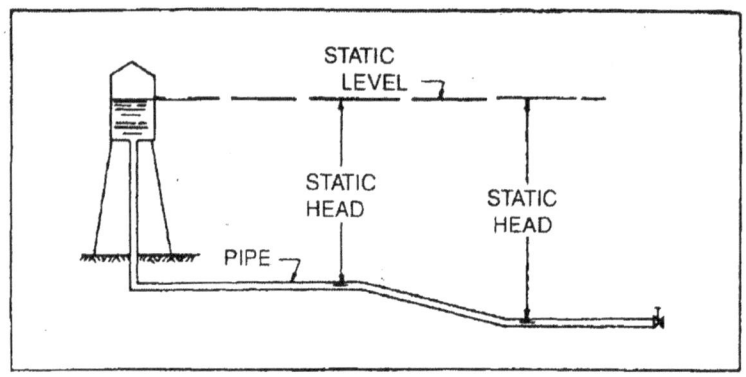

STATIC HEAD

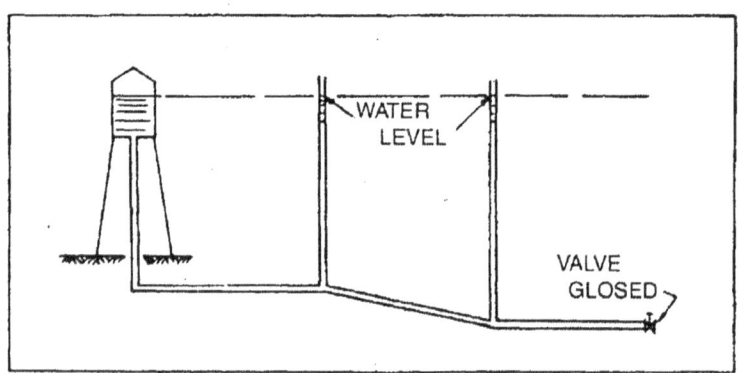

WATER LEVEL, NO FLOW IN PIPE

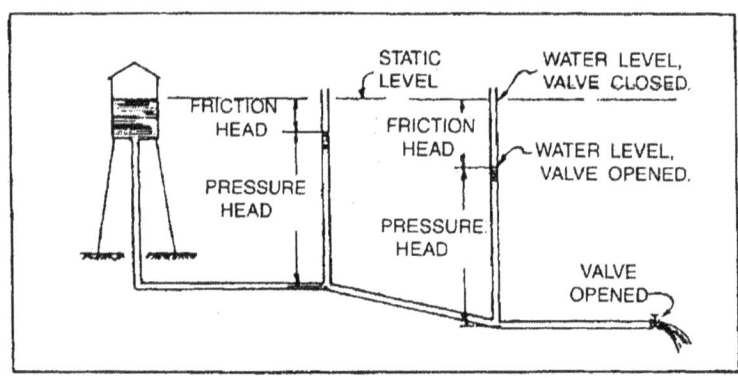

PRESSURE HEAD

If vertical open pipes are attached in a pipe line as shown in Figure 6, the water level in the pipes will stand at a level even with the elevation of the water in the storage tank. If the outlet valve is opened to permit water to flow, the level of the water in the vertical pipes will drop. The drop in the level or loss in head is the "friction head" and represents the energy lost by friction of the water flowing through the pipe.

Power Requirements for Pumping. Work must be done to move liquid against the total heads (H) indicated in Figures 8 and 9. The unit of work is the foot pound which is the amount of work or energy required to lift one pound a vertical distance of one foot. The common unit of power or rate of doing work is horsepower (hp). One horsepower is equal to 33,000 ft. lbs. per minute. In electrical units, one horsepower is equivalent to 746 watts.

The power required to drive a pump can be computed as follows:
Work done by the pump (or water horsepower) = Whp

$$Whp = \frac{lbs. \text{ of water raised per minute} \times H}{33,000}$$

$$= \frac{gpm \times 8.34 \times H}{33,000} = \frac{gpm \times H}{3,960}$$

Example: The sum of the elevation, pressure, velocity and friction heads is 100 ft. What would be the work done by the pump or the horsepower required (water horsepower) if 50 gallons per minute is pumped?

$$Whp = \frac{gal/min \times lbs/gal \times ft\,lbs/lb}{ft\text{-}lbs/min}$$

$$= 1.26 \text{ horsepower}$$

Since all the power delivered by the driving unit cannot be converted to useful work, the ratio between output and input is called pump efficiency.

Power required to drive the pump, or "brake horsepower" is computed by this formula:

$$bhp = \frac{whp}{pump\ eff} = \frac{gpm \times 8.33 \times H}{33,000 \times pump\ eff} = \frac{gpm \times H}{3960 \times pump\ eff}$$

If the efficiency (eff) of the pump is 65%

$$\frac{1.26}{0.65} = 1.94 \text{ horsepower must be delivered to the pump.}$$

Again since motors are not 100% efficient

$$Motor\ hp = \frac{whp}{pump\ eff \times motor\ eff}$$

$$= \frac{gpm \times H}{3960 \times pump\ eff \times motor\ eff}$$

If the motor efficiency is 80%

$$\frac{1.26}{0.65 \times 0.80} = 2.425$$

horsepower must be delivered to the motor in order to pump 50 gpm against a total head of 100 feet.

Flow in Open Channels. Flow in open conduits and in partially filled pipes is affected by the same factors as in pipes flowing full. These factors determine the slope required for an open channel to maintain a certain flow and velocity. The velocity, is actually determined by the slope of the water surface, but this is usually also the slope of the bottom of the channel and the water flows at a constant depth. The slope of the water surface is called the hydraulic gradient. The friction between water and the conduit walls depends upon the roughness of the surface, but the formula for it is different because the liquid now has a free surface and the length of contact depends upon the shape of the channel and the depth of flow. These factors are combined in the " hydraulic radius," which is found by dividing the cross-sectional area of the flowing water by the distance around that area along the walls of the channel. This distance is called the "wetted perimeter" of the channel (see Figure 3). Thus,

Hyd Rad $r = \dfrac{A}{W}$ feet (figure 3)

From these considerations, there has been developed the Chezy formula:

$v = C\sqrt{rs}$ feet per sec

where C = coefficient based on roughness, slope and value of r.

s = slope of the hydraulic gradient or water surface in open channels, usually expressed as ft per foot or ft per thousand feet. Thus, a slope of .004 indicates a drop of four feet in a thousand foot length.

The two principal formulas for determining C, the Kutter and the Manning formulas, depend largely upon values of "n" which is the coefficient of friction. These values have become quite well known for various types of surfaces and materials. Thus n=.013 is commonly used for design of vitrified tile pipes and for large diameter pre-cast concrete pipes.

Tables and diagrams have been published from which velocities, rates of flow and slopes can be determined for various diameters of pipes and values of "n".

Weirs. There are numerous ways of measuring flowing water, but three devices most commonly used are weirs, Venturi meters, and Parshall flumes.

The weir consists of rectangular opening or V notch opening with sharp edges. The weir is set vertically so that the flow passes over it tnd falls away from it.

FIG. 6

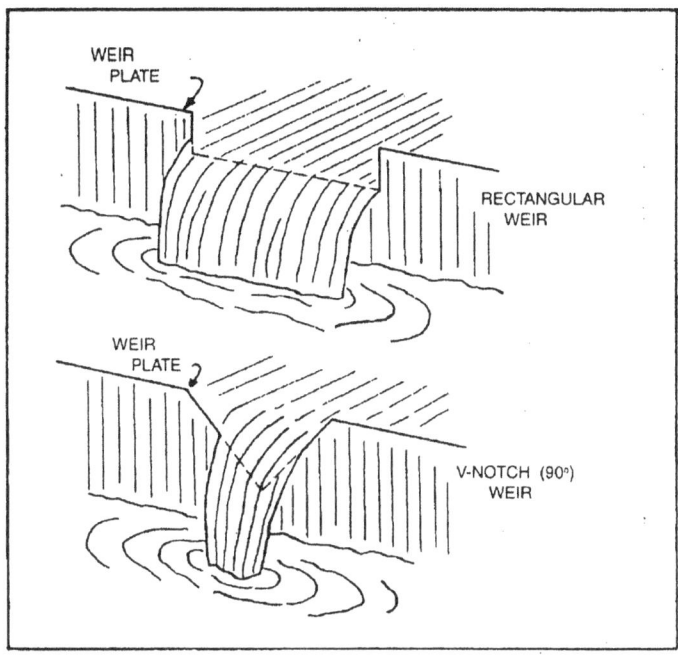

WEIRS

It is only necessary to measure the height of water above the crest of the weir at a point sufficiently upstream which avoids the curve of the water surface over the weir. In placing a weir, two points must be considered. First, the weir should be installed in the channel so that the velocity of the water approaching the weir is relatively low. Second, the "head" on the weir is not the depth of water as it passes over the weir proper but is the difference in elevation between the edge of the weir and the water upstream a short distance. In Figure 7 both of these points are illustrated. By using the head measurement the flow is determined from the formula:

Rate of flow $Q = 3.33 \, L \, h \sqrt{h}$ cfs (for a suppressed weir) and

$$Q = 3.33 \, (L - \frac{h}{5}) \, h \cdot \sqrt{h} \text{ cfs (for a contracted weir)}$$

where h = the height of horizontal water surface above crest of weir, L = horizontal length of weir.

The V notch weir is more accurate than the rectangular weir for small flows. For a 90 degree notch, the formula is: (Figure 8)

$Q = Ch^2 \sqrt{h}$ cfs where

C is a coefficient depending upon the material of the weir and the range of head. Values of C are given in handbooks for various materials and heads. The V notch weir is suitable for measuring flows from 10 to 3,500 gpm.

Another formula which may be used with a V notch weir with

90° angle is

$Q = 2.5 h^{5/2}$

where   Q = rate of discharge in cfs
        h = "head" on weir in feet (Figure 8)

Using the chart. (Figure 8)
If h is measured to be 0.20 feet then Q = .045cfs
= 21 gpm

FIG. 7

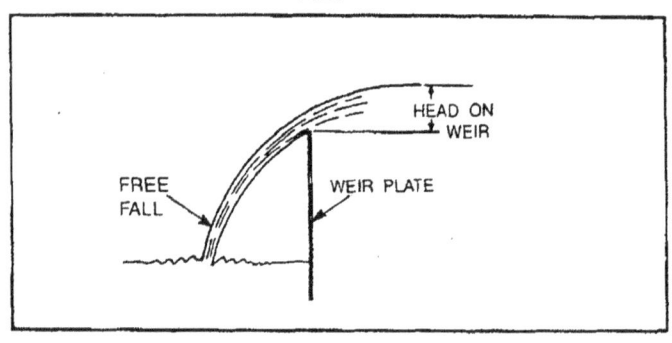

HEAD ON WEIR

FIG. 8

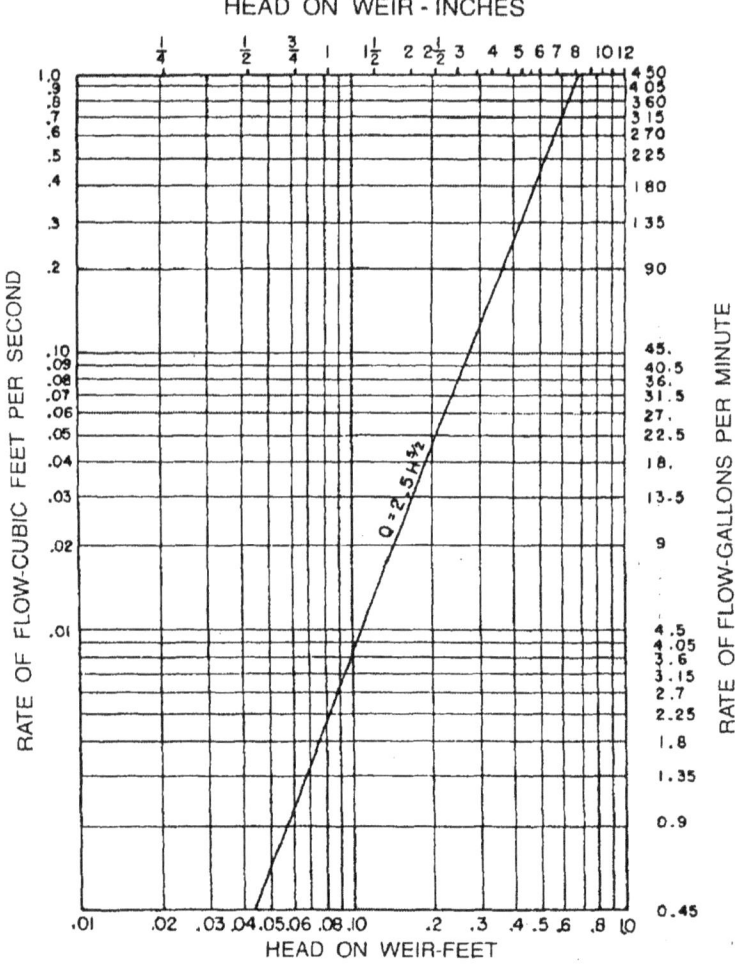

90° V-NOTCH WEIR FORMULA-Q=2.5H5/2

Venturi Meter. This type of flow measuring device is installed in a pipe line and consists of a throat carefully machined to a given inside diameter, a converging section which tapers from the pipe diameter to the throat and a diverging section from the throat to the pipe diameter. (See Figure 9) Taps are provided for measuring pressure head at points just before convergence and at the throat. The only measurement necessary to compute the flow is the difference in pressure head between the two tap points. Figure 10 shows graphically how pressure and velocity heads change in the Venturi Meter.

Parshall Flume. This type of flow measuring device was developed for measuring irrigation water in open channels where there may be debris and silt and where little loss of head can be permitted.

FIG. 9

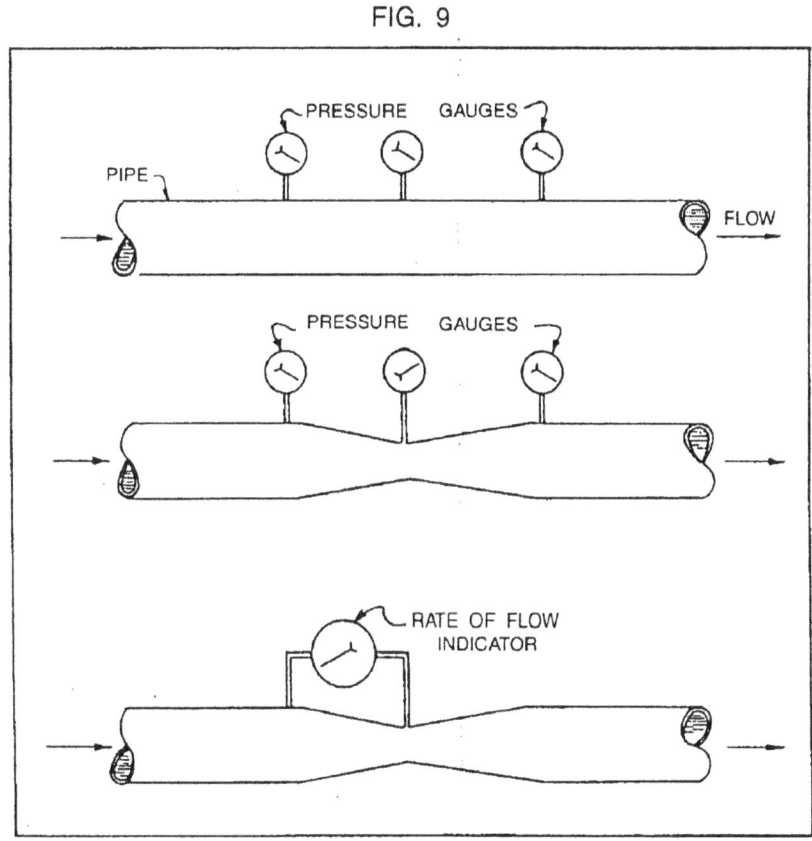

VENTURI TUBE

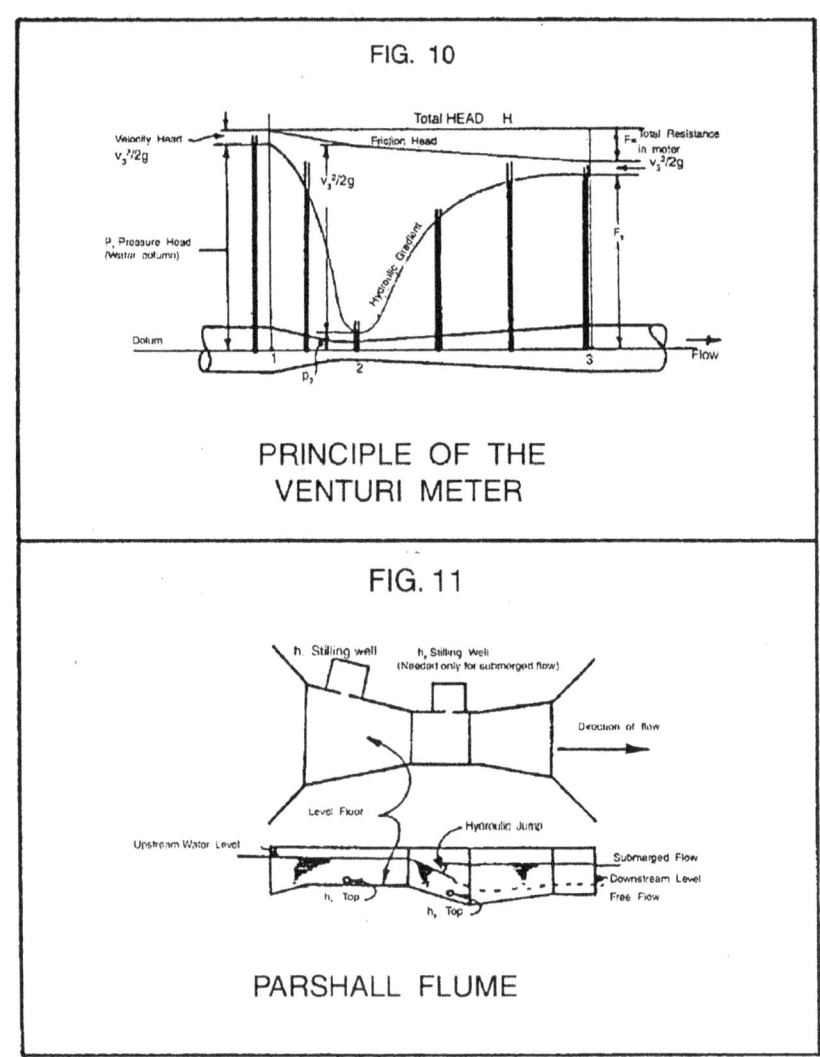

PRINCIPLE OF THE VENTURI METER

PARSHALL FLUME

In principle, the flume is similar to the Venturi meter. It has an inlet section with sides converging slowly to a throat of fixed dimensions and an outlet section diverging more rapidly to the original channel width. For the usual non-submerged condition only measurement of the depth of water at a fixed distance upstream from the throat is necessary to determine the flow. The flume may be constructed of almost any building material. For greatest accuracy the throat is often made to accurate dimensions from corrosion resistant metal. Figure 11 illustrates the Parshall Flume.

Magnetic Flow Meter. Bach of the previously described flow measuring devices involves an appreciable loss of head. A new development consists of a non-magnetic tube of the same internal diameter as the pipe line across which a magnetic field is established. Water flowing through the magnetic field produces a voltage proportional to the velocity. This voltage is converted by electrical and mechnical means to indicate and record the rate of flow.

An important operating and maintenance requirement of any flow measuring device is that pressure connecting stilling wells, floats and float tubes must be kept clean.

Rate of Flow Controllers. These are used to maintain flows at constant rates. Generally, all of the newer models depend on the Venturi principle to control a movable diaphragm or a pilot valve. This in turn actuates a main valve so as to control the size of an opening so that the desired amount of water is passed. Figure 12 shows a section through one type of controller. Actually this particular type of controller has two valves on the vertical stem and two valve seats but, for simplification, only one has been shown.

FIG. 12

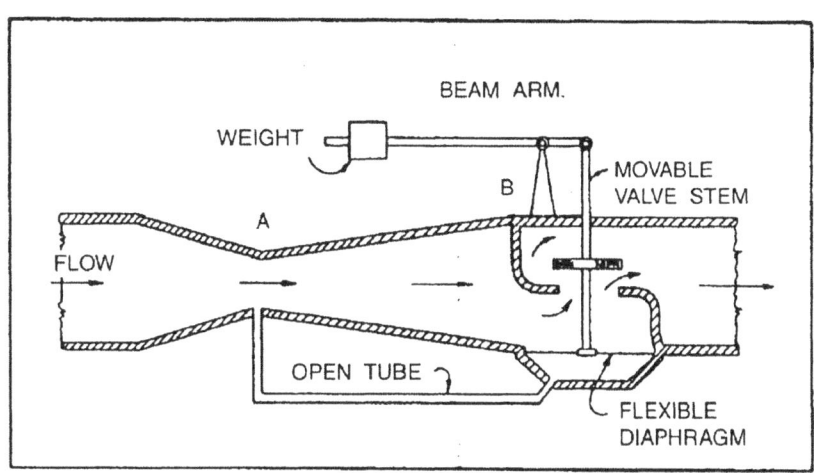

RATE OF FLOW CONTROLLER

The weight is placed at the desired point on the beam arm which corresponds to a certain rate of flow through the valve. At this particular rate of flow the unit pressure at point "A" will be less than the unit pressure at point "B". The unit pressure at point A is transferred, by means of the small open tube, to the compartment below the flexible diaphragm. The downward total pressure on the diaphragm is then greater than the upward total pressure. This results in a tendency for the valve stem to move downward. This tendency is counteracted by the weight at the proper location on the beam arm. At the desired rate of flow everything is in balance.

Pumps. Pumps have many uses in waterworks practice. Though there are many types, practically all water pumps may be classified into two general categories: displacement pumps and velocity pumps.

Displacement pumps employ some mechanical means (plungers, pistons, gears or cams) for forcing specific volumes of water through the units. Velocity pumps impart a high velocity to water and convert the velocity head into pressure head which forces the water through the apparatus.

Either type of pump raises the pressure on inlet side to a higher pressure on the outlet side. The specific means for bringing this about are quite different for the two types. Displacement type pumps, when operating at a particular speed, will take specific unit volumes of water and mechanically force the water out of the pump at a certain rate without regard to conditions beyond the pumping unit. When the resistance to flow beyond the pump is increased, the pressure will be increased. The only limit is the available horsepower and the physical strength of the discharge pipe or the pump. In other words, if something goes wrong on the discharge side of the pump to stop the flow, something may have to "give" and serious damage may result.

This is not the case with a velocity pump. A velocity pump merely causes the water to move with a very high velocity within the pump, usually in a circular direction. Under most conditions the amount of water which passes through the pump depends upon the resistance to flow on the discharge side. If the resistance is too great, for example if a valve is closed, the pump will continue to operate. This will produce the maximum pressure obtainable from that particular pump and speed of operation, but no wa.ter will pass through the pump. Probably no damage will result unless the pump is allowed to run until it over heats.

Displacement pumps may be subdivided into two general types-reciprocating and rotary. The reciprocating type, equipped with either plungers or pistons, includes direct acting, single or duplex, steam pumps, crank and flywheel pumps, and plunger pumps. Rotary pumps may be either cam, screw or gear types.

Velocity pumps may be subdivided into several general types including centrifugal, propeller, mixed flow, and turbine units.

Displacement pumps have certain advantages over velocity types. In displacement pumps the quantity of liquid delivered does not vary with the discharge head; they are easily primed; many act like air pumps and prime themselves when the suction head is low. They will operate smoothly on high suction lifts up to 25 feet or so. For high heads and small quantities the reciprocating pump is probably still the best. For many applications, the velocity pump, particularly the centrifugal pump, has displaced the reciprocating pump. Advantages of velocity pumps are lower initial cost, generally higher efficiency and easier installation and maintenance.

FIG. 13

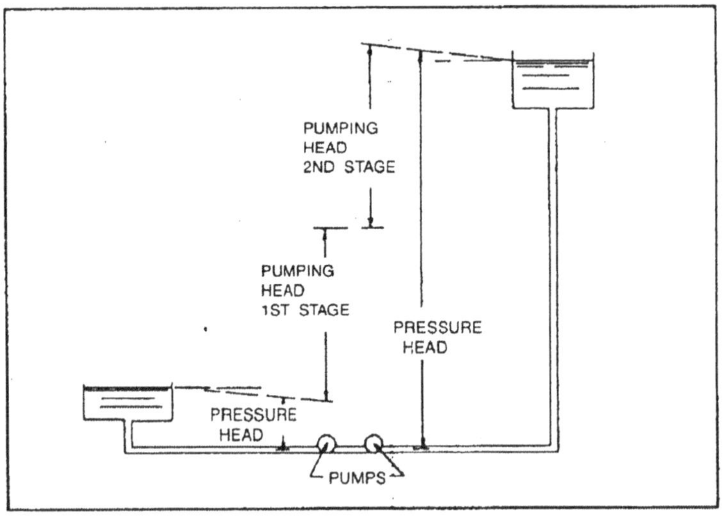

TWO STAGE PUMPING

Centrifugal Pumps. In the centrifugal pump, pressure is developed almost entirely by centrifugal force. Water enters at the center of an impeller which is rotated at high speed. Pressure is exerted and water moves to the outside. A specially shaped casing around the impeller discharges the water through a single opening to discharge line. There are various types of impellers. These include the open type which is commonly" used for pumping sewage and the closed type which is commonly used for pumping clear water. The water may enter at one side of the impeller in the side suction pump or on both sides in the double suction pump. Two or more pumps are used in stages when pumping against high heads. More than one stage can be obtained by using several impellers mounted on a single shaft. Also, two individual pumps can be mounted on a single shaft, driven by one motor, when the head conditions are high. The application of a multistage layout is illustrated in Figure 13.

Centrifugal pumps may be operated with'suction lifts. With all but minimum lifts, priming arrangements may be required.

The performance and operating characteristics are given on a pump curve sheet supplied by the manfacturer for each pump. On Figure 14 the curves show the discharge in gallons per minute (gpm) of the pump at various heads, the pump efficiency under different head-discharge conditions and the brake horsepower under various head-discharge conditions. As the head increases the discharge decreases until the shut-off head is reached.

FIG. 14

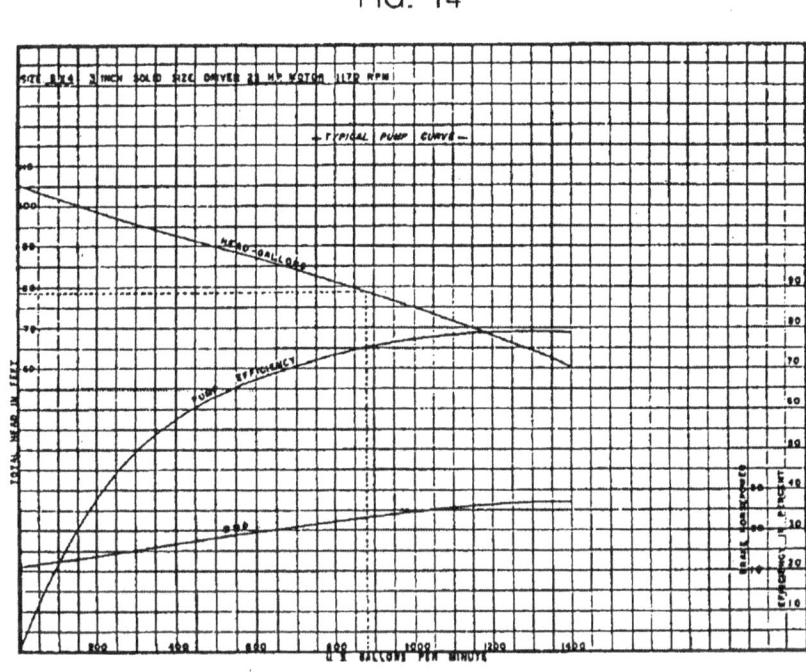

TYPICAL PUMP CURVE

On the pump curves, Figure 14, dotted lines indicate how values can be read from these curves. The pump for which these curves were prepared, when operated at 1170 revolutions per minute (rpm), will deliver 880 gpm at a total head of 79 feet. The brake horsepower (bhp) of the pump is 23 and the pump efficiency 75%. For a motor with an efficiency of 92 percent, the mhp (motor horsepower) should be 25. (Refer to power requirement for pumping). The shutoff head at which no water is delivered is 105 feet.

Large centrifugal pumps usually operate at slow speeds to minimize wear and maintenance costs.

The other velocity pumps have, in general, similar operating characteristics. They may vary considerably in construction and have different applications to water pumping problems. Propeller types are usually limited to low heads and the turbine type, with several stages, is most often used as a deep well pump.

18
Electricity

Electrical Units. The volt, as indicated in the introduction to this chapter, expresses electrical pressure just as feet, head or psi expresses water pressure. It is represented by the symbol "E", or sometimes emf, the abbreviation for electro-motive force.

For years, standard voltages have been 110, 220, 440, 2,200, 4,400 and 13,200. In water plants the voltage seldom exceeds 440. Higher voltages are used primarily for transmission lines. In some places the 110 and 220 standards have been replaced by 120 and 208. High voltages require proper equipment to prevent leaks (short circuits), and must be respected for personal-safety. Even pressures as low as 110 volts can be fatal.

Proper equipment should be used for the voltage furnished. If the average voltage is 120 on lighting circuits, then 120 and not 110 volt lamps should be used. They will last about three times as long.

For motors over 50 hp, voltages in excess of 440 is desirable. For 5 to 50 hp motors, economy dictates the use of 220 and 440 volts.

The ampere (amp) in electricity expresses the rate of flow, as gpm expresses water flows. In equations, the ampere is represented by I. Just as large pipes are required for large flows of water, large wire sizes are required for hea.vy amperages to keep down the losses due to resistance. Voltage drop due to resistance is similar to head loss due to friction in a pipe line.

Every electrical device has a current rating depending upon its design and resistance to flow. In motors the current varies with the load. Wires, fuses and switches are rated as to the current which they may safely carry. These ratings are fixed by a National Electric Code and should not be exceeded. An appliance rated for 25 amps should be protected by a fuse of that capacity to act as a safety valve. When carrying more than their rated capacity, wires and appliances overheat and may burn out or cause fires.

The ohm is the unit of electrical resistance. In electrical circ-cuits the loss of voltage, voltage drop, or loss in pressure is proportional to the resistance and the rate of current flow. Thus we have the simple relation known as Ohm's Law: E = RI. Values of resistance R for unit lengths or conductors of various sizes and materials are found in handbooks.

Direct and Alternating Currents. If the current flows first in one and then the other direction, it is known as alternating current and the number of times per second that it flows in each direction determines the number of cycles. A current that flows in any one direction 60 times per second is called 60 cycle. This is the standard for alternating current in this country.

Transformers are used to increase or decrease voltage. They consist of two stationary coils of wire insulated from each other but wound around a common iron core. Current flowing through the primary coil induces a current in the secondary with a voltage related to the number of turns of wire on the primary and secondary coils.

The Watt (W) is the unit of electrical power (P) and is most commonly used as a thousand watts or the kilowatt (KW). The mechanical unit of power or horsepower (HP) is equivalent to 746 watts. For rough computation it can be remembered that horsepower is approximately equivalent to three-quarters of a KW. Since the efficiency of many small motors is about 75%, one kilowatt in-put is roughly equivalent to one HP out-put.

For direct current:
P = E I. By substitution for E,
P = R I^2, or by substitution for I
$$P = \frac{E^2}{R}$$

From these expressions it can be seen that power varies directly with both current and voltage if resistance is not considered, but as the square of either one when resistance is considered.

The "kilowatt hour" is the unit of cost for electricity. As the term indicates, it is the average power requirement in KW multiplied by the time in hours over which it is used.

The "single phase circuit" or two-wire system shown in Figure 15 is the simplest circuit. Figure 15 shows a single phase, three-wire system that can furnish two voltages. The three phase (three-wire) is the standard system for large motors. There are two different arrangements of leads from generators or transformers known as delta, Figure 16 and Y shown in Figure 16. Lighting circuits can be taken off as shown. However, unless motors are small, it is better to separate power and lighting circuits to avoid dimming of the lights when motors start.

Circuit protection is provided by fuses enclosed in some type of flame-proof case. They are not always suitable and more complicated thermal relays, air circuit breakers or oil breakers, are required to allow a heavy flow of current for a short time before acting. To allow for a heavy flow, these devices are needed with large motors. A special oil is used in circuit breakers. No other should be used. When a circuit breaker operates frequently, cause should be investigated and corrective steps taken. Protective devices should never be "jumped."

Grounding is extremely important and must be maintained.

Most alternating current "motors" are either of the induction or synchronous type. Synchronous motor speed is determined by the formula,

$N = 120 F/P$ when

N = revolutions of motor per minute (rpm)

F = frequency, cycles per second

P = number of poles

For 60 cycles, $N = 7200/P$

Thus, the fewer the poles, the faster the speed and the smallest possible number of poles is two. Since there must be an even number of poles, the greatest synchronous speed possible for 60 cycles is 3,600 r.p.m. Other possible speeds are 1,800 r.p.m., 1,200 r.p.m., 900 r.p.m., 450 r.p.m. and so forth. The synchronous motor operates accurately at the given speed. This is valuable for clocks and timing devices. However, the synchronous motor has definite poles which must be excited or magnetized by some source of direct current. Synchronous motors have low starting torque (or power), which makes them unsatisfactory for many loads. For this reason it is fortunate that centrifugal pumps can usually be started with small load. Synchronous motors are sometimes used because of their favorable power factor on extremely large pumps.

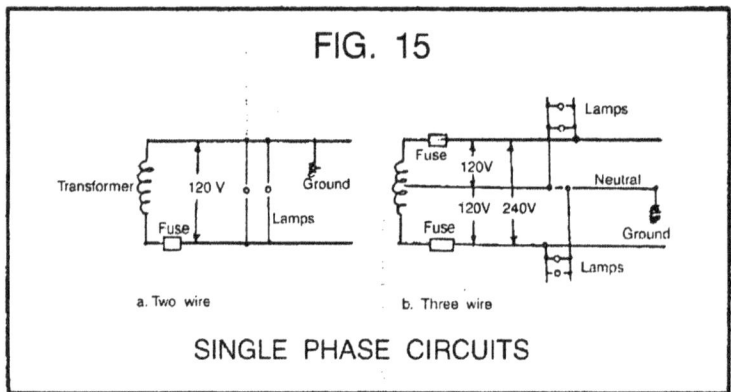

ELECTRIC CIRCUITS

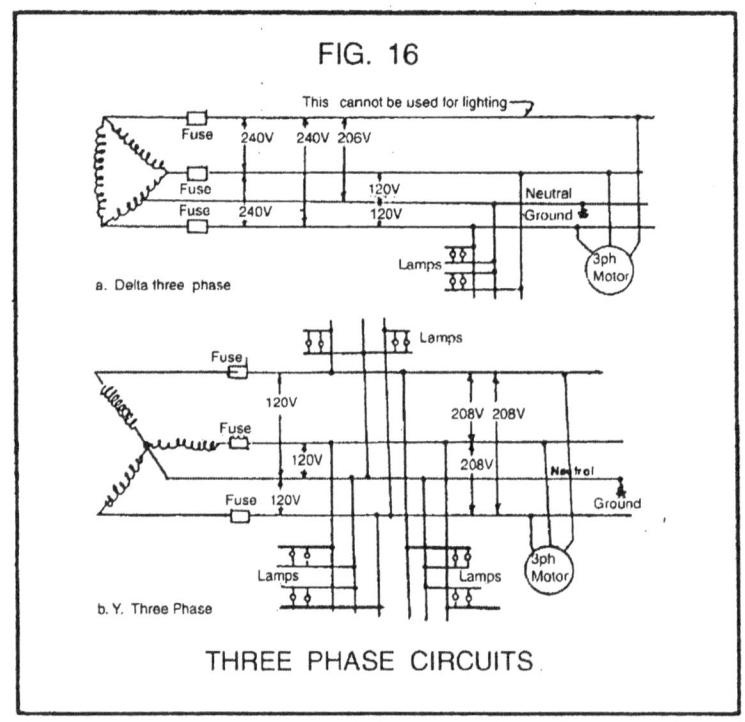

Induction motors. These motors have no poles which need excitation, and can be operated at variable speeds. They are sometimes called squirrel cage motors, because the rotor is made up of bars parallel to the shaft. Without a load, this type of motor will run at a speed close to the synchronous speed. As the load increases, the speed is reduced until at full load the speed is from 2% to 4% less than the synchronous speed. If the load is sufficiently increased, the motor will stop, or "pull out".

Induction motors require relatively small starting currents. Maintenance calls for keeping air ducts and windings of the motor clean. Oil in bearings should be flushed and changed at least once per year. The smaller motors require no special starting devices, and may be started directly across the line. Larger motors usually require reduced voltage for starting.

Variable speed is obtained in an induction motor by having a wound rotor, in whose circuit an external resistance may be added.

Thus a manufacturer can build a motor with external controls to give any speed and power which is required.

"Motor ratings", as well as the ratings for other electrical equipment, are based upon the temperature rise which will occur during operation continuously at normal full load and proper voltage. This rise is usually limited to 40 or 45 degrees centigrade. Thus, a motor may run hot to the touch and still be within its safe rating. A thermometer should be used to check the temperature on small motors. Large motors usually have temperature measuring devices built into them.

GLOSSARY OF BRIDGE ENGINEERING AND INSPECTION TERMS

	Page
Abutment ...... Aggregate	1
Allowable Unit Stress ...... Arch, Circular	2
Arch, Multi-Centered ...... Backstay	3
Backwall ...... Batter Pile	4
Bay ...... Berm	5
Blanket ...... Bracing	6
Bracing, (cont'd) ...... Brush Curb	7
Buckle ...... Cantilever Beam, Girder, or Truss	8
Cantilever Span ...... Check Analysis	9
Chord ...... Coefficient of Thermal Expansion	10
Cofferdam ...... Coping	11
Corbel ...... Covered Bridge	12
Cracking (reflection) ...... Curves in Plan and Profile	13
Cut ...... Diaphragm	14
Diaphragm Wall ...... Double Movable Bridge	15
Dowel ...... Drip Bead	16
Drip Hole ...... Expansion Dam	17
Expansion Joint ...... Falsework	18
Fascia ...... Fixed Bearing	19
Fixed Bridge ...... Foundation	20
Consolidated Soil Foundation ...... Girder Bridge	21
Girder Span ...... Guide Roller	22
Gusset ...... Hook Belt	23
Howe Truss ...... Joint	24
Keystone ...... Lateral Bracing	25
Lattice ...... Lock Device	26
Locking Mechanism ...... Pontoon Bridge	27
Retractile Draw Bridge ...... Overpass	28
Packing Ring ...... Pedestal Pier	29
Pile Pier or Bent ...... Pin Joint	30
Pin Packing ...... Priming Coat	31
Protection Fence ...... Reinforced Concrete Cantilever Wall	32
Rigid Frame Bridge ...... Rocker and Camshaft	33
Rolled Beams, Rolled Shapes ...... Sag Rod	34
Sash Brace ...... Shafts	35
Shear Lock ...... Skew Angle	36
Skewback ...... Span	37
Spandrel ...... Spreader	38
Springing Line ...... Stress	39
Stress (cont'd) ...... Sump	40
Superelevation ...... Sway Brace	41
Sway Frame ...... Toggle Joint	42
Tolerance ...... Truss	43
Truss Bridge ...... Warren Truss	44
Washer ...... Weep Hole	45
Weld ...... Wing Wall	46
Wing Wall (cont'd) ...... Working Stress	47

GLOSSARY OF BRIDGE ENGINEERING AND INSPECTION TERMS

A

Abutment. A substructure composed of stone, concrete, brick, or timber supporting the end of a single span or the extreme end of a multispan superstructure and, in general, retaining or supporting the approach embankment placed in contact therewith. (See also RETAINING WALLS, WING WALLS.)

The following types are now commonly used:

Cantilever Abutments. An abutment in which the stem or breast wall is fixed rigidly to the footing. The stem, acting as a cantilever beam transmits the horizontal earth pressure to the footing, which maintains stability by virtue of the dead weight of the abutment and of the soil mass resting on the rear portion, or heel, of the footing.

Cellular Abutment. An abutment in which the space between wings, breast wall, approach slab, and footings, instead of containing the approach fill, is hollow. This amounts to an R/C box or boxes comprising the abutment. On some bridges curtain walls are placed between the pier and abutment to simulate a cellular abutment.

Counterforted Abutment. An abutment which develops resistance to bending moment (or horizontal force) in the stem by use of counterforts. This permits the breast wall to be designed as a horizontal beam or slab spanning between counterforts, rather than as a vertical cantilever slab.

Gravity Abutment. A heavy abutment which resists the horizontal earth pressure by its own dead weight.

Integral Abutment. A small abutment cast monolithically with the end diaphragm of the deck. Although such abutments usually encase the ends of the deck beams and are pile supported, spread footings with a combination backwall and end diaphragm may also be used.

L-Abutment. A cantilever abutment with the stem flush with the toe of the footing, forming an L in cross section.

Spill-Thru Abutment. Consists essentially of two or more columns supporting a grade beam spanning the space between them. The approach embankment is retained only in part by the abutment since the embankment's sloped front and side portions extend with their normal slope to envelop the columns. Also called an arched abutment.

Shoulder Abutment. (*Full-Height Abutment.*) A cantilever abutment extending from the grade line of the road below to that of the road overhead. Usually set just off the shoulder.

Semi-Stub Abutment. Cantilever abutment founded part way up the slope, intermediate in size between a shoulder abutment and a stub abutment.

Straight Abutment. (*Trapezoidal or Block.*) An abutment whose stem and wings are in the same plane or whose stem is included within a length of retaining wall. In general, the stem wall is straight but will conform to the alignment of the retaining wall.

Stub Abutment. (*Perched Abutment, Dwarf Abutment.*) An abutment within the topmost portion of the end of an embankment or slope and, therefore, having a relatively small vertical height. While often engaging and supported upon piles driven through the underlying embankment or in-situ material, stubs may also be founded on gravel fill, the embankment, or natural ground itself.

Aggregate. The sand, gravel, broken stone, or combinations thereof with which the cementing material is mixed to form a mortar or concrete. The fine material used to produce mortar for stone and brick masonry and for the mortar component of concrete is commonly termed "fine aggregate" while the coarse material used in concrete only is termed "coarse aggregate."

Allowable Unit Stress. See STRESS.

Anchorage. The complete assemblage of members and parts whether composed of metal, masonry, wood or other material designed to hold in correct position the anchor span of a cantilever bridge, the end of a suspension span cable or a suspension span backstay; the end of a restrained beam, girder or truss span; a retaining wall, bulkhead, or other portion or part of a structure.

Anchor Span. The span which in conjunction with the uplift resisting anchorage device (if any) located at its outermost end, counterbalances and holds in equilibrium the fully cantilevered portion or arm extending in the opposite direction from the major point of support. See CANTILEVER BEAM, GIRDER, OR TRUSS.

Anchor Bolt. A bolt-like piece of metal commonly threaded and fitted with a nut, or a nut and washer at one end only, used to secure in a fixed position upon the substructure the end of a truss or girder, the base of a column, a pedestal, shoe, or other member of a structure. The end intended to engage the masonry may be formed in various ways depending somewhat upon the conditions attending its setting in final position. Among these are the following:

Hooked. Bent either cold or in a heated condition to form a hook-like anchorage. The hooked bolt is commonly built into the masonry preliminary to the placing of the member to be anchored and it may, therefore, be utilized to engage an anchor bar or other device imbedded in the masonry.

Ragged, Barbed or Fanged. Cut with a chisel to produce fin-like projections upon the surface.

Threaded. Shaped with a machine-cut thread. The thread anchorage is commonly supplemented by a nut, or a nut and anchor plate, when the bolt is to be built into the masonry instead of being set in a drilled hole.

Swedged. (*Notched, Hacked.*) Indented and bulged by swedging or nicked transversely and diagonally, or both, by cutting with a chisel.

Angle of Repose. (*Angle of Internal Friction.*) As applied to approach embankments or other earthwork construction: the batter or slope angle with the horizontal at which a given earth material will slide upon itself from a higher to a lower elevation. At all angles less than the angle of repose, the particles of earth are held in equilibrium by the forces of gravity and friction. Relatively slight variations in the quantity of contained moisture produce marked differences in the angle of repose. The inclined surface of a cut or of an embankment either naturally or artificially produced at the angle of repose is commonly described as being at "natural slope."

Anisotropy. The property of some engineering materials, such as wood, exhibiting different strengths in different directions.

Approach Slab. A heavy R/C slab placed on the approach roadway adjacent to and usually resting upon the abutment back wall. The function of the approach slab is to carry wheel loads on the approaches directly to the abutment, preventing the transfer of a horizontal dynamic force through the approach fill to the abutment stem.

Apron. A waterway bed protection consisting of timber, concrete, riprap, paving or other construction placed adjacent to substructure abutments and piers to prevent undermining by scour.

Arch. In general, any structure producing at its supports reactions having both vertical and horizontal components. However, this definition is not intended to include structures of the rigid frame type, although applicable thereto, but instead to apply only to those having throughout their length a curved shape, either actual or approximated.

Specific types of arches adapted to bridge construction derive their names either from the form of curve (or combination of curves assumed for the development of their intradosal surfaces), the support conditions, or their type of construction. The following constitute a portion of the types in use:

Elliptic Arch. One in which the intrados surface is a full half of the surface of an elliptical cylinder. This terminology is sometimes incorrectly applied to a multicentered arch. (An elliptic arch is fitted to stone masonry arches.)

Circular Arch. One in which the intrados surface is a portion of the surface of a right circular cylinder.

Multi-Centered Arch. One in which the intrados surface is outlined by two or more arcs having different radii by intersection tangentially and disposed symmetrically.

Open Spandrel Arch. An arch having spandrel walls with its spandrel unfilled. The arch ring receives its superimposed loads through these walls and, if necessary, through interior spandrel walls, tie or transverse walls, and/or interior columns.

A structure having the spandrel walls replaced by bays or panels with arches, lintel spans, or other constructions supporting the deck construction and these in turn supported by cross walls or columns resting upon the arch ring. See OPEN SPANDREL RIBBED ARCH.

Open Spandrel Ribbed Arch. A structure in which two or more comparatively narrow arch rings function in the place of an arch barrel. The ribs are rigidly secured in position by arch rib struts located at intervals along the length of the ring. The arch rings support a column type open spandrel construction sustaining the floor system and its loads.

Parabolic Arch. One in which the intrados surface is a segment of a symmetrical parabolic surface (suited to concrete arches).

Spandrel Arch. A stone or reinforced concrete arch span having spandrel walls to retain the spandrel fill or to support either entirely or in part the floor system of the structure when the spandrel is not filled.

Segmental Arch. An arch in which the intrados surface is less than half of the surface of a cylinder or cylindroid. Likewise it may take shape wherein any right section will show a parabolic curvature.

Two-Hinged Arch. An arch which is supported by a pinned connection at each support.

Three-Hinged Arch. An arch with end supports pinned and a third hinge (or pin) located somewhere near mid-span making the structure determinate.

Voussoir Arch. A hingeless arch with both supports fixed against rotation. Originally built of wedge-shaped stone blocks or voussoirs, the hingeless arch may also be built of concrete.

Arch Barrel. An arch ring that extends the width of the structure.

Arch Rib. An arch ring unit used in unfilled and open spandrel arch construction in reinforced concrete. Two or more relatively narrow arch ring units or sections support the columns of the bays or panels. The construction may involve a combination of arch ribs with spandrel walls providing an outward appearance akin to that of an unfilled spandrel arch.

One of the arched girders of a plate girder rib arch.

Arm. 1. The portion of a swing bridge or of a retractile draw bridge which forms the span or a portion of the span of the structure. 2. The rear or counterweight leaf of a bascule span. 3. The overhanging (or cantilever) portion of a cantilever bridge which supports the suspended span. 4. In statics, the perpendicular distance between the two parallel equal and opposite forces of a moment.

Armor. A secondary steel member installed to protect a vulnerable part of another member, e.g., steel angles placed over the edges of a joint.

Axle Load. The load borne by one axle of a traffic vehicle, a movable bridge, or other motive equipment or device and transmitted through a wheel or wheels to a supporting structure.

B

Back. See EXTRADOS.

Backfill. Material placed adjacent to an abutment, pier, retaining wall or other structure or part of a structure to fill the unoccupied portion of the foundation excavation.

Soil, usually granular, placed behind and within the abutment and wingwalls.

Backstay. The portion of the main suspension member of a suspension bridge extending between the tower and the anchorage. When this member continues over the towers from anchorage to anchorage, it does not support any portion of the bridge floor system which may be located between the tower and anchorage members of the structure.

A cable or chain attached at the top of a tower and extending to and secured upon the anchorage to resist overturning stresses exerted upon the tower by the suspension span attached to and located between towers.

Backwall. The topmost portion of an abutment above the elevation of the bridge seat, functioning primarily as a retaining wall with a live load surcharge. It may serve also as a support for the extreme end of the bridge deck and the approach slab.

Backwater. The water of a stream retained at an elevation above its normal level through the controlling effect of a condition existing at a downstream location such as a flood, an ice jam or other obstruction.

The increase in the elevation of the water surface above normal produced primarily by the stream width contraction beneath a bridge. The wave-like effect is most pronounced at and immediately upstream from an abutment or pier but extends downstream to a location beyond the body of the substructure part.

Balance Blocks. Blocks of cast iron, stone, concrete or other heavy weight material used to adjust the counterbalance of swing and lift spans.

Balance Wheel. (*Trailing Wheel.*) One of the wheels attached to the superstructure, normally having only a trailing contact upon a circular track surrounding the pivot of a center bearing swing bridge. These wheels maintain the proper balance and lateral stability of the superstructure by preventing excessive rocking or other motion due to wind pressures, shock from operating irregularities, or other causes. When correctly adjusted, a balance wheel will transmit only its own weight to the track and will revolve without load upon its axle.

Balancing Chain. See COUNTERBALANCING CHAIN.

Ballast. Filler material, usually broken stone or masonry, used either to stabilize a structure (as in filling a crib) or to transmit a vertical load to a lower level (as with a railroad track ballast).

Baluster. One of the column-like pieces composing the intermediate portion of a balustrade. Balusters may be varied in cross-sectional shape from round to square. See BALUSTRADE.

Balustrade. A railing composed of brick, stone or reinforced concrete located upon the retaining wall portion of an approach cut, embankment or causeway or at the outermost edge of the roadway or the sidewalk portion of a bridge to serve as a protection to vehicular and/or pedestrian traffic. Its major elements are: (1) plinth, (2) balusters, and (3) capping. However, the web portion may be built without openings instead of balustered or other open construction. See PARAPET.

Base Metal, Structure Metal, Parent Metal. The metal at and closely adjacent to the surface to be incorporated in a welded joint which will be fused, and by coalescence and interdiffusion with the weld will produce a welded joint.

Base Plate. A plate-shaped piece of steel, whether cast, rolled or forged, riveted upon or by other means made an integral part of the base portion of a column, pedestal or other member to transmit and distribute its load either directly or otherwise to the substructure or to another member.

Batten Plate. 1. A plate used to cover the joint formed by two abutting metal plates or shapes but ordinarily not considered as serving to transmit stress from one to the other. 2. A plate used in lieu of lacing to tie together the shapes comprising a built-up member. 3. A term sometimes used as synonymous with Stay Plates to indicate a plate in which the bar latticing or lacing of a bolted, riveted, or welded member terminates.

Batter. The inclination of a surface in relation to a horizontal or a vertical plane or occasionally in relation to an inclined plane. Batter is commonly designated upon bridge detail plans as so many inches to one foot. See RAKE.

Batter Pile. A pile driven in an inclined position to resist forces which act in other than a vertical direction. It may be computed to withstand these forces or, instead, may be used as a subsidiary part or portion of a structure to improve its general rigidity.

When driven and made fast upon the end of a pile bent or a piled pier located in a stream, river, or other waterway, it functions as a cutwater in dividing and deflecting floating ice and debris.

Bay. As applied to a stringer of multibeam structure, the area between adjacent stringers.

Bead. (*Run.*) A narrow continuous deposit of weld metal laid down in a single pass of fused filler metal.

Beam. 1. A simple or compound piece receiving and transmitting transverse or oblique stresses produced by externally applied loads, when supported at its end or at intermediate points and ends. The beam derives its strength from the development of internal bending or flexural stresses. 2. A rolled metal I-shaped or H-shaped piece. 3. An I-shaped piece or member composed of plates and angles or other structural shapes united by bolting, riveting or welding. In general, such pieces or members are described as built-up beams. These terms are applied to and define, in general terms only, variations in shape, size and arrangement of beam type members of reinforced concrete structures.

Reinforced Concrete Beam. Reinforced concrete beam is a construction wherein the tensile stresses, whether resulting from bending, shear, or combinations thereof produced by transverse loading, are by design carried by the metal reinforcement. The concrete takes compression (and some shear) only. It is commonly rectangular or Tee-shaped with its depth dimension greater than its stem width.

Reinforced Concrete T-Beam. Reinforced concrete T-beam derives its name from a similarity of shape to the letter "T," the head or topmost element of the letter consisting of a portion of the deck slab which is constructed integrally with the R/C beam stem.

Bearing Failure. Concerning the usual materials of construction, a crushing under extreme compressive load on an inadequate support; concerning soil, a shear failure in the supporting soil caused by excessively high pressures applied by a footing or pile.

Bearing. (*Fixed.*) A bearing which does not allow longitudinal movement.

Bearing Pad. A thin sheet of material placed between a masonry plate and the masonry bearing surface used to fill any voids due to imperfection of the masonry plate and bearing surface, to seal the interface, and to aid in even distribution of loads at the interface. The bearing pads may be made of alternating layers of red lead and canvas, of sheet lead, or of preformed fabric pads.

Bearing Seat. Top of masonry supporting bridge bearing.

Bearings. (*Live Load, Front Load, Outer.*) Live load bearings are a class of special bearings or supports installed on movable swing and bascule spans. These are engaged when the bridge is in the closed position taking the load off the trunnions and center pivot and preventing the outer end of the lift span from hammering on the rest pier under live load. Front load bearings are live load bearings placed on the support pier of a bascule bridge, and outer bearings are those on swing span and bascule rest piers.

Bed Rock. (*Ledge Rock.*) A natural mass formation of igneous, sedimentary, or metamorphic rock material either outcropping upon the surface, uncovered in a foundation excavation, or underlying an accumulation of unconsolidated earth material.

Bench Mark. A point of known elevation.

Bent. A supporting unit of a trestle or a viaduct type structure made up of two or more column or column-like members connected at their topmost ends by a cap, strut, or other member holding them in their correct positions. This connecting member is commonly designed to distribute the superimposed loads upon the bent, and when combined with a system of diagonal and horizontal bracing attached to the columns, the entire construction functions somewhat like a truss distributing its loads into the foundation.

When piles are used as the column elements, the entire construction is designated a "pile bent" or "piled bent" and, correspondingly, when those elements are framed, the assemblage is termed a "frame bent."

Berm. (*Berme.*) The line, whether straight or curved, which defines the location where the top surface of an approach embankment or causeway is intersected by the surface of the side slope. This term is synonymous with "Roadway Berm."

A horizontal bench located at the toe of slope of an approach cut, embankment or causeway to strengthen and secure its underlaying material against sliding or other displacement into an adjacent ditch, borrow pit, or other artificial or natural lower lying area.

Blanket. A protection against stream scour placed adjacent to abutments and piers and covering the stream bed for a distance from these structures considered adequate for the stream flow and stream bed conditions. The stream bed covering commonly consists of a deposit of stones of varying sizes which, in combination, will resist the scour forces. A second type consists of a timber framework so constructed that it can be ballasted and protected from displacement by being loaded with stones or with pieces of wrecked concrete structures or other adaptable ballasting material.

Boster. A block-like member composed of wood, metal, or concrete used to support a bearing on top of a pier cap or abutment bridge seat. It may adjust bearing heights and avoid constructing the bridge seat to the crown of the roadway, provide an area that may be ground to a precise elevation, or raise a bearing above moisture and debris that may collect on the bridge seat. See also BRIDGE PAD and BRIDGE SEAT PEDESTAL.

Bolted Joint. See RIVETED JOINT.

Bond. 1. In reinforced concrete, the grip of the concrete on the reinforcing bars, thereby preventing slippage of the bars. 2. The mechanical bond resulting from irregularities of surface produced in the manufacturing operations is an important factor in the strength of a reinforced concrete member. For plain round bar reinforcement, it is the difference between the force required to produce initial slip and the ultimate, producing failure. "Deformed" bars utilize this mechanical bond in conjunction with the surface bond. 3. The mechanical force developed between two concrete masses when one is cast against the already hardened surface of the other.

Bond Stress. A term commonly applied in reinforced concrete construction to the stress developed by the force tending to produce movement or slippage at the interface between the concrete and the metal reinforcement bars or other shapes.

Bowstring Truss. A general term applied to a truss of any type having a polygonal arrangement of its top chord members conforming to or nearly conforming to the arrangement required for a parabolic truss.

A truss having a top chord conforming to the arc of a circle or an ellipse. See PARABOLIC TRUSS.

Box Beam. A rectangular-shaped precast, and usually prestressed, concrete beam. These beams may be placed side by side, connected laterally, and used to form a bridge deck, with or without a cast-in-place slab or topping. In such cases, the beam units act together similar to a slab. Where a C-I-P slab is used and the units are spread, they act as beams.

Box Girder (concrete). A large concrete box-shaped beam, either reinforced or prestressed, usually multi-celled with several interior webs. The bottom slab of the girder serves as a flange only, while the top slab is both a flange and a transverse deck slab.

Box Girder (steel). A steel beam or girder, with a rectangular or trapezoidal cross section, composed of plates and angles or other structural shapes united by bolting, riveting, or welding, and having no interior construction except stiffeners, diaphragms, or other secondary bracing parts.

Recently, large steel multi-cell boxes with interior webs have been used as have composite steel box girders in which the concrete slab forms the top side of the box.

Bracing. A system of tension or of compression members, or a combination of these, forming with the part or parts to be supported or strengthened a truss or frame. It transfers wind, dynamic, impact, and vibratory stresses to the substructure and gives rigidity throughout the complete assemblage. In general, the bracing of a girder or of a truss span employs:

(1) A system of horizontal bracing in the planes of the top and bottom flanges or chords, designated according to its location, the top flange, top chord, top or overhead lateral brac-

ing, and the bottom flange, bottom chord or lower lateral bracing.

(2) Cross or X-bracing when placed transversely in vertical planes between beams and stringers and having diagonal members crossed, sometimes termed "Cross Frame." It functions as a diaphragm.

(3) Sway or buck bracing when placed transversely in vertical or nearly vertical planes between trusses. The term "overhead bracing," when applied here, is more appropriate than when applied to the top chord lateral bracing.

(4) Portal bracing consisting of a system of struts, ties and braces placed in the plane of the end posts of the trusses. Portal bracing may be in the plane of one flange of the end posts and described as a "single plane" portal or it may engage both flanges and be described as a "box portal." Without regard to its shape or details the entire portal bracing member is frequently designated as a "portal."

In general, the bracing of trestle and viaduct bents and towers employs:

(1) Transverse bracing engaging the columns of bents and towers in planes located either perpendicular or slightly inclined and transversely to the bridge alignment.

(2) Longitudinal bracing engaging the columns of bents and towers in planes located either perpendicular or slightly inclined and lengthwise with the bridge alignment.

(3) Horizontal bracing engaging the strut members of the transverse and longitudinal bracing of towers. Commonly this bracing is located in a horizontal position and is supported against sagging by vertical hangers or ties.

Bracket. A projecting support or brace-like construction fixed upon two intersecting members to function: (1) as a means of transferring reactions or shear stress from one to the other, or (2) to strengthen and render more rigid a joint connection of the members, or (3) to simply hold one member in a fixed position with relation to the other.

Breast Wall. (*Face Wall, Stem.*) The portion of an abutment between the wings and beneath the bridge seat. The breast wall supports the superstructure loads, and retains the approach fill.

Brick Veneer. See STONE FACING.

Bridge. A structure providing a means of transit for pedestrians and/or vehicles above the land and/or water surface of a valley, arroyo, gorge, river, stream, lake, canal, tidal inlet, gut or strait; above a road, highway, railway or other obstruction, whether natural or artificial.

In general, the essential parts of a bridge are: (1) the substructure consisting of its abutments and pier or piers supporting the superstructure, (2) the superstructure slab, girder, truss, arch or other span or spans supporting the roadway loads and transferring them to the substructure, and (3) the roadway and its incidental parts functioning to receive and transmit traffic loads.

Bridge (composite). A bridge whose concrete deck acts structurally with longitudinal main carrying members.

Bridge (indeterminate). A structure in which forces in the members cannot be determined by static equations alone.

Bridge (prestressed). A bridge whose main carrying members are made of prestressed concrete.

Bridge Pad. The raised, levelled area upon which the pedestal, shoe, sole, plate or other corresponding element of the superstructure takes bearing by contact. Also called Bridge Seat Bearing Area.

Bridge Seat. The top surface of an abutment or pier upon which the superstructure span is placed and supported. For an abutment it is the surface forming the support for the superstructure and from which the backwall rises. For a pier it is the entire top surface.

Bridge Site. The selected position or location of a bridge.

Bridging. A carpentry term applied to the cross-bracing, nailed or otherwise, fastened between wooden floor stringers, usually at the one-third span points, to increase the rigidity of the floor construction and to distribute more uniformly the live load and minimize the effects of impact and vibration.

Brush Curb. A narrow curb, 9 inches or less in width, which prevents a vehicle from brushing against the railing or parapet.

Buckle. To fail by an inelastic change in alignment (usually as a result of compression).

Buffer. (*Bumper.*) A mechanism designed to absorb the concussion or impact of a moving superstructure or other moving part when it swings, rises or falls to its limiting position of motion.

Built-Up Column. (*Built-Up Girder.*) A column, beam or girder, as the case may be, composed of plates and angles or other structural shapes united by bolting, riveting or welding to render the entire assemblage a unit. A built-up girder is commonly described as a plate girder.

Bulkhead. 1. A retaining wall-like structure commonly composed of driven piles supporting a wall or a barrier of wooden timbers or reinforced concrete members functioning as a constraining structure resisting the thrust of earth or of other material bearing against the assemblage. 2. A retaining wall-like structure composed of timber, steel, or reinforced concrete members commonly assembled to form a barrier held in a vertical or an inclined position by members interlocking therewith and extending into the restrained material to obtain the anchorage necessary to prevent both sliding and overturning of the entire assemblage.

Bumper. See BUFFER.

Buttress. A bracket-like wall, of full or partial height, projecting from another wall. The buttress strengthens and stiffens the wall against overturning forces applied to the opposite face by virtue of its depth in the direction of the loads. A buttress may be either integral with or independent of, but must be in contact with, the wall it is designed to reinforce. All parts of a buttress act in compression.

Buttressed Wall. See RETAINING WALL.

Butt Weld. A weld joining two abutting surfaces by depositing weld metal within an intervening space. This weld serves to unite the abutting surfaces of the elements of a member or to join members or their elements abutting upon or against each other.

C

Cable. One of the main suspension members of a suspension type bridge. Its function is to receive the bridge floor loads and transmit them to the towers and anchorages. See SUSPENSION BRIDGE.

Cable Band. The attachment device serving to fix a floor suspender upon the cable of a suspension bridge. In general this device consists of a steel casting provided with bolts or other appliances to securely seize it upon the cable and prevent the bank from slipping from its correct location.

Camber. The slightly arched form or convex curvature, provided in a single span or in a multiple span structure, to compensate for dead load deflection and to secure a more substantial and aesthetic appearance than is obtained when uniformly straight lines are produced. In general, a structure built with perfectly straight lines appears slightly sagged. This optical illusion is unsatisfactory and is most manifest in relatively long structures over rivers or other water areas.

The superelevation given to the extreme ends of a swing span during erection to diminish the deflection or "droop" of the arms when in open position-cantilevered from the center bearing. The decreased deformation below the normal position reduces the energy required to raise the ends in the closed position to permit the arms to function as simple spans.

Cantilever. A projecting beam, truss, or slab supported at one end only.

Cantilever Abutment. See ABUTMENT.

Cantilever Bridge. A general term applying to a bridge having a superstructure of the cantilever type.

Cantilever Beam, Girder, or Truss. A girder or truss having its members or parts so arranged that one or both of its end portions extend beyond the point or points of support. In general, it may have the following forms: (1) two projecting ends counterbalanced over a center support; (2) a projecting end counterbalanced in part by a portion extending beyond the point of support in the opposite direction, and having at its end an uplift resisting anchorage to complete the condition of equilibrium or, instead, the counterbalancing portion or anchor arm may in itself be adequate to counteract the projecting portion; (3) two projecting ends with an intermediate suspended portion, whose weight is completely counterbalanced by the anchor spans and/or anchorages. The end portions may or may not be alike in design.

Cantilever Span. A superstructure span of a cantilever bridge composed of two cantilever arms or of a suspended span connected with one or two cantilever arms.

Cap. (*Cap Beam, Cap Piece.*) The topmost piece or member of a viaduct, trestle, or frame bent serving to distribute the loads upon the columns and to hold them in their proper relative positions.

The topmost piece or member of a pile bent in a viaduct or trestle serving to distribute the loads upon the piles and to hold them in their proper relative positions. See PIER CAP and PILE CAP.

Capillary Action. The process by which water is drawn from a wet area to a dry area through the pores of a material.

Capstone. 1. The topmost stone of a masonry pillar, column or other structure requiring the use of a single capping element. 2. One of the stones used in the construction of a stone parapet to make up its topmost or "weather" course. Commonly this course projects on both the inside and outside beyond the general surface of the courses below it.

Carnegie Beam. See WIDE FLANGE.

Catch Basin. A receptacle, commonly box-shaped and fitted with a grilled inlet and a pipe outlet drain designed to collect the rain water and floating debris from the roadway surface and retain the solid material so that it may be removed at intervals. Catch basins are usually installed beneath the bridge floor or within the approach roadway with the grilled inlet adjacent to the roadway curb.

Catchment Area. See DRAINAGE AREA.

Catwalk. A narrow walkway for access to some part of a structure.

Cement Paste. The plastic combination of cement and water that supplies the cementing action in concrete.

Cement Matrix. The binding medium in a mortar or concrete produced by the hardening of the cement content of the mortar, concrete mixture of inert aggregates, or hydraulic cement and water.

Center Bearing. The complete assemblage of pedestal castings, pivot, discs, etc., functioning to support the entire dead load of a swing span when the end lifts are released or the span is revolving to "open" or to "closed position."

Center Discs. The assemblage of bronze, steel or other metal discs enclosed in the pivot of a center bearing swing span to reduce the frictional resistance in the operation of the span.

Center Lock. A locking device that transmits shear at the centerline of a double leaf bascule or double swing span bridge. This eliminates deflection and vibration at the center of the span.

Center Wedges. On a swing bridge, the assembly of pedestals and wedges located upon the pivot pier beneath the loading girder and operated mechanically to receive the pivot pier live loads and transmit them direct to the substructure, thus relieving the pivot casting from all, or nearly all, live load stress.

Centering. The supporting structure upon which the arch ring is constructed. This commonly consists of timber or metal framework having its topmost portion shaped to conform with the arch intrados and finished by covering with lagging or with bolsters, the latter being spaced to permit treatment of the mortared joints of stone masonry.

Support for formwork for any slab, beam, or other generally horizontal concrete structure.

Centering Device. The mechanical arrangement or device which guides the span of a bascule or a vertical lift span to its correct location upon its supports when being moved from open to closed position.

Channel Profile. Longitudinal section of a channel.

Chase. A channel, groove or elongated recess built into a structure surface for 1) the reception of a part forming a joint or (2) the installation of a member or part of the structure.

Check Analysis. See LADLE ANALYSIS.

Chord. In a truss, the upper and the lower longitudinal members, extending the full length and carrying the tensile and compressive forces which form the internal resisting moment, are termed chords. The upper portion is designated the upper, or top, chord and correspondingly the lower portion is designated the lower, or bottom, chord. The chords may be paralleled, or the upper one may be polygonal or curved (arched) and the lower one horizontal, or both may be polygonal. In general, the panel points of polygonal top chords are designed to follow the arc of a parabola and are, therefore, truly parabolic chords. Polygonal shaped chords are commonly described as "broken chords."

Chord Members. Trusses are commonly divided lengthwise into panels, the length of each being termed a panel length. The corresponding members of the chords are described as upper, or top, chord members and lower, or bottom, chord members.

Clearance. The unobstructed space provided: (1) in a through or half-through truss or a through plate girder type bridge, and (2) upon a deck truss or girder type bridge for the free passage of vehicular and pedestrian traffic. Clearance is measured in vertical and horizontal (lateral) dimensions and may or may not be determined or regulated by standard (clearance diagram) requirements. Vertical clearance for vehicles is measured above the elevation of the floor surface at its crown dimension while horizontal clearance is commonly measured from or with reference to the edge of travelway.

The unobstructed space provided below a bridge superstructure for (1) the passage of a river or stream with its surface burden of floating debris; (2) the passage of navigation craft commonly designated "clear headway" and (3) the passage of vehicular and pedestrian traffic. This form of clearance is frequently designated "under-clearance" to differentiate it from the provision for the requirements of the transportation service supported by the structure.

The space allowed for (1) the tolerance permitted in the dimensions of structural shapes; (2) the free assembling and adjustment of the elements of members or the members of a structure; and (3) the variations in dimensions incident to workmanship, temperature changes and minor irregularities. Among shop and field workers this condition is sometimes described as "the go and come" or "the play" allowance.

Clear Headway. (*Headway.*) The vertical clearance beneath a bridge structure available for the use of navigation. See CLEARANCE. In tidal waters headway is measured above mean high tide elevation.

Clear Span. The unobstructed space or distance between the substructure elements measured, by common practice, between faces of abutments and/or piers. However, when a structure is located upon a stream, river, tidal inlet or other waterway used by navigation, the clear span dimension is measured at mean low water elevation and may be the distance between guard or fender piers, dolphins or other constructions for the protection of navigation.

Clevis. A forked device used to connect the end of a rod upon a gusset plate or other structural part by means of a pin. It commonly consists of a forging having a forked end arranged to form two eyes or eyelets for engaging a pin and a nut-like portion, constructed integrally therewith, for engaging the correspondingly threaded end of a rod. However, the forked end (clevis) may form an integral portion of a rod without provision for adjustment of its length. An adjustable member having a fixed clevis at one end may be fitted with a thread and nut at its opposite end while one having fixed clevises at its ends may be fitted with either a sleeve nut or a turnbuckle in its midlength portion. Lateral bracing and tie-rod diagonals on old steel trusses often use clevises.

Clevis Bar. A member consisting of a rod having upset threaded ends fitted with clevises for engaging end connection pins. To render a clevis bar adjustable after assembling in a structure its ends are right and left threaded, or it may be constructed with a sleeve nut or a turnbuckle within its length, the end threads upon each of its sections being right and left hand and its clevises forged integrally with the body sections of the bar.

Clip Angle. See CONNECTION ANGLE.

Coefficient of Thermal Expansion. The unit strain produced in a material by a change of one degree in temperature.

Cofferdam. In general, an open box-like structure constructed to surround the area to be occupied by an abutment, pier, retaining wall or other structure and permit unwatering of the enclosure so that the excavation for the preparation of a foundation and the abutment, pier, or other construction may be effected in the open air. In its simplest form, the dam consists of interlocking steel sheet piles. See SHEET PILE COFFERDAM.

Collision Strut. A redundant member intended to reinforce the inclined end post of a through truss against damage from vehicular traffic. It joins the end post at a height above the roadway conceived to be the location of collision contact and, commonly, connects it with the first interior bottom chord panel point. The use of collision struts in highway bridges is limited.

Cold Work. The forming, such as rolling or bending, of a material at ordinary room temperature. Also applied to such deformation of steel elements in service under concentrated forces.

Column. A general term applying to a member resisting compressive stresses and having, in general, a considerable length in comparison with its transverse dimensions. This term is sometimes used synonymously for "post."

A member loaded primarily in compression. See also STRUT, POST, PILLAR.

Composite Joint. A joint in which the strength, rigidity or other requisites of its function are developed by combined mechanical devices, or by a fusion weld in conjunction with one or more mechanical means or appliances. The uncertain functioning of joints of this type makes their use undesirable.

Compound Roller. A roller consisting of a large solid cylinder at the center surrounded by a nest of smaller solid rollers having circular spacing bars engaging their ends and enveloped in a large hollow cylinder which forms the exterior surface of the assemblage. The large roller is commonly bored throughout its length at its center to permit observation of its interior material.

Compression (inelastic). Compression beyond the yield point.

Concrete. A composite material consisting essentially of a binding medium within which are embedded particles or fragments of a relatively inert mineral filler. In portland cement concrete, the binder or matrix, either in the plastic or the hardened state, is a combination of portland cement and water. The filler material, called aggregate, is generally graded in size from fine sand to pebbles or stones which may, in some concrete, be several inches in diameter.

Concrete is used in conjunction with stone fragments or boulders, of "one man" size or larger, imbedded therein to produce "cyclopean" or "rubble" concrete.

Connection Angle. (*Clip Angle.*) A piece or pieces of angle serving to connect two elements of a member or two members of a structure.

Consolidation. The time-dependent change in volume of a soil mass under compressive load caused by pore-water slowly escaping from the pores or voids of the soil. The soil skeleton is unable to support the load by itself and changes structure, reducing its volume and usually producing vertical settlements.

Continuous Girder. A general term applied to a beam or girder constructed continuously over one or more intermediate supports.

Continuous Spans. A beam, girder, or truss type superstructure designed to extend continuously over one or more intermediate supports.

Continuous Truss. A truss having its chord and web members arranged to continue uninterruptedly over one or more intermediate points of support, i.e., having three or more points of support.

Continuous Weld. A weld extending throughout the entire length of a joint.

Coping. A course of stone laid with a projection beyond the general surface of the masonry below it and forming the topmost portion of a retaining wall, pier, abutment, wingwall, etc. In general, the top surface is battered (washed) to prevent accumulation of rain or other moisture thereon.

A course of stone capping the curved or V-shaped extremity of a pier, providing a transition to the pier head proper. When so used it is commonly termed the "starling coping," "nose coping," the "cut-water coping" or the "pier extension coping."

In concrete construction the above terms are used without change.

Corbel. A piece or part constructed to project from the surface of a wall, column or other portion of a structure to serve as a support for a brace, short, beam or other member.

A projecting course or portion of masonry serving: (1) as a support for a superimposed member or members of a structure, or (2) as a part of the architectural treatment of a structure. In stone and brick masonry construction, this form of corbel is termed a "corbel course" implying greater length than that of a simple corbel.

Corrosion. The general disintegration and wasting of surface metal or other material through oxidation, decomposition, temperature, and other natural agencies.

Corrosion (electrolytic). Corrosion resulting from galvanic action.

Cotter Bolt. A bolt having a head at one end and near the opposite end a round hole or a hexagonal slot fitted with a cotter pin in the former or a tapered wedge in the latter. A cotter pin is usually formed by bending a piece of half-round rod to form a loop eye and a split body permitting its end to be splayed, thus holding it in position while a cotter wedge may be split for the same purpose, but either of these locking devices may be undivided and only bent sharply to prevent withdrawal. Cotter bolts are commonly fitted with one or two washers.

A cotter bolt fitted with a key is sometimes termed a "key bolt."

Counter. A truss web member which functions only when the span is partially loaded and shear stresses are opposite in sign to the normal conditions. The dead load of the truss does not stress the counter. See WEB MEMBERS.

Counterbalancing Chain. (*Balancing Chain.*) The chains made a part of the operating equipment of a vertical lift bridge to function as a weight counteracting the varying weight of the supporting cables incidental to the movements of the span.

Counterfort. A bracket-like wall projecting from another wall to which it adds stability by being integrally built with or otherwise securely attached to the side to which external forces are applied tending to overturn it. A counterfort, as opposed to a buttress, acts entirely to resist tensile and bending stresses. It may extend from the base either part or all the way to the top of the wall it is designed to reinforce.

Counterforted Wall. See RETAINING WALL.

Counterweight. A weight placed in position so as to counter balance the weight of a movable part (such as bascule leaf or vertical lift span).

Counterweight Well. (*Tail Pit.*) The enclosed space located beneath the bridge floor at the approach end to accommodate the counterweight and its supporting frame during the opening-closing cycle of the movable span of certain types of bascule bridge structures.

Course. In stone masonry, a layer of stone composed of either cut or uncut pieces laid with horizontal or slightly longitudinally inclined joints.

In brick masonry, a layer of bricks bedded in mortar.

Cover. In reinforced concrete, the clear thickness of concrete between a reinforcing bar and the surface of the concrete.

Cover Plate. A plate used in conjunction with flange angles or other structural shapes to provide additional flange section upon a girder, column, strut or similar member.

Covered Bridge. An indefinite term applied to a wooden bridge having in its construction a truss of any type adaptable to its location requirements. To prevent or delay deterioration of the timbers through infiltration of moisture into the framed or other joints, the entire structure, or instead, only its trusses are covered by a housing consisting of boards and shingles or other covering materials, fastened upon the side girts, rafters, purlins, or other parts intended to receive them. A covered bridge may be either a through or a deck structure. The former may be constructed with pony trusses.

Cracking (reflection). Visible cracks in an overlay indicating cracks in the concrete underneath.

Creep. An inelastic deformation that increases with time while the stress is constant.

Crib. A structure consisting of a foundation grillage combined with a superimposed framework providing compartments or coffers which are filled with gravel, stones, concrete or other material satisfactory for supporting the masonry or other structure to be placed thereon. The exterior portion may be planked or sheet-piled to protect the crib against damage by erosion or floating debris.

A structure consisting of a series of box-like compartments built of round or squared timbers having the crosstimbers (compartment division and end wall timbers) drift bolted and dove-tail framed or half framed to interlock with the side timbers, thus producing a rigid framework of the height desired. A portion of the compartment is constructed with floors to serve as ballast boxes for loading and sinking the crib in its final position after which the remaining compartments are filled or partially filled with gravel, stones or other material to render the entire structure stable against the forces to which it may be subjected.

This latter type of crib is used as a protection against wave action and stream currents producing scour and erosion adjacent to bridge structures to prevent undermining of abutments and piers or other substructure elements and also to serve as a training wall averting changes in shore and bank locations.

Cribbing. A construction consisting of wooden, metal or reinforced concrete units so assembled as to form an open cellular-like structure for supporting a superimposed load or for resisting horizontal or overturning forces acting against it.

Cross Frames. Transverse bracings between two main longitudinal members. See DIAPHRAGM and BRACING.

Cross Girder, Transverse Girder. A term applied to large timber members and to metal and reinforced concrete girder-like members placed generally perpendicular to and connected upon the main girders or trusses of a bridge span, including intermediate and end floor beams.

Cross Wall. See DIAPHRAGM WALL.

Crown of Roadway. 1. The crest line of the convexed surface. 2. The vertical dimension describing the total amount the surface is convexed or raised from gutter to crest. This is sometimes termed the cross fall of roadway.

Culvert. A small bridge constructed entirely below the elevation of the roadway surface and having no part or portion integral therewith. Structures over 20 feet in span parallel to the roadway are usually called bridges, rather than culverts; and structures less than 20 feet in span are called culverts even though they support traffic loads directly.

Curb. A stone, concrete or wooden barrier paralleling the side limit of the roadway to guide the movement of vehicle wheels and safeguard bridge trusses, railings or other constructions existing outside the roadway limit and also pedestrian traffic upon sidewalks from collision with vehicles and their loads.

Curb Inlet. See SCUPPER.

Curtain Wall. A term commonly applied to a thin masonry wall not designed to support superimposed loads either vertically or transversely.

A thin vertically placed and integrally built portion of the paving slab of a culvert intended to protect the culvert against undermining by stream scour. A similar construction placed in an inclined position is termed an "apron wall" or "apron."

A wall uniting the pillar or shaft portions of a dumbbell pier. However, its service function is that of a frame composed of struts and braces rendering the entire structure integral in its action. As here applied the term is synonymous with "diaphragm wall."

Curve Banking. See SUPERELEVATION.

Curves in Plan and Profile. A roadway may be curved in its lateral alignment, its vertical contour, or in both alignment and contour combined. The primary curves are described as:

1. Horizontal Curve. A curve in the plan location defining the alignment.

2. Vertical Curve. A curve in the profile location defining the elevation.

Cut. (*Cutting.*) That portion of a highway, railway, canal, ditch or other artificial construction of similar character produced by the removal of the natural formation of earth or rock whether sloped or level. The general terms "side hill cut" and "through cut" are used to describe the resulting cross sections of the excavations commonly encountered.

Cut Slope. A term applied to the inclined surface of an approach cut terminating in the ditch or gutter at its base, which in turn serves to remove accumulations of water from all areas drained into it.

Cylinder Pier. See PIER.

D

Dead Load. A static load due to the weight of the structure itself.

Dead Man. A general term applied to an anchorage member engaging the end of a stay rod, cable or other tie-like piece or part. The anchorage member is made secure through the resistance to movement produced by the earth, stone, brickbats, or other material used to embed and cover the anchor piece which may consist of a wooden log or timber, a metal beam or other structural shape, a quarried stone boulder or any other adaptable object. This type of anchor member is used to restrain and hold in position piles, bulkheads, cribs, and other constructions against horizontal movement as well as to resist the stresses of tie members acting in inclined and vertical directions.

Debris Rack. A grill type barrier used to intercept debris above a sewer or culvert inlet.

Deck. That portion of a bridge which provides direct support for vehicular and pedestrian traffic. The deck may be either a reinforced concrete slab, timber flooring, a steel plate or grating, or the top surface of abutting concrete members or units. While normally distributing load to a system of beams and stringers, a deck may also be the main supporting element of a bridge, as with a reinforced concrete slab structure or a laminated timber bridge.

Deck Bridge. A bridge having its floor elevation at, nearly at, or above the elevation of the uppermost portion of the superstructure.

Decking. A term specifically applied to bridges having wooden floors and used to designate the flooring only. It does not include the floor stringers, floor beams, or other members serving to support the flooring.

Deformation (elastic). Deformation occurring when stress in a material is less than the yield point. If the stress is removed, the material will return to its original shape.

Depth of Truss. As applied to trusses having parallel chords and to polygonal trusses having a midspan length with parallel chords; the vertical distance between the centerlines of action of the top and bottom chords.

Design Load. The loading comprising magnitudes and distributions of wheel, axle or other concentrations used in the determination of the stresses, stress distributions and ultimately the cross-sectional areas and compositions of the various portions of a bridge structure.

The design loading or loadings fixed by a specification are very commonly composite rather than actual, but are predicated upon a study of various types of vehicles. In lieu of a loading so determined for use as "standard," an equivalent uniform load designed to produce resulting structures practically identical with those evolved by the use of such loadings may be used. One or more concentrated loads may be used in conjunction with the uniform load to secure the effect corresponding to the incorporation of especially heavy vehicles within the normally maximum traffic considered as likely to pass upon a given bridge or a series of bridges. Such equivalent loadings are merely a convenience facilitating design operations.

In rating bridges for the Bridge Inspection Manual, either the H or HS trucks with their alternate lane loadings may be used. Or, if desired, the special legal limit trucks: Type 3, Type 3S 2, and Type 3–3, may be used.

Diagonal. See WEB MEMBERS.

Diagonal Stay. A cable support in a suspension bridge extending diagonally from the tower to the roadway system to add stiffness to the structure and diminish the deformations and undulations resulting from traffic service.

Diaphragm. A reinforcing plate or member placed within a member or deck system, respectively, to distribute stresses and improve strength and rigidity. See BRACING.

Diaphragm Wall (cross wall). A wall built transversely to the longitudinal centerline of a spandrel arch serving to tie together and reinforce the spandrel walls together with providing a support for the floor system in conjunction with the spandrel walls. To provide means for the making of inspections the diaphragms of an arch span may be provided with manholes.

The division walls of a reinforced concrete caisson dividing its interior space into compartments and reinforcing its walls. A wall serving to subdivide a box-like structure or portion of a structure into two or more compartments, or sections.

Dike. (*Dyke*). An earthen embankment constructed to provide a barrier to the inundation of an adjacent area which it encloses entirely or in part.

When used in conjunction with a bridge, its functions are commonly those of preventing stream erosion and localized scour and/or to so direct the stream current that debris will not accumulate upon bottom land adjacent to approach embankments, abutments, piers, towers, or other portions of the structure.

This term is occasionally misapplied to crib construction used to accomplish a like result. See CRIB.

Spur Dike. A projecting jetty-like construction placed adjacent to an abutment of the "U," "T," block or arched type upon the upstream and downstream sides, but sometimes only on the upstream side, to secure a gradual contraction of the stream width and induce a free even flow of water adjacent to and beneath a bridge. They may be constructed in extension of the wing wall or a winged abutment.

The common types of construction used for water wings are: (1) Wooden cribs filled with stones; (2) embankments riprapped on the waterway side; and (3) wooden and metal sheet piling.

Spur dikes serve to prevent stream scour and undermining of the abutment foundation and to relieve the condition which otherwise would tend to gather and hold accumulations of stream debris against and adjacent to the upstream side of the abutment.

Dimension Stone. A stone of relatively large dimensions, the face surface of which is either chisel or margin drafted but otherwise rough and irregular, commonly called either "rock face" or "quarry face."

Stones quarried with the dimensions large enough to provide cut stones with given finished dimensions.

Distribution Girder. A beam or girder-like member forming a part of the frame by which the dead and live loads are transmitted to the drum girder of a rim-boaring swing span.

Ditch. See DRAIN.

Diversion Drain. (*Diversion Flume.*) An open top paved drain constructed for the purpose of diverting and conveying water from a roadway gutter down the inclined surface of a bridge approach embankment or causeway.

Dolphin. A group or cluster of piles driven in one to two circles about a center pile and drawn together at their top ends around the center pile to form a buffer or guard for the protection of channel span piers or other portions of a bridge exposed to possible injury by collision with waterbound traffic. The tops of the piles are served with a wrapping consisting of several plies of wire, rope, coil, twist link, or stud link anchor chain, which, by being fastened at its ends only, renders itself taut by the adjustments of the piles resulting from service contact with ships, barges, or other craft. The center pile may project above the others to serve as a bollard for restraining and guiding the movements of water-borne traffic units.

Single steel and concrete piles of large size may also be used as dolphins.

Double Movable Bridge. A bridge in which the clear span for navigation is produced by joining the arms of two adjacent swing spans or the leaves of two adjacent bascule spans at or near the center of the navigable channel. The arms or leaves may act as cantilevers with a shear lock at their junction to provide for the passage of traffic over the joint. The leaves of bascules may be equipped to act as a hinged arch. Spans comprised of two bascule leaves are called double leaf bascule bridges. See MOVABLE BRIDGE.

Dowel. A short length of metal bar, either round or square, used to attach and prevent movement and displacement of wooden, stone, concrete, or metal pieces when placed in a bored, drilled, or cored hole located in their contact surfaces. A dowel may or may not be sized to provide a driving fit in the hole. In stone and premolded concrete structures the dowels are commonly set in lead, mortar, or other material filling the portions of the holes not occupied by the dowels. In concrete construction the plastic concrete is usually either placed around a dowel or the dowel is thrust into it.

In general, dowels function to resist shear forces, although footing dowels in reinforced concrete walls and columns resist bending forces.

Drain. (*Ditch, Gutter.*) A trench or trough-like excavation made to collect water. In general a drain is considered as functioning to collect and convey water whereas a ditch may only serve to collect it.

A gutter is a paved drain commonly constructed in conjunction with the curbs of the roadway or instead built closely adjacent to the paved portion of the roadway.

Drain Hole. (*Drip Hole.*) An aperture extending through a wall to provide an egress for water which might otherwise accumulate upon one of its sides. In this connection the term "weep hole" and "drain hole" are commonly used. See WEEP HOLE.

A cored, punched or bored hole in a box or trough shaped member or part to provide means for the egress of accumulated water or other liquid matter. In areas exposed to freezing temperatures, these holes are used to prevent damage by the expansive force incident to the freezing of water accumulations.

Drainage. The interception and removal of water from the roadway and/or sidewalk surfaces of a bridge or its approaches; from beneath the paved or otherwise prepared roadway and/or sidewalk surfaces of the approaches and from the sloped surfaces of hillsides, cuts, embankments, and causeways; from the backfill or other material in contact with abutments, retaining walls, counterweight wells or parts of a bridge or incidental structure.

A ditch, drain, gutter, gully, flume, catch basin, downspout, scupper, weep hole, or other construction or appliance facilitating the interception and removal of water.

Drainage Area, Catchment Area. The area from which the run-off water passing beneath a bridge or passing a specific location in a river or stream is produced.

Drawbridge. A general term applied to a bridge over a navigable stream, river, lake, canal, tidal inlet, gut or strait having a movable superstructure span of any type permitting the channel to be freed of its obstruction to navigation. A popular but imprecise term.

Probably the earliest use of a drawbridge was for military purposes, utilizing a single leaf hinged frame lifted up or let down by a comparatively simple manually operated mechanism.

Draw Rest. A support constructed upon a fender or guard pier and equipped with a latch block for holding a swing span in open position. This support may consist of a block of masonry, a rigid metal frame or other construction adapted to the service requirements.

Draw Span. A general term applied to either a swing or a retractile type movable superstructure span of a bridge over a navigable stream, river, lake, canal, tidal inlet, gut or strait. See MOVABLE BRIDGE.

Drift Bolt. A short length of metal bar, either round or square, used to connect and hold in position wooden members placed in contact. It may or may not be made with a head and a tapered point. Drift bolts are commonly driven in holes having a diameter slightly less than the bolts. This condition appears to be the recognized practical difference between a drift bolt and a dowel. The difference is more a matter of usage of terms rather than of functions to be performed.

Drip Bead. A channel or groove in the under side of a belt course, coping, or other protruding exposed portion of a masonry structure intended to arrest the downward flow of rain water and cause it to drip off free from contact with surfaces below the projection.

Drip Hole. See DRAIN HOLE.

Drop Inlet. A box-like construction commonly built integrally with the upstream end of a culvert with provision for the water to flow in at its top and to enter the culvert proper at its bottom or within its bottom portion. Vegetable or other material likely to become lodged in the culvert may be retained in the base portion of this receiving device by constructing its base to form a sump below the inlet elevation of the culvert. The culvert inlet may or may not be provided with a grating.

Drum Girder. (*Rim Girder.*) The circular plate girder forming a part of a swing bridge turntable transferring its loadings to the rollers and to the circular track upon which they travel. When the swing span is in "closed" position the drum girder track receives the superstructure dead and live loads and transmits these to the substructure bearing area beneath the track.

Ductility. The ability to withstand non-elastic deformation without rupture.

Dyke. See DIKE.

E

Efflorescence. A white deposit on concrete or brick caused by crystallization of soluble salts brought to the surface by moisture in the masonry.

Elastic Deformation. See DEFORMATION.

Elastomer. A natural or synthetic rubber-like material.

Electrolytic Corrosion. See CORROSION (ELECTROLYTIC).

Element. Metal Structures. An angle, beam, plate or other rolled, forged or cast piece of metal forming a part of a built piece. For Wooden Structures. A board, plank, joist, scantling or other fabricated piece forming a part of a built piece.

End Block. On a prestressed concrete beam, the thickening of the web or increase in beam width at the end to provide adequate anchorage bearing for the post-tensioning wires, rods, or strands.

End Hammer. The hammering action of an end lift device upon its pedestal or bearing plate resulting from the deflections and vibrations set up by the movements of traffic upon a swing span when the lifting device is improperly adjusted.

End Lift. The mechanism consisting of wedges, toggles, link-and-roller, rocker-and-eccentric or other devices combined with shafts, gears, or other operating parts requisite to remove the camber or "droop" of a swing span.

End Post. The end compression member of a truss, either vertical or inclined in position and extending from chord to chord, functioning to transmit the truss end shear to its end bearing.

Epoxy. A synthetic resin which cures or hardens by chemical reaction between components which are mixed together shortly before use.

Equalizer. A balance lever engaging the counterweight and the suspending cables of a vertical lift span as a means of adjustment and equalization of the stresses in the latter.

Equilibrium. In statics, the condition in which the forces acting upon a body are such that no external effect (or movement) is produced.

Equivalent Uniform Load. A load having a constant intensity per unit of its length producing an effect equal or practically equal to that of a live load consisting of vehicle axle or wheel concentrations spaced at varying distances apart, when used as a substitute for the latter in determining the stresses in a structure.

Expansion Bearing. A general term applied to a device or assemblage designed to transmit a reaction from one member or part of a structure to another and to permit the longitudinal movements resulting from temperature changes and superimposed loads without transmitting a horizontal force to the substructure.

The expansion bearing is designed to permit movement by overcoming sliding, rolling or other friction conditions. In general, provision is made for a movement equal to $1\frac{1}{4}''$ in 100', thus providing for ordinary irregularities in field erection and adjustment.

Expansion Dam. The part of an expansion joint serving as an end form for the placing of concrete at a joint. Also applied to the expansion joint device itself.

Expansion Joint. A joint designed to provide means for expansion and contraction movements produced by temperature changes, loadings or other agencies.

Expansion Rocker. An articulated assemblage forming a part of the movable end of a girder or truss and facilitating the longitudinal movements resulting from temperature changes and superimposed loads. Apart from its hinge connection the rocker proper is a cast or built-up member consisting essentially of a circular segment integrally joined by a web-like portion to a hub fitted for hinge action either with a pin hole or by having its ends formed into trunnions. In its service operation the rocker is commonly supported upon a shoe plate or pedestal. Strictly speaking, this is a segment of a roller. A short cast or built-up member hinged at both ends, or instead hinged at one end and provided with a circular segment or spherical type bearing at the other to facilitate expansion and contraction on other longitudinal rotational movements.

Expansion Roller. A cylinder so mounted that by revolution it facilitates expansion, contraction or other movements resulting from temperature changes, loadings or other agencies.

Expansion Shoe. (*Expansion Pedestal.*) An expansion bearing member or assemblage designed to provide means for expansion and contraction or other longitudinal movements. In general, the term "shoe" is applied to an assemblage of structural plates or plate-like castings permitting movement by sliding while the term "pedestal" is used to describe assemblages of castings or built-up members securing a somewhat greater total depth and providing for movement either by sliding or by rolling.

The masonry plate or casting is commonly held in a fixed position by anchor bolts and the superimposed shoe plate or pedestal is free to move longitudinally upon it or upon intervening rollers but is restrained from transverse movement either by a rib and slot, by pintles, by anchorage or by anchorage in combination with one of the first two mentioned. The term "bed plate" is sometimes used to designate the bottom portion of the assemblage.

Extrados. (*Back.*) 1. The curved surface of an arch farthest from its longitudinal construction axis or axes. 2. The curve defining the exterior surface of an arch.

Eyebar. A member consisting of a rectangular bar body with enlarged forged ends or heads having holes through them for engaging connecting pins.

An adjustable eyebar is composed of two sections fitted with upset threaded ends engaging a sleevenut or a turnbuckle.

Eyebolt. (*Ringbolt.*) A bolt having a forged eye at one end used, when installed in a structure, to provide means for making fast the end of a cable, a hooked rod or other part or portion of the bridge, or instead to provide a means of anchorage for unrelated equipment or structures.

A ringbolt is essentially an eyebolt fitted with a ring to serve the same purpose as described above for an eyebolt with added articulation.

F

Face Stones. The stones exposed to view in the face surfaces of abutments, piers, arches, retaining walls or other stone structures.

Face Wall.

    Abutment. See BREAST WALL.

    Spandrel Arch Structure. The outermost spandrel walls providing the face surfaces of the completed structure. See SPANDREL ARCH.

Factor of Safety. A factor or allowance predicated by common engineering practice upon the failure stress or stresses assumed to exist in a structure or a member or part thereof. Its purpose is to provide a margin in the strength, rigidity, deformation and endurance of a structure or its component parts compensating for irregularities existing in structural materials and workmanship, uncertainties involved in mathematical analysis and stress distribution, service deterioration and other unevaluated conditions.

Falsework. A temporary wooden or metal framework built to support without appreciable settlement and deformation the weight of a structure during the period of its construction and until it becomes self-supporting. In general, the arrangement of its details are devised to facilitate the construction operations and provide for economical removal and the salvaging of material suitable for reuse.

Fascia. An outside, covering member designed on the basis of architectural effect rather than strength and rigidity although its function may involve both.

A light, stringer-like member spanning longitudinally between cantilever brackets which support large overhangs on girder or beam bridges.

Fascia Girder. As exposed outermost girder of a span sometimes treated architecturally or otherwise to provide an attractive appearance.

Fatigue. The tendency of a member to fail at a lower stress when subjected to cyclical loading than when subjected to static loading.

Felloe Guard. See WHEEL GUARD.

Fender. 1. A structure placed at an upstream location adjacent to a pier to protect it from the striking force, impact and shock of floating stream debris, ice floes, etc. This structure is sometimes termed an "ice guard" in latitudes productive of lake and river ice to form ice flows. 2. A structure commonly consisting of dolphins, capped and braced rows of piles or of wooden cribs either entirely or partially filled with rock ballast, constructed upstream and downstream from the center and end piers (or abutments) of a fixed or movable superstructure span to fend off water-borne traffic from collision with these substructure parts, and in the case of a swing span, with the span while in its open position.

Fender Pier. A pier-like structure which performs the same service as a fender but is generally more substantially built. These structures may be constructed entirely or in part of stone or concrete masonry. See GUARD PIER.

Field Coat. A coat of paint applied upon the priming or base coat or upon a coat subsequently applied and, generally, after the structure is assembled and its joints completely connected by bolts, rivets or welds. This application is quite commonly a part of the field erection procedure and is, therefore, termed field painting.

Fill. (*Filling.*) Material, usually earth, used for the purpose of raising or changing the surface contour of an area, or for constructing an embankment.

Filler (Filler Plate). In wooden and structural steel construction. A piece used primarily to fill a space beneath a batten, splice plate, gusset, connection angle, stiffener or other element.

Filler Metal. Metal prepared in wire, rod, electrode or other adaptable form to be fused with the structure metal in the formation of a weld.

Filler Plate. See FILLER.

Fillet. 1. A curved portion forming a junction of two surfaces which would otherwise intersect at an angle. 2. In metal castings and rolled structural shapes a fillet is used to disseminate and relieve the shrinkage or other stresses tending to overstress and, perhaps, rupture the junction material. In castings it may also provide means for movement to take place at locations where the rigidity of the mold would otherwise resist and obstruct this action. 3. In concrete construction the use of mitered fillets in internal corners of forms not only serves the purposes applying to castings but also facilitates both the placing of concrete and the subsequent removal of forms.

Fillet Weld. A weld joining intersecting members by depositing weld metal to form a near-triangular or fillet shaped junction of the surfaces of the members so joined. This weld serves to unite the intersecting surfaces of two elements of a member.

Filling. See FILL.

Finger Dam. Expansion joint in which the opening is spanned by meshing steel fingers or teeth.

Fish Belly. A term applied to a girder or a truss having its bottom flange or its bottom chord, as the case may be, constructed either haunched or bow-shaped with the convexity downward. See LENTICULAR TRUSS.

Fixed-Ended Arch. See VOUSSOIR ARCH.

Fixed Bearing. The plates, pedestals, or other devices designed to receive and transmit to the substructure or to another supporting member or structure the reaction stresses of a beam, slab, girder, truss, arch or other type of superstructure span.

The fixed bearing is considered as holding the so-termed "fixed end" of the structure rigidly in position, but in practice the clearance space commonly provided in the anchorage may permit a relatively small amount of movement.

Fixed Bridge. A bridge having its superstructure spans fixed in position except that provision may be made in their construction for expansion and contraction movements resulting from temperature changes, loadings, or other agencies.

Fixed Span. A superstructure span having its position practically immovable, as compared to a movable span.

Flange. The part of a rolled I-shaped beam or of a built-up girder extending transversely across the top and bottom edges of the web. The flanges are considered to carry the compressive and tensile forces that comprise the internal resisting moment of the beam, and may consist of angles, plates, or both.

Flange Angle. An angle used to form a flange element of a built-up girder, column, strut or similar member.

Floating Bridge. In general this term means the same as "Pontoon Bridge." However, its parts providing buoyancy and supporting power may consist of logs or squared timbers, held in position by lashing pieces, chains or ropes, and floored over with planks, or the bridge itself may be of hollow cellular construction.

Floating Foundation. A term sometimes applied to a "foundation raft" or "foundation grillage." Used to describe a soil-supported raft or mat foundation with low bearing pressures.

Flood Gate. (*Tide Gate.*) An automatically operated gate installed in a culvert or bridge waterway to prevent the ingress of flood or tide water to the area drained by the structure.

Floor. See DECK.

Floor Beam. A beam or girder located transversely to the general alignment of the bridge and having its ends framed upon the columns of bents and towers or upon the trusses or girders of superstructure spans. A floor beam at the extreme end of a girder or truss span is commonly termed an end floor beam.

Floor System. The complete framework of floor beams and stringers or other members supporting the bridge floor proper and the traffic loading including impact thereon.

Flow Line. The surface of a water course.

Flux. A material which prevents, dissolves, and removes oxides from metal during the welding process. It may be in the coating on a metal stick electrode or a granular mass covering the arc in submerged arc welding and protects the weld from oxidation during the fusion process.

Footbridge. (*Pedestrian Bridge.*) A bridge designed and constructed to provide means of traverse for pedestrian traffic only.

Footing. (*Footing Course, Plinth.*) The enlarged, or spread-out, lower portion of a substructure, which distributes the structure load either to the earth or to supporting piles. The most common footing is the concrete slab, although stone piers also utilize footings. Plinth refers to stone work as a rule. "Footer" is a local term for footing.

Foot Wall. See TOE WALL.

Forms. (*Form Work, Lagging, Shuttering.*) The constructions, either wooden or metal, providing means for receiving, molding and sustaining in position the plastic mass of concrete placed therein to the dimensions, outlines and details of surfaces planned for its integral parts throughout its period of induration or hardening.

The terms "forms" and "form work" are synonymous. The term "lagging" is commonly applied to the surface shaping areas of forms producing the intradoses of arches or other curved surfaces, especially when strips are used.

Forms. (SIP, Stay-in-Place.) A prefabricated metal concrete deck form that will remain in place after the concrete has set.

Form Work. See FORMS.

Foundation. The supporting material upon which the substructure portion of a bridge is placed. A foundation is "natural" when consisting of natural earth, rock or near-rock material having stability adequate to support the superimposed loads without lateral displacement or compaction entailing appreciable settlement or deformation. Also, applied in an imprecise fashion to a substructure unit.

Consolidated Soil Foundation. A foundation of soft soil rendered more resistant to its loads by (1) consolidating the natural material, (2) by the incorporation of other soil material (sand, gravel, etc.) into the soft material, and (3) by the injection of cementing materials into the soil mass which will produce consolidation by lapidification.

Pile or Piled Foundation. A foundation reinforced by driving piles in sufficient number and to a depth adequate to develop the bearing power required to support the foundation load.

Foundation Excavation. (*Foundation Pit.*) The excavation made to accommodate a foundation for a retaining wall, abutment, pier or other structure or element thereof.

Foundation Grillage. A construction consisting of steel, timber, or concrete members placed in layers. Each layer is normal to those above and below it and the members within a layer are generally parallel, producing a crib or grid-like effect. Grillages are usually placed under very heavy concentrated loads.

Foundation Load. The load resulting from traffic, superstructure, substructure, approach embankment, approach causeway, or other incidental load increment imposed upon a given foundation area.

Foundation Pile. A pile, whether of wood, reinforced concrete, or metal used to reinforce a foundation and render it satisfactory for the supporting of superimposed loads.

Foundation Pit. See FOUNDATION EXCAVATION.

Foundation Seal. A mass of concrete placed underwater within a cofferdam for the base portion of an abutment, pier, retaining wall or other structure to close or seal the cofferdam against incoming water from foundation springs, fissures, joints or other water carrying channels. See TREMIE.

Foundation Stone. The stone or one of the stones of a course having contact with the foundation of a structure.

Frame. A structure having its parts or members so arranged and secured that the entire assemblage may not be distorted when supporting the loads, forces, and physical pressures considered in its design. The framing of a truss relates to the design and fabrication of the joint assemblages.

Framing. The arrangement and manner of joining the component members of a bent, tower, truss, floor system or other portion of a bridge structure to insure a condition wherein each element and member may function in accord with the conditions attending its design. Framing must be interpreted as including both design and fabrication for the complete structure.

Friction Roller. A roller placed between parts or members intended to facilitate change in their relative positions by reducing the frictional resistance to translation movement.

Frost Heave. The upward movement of and force exerted by soil due to alternate freezing and thawing of retained moisture.

Frost Line. The depth to which soil may be frozen.

G

Galvanic Action. Electrical current between two unlike metals.

Gauge. The distance between parallel lines of rails, rivet holes, etc. A measure of thickness of sheet metal or wire.

Girder. A flexural member which is the main or primary support for the structure, and which usually receives loads from floor beams and stringers.

Any large beam, especially if built up.

Girder Bridge. A bridge whose superstructure consists of two or more girders supporting a separate floor system of slab and floor beams, or slab, stringer, and floor beam, as differentiated from a multi-beam bridge or a slab bridge.

Any bridge utilizing large, built-up steel beams, prestressed concrete beams, or concrete box girders.

With reference to the vertical location of the floor system, plate girder spans are divided into two types, viz.:

1. Through bridges having the floor system near the elevation of the bottom flanges, whereby traffic passes between the top flanges.

2. Deck bridges having the floor system at or above the elevation of the top flanges whereby traffic passes above the girders.

Girder Span. A span in which the major longitudinal supporting members are girders. It may be simple, cantilever or continuous in type.

Gothic Arch. (*Pointed Arch.*) An arch in which the intrados surface is composed of two equal cylinder segments intersecting obtusely at the crown.

The Tudor Arch is a modification of the Gothic, produced by the introduction of shorter radius cylinder segments at the haunches thus rendering it a four-centered form or type.

Grade Crossing. A term applicable to an intersection of two or more highways, two railroads or one railroad and one highway at a common grade or elevation; now commonly accepted as meaning the last of these combinations.

Grade Intersection. The location where a horizontal and an inclined length of roadway or, instead, two inclined lengths meet in profile. To provide an easy transition from one to the other they are connected by a vertical curve and the resulting profile is a sag or a summit depending upon whether concaved or convexed upward.

Grade Separation. A term applied to the use of a bridge structure and its approaches to divide or separate the crossing movement of vehicular, pedestrian or other traffic, by confining portions thereof to different elevations. See OVERPASS.

Gradient. The rate of inclination of the roadway and/or sidewalk surface(s) from horizontal applying to a bridge and its approaches. It is commonly expressed as a percentage relation of horizontal to vertical dimensions.

Gravity Wall. See RETAINING WALL.

Grillage. A platform-like construction or assemblage used to insure distribution of loads upon unconsolidated soil material. See FOUNDATION GRILLAGE.

A frame composed of I-beams or other structural shapes rigidly connected and built into a masonry bridge seat, skewback or other substructure support to insure a satisfactory distribution of the loads transmitted by the superstructure shoes, pedestals, or other bearing members.

Grout. A mortar having a sufficient water content to render it a free-flowing mass, used for filling (grouting) the interstitial spaces between the stones or the stone fragments (spalls) used in the "backing" portion of stone masonry; for fixing anchor bolts and for filling cored spaces in castings, masonry, or other spaces where water may accumulate.

Guard Pier. (*Fender Pier.*) A pier-like structure built at right angles with the alignment of a bridge or at an angle therewith conforming to the flow of the stream current and having adequate length, width, and other provisions to protect the swing span in its open position from collision with passing vessels or other water-borne equipment and materials. It also serves to protect the supporting center pier of the swing span from injury and may or may not be equipped with a rest pier upon which the swing span in its open position may be latched. The type of construction varies with navigation and stream conditions from a simple pile and timber structure or a wooden crib-stone ballasted structure to a solid masonry one, or to a combination construction. In locations where ice floes or other water-borne materials may accumulate upon the upstream pier end, a cutwater or a starling is an essential detail. See FENDER PIER.

Guard Railing. (*Guard Rail, Guard Fence, Protection Railing.*) A fencelike barrier or protection built within the roadway shoulder area and intended to function as a combined guide or guard for the movement of vehicular and/or pedestrian traffic and to prevent or hinder the accidental passage of such traffic beyond the berm line of the roadway.

Guide. A member or element of a member functioning to hold in position and direct the movement of a moving part.

Guide Roller. A roller fixed in its location or position and serving both as a friction roller and as a pilot or guide for a part or member in contact with it.

Gusset. A plate serving to connect or unite the elements of a member or the members of a structure and to hold them in correct alignment and/or position at a joint. A plate may function both as a gusset and splice plate while under other conditions it may function as a gusset and stay plate. See SPLICE PLATE and STAY PLATE.

Gutter. See DRAIN.

Gutter Grating. A perforated or barred cover placed upon an inlet to a drain to prevent the entrance of debris gathered and brought to the inlet by the water stream.

Guy. A cable, chain, rod or rope member serving to check and control undulating, swaying or other movements, or to hold a fixed alignment or position a structure or part thereof by having one of its ends bolted, clamped, tied or otherwise fastened upon it, the other end being secured upon a part or member of the structure or upon a disconnected anchorage.

H

H-Beam. (*H-Pile.*) A rolled steel bearing pile having an H-shaped cross section.

Hand Hole. Holes provided in cover plates of built-up box sections to permit access to the interior for maintenance and construction purposes.

Hand Operated Span. A manpower-operated movable span to which the force for operating is applied upon a capstan, winch, windlass or wheel.

The terms "Hand Draw Bridge," "Hand Swing Bridge" and "Lever Swing Bridge" are applied to swing spans of hand-operated type.

Hand Rail. See RAILING.

Hanger. A tension element or member serving to suspend or support a member attached thereto. A tension member, whether a rod, eyebar, or built-up member supporting a portion of the floor system of a truss, arch or suspension span. In suspension bridge construction wire cable is used and the complete member is commonly termed a "suspender."

Haunch. A deepening of a beam or column, the depth usually being greatest at the support and vanishing towards or at the center. The curve of the lower flange or surface may be circular, elliptic, parabolic, straight or stepped.

Head. A measure of water pressure expressed in terms of an equivalent weight or pressure exerted by a column of water. The height of the equivalent column of water is the head.

Headwater. The depth of water at the inlet end of a pipe, culvert, or bridge waterway.

Headway. See CLEAR HEADWAY.

Heat Treatment. Any of a number of various operations involving heating and cooling that are used to impart specific properties to metals. Examples are tempering, quenching, annealing, etc.

Heel of Span. The rotation end of a bascule span.

Heel Stay. See SHEAR LOCK.

Hemispherical Bearing. A bearing which utilizes the ball and socket principle by having male and female spherical segments forming the bearing areas or surfaces of the interlocking elements, thus providing for movements by revolution in any direction.

In order to insure accurate adjustment of the mating elements it is essential that a pintle or other self-centering device be provided as a part of the construction details.

Hinged Joint. A joint constructed with a pin, cylinder segment, spherical segment or other device permitting movement by rotation.

Hip Joint. (*The Hip of Truss.*) The juncture of the inclined end post with the end top chord member of a truss. In the truss of a swing span, the juncture of the inclined end post located adjacent to the center of span, with the combined top chord and the connecting tie member between the swing span arms, is designated an "interior hip joint" or an "interior hip of truss."

Hip Vertical. The vertically placed tension member engaging the hip joint of a truss and supporting the first panel floor beam in a through truss span, or instead, only the bottom chord in a deck truss span.

Hook Bolt. 1. A bolt having a forged hook at one end used for essentially the same purposes as described for an eyebolt. See EYEBOLT. 2. A bolt having its head end bent at or nearly at a right angle with its body portion and, when in use, acting as a clamp.

Howe Truss. A truss of the parallel chord type originally adapted to wooden bridge construction but with the later development of metal bridge trusses it was adopted only to a limited extent due to the uneconomical use of metal in its compression members. The web system is composed of vertical (tension) rods at the panel points with an X pattern of diagonals.

Hydrolysis. A chemical process of decomposition in the presence of elements of water.

Hydroplaning. Loss of contact between a tire and the deck surface when the tire planes or glides on a film of water covering the deck.

I

Ice Guard. See FENDER.

Impact. As applied to bridge design—a dynamic increment of stress equivalent in magnitude to the difference between the stresses produced by a static load when quiescent and by a load moving in a straight line.

Impact Load. (*Impact Allowance.*) A load allowance or increment intended to provide for the dynamic effect of a load applied in a manner other than statically.

Indeterminate Stress. A stress induced by the incorporation of a redundant member in a truss or of an additional reaction in a beam rendering stress distributions indeterminate by the principles of statics.

In redundant beams or trusses the distribution of the stresses depends upon the relative stiffnesses or areas of the members.

Inelastic Compression. See COMPRESSION (INELASTIC).

Inspection Ladders. (*Inspection Platforms and Walks.*) Special devices or appliances designed to afford a safe and efficient means for making inspections and tests to determine the physical condition of a structure and to facilitate repair operations incident to its maintenance which must include these service conveniences. To prevent displacement they will be, in general, rigidly fixed upon the structure. However, certain types of structures are adapted to the use of movable platform devices for suspension from the railings or other parts which are or may be adapted thereto.

The term "catwalk" is applied to narrow permanent walks supported, usually, by brackets or by hangers and located below and/or above the bridge floor. This term is also applied to temporary walks used in the construction of suspension and other types of bridges as utilities facilitating the movements of labor and materials, and the supervision and inspection operations.

Intercepting Ditch. A ditch constructed to prevent surface water from flowing in contact with the toe of an embankment or causeway or down the slope of a cut.

Intergranular Pressure. Pressure between soil grains.

Intermittent Weld. A noncontinuous weld commonly composed of a series of short welds with intervening spaces arranged with fixed spacing and length.

Intrados. (*Soffit.*) The curved surface of an arch nearest its longitudinal (constructional) axis or axes. Properly speaking the intrados is the curve defining the interior surface of the arch.

J

Jack Stringer. The outermost stringer supporting the bridge floor in a panel or bay. It is commonly of less strength than a main stringer.

Joint. In Stone Masonry. The space between individual stones.

In Concrete Construction. The divisions or terminations of continuity produced at predetermined locations or by the completion of a period of construction operations. These may or may not be open.

In a Truss or Frame Structure. (1) A point at which members of a truss or frame are joined, (2) the composite assemblage of pieces or members around or about the point of intersection of their lines of action in a truss or frame.

K

Keystone. A stone of the crown string course of an arch. However, this term is most commonly applied to the symmetrically shaped wedge-like stone located in a head ring course at the crown of the arch, which thus exposed to view produces desired architectural effects. This head ring stone commonly extends short distances above and below the extradosal and intradosal limits of the voussoirs of adjoining string courses. The final stone placed, thereby closing the arch.

King-Post. (*King Rod.*) The post member in a "King-post" type truss or in a "King-post" portion of any other type of truss.

King-Post Truss. A truss adapted to either wooden or metal bridge construction. It is composed of two triangular panels with a common vertical. A beam or chord extends the full truss length.

In the through form of this truss the inclined members are struts and the vertical or King-post is a hanger. In the deck truss, the two inclined members become tie (tension) members and the vertical becomes a post (compression) member.

The King-post truss is the simplest of trusses belonging to the triangular system. However, it is described with equal accuracy as a trussed girder.

K-Truss. A truss having a web system wherein the diagonal members intersect the vertical members at or near the mid-height. When thus arranged the assembly in each panel forms a letter "K"; hence the name "K-Truss."

Knee Brace. A member usually short in length, engaging at its ends two other members which are joined to form a right angle or a near-right angle. It thus serves to strengthen and render more rigid the connecting joint.

Knee Wall. A return of the abutment backwall at its ends to enclose the bridge seat on three of its sides. The returned ends may or may not serve to retain a portion of the bridge approach material, but do hide the bridge seat, beam ends, and bearings.

Knuckle. An appliance forming a part of the anchorage of a suspension bridge main suspension member permitting free longitudinal movement of the anchorage chain at locations where it changes its direction and providing for elastic deformations induced by temperature changes and the pull exerted by the suspension member.

L

Lacing. See LATTICE.

Ladle Analysis. (*Ladle Test, Check Analysis.*) As applied to the chemical determination of the constituents of steel or other ferrous metals, the terms "ladle analysis" and "ladle test" are synonymous and are used to designate the analysis of drillings or chips taken from the small ingot or ingots cast from a spoon sample taken from each melt during the pouring (teeming) operation.

The term "check analysis" is applied to the analysis of drillings taken from the finished material after being rolled, forged or otherwise worked. It is primarily intended as a check determination of the results secured from the ingots made at the furnace. Specifications may provide a tolerance or margin of variation between the ingot and the finished material analyses.

Lagging. See FORMS.

Laminated Timber. Timber planks glued together to form a larger member. Laminated timber is used for frames, arches, beams, and columns.

Lap Joint. A joint in which a splice is secured by fixing two elements or members in a position wherein they project upon or overlap each other.

Latch. (*Latch Block.*) The device or mechanism commonly provided at one or both ends of a swing span to hold the span in its correct alignment when in its closed position, and in readiness for the application of the end wedges or lifts.

Latch Lever. A hand-operated lever attached by a rod, cable or chain to the latching device of a movable span and used to engage and to release the latch.

Lateral Bracing. (*Lateral System.*) The bracing assemblage engaging the chords and inclined end posts of truss and the flanges of plate girder spans in the horizontal or inclined planes of these members to function in resisting the transverse forces resulting from wind, lateral vibration, and traffic movements tending to produce lateral movement and deformation. See BRACING.

Lattice. (*Latticing, Lacing.*) An assemblage of bars, channels, or angles singly or in combination bolted, riveted or welded in inclined position upon two or more elements of a member to secure them in correct position and assure their combined action. When the bars form a double system by being inclined in opposite directions the assemblage is termed "double lattice." When so arranged the bars are commonly connected at their intermediate length intersections.

Lattice Truss. In general, a truss having its web members inclined but more commonly the term is applied to a truss having two or more web systems composed entirely of diagonal members at any interval and crossing each other without reference to vertical members. Vertical members when used perform the functions of web stiffeners. They may be utilized for connecting vertically placed brace frames to the girders.

Leaf. The portion of a bascule bridge which forms the span or a portion of the span of the structure.

Ledge Course. In masonry or concrete construction, a course forming a projection beyond the plane of a superimposed course or courses. The projecting portion may be wash dressed to permit an unobstructed flow of rain water down the wall surface. A ledge course differs from a belt or string course in having a projection only upon its topmost bed. This construction is also known as a "Ledger Course."

Ledge Rock. See BED ROCK.

Lenticular Truss. (*Fish Belly Truss.*) A truss having polygonal top and bottom chords curved in opposite directions with their ends meeting at a common joint. The chords nearly coincide with parabolic arcs. In through spans the floor system is suspended from the joints of the bottom chord and the end posts are vertical.

Lifting Girder. A girder or girder-like member engaging the trusses or girders of a vertical lift span and to which the suspending cables are attached.

Lift Span. A superstructure span moved by revolution in a vertical plane or by lifting in a vertical direction to free a navigable waterway of the obstruction it presents to navigation. See MOVABLE BRIDGE.

Link and Roller. An adjustable device or assemblage consisting of a hinged strut-like link fitted with a roller at its bottom end, supported upon a shoe plate or pedestal and operated by a thrust strut serving to force it into a vertical position and to withdraw it therefrom. When installed at each outermost end of the girders or the trusses of a swing span their major function is to lift them to an extent that their camber or droop will be removed and the arms rendered free to act as simple spans. When the links are withdrawn to an inclined position fixed by the operating mechanism the span is free to be moved to an open position.

Lintel Bridge. A bridge having a single span or a series of spans composed of slabs of stone or reinforced concrete spanning the interval or intervals between its substructure elements.

Lintel Stone. A stone used to support a wall over an opening.

Live Load. A dynamic load such as traffic load that is supplied to a structure suddenly or that is accompanied by vibration, oscillation or other physical condition affecting its intensity.

Loading Girder. A term applied to the girder or girders of a center bearing type swing span, located above the pivot pier and functioning to concentrate the superimposed load upon the pivot.

Location. The longitudinal line assumed for construction purposes, which may or may not coincide with the center line of bridge; together with the gradients upon the bridge and its approaches established upon the construction plans and/or on the bridge site preparatory to construction operations.

Lock Device. A mechanism which locks the movable span of a bridge in its "closed" position and prevents movement to "open" position until released. The device on a swing span may also be used to lock the span in its "open" position at times when wind or other conditions render this prevention of movement desirable.

Locking Mechanism. A general term applied to the various devices used for holding in their closed or traffic service position a bascule, vertical lift or swing span of any type. This term applies not only to the locking or latching appliance but includes also the levers, shafts, gears or other parts incidental to their service operation.

Longitudinal Bracing. (*Longitudinal System.*) The bracing assemblage engaging the columns of trestle and viaduct bents and towers in perpendicular or slightly inclined planes located lengthwise with the bridge structure and functioning to resist the longitudinal forces resulting from traffic traction and momentum, wind or other forces tending to produce longitudinal movement and deformation. See BRACING.

M

Margin. See TOLERANCE.

Masonry. A general term applying to abutments, piers, retaining walls, arches and allied structures built of stone, brick or concrete and known correspondingly as stone, brick or concrete masonry.

Masonry Plate. A steel plate or a plate-shaped member whether cast, rolled or forged, built into or otherwise attached upon an abutment, pier, column, or other substructure part to support the rocker, shoe, or pedestal of a beam, girder or truss span and to distribute the load to the masonry beneath.

Mattress. A mat-like protective covering composed of brush and poles, commonly willow, compacted by wire or other lashings and ties and placed upon river and stream beds and banks; lake, tidal or other shores to prevent erosion and scour by water movement action.

Meander. The tortuous channel that characterizes the serpentine curvature of a slow flowing stream in a flood plain.

Member. An individual angle, beam, plate forging, casting or built piece, with or without connected parts for joints, intended utlimately to become an integral part of an assembled frame or structure.

Milled. In steel fabrication, a careful grinding of an edge or surface to assure good bearing or fit.

Mortar. An intimate mixture, in a plastic condition, of cement, or other cementitious material with fine aggregate and water, used to bed and bind together the quarried stones, bricks, or other solid materials composing the major portion of a masonry construction or to produce a plastic coating upon such constructions.

The indurated jointing material filling the interstices between and holding in place the quarried stones or other solid materials of masonry construction. Correspondingly, this term is applied to the cement coating used to produce a desired surface condition upon masonry constructions and is described as the "mortar finish," "mortar coat," "floated face or surface," "parapet," etc.

The component of concrete composed of cement, or other indurating material with sand and water when the concrete is a mobile mass and correspondingly this same component after it has attained a rigid condition through hardening of its cementing constituents.

Movable Bridge. A bridge of any type having one or more spans capable of being raised, turned, lifted, or slid from its normal vehicular and/or pedestrian service location to provide for the passage of navigation. The movements of the superstructure may be produced either manually or by engine power.

Bascule Bridge. A bridge having a superstructure designed to swing vertically about a fixed or a moving horizontal axis. The axis may be the center of a hinge pin or trunnion, or it may be only a line fixing the center of a circular rotation combined with translation, (rolling lift bridge).

Vertical Lift Bridge. A bridge having a superstructure designed to be lifted vertically by cables or chains attached to the ends of the movable span and operating over sheaves placed upon the tops of masts or towers or by other mechanical devices functioning to lift the span to "open" position and to lower it into its "closed" position with its ends seated upon bridge seat pedestals.

Pontoon Bridge. A bridge ordinarily composed of boats, scows or pontoons so connected to the deck or floor construction that they are retained in position and serve to support vehicular and pedestrian traffic. A pontoon bridge may be so constructed that a portion is removable and thus serve to facilitate navigation. Modern floating bridges may have pontoons built integrally with the deck.

Retractile Draw Bridge. (*Traverse Draw Bridge.*) A bridge having a superstructure designed to move horizontally either longitudinally or diagonally from "closed" to "open" position, the portion acting in cantilever being counterweighted by that supported upon rollers.

Rolling Lift Bridge. A bridge of the bascule type devised to roll backward and forward upon supporting girders when operated throughout an "open and closed" cycle.

Swing Bridge. A bridge having a superstructure designed to revolve in a horizontal plane upon a pivot from its "closed" position to an "open" one wherein its alignment is normal or nearly normal to the original alignment. For a structure having its substructure skewed the design commonly provides for revolution in one direction only and through an arc less than 90°. The superstructure is balanced upon a center and its ends acting as cantilevers when the end bearings are released may be either equal in length or unequal with the shorter one counterweighted to permit free revolution movement. A swing bridge with its end bearings released may be supported: (1) upon a single center bearing; (2) upon a circular rim or drum supported upon rollers and (3) upon a center bearing and rim in combination.

Movable Span. A general term applied to a superstructure span designed to be withdrawn, swung, lifted or otherwise moved longitudinally, horizontally or vertically to free a navigable waterway of the obstruction it presents to navigation.

Mud Sill. A single piece of timber or a unit composed of two or more timbers placed upon a soil foundation as a support for a single column, a framed trestle bent, or other similar member of a structure.

A load distribution piece aligned with and placed directly beneath the sill piece of a framed bent is termed a "Sub-sill" although it may serve also as a mud sill.

N

N-Truss. See PRATT TRUSS.

Natural Slope. See ANGLE OF REPOSE.

Neat Line. (*Neat Surface.*) The general alignment position or the general surface position of a face or other surface exlusive or regardless of the projections of individual stones, belts, belt courses, copings or other incidental or ancillary projections in a masonry structure.

Neutral Axis. The axis of a member in bending along which the strain is zero. On one side of the neutral axis the fibers are in tension, on the other side in compression.

Normal Roadway Cross Section. The roadway cross section with its crown in countradistinction to the superelevated cross sections used upon horizontal curves of different degrees of curvature and the transition lengths required for their development.

Nose. A projection acting as a cut water on the upstream end of a pier. See STARLING.

Notch Effect. Stress concentration caused by an abrupt discontinuity or change in section. Such concentrations may have a marked effect on fatigue strength of a member.

O

Operator's House. (*Operator's Cabin.*) The building containing the power plant and operating machinery and devices required for the operator's (bridge tender's) work in executing the complete cycle of opening and closing a movable bridge span.

Overpass. (*Underpass.*) The applications of these terms are definitely indicated by their constructions. For any given combination of highways, railways, and canals, the basic element is a separation of grades. The use of these terms is fixed by the relative elevations of the traffic ways involved; for the lower roadway, the structure is an underpass; for the upper roadway, an overpass.

P

Packing Ring. See SEPARATOR.

Paddleboard. Striped, paddle-shaped signs or boards placed on the roadside in front of a narrow bridge as a warning.

Panel. (*Sub-Panel.*) The portion of a truss span between adjacent points of intersection of web and chord members and, by common practice, applied to intersections upon the bottom chord. A truss panel divided into two equal or unequal parts by an intermediate web member, generally by a subdiagonal or a hanger, forms the panel division commonly termed "subpanels."

Panel Point. The point of intersection of primary web and chord members of a truss.

Parabolic Truss. (*Parabolic Arched Truss.*) A polygonal truss having its top chord and end post vertices coincident with the arc of a parabola; its bottom chord straight and its web system either triangular or quadrangular.

Parapet. A wall-like member composed of brick, stone or reinforced concrete construction upon the retaining wall portion of an approach cut, embankment or causeway or along the outermost edge of the roadway or the sidewalk portion of a bridge to serve as a protection to vehicular and/or pedestrian traffic. While the terms balustrade and parapet are used, in a measure, synonymously, the latter is commonly regarded as applying to barriers of the block type without openings within the body portion. See BALUSTRADE.

Parker Truss. See PRATT TRUSS.

Pedestal. A cast or built-up metal member or assemblage functioning primarily to transmit load from one member or part of a structure to another member or part. A secondary function may be to provide means for longitudinal, transverse or revolution movements.

A block-like construction of stone, concrete or brick masonry placed upon the bridge seat of an abutment or pier to provide a support for the ends of the beams.

Pedestrian Bridge. See FOOT BRIDGE.

Penetration. When Applied to Creosoted Lumber. The depth to which the surface wood is permeated by the creosote oil.

When Applied to Welding. The depth to which the surface metal of the structure part (Structure metal) is fused and coalesced with the fused weld metal to produce a weld joint. See WELD PENETRATION.

When Applied to Pile Driving. The depth a pile tip is driven into the ground.

Pier. A structure composed of stone, concrete, brick, steel or wood and built in shaft or block-like form to support the ends of the spans of a multi-span superstructure at an intermediate location between its abutments.

The following types of piers are adapted to bridge construction. The first three are functional distinctions, while the remaining types are based upon form or shape characteristics.

Anchor Pier. A pier functioning to resist an uplifting force, as for example: The end reaction of the anchor arm of a cantilever bridge. This pier functions as a normal pier structure when subjected to certain conditions of superstructure loading.

Pivot Pier. Center Pier. A term applied to the center bearing pier supporting a swing span while operating throughout an opening-closing cycle. This pier is commonly circular in shape but may be hexagonal, octagonal or even square in plan.

Rest Pier. A pier supporting the end of a movable bridge span when in its closed position.

Cylinder Pier. A type of pier produced by sinking a cylindrical steel shell to a desired depth and filling it with concrete. The foundation excavation may be made by open dredging within the shell and the sinking of the shell may proceed simultaneously with the dredging.

Dumbbell Pier. A pier consisting essentially of two cylindrical or rectangular shaped piers joined by a web constructed integrally with them.

Hammerhead Pier. (*Tee Pier.*) A pier with a cylindrical or rectangular shaft, and a relatively long, transverse cap.

Pedestal Pier. A structure composed of stone, concrete or brick built in block-like form—supporting a column of a bent or tower of a viaduct. Foundation conditions or other practical considerations may require that two or more column supports be placed upon a single base or footing section. To prevent accumulation of stream debris at periods of high water or under other conditions the upstream piers may be constructed with cut-waters and in addition the piers may be connected by an integrally built web between them. When composed only of a wide blocklike form, it is called a wall or solid pier.

Pile Pier or Bent. A pier composed of driven piles capped or decked with a timber grillage or with a reinforced concrete slab forming the bridge seat.

Rigid Frame Pier. Pier with two or more columns and a horizontal beam on top constructed to act like a frame.

Pier Cap. (*Pier Top.*) The topmost portion of a pier. On rigid frame piers, the term applies to the beam across the column tops. On hammerhead and tee piers, the cap is a continuous beam.

Pilaster. A column-like projection upon a face surface rarely intended to serve as a structural member but instead functioning as an architectural treatment to relieve the blankness of a plane surface.

Pile. A rod or shaft-like linear member of timber, steel, concrete, or composite materials driven into the earth to carry structure loads thru weak strata of soil to those strata capable of supporting such loads. Piles are also used where loss of earth support due to scour is expected.

Bearing Pile. One which receives its support in bearing through the tip (or lower end) of the pile.

Friction Pile. One which receives its support through friction resistance along the lateral surface of the pile.

Sheet Piles. Commonly used in the construction of bulkheads, cofferdams, and cribs to retain earth and prevent the inflow of water, liquid mud, and fine grained sand with water, are of three general types, viz.: (1) Timber composed of a single piece or of two or more pieces spiked or bolted together to produce a compound piece either with a lap or a tongued and grooved effect. (2) Reinforced concrete slabs constructed with or without lap or tongued and grooved effect. (3) Rolled steel shapes with full provision for rigid interlocking of the edges.

Pile Cap. Concrete footings for a pier or abutment supported on piles. Also applied to the concrete below the pile tops when footing reinforcing steel is placed completely above the piles.

Pile Cut-Off. The portion of a pile removed or to be removed from its driven butt end to secure the elevation specified or indicated.

Pile Shoe. A metal piece fixed upon the point or penetration end of a pile to protect it from injury in driving and to facilitate penetration in every dense earth material.

Pile Splice. One of the means of joining one pile upon the end of another to provide greater penetration length.

Piling. (*Sheet Piling.*) General terms applied to assemblages of piles in a construction. See PILE.

Pin. A cylindrical bar used as a means of connecting, holding in position, and transmitting the stresses of, the members forming a truss or a framed joint. To restrain the pin against longitudinal movement its ends are fitted with pin nuts, cotter bolts, or both. The nuts are commonly of the recessed type taking bearing at their edges upon the assemblage of members. To prevent the loosening of the nuts and the displacement of the pins by vibration, joint movements, and other service conditions, the pin ends may be burred or they may be fitted with cotters.

Pin-Connected Truss. A general term applied to a truss of any type having its chord and web members connected at the truss joints by pins.

Pinion. The small driving gear on the powertrain of a movable bridge.

Pinion Bracket. The frame supporting the turning pinion with its shaft and bearings upon the drum girder or the loading girder of a swing span.

Pin Joint. A joint in a truss or other frame in which the members are assembled upon a cylindrical pin.

Pin Packing. An arrangement of truss members on a pin at a pinned joint.

Pin Plate. A plate or shape riveted or otherwise rigidly attached upon the end of a member to secure a desired bearing upon a pin or pin-like bearing; to develop and distribute the stress of the joint and/or secure additional strength and rigidity in the member.

Pintle. A small steel pin or stud, engaging the rocker in an exansion bearing, thereby permitting rotation, transferring shear, and preventing translation.

Pitch. The longitudinal spacing between rivets, studs, bolts, holes, etc., which are arranged in a straight line.

Plate Girder. An I-shaped beam composed of a solid plate web with either flange plates or flange angles bolted, riveted or welded upon its edges. Additional cover plates may be attached to the flanges to provide greater flange area.

Plinth. See FOOTING.

Plinth Course. The course or courses of stone forming the base portion of an abutment, pier, parapet or retaining wall and having a projection or extension beyond the general surface of the main body of the structure. See also BASE and FOOTING.

Plug Weld. (*Slot Weld.*) A weld joining two elements of a member or two members so assembled that an area of contact will be secured and the weld produced by depositing weld metal within circular, square, slotted or other shaped holes cut through one or more of the elements or members. This weld serves to unite the elements of a member or to join the members intersecting at truss at other joints of a structure.

Pointed Arch. See GOTHIC ARCH.

Pointing. The operations incident to the compacting of the mortar in the outermost portion of a joint and the troweling or other treatment of its exposed surface to secure water tightness or desired architectural effect or both.

Polygonal Truss. A general term applied to a truss of any type having an irregular or "broken" alignment of straight top chord members which forms with the end posts and the bottom chord the perimeter of a polygon.

Pony Truss. A general term applied to a truss having insufficient height to permit the use of an effective top chord system of lateral bracing above the bridge floor.

Pop-Out. Conical fragment broken out of concrete surface. Normally about one inch in diameter. Shattered aggregate particles usually found at bottom of hole.

Portable Bridge. A bridge so designed and constructed that it may be readily erected for a temporary communication-transport service; disassembled and its members again reassembled and the entire structure rendered ready for further service.

Portal. The clear unobstructed space of a through bridge forming the entrance to the structure.

The entire portal member of the top chord bracing which fixes the uppermost limit of the vertical clearance. See BRACING. The portal of a skew bridge is described as a "skew portal."

Post. A term commonly applied to a relatively short member resisting compressive stresses, located vertical or nearly vertical to the bottom chord of a truss and common to two truss panels. Sometimes used synonymously for column. See COLUMN.

Posted. A limiting dimension, speed, or loading, e.g., posted load, posted clearance, posted speed, indicating larger dimensions and higher speeds and loads can not be safely taken by the bridge.

Pot Holes. Small worn or distintegrated areas of bridge floor or approach surface concaved by the wearing action of vehicle wheels.

Pratt Truss. (*N-Truss.*) A truss with parallel chords and a web system composed of vertical posts with diagonal ties inclined outward and upward from the bottom chord panel points toward the ends of the truss except the counters required in midlength panels. The Parker Truss is an adaptation of the Pratt Truss by making the top chord polygonal in shape.

Priming Coat. (*Base Coat.*) The first coat of paint applied to the metal or other material of a bridge. For metal structures this is quite commonly a fabricating shop application and is, therefore, termed the "shop coat."

Protection Fence. See GUARD RAILING.

Protection Railing. See GUARD RAILING.

Q

Queen-Post Truss. A parallel chord type of truss adapted to either timber or metal bridge construction, having three panels with one of the chords occupying only the length of the center panel. Unless center panel diagonals are provided, it is a trussed beam.

R

Rack. A bar with teeth on one of its sides, designed to mesh with the gears of a pinion or worm. The rack is usually attached to the moving portion of a movable bridge and receives the motive power from the pinion.

Radial Rod. (*Spider Rod.*) A radially located tie rod connecting the roller circle of a rim-bearing swing span with the center pivot or center bearing casting.

Radial Strut. A radially located brace member of the drum construction of a rim-bearing swing span.

Railing. (*Handrail.*) A wooden, brick, stone, concrete or metal fence-like construction built at the side of the roadway, or the sidewalk, upon the retaining wall portion of an approach cut, embankment, or causeway or at the outermost edge of the roadway or the sidewalk portion of a bridge to guard or guide the movement of both pedestrian and vehicular traffic and to prevent the accidental passage of traffic over the side of the structure.

The term "handrail" is commonly applied only to railing presenting a latticed, barred, balustered or other open web construction.

Rake. The slope, batter or inclination from a horizontal, vertical or other assumed plane, of the sides of an embankment or other inclined earth construction; the batter of a face or other surface of masonry; of the plane of a truss side of a tower or other portion of a bridge superstructure or of any member thereof.

Ramp. An inclined traffic-way leading from one elevation to another. The general term used to designate an inclined roadway and/or sidewalk approach to a bridge and commonly applied to a rather steep incline.

Random Stone. A general term applied to quarried stone block of any dimensions whether intended for ashlar or for random masonry construction.

Range of Stress. The algebraic difference between the minimum and maximum stresses in a member or in an element or part thereof either computed to be produced by a given condition of loading or produced by its actual service loading.

Rebar. A steel reinforcing bar.

Redundant Member. A member in a truss or frame which renders it a statistically indeterminate structure. The structure would be stable without the redundant member whose primary purpose is to reduce the stresses carried by the determinate structure.

Re-Entrant Corner. A corner with more than 180° of material and less than 180° of open space.

Reinforcing Bar. A steel bar, plain or with a deformed surface, which bonds to the concrete and supplies tensile strength to the concrete.

Retaining Wall. A structure designed to restrain and hold back a mass of earth.

  Buttressed Wall. A retaining wall designed with projecting buttresses to provide strength and stability.

  Counterforted Wall. A retaining wall designed with projecting counterforts to provide strength and stability.

  Gravity Wall. A wall composed of brick, stone or concrete masonry designed to be stable against sliding and rotation (overturning) upon its foundation or upon any horizontal plane within its body by virtue of its shape and weight.

  Reinforced Concrete Cantilever Wall. A wall consisting of a base section integral with stem constructed approximately at a right angle thereto giving its cross section a letter "L" or an inverted "T" shape. The stem portion resists the horizontal or other forces tending to produce overturning by acting as a cantilever beam.

Rigid Frame Bridge. A bridge with rigid or moment resistant connections between deck slabs or beams and the substructure walls or columns, producing an integral, elastic structure. The structure may be steel or concrete.

In general this type of bridge may be regarded as a form of arch or curved beam having its intermediate intradosal section or portion either straight or slightly curved and its end sections located normal to the straight portion or to the tangent of the curved one at its center length position.

Rim Girder. See DRUM GIRDER.

Rim Plate. Toothed or plain segmental rim on a rolling lift bridge.

Ringbolt. See EYEBOLT.

Ring Stone. See VOUSSOIR.

Riprap. Brickbats, stones, blocks of concrete or other protective covering material of like nature deposited upon river and stream beds and banks, lake, tidal or other shores to prevent erosion and scour by water flow, wave or other movement.

Rise of an Arch. For a symmetrical arch; the vertical distance from the chord through its springing lines to the intrados at its crown.

For an unsymmetrical arch, assumed to be in a normal vertical position, the vertical distances from its springing lines to the intrados at its crown.

Riveted Joint. (Bolted Joint.) A joint in which the assembled elements and members are united by rivets. The design of a riveted joint contemplates a proper distribution of its rivets to develop its various parts with relation to the stresses and the purposes which each must serve.

A bolted joint differs from a riveted one only in the use of bolts as the uniting medium instead of rivets. The conditions of design are generally the same, but different allowable unit stresses are employed.

Roadway. (*Travel Way.*) 1. The portion of the deck surface of a bridge intended for the use of vehicular or vehicular and pedestrian traffic. 2. The top surface portion of an approach embankment, causeway or cut intended for the general use of vehicular or vehicular and pedestrian traffic. In general, its width corresponds (1) to the distance curb to curb; (2) to the distance between the outside limits of sidewalks; or (3) to the width of the roadway pavement or traveled way when no curbs exist.

Roadway Shoulder Area. (*Shoulder Area.*) The portion or area of the top surface of an approach embankment, causeway, or cut immediately adjoining the roadway, used to accommodate stopped vehicles in emergencies and to laterally support base and surface courses.

Rocker Bearing. A cylindrical, sector-shaped member attached by a pin or trunnion at its axis location to the expansion end of a girder or truss and having line bearing contact upon its perimetral surface with the masonry plate or pedestal, thus providing for the longitudinal movements resulting from temperature changes and superimposed loads by a wheel-like translation.

The design condition that the entire reaction stress is concentrated upon a line contact renders it especially essential that the masonry plate or pedestal be accurately leveled and that the rocker be carefully adjusted to secure a uniform even bearing thereon. A relatively large percentage of this type of bearings lack correct adjustment.

Rocker Bent. A bent composed of metal, reinforced concrete or timber, hinged or otherwise articulated at one or both ends to provide the longitudinal movements resulting from temperature changes and the superimposed loads of the span or spans supported thereon.

Rocker and Camshaft. An adjustable bearing device or assemblage consisting of a rocker bearing combined with a camshaft, properly mounted and geared to produce by its rotation a vertical lifting action, reacting upon a shoe plate or pedestal fixed upon the bridge seat. When installed at each outermost end of the girders, or the trusses of a swing span, the lifting action raises them to an extent that their camber or droop will be removed and the areas rendered free to act as simple spans. When the camshafts are revolved through an angle of 180° from their total or full lift position the rocker bearings are released and lifted and the span is free to be moved to "open" position.

Rolled Beams, Rolled Shapes. See STRUCTURAL SHAPES, WIDE FLANGE BEAMS.

Roller. 1. A steel cylinder forming an element of a roller nest or any other device or part intended to provide movements by rolling contact. The so-termed "segmental roller" consisting essentially of two circular segments integrally joined by a web-like portion is used in the construction of roller nests requiring relatively large bearing length with the least practicable shoe plate area and a correspondingly decreased weight of metal in the entire assemblage. 2. One of the wheel-like elements forming the roller circle of a rim-bearing swing span.

Roller Bearing. A single roller or a group of rollers so housed as to permit movement of a part or parts of a structure thereon.

Roller Nest. A group of steel cylinders forming a part of the movable end of a girder or truss and located between the masonry plate and shoe or pedestal to facilitate the longitudinal movements resulting from temperature changes and superimposed loads. Commonly the rollers are assembled in a frame or a box. Roller nests may be used for other services than those herein described. The term "Expansion Rollers" is sometimes used synonymously for roller nest.

Roller Track. The circular track upon which the drum rollers of a rim-bearing swing span travel. This is sometimes described as the lower track.

Roller Tread. See TREAD PLATES.

Rolling Lift Bridge. See MOVABLE BRIDGE.

Rubble. Irregularly shaped pieces of stone in the undressed condition obtained from the quarry and commonly ranging in size from relatively small usable pieces to one-man or two-man stones. This term is also applied to large boulders and fragments requiring mechanical equipment for handling. When shaped ready for use in rubble masonry, this stone is commonly described as "worked" or "dressed" rubble.

Run-Off. As applied to bridge design, the portion of the precipitation upon a drainage (catchment) area which is discharged quickly by its drainage stream or streams and which, therefore, becomes a factor in the design of the effective water discharge area of a bridge. Run-off is dependent upon soil porosity (varied by saturated or frozen condition), slope or soil surfaces, intensity of rainfall or of melting snow conditions, and other pertinent factors.

S

Saddle. A member located upon the topmost portion of the tower of a suspension bridge, designed to support the suspension cable or chain and to provide for its horizontal movements resulting from elastic deformations induced by temperature changes and the stresses incident to the service loadings.

Safe Load. The maximum loading determined by a consideration of its magnitudes and distributions of wheel, axle or other concentrations as productive of unit stresses in the various members and incidental details of a structure, permissible for service use, due consideration being given to the physical condition of the structure resulting from its previous service use.

Safety Curb. A narrow curb between 9 inches and 24 inches wide serving as a refuge or walkway for pedestrians crossing a bridge.

Sag. A deformation of an entire span; of any part of a span, or of one or more of its members from the horizontal, vertical, or inclined position intended as a condition of its original design and construction. This variation may result from elastic deformation of structural material; from irregularities produced by inadequate temporary supports during the progress of construction operations; or from incorrect adjustments and unworkmanlike procedures made a part of the work.

In existing structures sag may be attributable to (1) original construction irregularities; (2) to excessive stresses resulting from overloading; (3) to corrosion, decay or other deterioration of the structure materials, and (4) plastic flow of material.

The total deflection of the cable members of a suspension bridge. The so-termed "sag ratio" is the relation existing between the sag and the length of span.

Sag Rod. A rod usually fitted with threads and nuts at its ends; used to restrain a structure member from sagging due to its own weight or to external force or forces.

Sash Brace. (*Sash Stay, Sash Strut.*) A horizontal or nearly horizontal piece bolted or otherwise secured upon the side of a pile or framed bent between the cap and ground surface or the cap and sill, as the case may be, thus adding rigidity to the assemblage.

The horizontal member in a tier of bracing attached to a timber, reinforced concrete, or metal trestle bent or tower.

Scab. (*Scab Piece.*) A plank spiked or bolted over the joint between two members to hold them in correct adjustment and strengthen the joint.

A short piece of I-beam or other structural shape bolted, riveted or welded upon the flange and/or web of a metal pile to increase its resistance to penetration. Similarly, for the same purpose, a piece of dense hardwood fitted upon the flange and/or web and having bearing upon a lug angle at one or both its ends.

Scour. An erosion of a river, stream, tidal inlet, lake or other water bed area by a current, wash or other water in motion, producing a deepening of the overlying water, or a widening of the lateral dimension of the flow area.

Screw Jack and Pedestal. An adjustable device or assemblage consisting of a screw operated within a fixed nut and having upon its bottom end a pedestal-like bearing conjoined with it by a ball and socket or other equally adaptable articulation permitting its adjustment upon a shoe plate or pedestal fixed upon the bridge seat. When installed at each outermost end of the girders or the trusses of a swing span their major function is to lift them to an extent that their camber or droop will be removed and the arms rendered free to act as simple spans.

Scupper. (*Curb Inlet.*) An opening in the floor portion of a bridge, commonly located adjacent to the curb or wheel guard, to provide means for rain or other water accumulated upon the roadway surface to drain through it into the space beneath the structure. Bridges having reinforced concrete floors with concrete curbs may be effectively drained through scuppers located within the curb face surfaces.

Scupper Block. One of the short wooden pieces fixed between the wooden planks of a bridge floor and the bottom side of the wheel guard to provide open spaces beneath the latter for draining rain or other water accumulation from the floor surface.

Seam Weld. A weld joining the edges of two elements of a member or of two members placed in contact. This weld serves to form a continuous surface whether plane or curved, and to prevent infiltration of moisture between the parts. In general, it is not a stress carrying weld.

Seat Angle. (*Shelf Angle.*) A piece of angle attached upon the side of a column girder or other member to provide support for a connecting member either temporarily during its erection or permanently. The outstanding leg of the angle may be strengthened by a stiffener placed vertically beneath it.

Segmental Girder and Track Girder. These terms apply to the rolling lift type of bascule bridge combining circular rotation and translation movements in the "opening-closing" cycle.

The term "segmental girder" is used to designate one of the movable operating girders of a span or leaf to which a span girder or truss is rigidly attached. It commonly consists of a plate girder having its bottom flange curved to form a segment of a circle. This curved flange is fitted with tread castings which take line bearing contact upon the tread castings fitted upon the top flange of the supporting track girder with which they interlock to insure positive translation movement.

The term "track girder" is used to designate one of the plate girders or trusses intended to provide support for the movable span throughout an "opening-closing" cycle. Its tread castings fitted upon its top flange or chord form the track upon which the segmental girder moves by a rack and pinion-like action.

Segmental Rim. The curved rim or circular segment of a rolling lift bridge.

Seizing. The ligature of wire or other material applied upon a suspension bridge cable to hold the individual wires in satisfactory contact condition.

Separator. See SPREADER.

Shafts. Pieces conveying torsion stress only, which are, in general, used only in movable structures.

Shear Lock. (*Heel Stay, Tail-Lock.*) The device or mechanism provided at the heel of a bascule span to engage and hold the leaf in its closed position and prevent rotation.

Sheave. A wheel having a groove or grooves in its face surface. This term may be applied collectively to include both the sheave and its housing block.

Sheave Girder. A girder or girder-like member supporting the operating cable sheaves at the top of a tower of a vertical lift bridge.

Sheave Hood. A protecting covering placed above a sheave engaging the suspending cables of a vertical lift bridge to prevent accumulations of moisture, sleet and ice upon the sheave face.

Sheet Pile Cofferdam. In general a wall-like, watertight or nearly watertight barrier composed of driven timber or metal sheet piling constructed to surround the area to be occupied by an abutment, pier, retaining wall or other structure and permit unwatering of the enclosure so that the excavation for the preparation of a foundation and the abutment, pier or other construction may be produced in the open air. The alignment of the piles may be facilitated by the use of walers, struts and ties.

This type of dam is adapted to construction located in still or slow flowing shallow water. Its watertightness is sometimes rendered more complete by depositing earth material against the exterior side of the dam.

Sheet Piling. (*Sheeting.*) A general or collective term used to describe a number of sheet piles taken together to form a crib, cofferdam, bulkhead, etc.

Shelf Angle. See SEAT ANGLE.

Shim. A comparatively thin piece of wood, stone, or metal inserted between two elements, pieces or members to fix their relative position and/or to transmit bearing stress.

Shoe. In general, a pedestal-shaped member at the end of a plate girder or truss functioning to transmit and distribute its loads to a masonry bearing area or to any other supporting area or member. A shoe may be a cast or a built-up member; the base plate or plate-like part of which is commonly termed the "shoe plate," which may take bearing directly upon a masonry plate or upon an intervening expansion device.

Shore. A strut or prop placed in a horizontal, inclined or vertical position against or beneath a structure or a portion thereof to restrain movement.

Shoulder Area. See ROADWAY SHOULDER AREA.

Sidewalk. The portion of the bridge floor area serving pedestrian traffic only and, for safety and convenience to its users, commonly elevated above the portion occupied by vehicles.

Sidewalk Bracket. As applied to metal structures: A trianguar shaped frame attached to and projecting from the outside of a girder, truss or bent to serve as a support for the sidewalk stringers, floor and railing or parapet. In general, these brackets are in effect a cantilevered extension of the floor beams and are commonly connected to them by bars or other tension pieces designed to sustain the bending moment at the junction plane.

As applied to reinforced concrete structures: A cantilever beam commonly triangular in shape, attached to and projecting from the outside of a girder, truss, or bent to serve as a support for the sidewalk floor slab and the railing or parapet.

Sill. (*Sill Piece.*) The base piece or member of a viaduct or trestle bent serving to distribute the column loads directly upon the foundation or upon mud sills embedded in the foundation soil transversely to the alignment of the bent.

Silt. Very finely divided siliceous or other hard and durable rock material derived from its mother rock through attritive or other mechanical action rather than chemical decomposition. In general, its grain size shall be that which will pass a Standard No. 200 sieve.

Simple Span. A superstructure span having, at each end, a single unrestraining bearing or support and designed to be unaffected by stress transmission to or from an adjacent span or structure.

S-I-P Forms. See FORMS.

Skew Angle. As applied to oblique bridges; the skew angle, angle of skew or simply "skew" is the acute angle subtended by a line normal to the longitudinal axis of the structure and a line parallel to or coinciding with the alignment of its end.

Skewback. The course of stones, in an abutment or pier, located at the extremity of an arch and having its beds inclined (battered) as required to transmit the stresses of the arch. The bed adjoining the voussoirs forming the first string course of the arch ring will be normal to the axis of the arch. The individual stones of the skewback course are designated "skewback stones."

A casting or a combination of castings; or a built-up member designed to function as a skewback.

Skewback Shoe. (*Skewback Pedestal.*) The shoe or pedestal member, transmitting the thrust of a trussed arch or a plate girder arch to the skewback course or cushion course of an abutment or pier. Skewback shoes and pedestals are commonly hinged.

Slab. A thick plate, usually of reinforced concrete, which supports load by flexure. It is usually treated as a widened beam.

Slab Bridge. A bridge having a superstructure composed of a reinforced concrete slab constructed either as a single unit or as a series of narrow slabs placed parallel with the roadway alignment and spanning the space between the supporting abutments or other substructure parts. The former is commonly constructed in place but the latter may be precast.

Slag Inclusion. Small particles of slag trapped inside a weld during the fusion process.

Sleeve Nut. A device used to connect the elements of an adjustable rod or bar member. It consists of a forging having an elongated nut-shaped body with right- and left-hand threads within its end portions, thus permitting its adjustment with a wrench to provide a desired tension in the member.

Slenderness Ratio. Measure of stiffness of a member, expressed as the length of the member divided by its radius of gyration.

Slope. A term commonly applied to the inclined surface of an excavated cut or an embankment.

Slope Pavement. (*Slope Protection.*) A thin surfacing of stone, concrete or other material deposited upon the sloped surface of an approach cut, embankment or causeway to prevent its disintegration by rain, wind or other erosive action.

Slot Weld. See PLUG WELD.

Soffit. See INTRADOS.

Sole Plate. A plate bolted, riveted, or welded upon the bottom flange of a rolled beam, plate girder, or truss to take direct bearing upon a roller nest, bearing pedestal, or masonry plate. It distributes the reaction of the bearing to the beam, girder, or truss member. The sole plate may also function as a combined sole and masonry plate at the fixed end of a beam, girder, or truss.

Soldier Beam. A steel pile driven into the earth with its butt end projecting, used as a cantilever beam to support horizontal lagging retaining an excavated surface.

Spalls. Circular or oval depression in concrete caused by a separation of a portion of the surface concrete, revealing a fracture parallel with or slightly inclined to the surface. Usually part of the rim is perpendicular to the surface.

The pieces of spalled concrete themselves.

Span. This term has various applications depending upon its use whether in design, in field construction, or in its common nontechnical application, viz.:

When applied to design of a beam, girder, truss or arch structure. The distance center to center of the end bearings or the distance between the lines of action of the reactions whether induced by substructure or other supporting members.

When applied to the field construction of substructure abutments and piers. The unobstructed space or distance between the faces of the substructure elements. For arch structures this length is measured at the elevation of the springing lines. These lengths or dimensions are commonly referred to as "clear span length." See CLEAR SPAN.

The complete superstructure of a single span bridge or a corresponding integral part or unit of a multiple span structure. This application of "span" is rendered more specific when subdivided into: (a) Fixed Span: A superstructure anchored in its location upon the substructure and (b) Movable Span: A superstructure intended to be swung or lifted to provide an unobstructed waterway space for the passage of waterborne traffic.

Spandrel. The space bounded by the arch extrados, the substructure abutments and/or pier(s), and the roadway surface or other elevation limit fixed by the construction details.

Spandrel Column. A column superimposed upon the ring or a rib of an arch span and serving as a support for the deck construction of an open spandrel arch. See OPEN SPANDREL ARCH.

Spandrel Fill. The filling material placed within the spandrel space of a spandrel arch.

Spandrel Tie. A wall or a beam-like member connecting the spandrel walls of an arch and securing them against bulging and other deformation. In stone masonry arches the spandrel tie walls served to some extent as counterforts. In reinforced concrete spandrel arch spans spandrel tie walls may likewise serve as counterforts. See TIE WALLS.

Spandrel Wall. A wall built upon an arch to function as a retaining wall for the spandrel fill and the roadway in a spandrel filled structure; but, when the spandrel is not filled, to support the floor system and its loads. In wide structures having unfilled spandrels one or more interior walls may be used, thus providing a cellular construction when combined with tie walls. See TIE WALLS.

Specifications. A detailed enumeration of the chemical and physical properties determining the quality of construction materials together with requirements for handling, shipping and storage thereof; the conditions governing the loads, load applications and unit stress considerations of bridge foundation, substructure and superstructure design; the development of construction details and their applications incident to fabrication; erecton or other construction procedures pertinent to the production of serviceable bridge structures.

When general or so called "standard" specifications are used, it occasionally becomes necessary to supplement the requirements by items having specific application to a given bridge structure or group of structures. The special items may either designate and authorize departures from the "standard" or apply entirely to requirements and conditions not dealt with therein. The status of these supplemental or special specifications is commonly fixed by the "standard" specifications. Likewise the "standard" specification commonly recognizes the possibility of discrepancies between the specifications and the general plans and working (detail) drawings by fixing a coordination status for such occurrences.

Spider. The collar-like plate connecting the spider frame of a rim bearing or a combined rim and center bearing swing span to the pivot.

Spider Frame. The frame assemblage of struts, radial rods, spacer rings and roller adjusting devices holding the conical roller ring of a rim bearing or a combined rim and center bearing swing span in correct position with relation to the pivot.

Spider Rod. See RADIAL ROD.

Splay Saddle. A member at the anchorage ends of suspension bridge cables which permits the wires or strands to spread so that they may be connected to the anchorage.

Splice. This term has two applications depending upon its use whether in design or in shop and field construction, viz.:

When applied to design and the development of construction details: The joining or uniting of elements of a member, parts of a member or members of a structure to provide desired conditions for the transmittal of stress and the development of rigidity and general strength fulfilling the service requirements of the member or of the structure of which it is a part.

When applied to shop and field construction: the complete assemblage of parts used in producing the union of elements of a member or members of a structure.

Splice Joint. A joint in which the elements of a member or the members of a structure are joined by a splice plate or by a part or piece functioning to secure a required amount of strength and stability.

Spreader. 1. A cast or fabricated piece used to hold angles, beams, channels or fabricated pieces or parts in the locations or positions in which they function as parts of a member or structure. 2. A ring-like or sleeve-like piece placed upon a pin to hold the eyebars or other members assembled upon it in their correct member positions. This piece is sometimes described as a "pin-filler," or "packing ring."

Springing Line. The line within the face surface of an abutment or pier at which the intrados of an arch takes its beginning or origin.

Starling. An extension at the upstream end only, or at both the upstream and downstream ends of a pier built with surfaces battered thus forming a cutwater to divide and deflect the stream waters and floating debris and, correspondingly, when on the downstream end, functioning to reduce crosscurrents, swirl and eddy action which are productive of depositions of sand, silt and detritus downstream from the pier.

Statics. The branch of physical science which is concerned with bodies acted on by balanced forces. Therefore, these bodies are either at rest or static.

Stay-In-Place Forms. See FORMS.

Stay Plate. (*Tie Plate.*) A plate placed at or near the end of a latticed side or web of a compression or other member and also at intermediate locations where connections for members interrupt the continuity of the latticing. This plate serves to distribute the lattice bar stress to the elements of the member and adds stiffness and rigidity to joint assemblages.

Stem. The vertical wall portion of an abutment retaining wall, or solid pier. See also BREASTWALL.

Stiffener. An angle, tee, plate or other rolled section riveted, bolted or welded upon the web of a plate girder or other "built-up" member to transfer stress and to prevent buckling or other deformation.

A stiffener forged at its ends to fit upon the web and the web-legs of the flange angles of a plate girder is termed "crimped."

Stiffening Girder, Stiffening Truss. A girder or truss incorporated in a suspension bridge to function in conjunction with a suspension cable or chain by restraining the deformations of the latter and by distributing the concentrated or other irregularly distributed loads thus resisting and controlling the vertical oscillations of the floor system imparted to it by the cable or chain deformations.

Stirrup. In timber and metal bridges: A U-shaped rod, bar or angle piece providing a stirrup-like support for an element of a member or a member.

In reinforced concrete bridges: A U-shaped bar placed in beams, slabs or similar constructions to resist diagonal tension stresses.

Stirrup Bolt. A U-shaped rod or bar fitted at its ends with threads, nuts and washers and used to support streamer or other timber pieces of wooden truss structures suspended from the bottom chord.

Stone Facing. (*Stone Veneer, Brick Veneer.*) A stone or brick surface covering or sheath laid in imitation of stone or brick masonry but having a depth thickness equal to the width dimension of one stone or brick for stretchers and the length dimension for headers. The backing portion of a wall or the interior portion of a pier may be constructed of rough stones imbedded in mortar or concrete, cyclopean concrete, plain or reinforced concrete, brick bats imbedded in mortar, or even of mortar alone. The backing and interior material may be deposited as the laying of the facing material progresses to secure interlocking and bonding with it, or the covering material may be laid upon its preformed surface.

Strain. The distortion of a body produced by the application of one or more external forces and measured in units of length. In common usage, this is the proportional relation of the amount of distortion divided by the original length.

Stress. The resistance of a body tp distortion when in a solid or plastic state and when acting in an unconfined condition. Stress is produced by the strain (distortion) and holds in equilibrium the external forces causing the distortion. It is measured in pounds or tons. Within the elastic limit the strain in a member of a structure is proportional to the stress in that member.

Allowable Unit Stress. As applied to the investigation of an existing structure in determining its adequacy for existing or prospective service; it is the stress per unit of area of the material of the entire structure or any portion or member thereof which is determined to be a safe unit for service use, due consideration being given to the quality of the material, physical condition, the adequacy of the construction details or other physical factors incident or pertinent to the service conditions to which they are or will be subjected and, if necessary, to the conditions contemplated to exist in the event of repair, replacement or strengthening operations.

Unit Stress. The stress per square inch (or other unit of surface or crosssectional area). The Allowable Unit Stress is: (a) Assumed in determining the composition and construction details of a memer or the members of a proposed structure, or (b) assumed for judging the safe load-capacity of an existing structure; while working stress is (c) produced in the members and parts of an existing structure when subjected to loads, impacts and other stress-producing elements and factors to which the structure is proposed to be or may have been subjected.

Working Stress. The unit stress in a member under service or design load.

Stress Sheet. A drawing showing a structure in skeletal form sufficient only to impart or suggest in conjunction with notations thereon its general makeup, major dimensions and the arrangement and composition of its integral parts. Special construction details may be shown by section views and sketches with or without dimensional data. Upon the skeletal outline of the structure or in tabulated form the drawing should show the computed stresses resulting from the application of a system of loads together with the design composition of the individual members resulting from the application of assumed unit stresses for the material or materials to be used in the structures. The assumed design load or loads should appear either in diagrammatic form with dimensions and magnitudes, or reference be made to readily available information relating thereto by a special note conspicuously displayed upon the drawing. A future investigation of a given structure to determine its reliability for a given load or combination of loads may be greatly facilitated and expedited by an adequate stress sheet record of its original design conditions.

Stringer. A longitudinal beam supporting the bridge deck, and in large bridges or truss bridges, framed into or upon the floor beams.

Structural Members. Basically these are of three types, viz.: (1) Ties: Pieces subject to axial tension only; (2) Columns or Struts: Pieces subject to axial compression only; (3) Beams: Pieces transversely loaded and subject to both shear and bending moment.

However, the arrangement of the members of a structure and the application of its design loads may embody combinations of these basic stress types.

Structural Shapes. As applied to bridge structures: The various types and forms of rolled iron and steel having flat, round, angle, channel, "I", "H", "Z" and other cross-sectional shapes adapted to the construction of the metal members incorporated in reinforced foundations, substructures and superstructures.

Structural Tee. A tee-shaped rolled member formed by cutting a wide flange longitudinally along the centerline of web.

Strut. A general term applying to a piece or member acting to resist compressive stress.

Sub-Panel. See PANEL.

Subpunched and Reamed Work. A term applied to structural steel shapes having rivet holes punched a specified dimension less in diameter than the nominal size of the rivets to be driven therein and subsequently reamed to a specified diameter greater than the rivet size.

This term is also applied to completely assembled and riveted members and structures in which the rivet holes have been produced by subpunching and reaming procedure.

Substructure. The abutments, piers, grillage or other constructions built to support the span or spans of a bridge superstructure whether consisting of beam, girder, truss, trestle or other type or types of construction.

Sump. A pit or tank-like depression or receptacle into which water is drained. The removal of the water so accumulated may be effected by pumping or by siphoning.

Superelevation. (*Curve Banking.*) The transverse inclination of the roadway surface within a horizontal curve and the relatively short tangent lengths adjacent thereto required for its full development. The purpose of superelevation is to provide a means of resisting or overcoming the centrifugal forces of vehicles in transit.

Superstructure. The entire portion of a bridge structure which primarily receives and supports highway, railway, canal, or other traffic loads and in its turn transfers the reactions resulting therefrom to the bridge substructure. The superstructure may consist of beam, girder, truss, trestle or other type or types of construction.

A superstructure may consist of a single span upon two supports or of a combination of two or more spans having the number and distribution of supports required by their types of construction, whether consisting of simple, continuous, cantilever, suspension, arch or trestle span-tower-bent construction.

Surcharge. An additional load placed atop existing earth or dead loads. In the case of abutments and retaining walls, the surcharge load is assumed to be replaced by an earth load of equivalent total weight.

Suspended Span. A superstructure span having one or both of its ends supported upon or from adjoining cantilever arms, brackets or towers, and designed to be unaffected by other stress transmission to or from an adjacent structure. The ordinary use of a suspended span is in connection with cantilever span construction.

Suspender. A wire cable, a metal rod or bar designed to engage a cable band or other device connecting it to the main suspension member of a suspension bridge at one end and a member of the bridge floor system at the other thus permitting it to assist in supporting the bridge floor system and its superimposed loads by transferring loads to the main suspension members of the structure.

A member serving to support another member in a horizontal or an inclined position against sagging, twisting or other deformation due to its own weight.

Suspension Bridge. A bridge in which the floor system and its incidental parts and appliances are supported in practically a horizontal position by being suspended upon cables which are supported at two or more locations upon towers and are anchored at their extreme ends. The cables constitute the main suspension members and commonly their anchorage may be one of three forms, viz.: (1) By extension of these members beyond the towers to the anchorages; (2) By fixing their ends upon the towers and backstaying the towers against overturning by the suspension members pulling upon them; (3) By an integral inclusion of the anchorages within the structure whereby the entire horizontal and vertical components of the main suspension member stresses are resisted by a rigid floor system construction functioning as a column, upon the extreme ends of which the main suspension members are securely connected. This form is commonly described as "self anchored."

Suspension Cable. (*Suspension Chain.*) One of the main members upon which the floor system of a suspension bridge is supported. Its ends may be fixed at the tops of towers which are backstayed to resist the horizontal components of the cable or chain stresses or instead it may rest upon saddles at the tops of two or more towers and be extended and fixed upon anchorage members. When the extension portions from the tops of towers to the anchorages do not directly support any part of the bridge floor, they function essentially as backstays; but when they engage floor suspenders located between the towers and anchorages they function as suspension cables for the end spans of the structure.

Sway Anchorage. (*Sway Cable.*) A guy, stay cable or chain attached at an intermediate length location upon the floor system of a suspension bridge and anchored upon the end portion of an abutment or pier or in the adjacent land surface to increase the resistance of the suspension span to lateral movement.

Sway Brace. 1. A piece bolted, or otherwise secured in an inclined position upon the side of a pile or frame bent between the cap and ground surface or the cap and sills, as the case may be, to add rigidity to the assemblage. See BRAC-

ING. 2. An inclined member in a tier of bracing forming a part of a timber, metal, or R/C bent or tower. 3. One of the inclined members of the sway bracing system of a metal girder or truss span. In plate girder construction the term X-brace is sometimes used.

Sway Frame. A complete panel or frame of sway bracing. See BRACING.

Swedge Bolt. See ANCHOR BOLT.

Swing Span. A superstructure span designed to be entirely supported upon a pier at its center, when its end supports have been withdrawn or released, and equipped to be revolved in a horizontal plane to free a navigable waterway of the obstruction it presents to navigation when in its normal traffic service position. See MOVABLE BRIDGE.

Swing Span Pivot. The center casting upon or about which the movable portion of a swing span revolves in making an opening-closing cycle.

In the center bearing type span, this casting functions not only as a pivotal member but also as the support for the movable span when the end lifting device is released.

In the rim-bearing type span this casting functions as a pivotal anchor member regulating the location of the movable parts throughout an opening-closing cycle but does not support the movable span.

In the combined center and rim-bearing type this casting functions as a support for a portion of the weight of the movable span when the end lifting device is released.

T

Tack Weld. A weld of the butt, fillet or seam type intended only to fix an element of a member or a member of a structure in correct adjustment and position preparatory to fully welding. Tack welds may be used to restrain welded parts against deformation and distortion resulting from expansion of the metal by atmospheric and welding temperatures.

Tail Lock. See SHEAR LOCK.

Tail Pit. See COUNTERWEIGHT WELL.

Tail Water. Water ponded below the outlet of a culvert, pipe, or bridge waterway, thereby reducing the amount of flow through the waterway. Tailwater is expressed in terms of its depth. See also HEADWATER.

Temporary Bridge. A structure built for emergency or interim use to replace a previously existing bridge demolished or rendered unserviceable by flood, fire, wind or other untoward occurrence, or instead, to supply bridge service required for a relatively short period.

Tendon. A prestressing cable or strand.

Tension. An axial force or stress caused by equal and opposite forces pulling at the ends of the members.

Throat. Of a fillet weld. The dimension normal to the sloping face of a fillet weld between the heel of the weld and the sloping faces.

Through Bridge. A bridge having its floor elevation more nearly at the elevation of the bottom than at the top portion of the superstructure, thus providing for the passage of traffic between the supporting parts.

Tide Gate. See FLOOD GATE.

Tie Plate. See STAY PLATE.

Tie Rod. (*Tie Bar.*) A rod-like or bar-like member in a truss or other frame functioning to transmit tensile stress.

Tie Walls. (*Spandrel Tie Wall.*) One of the walls built at intervals above the arch ring to tie together and reinforce the spandrel walls. See DIAPHRAGM WALL.

Any wall designed to serve as a restraining member to prevent bulging and distortion of two other walls connected thereby.

Toe of Slope. The location defined by the intersection of the sloped surface of an approach cut, embankment or causeway or other sloped area with the natural or an artifical ground surface existing at a lower elevation.

Toe Wall. (*Footwall.*) A relatively low retaining wall placed near the "toe-of-slope" location of an approach embankment or causeway to produce a fixed termination or to serve as a protection against erosion and scour or, perhaps, to prevent the accumulation of stream debris.

Toggle Joint. A mechanical arrangement wherein two members are hinged together, in fact or in effect, at a central location and hinged separately at their opposite ends; their alignment forming an obtuse angle so that a force applied at the common hinge location will produce a thrust acting at the end hinges, laterally to the alignment or direction of the original force.

Tolerance. (*Margin.*) A range or variation in physical or chemical properties specified or otherwise determined as permissible for the acceptance and use of construction materials.

Tower. 1. A three dimension substructure framework in a viaduct type structure having the vertical bents at its ends joined longitudinally by struts and braces thus rendering the assemblage so formed effective in resisting forces acting longitudinally upon the structure. 2. A four-sided frame supporting the ends of two spans or instead one complete span (tower span) and the ends of two adjacent spans of a viaduct; having its column members strutted and braced in tiers and the planes of either two or four sides battered. 3. A pier or a frame serving to support the cables or chains of a suspension type bridge at the end of a span. 4. A frame functioning as an end support, guide frame and counterweight support for a vertical lift span during an operating cycle.

Track Girder. See SEGMENTAL GIRDER.

Track Plate. The plate, toothed or plain, upon which the segmental girder of a rolling lift span rolls.

Track Segment. One of the assemblage pieces of the circular track supporting the balance wheels of a center bearing swing span or the drum bearing wheels of a drum or combined center and drum bearing span.

Transition Length. The tangent length within which the change from a normal to a superelevated roadway cross section is developed.

Transverse Bracing. (*Transverse System.*) The bracing assemblage engaging the columns of trestle and viaduct bents and towers in perpendicular or slightly inclined planes and in the horizontal or nearly horizontal planes of their sash braces to function in resisting the transverse forces resulting from wind, lateral vibration and traffic movements tending to produce lateral movement and deformation of the columns united thereby. See BRACING.

Transverse Girder. See CROSS GIRDER.

Travel Way. See ROADWAY.

Tread Plates. (*Roller Tread.*) The plates attached upon the bottom flange of the drum girder; shaped to form a circular surface taking a uniform even bearing upon the drum rollers and thereby transferring to them the live and dead loads of the superimposed structure. The assemblage of tread plates is sometimes described as the "Upper Track."

Tremie. A long trunk or pipe used to place concrete under water. A tremie usually has a hopper at its upper end.

The concrete placed under water by use of a tremie is often called tremie concrete. In placing tremie concrete, it is important that the mouth of the tremie be kept immersed within the mass of concrete already deposited to prevent the water from mixing with the concrete, thereby weakening or destroying it.

Trestle. A bridge structure consisting of beam, girder or truss spans supported upon bents. The bents may be of the piled or of the frame type, composed of timber, reinforced concrete or metal. When of framed timbers, metal or reinforced concrete they may involve two or more tiers in their construction. Trestle structures are designated as "wooden," "frame," or "framed," "metal," "concrete," "wooden pile," "concrete pile," etc., depending upon or corresponding to the material and characteristics of their principal members.

Trailing Wheel. See BALANCE WHEEL.

Triangular Truss. See WARREN TRUSS.

Trunnion. As applied to a bascule bridge. The assemblage consisting essentially of a pin fitted into a supporting bearing and forming a hinge or axle upon which the movable span swings during an opening-closing cycle.

Trunnion Girder. The girder supporting the trunnions on a bascule bridge.

Truss. A jointed structure having an open built web construction so arranged that the frame is divided into a series of triangular figures with its component straight members primarily stressed axially only. The triangle is the truss element and each type of truss used in bridge construction is an assemblage of triangles. The connecting pins are assumed to be frictionless.

Truss Bridge. A bridge having a truss for a superstructure: The ordinary single span rests upon two supports, one at each end, which may be abutments, piers, bents or towers, or combinations thereof. The superstructure span may be divided into three parts, viz.: (1) the trusses, (2) the floor system and (3) the bracing.

Truss Panel. See PANEL.

Trussed Beam. A beam reinforced by one or more rods upon its tension side attached at or near its ends and passing beneath a support at the midlength of the span producing in effect an inverted King post truss. The support, if a wooden block, is commonly termed a "saddle block" but, if a cast iron or structural steel member it is termed a "stanchion."

Tubular Truss. A truss whose chords and struts are composed of pipes or cylindrical tubes.

Tudor Arch. See GOTHIC ARCH.

Turnbuckle. A device used to connect the elements of adjustable rod and bar members. It consists of a forging having nut-like end portions right and left hand threaded and integrally connected by two bars upon its opposite sides thus providing an intervening open space through which a lever may be inserted to adjust the tension in the member.

Turning Pinion and Rack. The pinion to which the power to operate a swing span is applied and the circular rack fixed upon the pivot pier upon which the pinion travels to produce its rotation movement. When a swing span requires a very considerable amount of power to operate it, two operating pinions located at opposite sides of the circular rack or nearly so are commonly used to distribute the operating force upon the rack and its anchorage.

U

U–Bolt. A bar, either round or square, bent in the shape of the letter "U" and fitted with threads and nuts at its ends.

Underpass. See OVERPASS.

Uplift. A negative reaction or a force tending to lift a beam, truss, pile, or any other bridge element upwards.

V

Vertical-Lift Bridge. See MOVABLE BRIDGE.

Viaduct. A bridge structure consisting of beam, girder, truss, or arch span supported upon abutments with towers or alternate towers and bents or with a series of piers (cylindrical, dumbbell, rectangular or other types), or with any combination of these types of supporting parts.

In general, a viaduct is regarded as having greater height than a trestle. However, this notion is inconsistent with bridge engineering practice. A viaduct may be in all respects like a multiple span bridge.

Vierendeel Truss. A rigid frame consisting essentially of an assemblage of rectangles and trapezoids with no diagonal members. Its service in a bridge is the same as that assigned to a plate girder or a truss.

Voided Unit. A precast concrete deck unit containing cylindrical voids to reduce dead load.

Voussoir. (*Ring Stone.*) One of the truncated wedge shaped stones composing a ring course in a stone arch. The facing or head voussoirs are those placed at the terminations of a ring course.

W

Wale. (*Wale-Piece, Waler.*) A wooden or metal piece or an assemblage of pieces placed either inside or outside, or both inside and outside, the wall portion of a crib, cofferdam or similar structure, usually in a horizontal position to maintain its shape and increase its rigidity, stability, and strength. An assemblage of wale pieces is termed a "waling," or "strake o' wail."

Warren Truss. (*Triangular Truss.*) A parallel chord truss developed for use in metal bridge structures, wherein the web system is usually formed by a single triangulation of members at an angle to each other. There are no counters but web members near the center of a span may be subject to stress reversals and are to be designed accordingly. Verticals may or may not be used.

Washer. A small metal disc having a hole in its center to engage a bolt or a rivet. It may be used beneath the nut or the head of a bolt or as a separator between elements of a member or the members of a structure.

Water Table. The upper limit or elevation of ground water saturating a portion of a soil mass.

Waterway. The available width for the passage of stream, tidal or other water beneath a bridge, if unobstructed by natural formations or by artificial constructions beneath or closely adjacent to the structure. For a multiple span bridge the available width is the total of the unobstructed waterway lengths of the spans. See CLEAR SPAN.

Wearing Surface. (*Wearing Course.*) The surface portion of a roadway area which is in direct contact with the means of transport and is, therefore, primarily subject to the abrading, crushing or other disintegrating effect produced by hammering, rolling, sliding or other physical action tending to induce attrition thereof.

A topmost layer or course of material applied upon a roadway to receive the traffic service loads and to resist the abrading, crushing or other distintegrating action resulting therefrom.

Web. The portion of a beam, girder or truss, located between and connected to the flanges or the chords. It serves mainly to resist shear stresses. The stem of a dumbbell or solid wall type pier.

Web Members. The intermediate members of a truss extending, in general, from chord to chord but not including the end posts. Inclined web members are termed diagonals. A "tie" is a diagonal in tension while a brace or strut is a diagonal in compression. A vertical web member in compression is commonly designated a post, while one in tension due entirely to the external forces applied at its lower end, is designated a hanger. The joint formed by the intersection of an inclined end post with the top chord is commonly designated the hip joint or "the hip" end and the vertical tension member engaging the hip joint is commonly known as the hip vertical or the first panel hanger.

Web Plate. The plate forming the web element of a plate girder, built-up beam or column.

Wedge and Pedestals. An adjustable bearing device or assemblage consisting of a wedge operating between an upper and a lower bearing block or pedestal, and when installed at each outermost end of the girders or the trusses of a swing span, functioning to lift them to an extent that their camber or "droop" will be removed and the arms rendered free to act as simple spans. Furthermore, when installed beneath the loading girder of a center bearing swing span they serve to relieve the pivot bearing from all or nearly all live load and to stabilize the center portion of the span. When the wedges are withdrawn and the end latching device released, the span is free to be moved to an "open" position.

Lifting devices of the wedge and pedestal type may be used under the loading girder of a center bearing swing span in conjunction with rocker and eccentric, link and roller, or other end lifting devices at the ends of the span.

However, some swing spans of short length and placed in rather unimportant locations are designed to support both dead and live loads upon the center pivot and the ends of span are inadequately lifted with the result that they "end hammer" upon their pedestals.

Wedge Stroke. The theoretical travel distance a wedge must move upon its pedestal to lift the end of the arm of a swing span a distance equal to the vertical camber or "droop" of the arm due to elastic deformation minus the portion assumed to be provided in the field erection operation.

The actual elastic deformation of the arms of a given swing span may vary considerably from the theoretical due probably to temperature variations during the periods in which fabrication and erection are in progress, or to variation in the friction developed between the elements combined to form joints and to other incidental irregularities.

Weep Hole. (*Weep Pipe.*) An open hole or an embedded pipe in a masonry retaining wall, abutment, arch or other portion of a masonry structure to provide means of drainage for the embankment, causeway, spandrel backfill or retained soil wherein water may accumulate.

Weld. The process of uniting portions of one or more pieces, the elements of a member, or the members of a structure in an intimate and permanent position or status by (1) the application of pressure induced by the blow of a hammer or by a pressure machine, the portions to be united having been previously heated to a so-called welding temperature and the junction areas cleaned and purified by the application of fluxing material, or by (2) the use of a high temperature flame to preheat the metal adjacent to the weld location and when it has attained a molten temperature to add molten weld metal, in conjunction with fluxing material, in sufficient quantity to produce a fully filled joint when cooled or by (3) the use of the electric arc to obtain a molten temperature in the metal closely adjacent to the weld location and to supply in the arc stream molten filler metal and fluxing material requisite to produce by coalescence of the structure and electrode metals a fully filled joint.

The joint produced by the application of a welding process.

Weld Layer. A single thickness of weld metal composed of beads (runs) laid in contact to form a pad weld or a portion of a weld made up of superimposed beads.

Weld Metal. The fused filler metal which is added to the fused structure metal to produce by coalescence and interdiffusion a welded joint or a weld layer.

Weld Penetration. The depth beneath the original surface, to which the structure metal has been fused in the making of a fusion weld. See PENETRATION.

Weld Sequence. The order of succession required for making the welds of a built-up piece or the joints of a structure to avoid, so far as practicable, the residual stresses producing or tending to produce individual joint distortions and deformations of the structure or its members.

Welded Bridge. (*Welded Structure.*) A structure wherein the metal elements composing its members and the joints whereby these members are combined into the structure frame, are united by welds.

Welded Joint. A joint in which the assembled elements and members are united through fusion of metal. The design of a welded joint contemplates a proper distribution of the welds to develop its various parts with relation to the stresses and the purpose which each must serve, due consideration being given to factors productive of secondary stresses through weld shrinkage, warping and other conditions attending weld fabrication.

Wheel Base. A term applied to the axle spacing or lengths of vehicles. When applied to automobiles and trucks having wheel concentrations at the ends of the front and rear axles it is the length center to center of axles or the longitudinal dimension center to center of front and rear wheels.

Wheel Concentration. (*Wheel Load.*) The load carried by and transmitted to the supporting structure by one wheel. This concentration may involve the wheel of a traffic vehicle, a movable bridge, or other motive equipment or device. See AXLE LOAD.

Wheel Guard. (*Filloe Guard.*) A timber piece placed longitudinally along the side limit of the roadway to guide the movements of vehicle wheels and safeguard the bridge trusses, railings and other constructions existing outside the roadway limit from collision with vehicles and their loads.

Whiteway Lighting. The lighting provided for nighttime illumination along a road or bridge, as distinguished from sign lighting or colored regulatory and warning lights.

Wide Flange. (*Carnegie Beam.*) A rolled member having an H-shaped cross section, differentiated from an I-beam in that the flanges are wider and the web thinner.

Wind Bracing. The bracing systems in girder and truss spans and in towers and bents which function to resist the stresses induced by wind forces.

Wing Wall. The retaining wall extension of an abutment intended to restrain and hold in place the side slope material of an approach causeway or embankment. When flared at an angle with the breast wall it serves also to deflect stream water and floating debris into the waterway of the bridge and thus protects the approach embankment against erosion. The general forms of wing walls are:

(1) Straight—in continuation of the breast wall of the abutment.

(2) U-type—placed parallel to the alignment of the approach roadway.

(3) Flared—forming an angle with the alignment of the abutment breast wall by receding therefrom.

(4) Curved—forming either a convex or concave arc flaring from the alignment of the abutment breast wall.

The footing of a full abutment height wing wall is usually a continuation of the base portion of the breast wall but may be stepped to a higher or lower elevation to obtain acceptable foundation conditions.

A stub type of straight wing wall is sometimes used in connection with a pier-like or bent-like abutment placed within the end of an embankment. This type, commonly known as "elephant ear" or as "butterfly wing" serves to retain the top portion of the embankment from about the elevation of the bridge seat upward to the roadway elevation. The top surface is battered to conform with the embankment side slope.

Working Stress. See STRESS.

www.ingramcontent.com/pod-product-compliance
Lightning Source LLC
Chambersburg PA
CBHW081801300426
44116CB00014B/2204